AND THE ORGANISATION OF SPACE • BUILDING

isation and DENTITIES AND SPACES •

UI DARY CROSSINGS: PRODUCING ORGANISED

tion of space

OF SPACE? • CONCLUSIONS: DISORGANISING SPACE

power, identity and materiality at work

Karen Dale and Gibson Burrell
University of Leicester

First published 2008 by
PALGRAVE MACMILLAN
Houndmills, Basingstoke, Hampshire RG21 6XS and
175 Fifth Avenue, New York, N.Y. 10010
Companies and representatives throughout the world

PALGRAVE MACMILLAN is the global academic imprint of the Palgrave
Macmillan division of St. Martin's Press, LLC and of Palgrave Macmillan Ltd.
Macmillan® is a registered trademark in the United States, United Kingdom
and other countries. Palgrave is a registered trademark in the European
Union and other countries.

ISBN-13: 978–0–230–57268–3

This book is printed on paper suitable for recycling and made from fully
managed and sustained forest sources. Logging, pulping and manufacturing
processes are expected to conform to the environmental regulations of the
country of origin.

A catalogue record for this book is available from the British Library.

A catalog record for this book is available from the Library of Congress.

10   9   8   7   6   5   4   3   2   1
17 16 15 14 13 12 11 10 09 08

For Rosie and Owain

contents

list of illustrations

acknowledgements

This book has been five years in the making, and has seen us move institutions and houses several times, enabling us to experience and sometimes analyse the effects of space and organisation at all too close quarters. During that time we have incurred a great debt of gratitude to colleagues, friends and family. We would like to thank a number of people who read drafts of the book for their generosity of time and support: Karen Legge, Barbara Townley, Colin Williams, Alan Whitaker and two anonymous reviewers on behalf of Palgrave. We are especially grateful to Martin Parker, whose comments on an early draft encouraged us to reshape the book and see things from new perspectives.

We have discussed the content of the book with a number of people who have also shared their stories and examples. We are very grateful to Tony Eastmond, Glenn Morgan, Peter Mack, Nick Ellis, Tom Keenoy, Peter Armstrong, Martin Corbett, Heather Ward, Melissa Tyler and Phil Hancock, and attendees at many a staff seminar in universities in the UK and at conferences abroad, including Dvora Yanow, Alfons van Marrewijk, and the participants in the 'space' stream at APROS in 2005. For some years we taught a module on space and architecture to masters students at Warwick Business School, and we would particularly like to thank Lorna Jones and Fergus McWilliams for interesting discussions. Earlier drafts of some of the material have appeared in journal articles and chapters in edited books. We have benefited greatly from the comments of editors and reviewers and would particularly like to thank Hugh Willmott, Mats Alvesson, Mahmood Ezzamel, Rick Delbridge, Mike Reed, Adrian Carr, Phil Hancock (again!) and Martin Parker (again and again!). We have also benefited enormously from conversations with John Holm and Frank Duffy of DEGW, facilities and buildings managers at various organisations, especially EnergyCo and a bank HQ in Melbourne, which must necessarily stay anonymous, but we are grateful nonetheless.

The patience of Steve Rutt, Ursula Gavin and Jacky Kipenberger at Palgrave Macmillan has been of truly legendary proportions and we wish to thank them for their support throughout the half decade.

The pictures which we use to illustrate some of the main themes of the book have been begged and borrowed (but not stolen!) from friends and relations. We thank Simon Eling for the great picture of Triangular Lodge; Gerald Pinkham for that of the Welsh Assembly Building; Phil Hancock for the BBC Media Village pictures; Rita and Ronnie Balderson for the photograph of the Ford and Edison Compounds; and Margaret Nix for the powerful image of Ground Zero, taken only a month after the collapse of the Twin Towers.

We would not have had the space to write this book without the inestimable help of Lilian Payne, Karen's mother, and also Margaret Nix, to whom we owe an enormous debt of gratitude for looking after our children so well. We would like to send our love to them, and to all our children and grandchildren: Clare, Anna, Katy, Rosie and Owain, and Megan, Jack and James.

Of course all remaining errors and infelicities are entirely our responsibility, and luckily, as co-authors and partners, we will have each other to blame!

preface

We are hopeful that this book will be of interest to a wide readership, including academics, students, practitioners, consultants and the general reader who wishes to understand more about how their everyday spaces are organised. With this broad appeal in mind, this preface aims to sketch out some of the main dimensions of the book.

First, the topic of 'space' is highly relevant to both current theory and practice. Crang and Thrift state that "space is the everywhere of modern thought" (2000: 1) and there has certainly been an explosion of interest in space across the social sciences, although less so within the fields of management and organisation studies. And in many ways this is odd, because it is within the business world that there have been many conscious attempts to re-order spatial practices. Contemporary practice within organisations is often driven by a consuming interest in space, both as an economic asset to be effectively utilised and as a social tool to achieve key organisational goals, such as commitment, creativity and innovation. There has been an accompanying proliferation of consultancy activity in this area by both designers and human resource management specialists, a growth in 'facilities management' as a key strategic concern, and even a keen interest by government in the advantages to be gained by manipulating space to reform civil service 'culture'. High-profile examples include the removal of seven miles of internal walls from the Treasury Building of the UK government (Allen *et al.* 2004), whilst in the private sector, Philips' 70,000 sq m Software Innovation Campus in Bangalore, India, was designed to facilitate "high levels of staff engagement" (www.degw.com). As we write this Preface in March 2007, the pest control company Rentokil is seeking to diversify its business to encompass a holistic approach to the sensory management of the office worker, which would include interior design, 'acoustic artwork', scent management, feng shui and 'wellness' (*The Times*, 16 March, 2007, p. 15). Jeff Mariola,

Managing Director of Rentokil's new division Ambius, proclaimed that "Rentokil is now in the business of seduction" (ESRC Conference, RIBA, London, 16 March, 2007). This explicit enlistment of the material spaces of organisation as a managerial tool is an important development in the restructuring of power, corporate culture and employee identities. To put it provocatively, management theory frequently lags behind management practice, so in discussing these developments we hope that the book provides a timely contribution to understanding organisational life.

However, this book aims to do far more than to introduce readers to current management practices. It actively seeks to theorise these practices within a broader understanding of managerial work as a social practice within a globalised political economy. In this it has a resonance with work on 'critical management studies'. This perspective of understanding management has led to an examination of issues which have often been assumed to be 'neutral' and 'apolitical' in much of management theory. Alvesson and Willmott (1992: 4), for example, talk of "breaking the mythic spell of conventional management theory" through exposing power asymmetries and critiquing the assumed "neutrality of management theory and the impartiality of management practice". Here, culture, identity and power become of central interest to understanding management and organisation. From our point of view this leads us to consider how spatial practices "produce people" (Alvesson and Willmott 1992: 5) and how organisational aesthetics is much more than a simple beautifying of the workplace, but is an issue of politics and power (Dale and Burrell 2003). In doing so, this book goes far beyond a simple consideration of the physical settings of organisations, extending to a thorough-going critique of the abstracted nature of much organisation and management studies, and integrates both current practice-based interventions in organisations with a re-thinking of dominant theoretical approaches.

By taking a more critical approach to management within a political economy, we wish to stress an analytical focus in understanding organisational activity, an appreciation of the strengths and limitations of both practice and theory, and a sensitivity to the complexity of social, political, ethical, economic and philosophical issues that shape contemporary organisational analysis. These are approaches which are central to much advanced-level teaching and research in management and organisation. Thus we see this book as being highly relevant for final-year undergraduate and specialist master's modules across management studies, organisational analysis, the sociology of industry and organisations, organisational psychology, and human resource management. It will also be useful for the growing number of advanced-level master's courses in management research (MRes) and taught PhD programmes.

Space, of course, is not just about the arrangement of the organisation's internal built environment, but about how organisations relate to each other and to the wider social world of which they are a fundamental part. We feel strongly that organisations should not be seen as isolated arenas of social activity, predominantly associated with the realms of 'production' or 'work'. Yes, in capitalist economies at least, the majority of people have to spend a large part of their daily lives working in order to live, and thus the organisation of production is still highly important. But we tend to forget all the other ways in which organisation produces our everyday lives: in leisure, media, religion, consumption, education and so much more. And thus organisation is integral to the construction of the spaces in which we live, ranging from the nature of globalised consumption, the cultural assumptions embedded in entertainment, heritage and leisure facilities, right to the supposed privacy of the home.

In demonstrating the crucial nature of organisation and management for understanding the social, spatial and the material relations of the societies in which we live, we believe that this book is relevant to readers from across a range of disciplines. These would include cultural studies, sociology, geography and urban studies. We also hope that it is read by architects and designers who are professionally interested in the social and political contexts and implications of the world that they are involved in constructing. As Cedric Price, a prominent British architectural thinker, has said, "Architects are being trained to produce sophisticated variations of enclosure and three-dimensional systems for organisations which themselves are being questioned as to their validity" ('Aiming to Miss' lecture series at the Architectural Association, London). Bearing this in mind then, there is much scope for bringing together the insights of social science and architecture. For example, an interdisciplinary project based in the Gothenberg Research Institute, Sweden, on 'managing big cities' aims to fuse these perspectives

> " This international research program aims at bridging the gap between two traditional big city studies: those that focus on the intentions of the planners (politicians, city planners, and architects) and those that focus on the citizens, as represented by sociologists, mass media and artists. In this case, the focus is city management, that is organizational practices within both private and public sector that together built an action net that constitutes the management of the modern big city. (www.hgu.gu.se/item.aspx?id=7706; Czarniawska 2004)

In dealing with such questions of the management of space, this book relates the materiality of organisation to issues in management theory such as power, identity and culture, and reasserts the significance of the physical and embodied nature of social relations. Further, it has an integrative approach to organisation and management, interrelating the spheres of production, consumption and reproduction, and demonstrating through their materiality their interdependence and the significance of management to diverse areas of social life. In this book, then, two major lines of argument intersect. The first is that space is central to organisation. The second is that organisation is fundamental to understanding social structures, processes and relations. In putting these arguments forward we hope to see the analysis of organisation become more aware of space, embodiment and materiality, and to see social theory become more aware of the significance of organisation as a social form or institution that facilitates collective action, and as a social ordering process that facilitates meaning and structure.

Triangular Lodge, Rushton, Northamptonshire, UK. Sir Thomas Tresham formulated the idea for the Triangular Lodge whilst imprisoned for his Catholic faith. On his release in 1593 he constructed the building as an equilateral triangle, where all features express the symbolism of the Trinity in combination with the Tresham family trefoil. The symbolic and material come together in expressing powerfully what had been suppressed. However, the Treshams should not be seen as wholly downtrodden, as they played their own part in the suppression of local peasantry, including the killing of 50 local protestors in the Newton Riots of 1607, caused in part by the enclosure of common lands. Triangular Lodge is near to where we live, and stands for us a remainder of the multiple ways in which space and architecture are woven together with issues of power, resistance, culture and identity: a fusion of the social and the material.

1 introduction: the spaces of organisation and the organisation of space

LDING• ORGANISATION: SECURING AND OBSCURING POWER • BUILDING PEOPLE: IDENTITIES AND SPACES • A POLITICAL ECONOMY OF ORGANISED SPACE • BOUNDARY CROSSINGS: THE POROUSNESS OF ORGANISED SPACE • BOUNDARY MATERIALITY: SPATIAL AND EMBODIED POLITICS IN ORGANISATION • ALTERNATIVE SPACES: THE RADICAL ORGANISATION OF SPACE? • CONCLUSIONS: DISORGANISING SPACE

> *A model of political culture appropriate to our own situation will necessarily have to raise spatial issues as its fundamental organizing concern.*
>
> (Jameson 1991: 51)

> *Our society is an organisational society. We are born in organisations, educated by organisations, and most of us spend much of our lives working for organisations. We spend much of our leisure time paying, playing and praying in organisations. Most of us will die in an organisation, and when the time comes for burial, the largest organisation of them all – the state – must grant official permission.*
>
> (Etzioni 1964: 1)

This is a book about the spaces of organisation and the organisation of space. Since earliest times, humans have worked upon their surroundings in order to fulfil their needs. But these constructions have never been solely functional. Through the adaptation of the physical world, the social and cultural worlds have also come into being. Materiality communicates and shapes. It consists not only of physical structures but is part of the inter-subjective and subjective realms that make up our social relations. And in turn, the physical world made social comes to constitute people through its very materiality. The spaces and places around us construct us as we construct them.

But what of the organisation of these spaces and places? Obviously there are the spaces of organisations, which in a mental map of 'organisation' usually translates to factories and offices. There is, indeed, a massive investment and interest in corporate architecture. The most talked about building on the London skyline in recent years has been Swiss Re's unique Norman Foster design, commonly known as the 'erotic gherkin', which won the Royal Institute of British Architecture's prize in 2004. The shortlist for the 2005 RIBA prize included no less than two industrial buildings out of six: the BMW Central Building in Leipzig designed by Zaha Hadid and the McLaren Technology Centre in Woking designed by Foster and Partners. On the inside, too, many organisations have been consciously and systematically reshaping their spaces. Consultancies such as DEGW and SpaceSyntax are engaged by corporations to help rethink how buildings are best utilised. Over seven miles of walls have been removed from inside the Treasury building in London in order to bring about significant 'cultural change' (Allen *et al.* 2004). Spatial interventions include those baldly designed to save money by maximising efficient use of expensive built assets as well as those which aim for cultural shift through changing spatial configurations. Often the two aspects, economic and social, are overlaid upon each other.

Yet, is it so obvious that organisation is contained solely in these buildings? Even 'work' has slipped outside the work*place* (Felstead *et al.* 2005). It is rapidly moving through trains and planes, sitting in cafes, displayed in shopping malls, it is busy in the home (Massey 1995b; 2005: 177), which in a multitude of ways it never wholly left (e.g. Hochschild 1989; Huws 1984; Phizacklea and Wolkowitz 1995). 'Workspace' as a distinctive bounded place has become a problematic concept. In the post-industrial era of consumption and the rise of the service sector, workspaces for many people are diverse and not bounded at all by the traditional separation of spheres of production, consumption and reproduction. From shops to museums, gyms to banks, hairdressers to heritage parks, workspaces are overlaid on other sorts of spaces. However, in all these spheres and spaces, organisation too makes its home – and, indeed, organisation is as much part of the home as the bricks and mortar that are themselves produced through organisation, transported and placed together in one location through organisation, set in particular designs and used to form specific sub-spaces through organisation.

These multiple spaces can also be seen to produce their own organisations. Whole industries have burgeoned around the desires of people to shape their material surroundings. These span the construction business, DIY superstores, garden centres, homeware shops, through to the media carnival of the imaginary desiring-spaces of home and garden magazines, design gurus and wall-to-wall home-interest television programmes. This all fits snugly with some of the major societal trends under advanced capitalism. Home fashion becomes an extension of the 'project of self', the material representation of an identity, a lifestyle, a position in society (Bourdieu 1984; Giddens 1991). It dovetails neatly into a society of consumption, where 'choice', possession and style communicate the loudest about who we are. It is part of a wider negotiation of an economic position where mass products and mass markets have to be transmuted into individuality and uniqueness, where sameness is somehow a mark of difference. A long-standing advertising campaign for bespoke 'Mark Wilkinson' kitchens captures this tension. Images of a kitchen that is distinctively 'of' that designer (someone attuned to the luxury interior market can spot a 'Mark Wilkinson' from a 'Smallbone' or a 'Chalon', and, indeed, another advertisement explicitly claims 'unmistakeably Mark Wilkinson') are headed with the byline 'It's what it says about you that makes a difference'. The designer himself even becomes caught up in this replication of the simulacrum of difference, when Wilkinson bemoans that his creativity is constrained by customers wanting what they have already seen him produce. This set of contradictions was illustrated for us at a personal level a few years ago when we decided we wanted a scarlet throw for the living room. That season all the reds were terracotta or aubergine, with not a scarlet to be had. 'Individual' constructions of space, however 'private' that space might be assumed to be, go through the medium of 'organisation' in a multiplicity of ways. No doubt if we had employed an interior designer with the right networks to 'source' a scarlet throw, or had been prepared to pay for bespoke furnishings, we could have fulfilled our immediate desires, but even these caveats drive us right back again to understanding how 'our' spaces are socially organised. As well as being the intimate spaces of dreams (Bachelard 1994) – and oppressions, as feminist writers have pointed out (e.g. Cowan 1983; Friedan 1963; Hochschild 1989) – those domestic places are *organised* spaces. And organised spaces are at once intensely personal and intensely political; they are material, social and imaginary.

Thus the interwoven nature of organisation, space and architecture profoundly affects our everyday lives, although we may rarely notice this, as the built environment becomes a taken-for-granted part of our daily experiences. As Brand says,

> The building industry is the second largest in the world (after agriculture). Buildings contain our lives and all civilisation. The problem is also intensely personal. If you look up from this book, what you almost certainly see is the inside of a building. Glance out of a window and the main thing you notice is the outside of other buildings. (1994: 2)

In this book two major lines of argument are interwoven. The first is that space is central to organisation. The second is that organisation is fundamental to understanding social structures, processes and relations. In putting these arguments forward, our intention is to encourage an analysis of organisation that is more aware of space, embodiment and materiality, and a social theory that is more aware of the significance of organisation as a social form or institution that facilitates collective action, and as a social ordering process that facilitates meaning and structure.

In the rest of this chapter, we discuss the conceptual framework for the rest of the book, in particular examining what we mean by the key terms 'space' and 'organisation'. We start this with the work of Henri Lefebvre, the French social and political thinker and activist, and possibly the most influential writer about space.

Social and theoretical productions of space: an introduction to Henri Lefebvre

It has been argued that 'space is the everywhere of modern thought' (Crang and Thrift 2000: 1). This at once presents a series of problems to anyone who wishes to research it. 'Space' is used in a multitude of ways, from the abstract and highly theoretical, through the symbolic, to the experientially concrete. However, Crang and Thrift argue that a larger problem is not the 'wide semantic field' of space (Soja 1980), but that it is used in a highly flexible way with no specific meaning in mind. Indeed, they highlight how in this generalised way it can be used to produce an enhanced impression of being up-to-date with theoretical trends and concerns (1980). 'Space' is used as a sign in other ways. Crang and Thrift go on to note that 'different disciplines do space differently' (1980) so that it signifies different theoretical shifts depending on its disciplinary context. Thus, they conclude, 'in all disciplines, space is a representational strategy' (1980). This lament is one shared by Massey in her book *For Space*. Here she, too, argues that the concept of space has become associated, and debased, by the way it constantly becomes elided into representation: 'over and over we tame the spatial into the textual and the conceptual; into representation' (2005: 20). In this connection, she maintains, space has come to be seen as fixed, stabilised, structure, in comparison with the active, agentic understanding of time (whether as history or consciousness or a fusion of the two). Yet the conjunction of space and time cannot be separated, except by theoretical sleight of hand. Thus the 'spatial turn' evidenced in many disciplines, presented as a development away from the dominance of time and history, can only be problematic.

As well as the theoretical tendency to produce a dichotomised relationship between 'space' and 'time', a bi-polar tension has been created between 'space' and 'place'. There is the story of the indigenous peoples who knew unequivocally that they were at the centre of their god's universe because they could see exactly the same distance in each direction. Knowing one's place is a part of this relationship to space. Place is seen as the private, cosy, warm side of geographical emplacement whereas space can hold within it the terror of boundless distance. The form of categorisation that characterises the dichotomy is the separation between categories that are at once mutually exclusive and hierarchically ordered. Casey's *The Fate of Place* (1998) argues that Western philosophy from Aristotle has denigrated 'place' in favour of 'space', although modern philosophers such as Heidegger, Merleau-Ponty and Irigaray start to provide a way of returning to place as central. Yi-Fu Tuan, in seeking to bring the 'perspective of experience' into our understanding of space and place, defines both of them in terms of the lived:

> " The ideas 'space' and 'place' require each other for definition. From the security and stability of place we are aware of the openness, freedom, and threat of space, and vice versa. Furthermore, if we think of space as that which allows movement, then place is pause; each pause in movement makes it possible for a location to be transformed into place. (1977: 6)

From both the philosophical and the experiential, space and place have an intimate and intertwined set of connections, both discursive and material. In the perspective on social space discussed below, we hope to develop a nuanced way of bringing together these aspects of space and place without the sharp dichotomy between them.

In this book, we aim to work with a conceptualisation of space that is specific rather than abstracted, embedded rather than symbolic. This involves a perspective on space as socially produced and simultaneously socially producing; as concurrently material and imaginary; as intimately connected to embodiment; and as irreducibly political. The theorist who has most influenced this perspective is Henri Lefebvre (1901–1991). In the specific context of space, he is most known through *The Social Production of Space*, published in France in 1974, belatedly produced in English in 1991. This work has diffused into geographical theorisation of space predominantly through the work of Soja (1989), Gregory (1994) and especially Harvey (e.g. 1985a, 1985b, 1989). Lefebvre, though, had a much longer and deeper impact on social theory. Over his years of activism and writing,[1] he remained rooted in Marxism, although he was to change and modify his understanding of what this meant in the light of changing political events, through the Cold War and the revolutionary days of 1968. He was also much influenced by Surrealism and especially the Situationists, even after his split with them in the 1960s. Situationist activism (which we will discuss briefly in Chapter 7) certainly demonstrates a spatial politics, in the attempt to rewrite dominant meanings spatially and create awareness of the taken-for-granted nature of power in urban space. The significance of this can be seen in the importance he placed on everyday life (2000/1969), both as an area relevant to analysis and for transformation. As Shields argues, Lefebvre focuses on the importance of the everyday – *le quotidien*. His is 'the politics of the banal' rather than 'the politics of the elite' (Shields 1999: 1, 66). Similarly, through his activism, Lefebvre lived his politics and philosophy, rather than just theorising it on the page. This 'engaged social science' (1999: 5) saw him spend many years of research in industrial and union settings. Shields argues that his work is a forerunner of industrial sociology (p. 20).

Lefebvre rejected a structuralist, Althusserian reading of Marx which dominated post-1968 Paris for a more Hegelian one (Gregory 1994). In explaining the failure of the Left in France at this time, in Lefebvre's view, the everyday lives and consciousness of people were central to changing the objective conditions of society, and he believed that the Soviet Revolution had not been radical enough because it failed to address this everyday experience. What Lefebvre was arguing can be seen in spatial form in the wholesale export of Fordist production architecture to the USSR in the 1930s by Albert Kahn, not to mention Ford's own propagandist crowing that he would not sell tractors to the USSR until they had effectively taken on board the complete spatial infrastructure required for a system of transport (Ford 1926: 7–8, see discussion of this in Chapter 4). Lefebvre located Marx's theory of alienation not only in the workplace, but also throughout modern life (Shields 1999: 40). This opening-up of everyday life is important for the development of our argument in this book, which also does not remain with the workplace but traces these connections throughout a multitude of differing yet related social-spatial practices of organisation. In this, we are indebted to Lefebvre's argument that modern forms of capitalism produce a certain form of social space that he characterises as 'abstract space'. Lefebvre has been criticised for tending to present this as an intentional capitalist 'strategy' (Gregory 1994; Shields 1999: 156). However, we believe the opposite tendency is as much if not more worrisome: the tendency to take the capitalist basis of the spatial organisation of everyday life as 'normal'.

Lefebvre argues that all space is socially produced. He recognises that this idea is not always straightforward to grasp. The idea of 'producing space' 'sounds bizarre, so great is the sway still held by the idea that empty space is prior to whatever ends up filling it' (1991: 15). But through this re-conceptualisation of space as socially produced, Lefebvre provides the tools for a subtle understanding of the social and material interplay in an active, social production of space. His work connects two aspects of materiality: the 'physicality' of materiality, its 'thingness', *and* the 'imaginary' aspect of materiality, that which conveys its social, cultural and historical meaning in, for example, the meanings and memories we associate with particular objects and places. He also argues for the reciprocal enfolding of these relations of the social and material, whereby 'space is produced by social relations that it also reproduces, mediates and transforms' (Natter and Jones III 1997: 149).

One of Lefebvre's endeavours in *The Production of Space* is to bring together understandings of space from disparate areas of thought and life. Although he takes an analogy from physics, and describes this as a 'unitary theory' (1991: 11), it is not a simplistic, all-inclusive, universalistic meta-theory of space that he is seeking. He argues that 'this search for a unitary theory in no way rules out conflicts within knowledge itself, and controversy and polemics are inevitable' (p. 13). Rather he attempts to bring together diverse understandings of space – physical, mental and social – that have been artificially separated by intellectual fields and classifications. He also seeks to move beyond an 'abstract' notion of space, which often may be discerned across these fields, that generalises and reduces space to a theoretical category. Thus, in the book he covers a multitude of aspects of socially produced space: abstract, absolute, mental, real, visible-readable, sensory-sensual, contradictory, differential and so on. Lefebvre's main characterisations of social space are developed deliberately as triads to avoid theoretical tendencies towards dualisms, dichotomies and antagonisms (1991: 39). Here we try to delineate some of these aspects and relate them to the organisation of space.

Lefebvre makes a distinction between space as perceived, conceived and lived, and relates these to three overlapping aspects of social space: spatial practice, representations of space and representational space. It is not always easy to tease out Lefebvre's analyses, but we shall try here to describe these three elements and to map them onto a spatial understanding of organisation. The first aspect, 'spatial practice', Lefebvre also links to 'perceived' space. Lefebvre describes it as both 'production and reproduction, and the particular locations and spatial sets characteristic of each social formation' (1991: 33). As Lefebvre characterises it as perceived space and gives an example of the life of a high-rise tenant, we take it to mean the spaces that we know and experience on a day-to-day level, including work, home, leisure and the linkages (routes) between each. Lefebvre also indicates it has elements of both daily routine and of being gradually developed through a society's history (p. 38). Thus as well as being phenomenologically experienced spaces, they may be taken for granted through the habits of the body. This should be compared with

Merleau-Ponty's 'knowing without knowing' (1962, 1973) and Bourdieu's 'habitus' (1984), made up of class- and gender-based sedimented bodily ways of engaging with the world. Thus our experience of organisations, of work or leisure, for example, is built up not only through our own individual habituated ways of engaging our bodies with a certain materiality, our 'knowing without knowing' of the spatial relations within a particular place; but also the historical embodiment of a 'workplace', a 'gym' or a 'department store' and how it is constructed spatially in certain ways so as to produce the meaning of that particular sort of social space.

The second element of Lefebvre's triad is 'representations of space', and he characterises this as 'conceived' space. These are spaces as planned and executed by planners, designers, architects and engineers and, although he does not include them, we could add managers. These are the deliberate constructions of space to embody certain conceptualisations (e.g. functionality, control) in materialised form. Lefebvre explicitly connects this with the 'dominant spaces in any society (or mode of production)' (1991: 39) and hence for us intimately connected with organisation. We characterise this element as 'organised space'. For example, the conscious spatial construction of sales has long been known, with its construction of image, placing (literally!) of product where it is most likely to be noticed, and sensory domination of space, as in for example, the dispersal of the smell of fresh bread in the direction of the customer. But in recent years, as we have noted, there has been a much more deliberate movement in the conscious design of workplaces to achieve certain values and business goals through the manipulation of space. This is not simply in terms of work ergonomics or to gain greater efficiency, but as an integral element to the impetus of capturing hearts and minds through the use of spatial politics in attempts to manufacture both organisational culture and appropriate employee identities. Later in the book, we will examine some of the design companies involved in this processing of people and the explicitly reconfigured workplaces achieved through their ministrations.

The final element of social space is 'representational space', characterised by Lefebvre as 'lived space'. This is phenomenologically experienced space overlaid with 'imaginary spaces'[2] whereby the material and the cultural are fused: the social creation of space so that signs, images and symbols are made material. In the workplace, we can see this in the use of larger offices and plush furniture as status symbols, and also in the less formal creation of spaces of resistance through, for example, cartoons, personal email messages and family photographs.

These three elements are of course difficult to disentangle in our embodied experience of social space, and Lefebvre recognises that there are contradictions within and between these elements of social space, and the 'dialectical relationship that exists within the triad of the perceived, the conceived and the lived' (1991: 39). But this is the consequence of attempting to develop a meaningful understanding of the different ways in which social space is shaped by and shapes everyday lives, without being reduced to an elegant but abstract model. For Lefebvre, theorising space is meaningless unless it can 'grasp the concrete' (p. 40).

These different elements of the construction of space provide us with some conceptual tools for understanding the spatial politics of organisation. Lefebvre explores the development of social space from classical times. His discussion of social space as constructed through the Roman Empire (1991: 241–6) is pertinent here, as it illustrates how these dimensions can contain different and diverse, even contradictory, aspects within them, even as they are involved in the production of a certain social space. The Roman Empire can be seen as a huge achievement of the 'space of power', with the scale and durability of its expansion. It may also be seen as a key exemplar of spatial organisation. Lefebvre points to the dual character of the three elements of social space in the Empire: in spatial practice he directs us to the Roman road which connects the urban to the countryside, allowing control through the assertion of the city as the political centre and a gateway marking power over entry, and yet also to the Roman house, which provides another locale of the established power of Law and Patrimony expressed through property. In terms of the dual nature of the representation of space, Lefebvre underscores the significance of the circular on the one hand (with the myth of Remus founding the city by drawing a circle with his plough, dividing a political space from a natural one) and on the other the strict grid of the military camp (which we will return to in Chapter 2), although again as a closed space. Representational space is dominated by the 'masculine', the authoritarian and the juridical, with the 'feminine' being integrated through the earth both as bringer forth of life and as burial place of the dead. Through this discussion, Lefebvre demonstrates how the original conceived and imposed system becomes literally incorporated into the *habitus* – a term also used by Bourdieu, and taken by Lefebvre to be defined as a 'mode of being' (1991: 259).

Lefebvre (1991: 164–5) develops these dimensions with relation to other concepts, most usefully perhaps his views on the domination and appropriation of social space, which relate to Marx's analogous concepts. Here he draws a distinction between 'dominated (and dominant) space, which is to say a space transformed – and mediated – by technology, by practice,' and appropriated space which is a space modified for the needs and possibilities of a particular group. He links the domination of space to military, political and state power, but it would seem reasonable to extend this description to organisations, particularly given the dominance of large capitalist corporations. Appropriation is a more ambiguous category, as he comments, 'Examples of appropriated spaces abound, but it is not always easy to decide in what respect, how, by whom and for whom they have been appropriated' (p. 165). Harvey further develops Lefebvre's strands by juxtaposing four dimensions of spatial practice across Lefebvre's triad to produce a grid (1989: 220–1). These dimensions are accessibility-distanciation (distance as a barrier to social interaction, and how this is overcome), appropriation of space, domination of space (both of these mirror Lefebvre's concepts) and future representations of space (how new systems, actual or imagined, arise).

These different aspects of social space will come together in our analysis of organisation and space. We can grasp some sense of how they work together in this illustration from Shields:

> it is not just a question of 'Space' but of overlaid 'Spaces'
> which are made up of multitudinous 'places', good and bad
> (the 'right' and 'wrong' sides 'of the tracks', 'dangerous' urban
> areas, ghettos, 'middle class enclaves', public squares, private
> yards, the sanctified space of a cathedral, the profane space of a
> tavern) and are criss-crossed by directional 'paths' ranging from
> natural paths (trails, mountain passes, river routes) through

physical pathways (roads, railways, canals) to abstract paths of air-route corridors, frequency delimited microwave transmission beams, electronic, satellite-based trans-border data flows. All these genres of space have the effect of fragmenting any overall vision of the socio-cultural system of spaces in which we live. (1997: 190)

As has already been alluded to above, especially in the importance of 'habitus' for understanding social space, Lefebvre believed that human embodiment was fundamental to the understanding of the social production of space. Indeed, he argues that 'the whole of (social) space proceeds from the body' (1991: 405). Lefebvre brings human embodiment into each of his elements of social space. He recognises that 'social practice presupposes the use of the body: the use of the hands, members, sensory organs and the gestures of work as of activity unrelated to work' (p. 40). He also recognises that representations of the body are multiple, coming from science, nature, culture and ideology. He goes further in this and appreciates that the body's lived experience is mediated by these representations, which may have long historical roots, such as those deriving from the Judeo-Christian tradition in western societies. This is human embodiment as simultaneously socially produced but also socially producing (Grosz 1994, 2001).

In conjunction with this emphasis on embodiment, Lefebvre rejects the Cartesian split of mind and body, along with the abstract construction of space that this entails. Here he has much in common with the French phenomenologist Merleau-Ponty, who also provides a radical critique of Cartesianism through the centrality of embodiment (Casey 1998; Williams and Bendelow 1998). Merleau-Ponty states in *The Phenomenology of Perception* that 'far from my body's being for me no more than a fragment of space, there would be no space at all for me if I had no body'. He argues that 'to be a body is to be tied to a certain world' (1962: 148), for perception of the world is always embodied perception, since 'the perceiving mind is an incarnated mind' (1989: 3). He sees embodiment as 'reversible', which emphasises the body as sentient and sensible, sees and is seen, hears and is heard, touches and is touched. Thus embodiment is neither ideas nor matter, subject nor object, but both at the same time. Merleau-Ponty 'identifies social, embodied action with the production of meaning. Meaning is not produced by a transcendental or constituting consciousness but by an engaged body-subject' (Crossley 1996: 101). In this conceptualisation of the embodied subject, then, we can see a tool for understanding the negotiation of the material and the social, the organisational and the subjective, in relation to the production of social space.

Lefebvre is highly critical of abstract conceptualisations of space that excise the role of embodiment in the production of space. He describes how the concept of space moved away from the space of social practice and was been taken over by metaphysical representations of space such as the Cartesian construction of space as 'absolute, infinite *res extensa*, a divine property which may be grasped in a single act of intuition because of its homogeneous (isotropic) character' (1991: 14). The critique of the conceptualisation of space as derived from Euclid and Descartes is significant because it lays the framework for the 'abstract space' that becomes the dominant social space of capitalism (p. 49).

Spaces and times of power: abstract space, capitalism and globalisation

One of the key themes in *The Production of Space* is the movement from 'absolute space' to 'abstract space'. 'Absolute space' is the space which came out of natural characteristics transformed by religious and political activity. It is 'a product of the bonds of consanguinity, soil and language' (Lefebvre 1991: 48). 'Abstract space' is the space of capitalism. It is based upon Marx's theory of accumulation, and 'it is in this space that the world of commodities is deployed, along with all that it entails: accumulation and growth, calculation, planning, programming' (1991: 307). It is an instrumental space, a space dominated by exchange relations, and thus closely connected with Marx's conceptualisation of alienation. Gregory argues that

> both Lefebvre and Foucault accentuate what Soja calls the 'inst-rumentality' of social space (1989: 50) – what they would refer to as its strategic function.... Lefebvre's account is based on the distinction between exchange value and use value that lies at

BOUNDARY CROSSINGS: REPRODUCING ORGANISED SPACE • BUILDING A SOCIAL MATERIALITY: SPATIAL AND EMBODIED POLITICS IN ORGANISATION • ALTERNATIVE SPACES: THE RADICAL ORGANISATION OF SPACE? • CONCLUSIONS: DISORGANISING SPACE

 13

> the heart of Marx's analysis of the commodity. Whereas Marx's critique of political economy privileged history over geography, Lefebvre, however, tries to make the 'silent spaces' of Capital speak. (1994: 275)

Abstract space is also a globalised space. Lefebvre talks of its 'worldwide strategies, as well as the power of money and that of the political state. This space is founded on the vast network of banks, business centres and major productive entities, as also on motorways, airports and information lattices' (1991: 53). Thus the analysis of abstract space has political significance for understanding the social-spatial relations of the modern world, as capitalism exerts a growing influence in economic and cultural terms, both at the level of the world system and for the individual sense of identity.

There are three elements that, Lefebvre argues, come to make up abstract space (1991: 285–91): the geometric format; the optical or visual format; and the phallic format. The first is the logico-mathematical, cognitive space that is based upon Euclidean–Cartesian geometry (p. 24). It comes from a mental projection of an imaginary space that is extended, homogenous and absolute, these properties allowing for its use as a space of mathematical and logical operations. It leads to the reduction of three-dimensional lived, embodied space to a two-dimensional representation, such as a plan or map. The second element relates to this, in that it is the dominance of the visual, subordinating the other senses. Lefebvre argues that the dependence on the written word (McLuhan 1962) and the spectacularisation of society (critiqued by Guy Debord (1967) and the Situationists) both stem from this, and that these relate to the two 'moments' of visualisation: the metaphoric, where the act of writing becomes focal, and the metonymic, where parts or fragments come to stand for the whole. Through these, he argues, 'all of social life becomes the mere decipherment of messages by the eyes, the mere reading of texts' (1991: 286). Here we can see frustration with those elements of structuralism and post-structuralism that become bound up with representation and nothing outside this, where the 'philosophico-epistemological notion of space is fetishized and the mental realm comes to envelop the social and physical one' (pp. 5–6; cf. Crang and Thrift, and Massey, discussed earlier). Lefebvre also points to the way that the ascendancy of the eye 'tends to relegate objects to the distance, to render them passive. That which is seen is reduced to an image – and to an icy coldness' (p. 286). It can also be understood as relating to the consequences of alienation on social relations, a theme that we take up in spatial terms in Chapter 4.

The final element, that of the phallic, is also connected to the metonymic and metaphoric urges of the 'logic of visualization'. Here the part taken as the whole symbolises 'force, male fertility, masculine violence' (1991: 287). In terms of the social production of abstract space, it is the form of political power, carried through by the state and its agencies such as the police, the army, and through bureaucracy. The phallic element also translates the lived body into an abstract 'coded and decodable system' (p. 310).

> The demise of the body has a dual character, for it is at once symbolic and concrete: concrete, as a result of the aggression to which the body is subject; symbolic, on account of the fragmentation of the body's living unity. This is especially true of the female body, as transformed into exchange value, into a sign of the commodity and indeed into a commodity *per se*. (Lefebvre 1991: 310)

The geometric-visual-phallic abstract space of capitalism presents itself as being homogeneous, transparent and thus readable. It implies a tacit agreement, reciprocity and consensus. Although in our view, perhaps the rhetorical self-justifying nature of the language of 'democracy' and 'freedom' has been somewhat blown apart in recent years in the debates over the legitimacy of the first election win of US President George W. Bush and the disenfranchisement of large numbers of poor and black voters, and the controversy over the war in Iraq and the lack of transparency of parliamentary information in the UK. Yet these debates assume that these are exceptional failures of capitalist democracies, but fundamental to their very operation. In contrast, Lefebvre sees a key characteristic of 'abstract space' is that it is deceptive, an illusion that hides the hierarchies, the inclusions and exclusions, the underpinning power and violence that are fundamental elements of capitalist spaces.

Whereas abstract space is seen as transparent, neutral and pure, it works in complex and apparently contradictory ways (1991: 56).

This abstract space of capitalism produces a form of social-spatial politics which hides its own operations of power under a cloak of transparency, visibility and openness. The ubiquity of the mobile phone/camera; the penetration of the media into nearly every living room; the spread-eagled products of the supermarket shelves telling the mantra of 'consumer choice' reflect these supposedly transparent, homogeneous spaces of capitalism. The secret of this illusion is in the very transparency itself. In Chapter 2, we explore further this simultaneous 'securing and obscuring' (Burawoy 1985: 82) of power in the development of capitalist organisation; the case study in Chapter 6 illustrates in practice the illusions of transparency and opacity (Lefebvre 1991: 27–30, 287–8) inherent in organisational representation.

Lefebvre sees everyday, embodied experience as being a key locus for understanding the conflict and contradictions inherent in the abstract spaces of capitalism. For Lefebvre, space is lived before it is perceived, and produced before it is read. Thus there is a fundamental and irresolvable tension between 'the "abstract space" of capitalism's economic and political systems – externalized, rationalized, sanitized – and the swirling, kaleidoscopic "lived space" of everyday life. The tension between these spaces transcodes a tension between integration and differentiation that admits of no final solution' (Gregory 1994: 275).

It is a similar tension to this that underpins debates around the extension of capitalism into every greater economic, geographic and imaginary spaces. The abstracted notion of 'globalisation' is presented as a homogeneous, universalising force, a movement of global capital that transforms all into sameness, sweeping away difference, local opacities and experience, and yet cannot be challenged since it somehow seems to be a natural and inevitable trajectory. However, Lefebvre's work provides an opening for understanding the interconnections between different levels of how social space is produced and reproduced; indeed, that all spaces are social, however global or abstract they might appear to be. He provides us with a way of understanding how all social space is what Massey (1995a) describes as 'hybrid space'.

Harvey (1989, 2000) has used Lefebvre's spatialised account of capitalism to develop a critique of contemporary globalisation. He points to the active organising and re-organising of space under capitalism: 'capitalism is under the compulsion to eliminate all spatial barriers, to "annihilate space through time" as Marx puts it, but it can do so only through the production of a fixed space. Capitalism thereby produces a geographical landscape (of space relations, of territorial organisation, and of systems of places linked in a "global" division of labour and of functions) appropriate to its own dynamic of accumulation at a particular moment of its history, only to have to destroy and rebuild that geographical landscape to accommodate accumulation at a later date' (2000: 59). This process is what Harvey describes as capitalism's 'spatial fix': 'capitalism cannot do without its "spatial fixes". Time and time again it has turned to geographical reorganisation (both expansion and intensification) as a partial solution to its crises and impasses. Capitalism therefore builds a geography in its own image' (p. 54). It is this process which, despite the rhetoric about the homogeneity of globalisation, produces different places as different in relation to the dynamics of accumulation. In other words, it produces an 'uneven geographical development'.

The significance of bringing to social analysis an understanding of the interconnections between the global and the local, the abstract and the everyday is further emphasised by Harvey, when he asks why the two overwhelming areas of intellectual interest in recent times have been on the one hand 'globalisation' and on the other the human body. He points out that

> 'Globalization' is the most macro of all discourses that we have available to us while that of 'the body' is surely the most micro from the standpoint of understanding the workings of society.... These two discursive regimes – globalisation and the body – operate at different ends of the spectrum in the scalar we might use to understand social and political life. But little or no systematic attempt has been made to integrate 'body talk' with 'globalisation talk'. (Harvey 2000: 15)

Thus Harvey points us to a form of analysis that seeks to explore the interconnections of these different levels of social relations: that of **scale**. This is widely used in geography, and it is useful because it moves away from the more dichotomised readings of space (macro) and place (micro), which tend to separate, differentiate and hierarchise conceptual relationships. It is also useful because it brings an expressly spatial and material orientation to the different levels of analysis, showing the relations between local, organisational, national and international interactions in a specific rather than an abstract way. It is this context, of course, that the expression 'uneven geographies of development' is more productive than the 'semantic peccadilloes' (Dicken *et al.* 1997: 158) of terms such as 'globalisation' that serve to obscure the social-spatial power relations and inequalities under a set of rhetorical myths (Castree *et al.* 2004; Harvey 2000).

However, scales are not to be seen as static and determined, as Swyngedouw argues,

> " spatial scales are never fixed, but are perpetually redefined, contested, and restructured in terms of their extent, content, relative importance, and interrelations. For example, the present struggle over whether the scale of social, labour, environmental and monetary regulation within the European Union should be local, national, or European indicates how particular geographical scales of regulation are perpetually contested and transformed. Clearly, relative social power positions will vary considerably depending on who controls what at which scale. (1997: 141)

As Harvey goes on to point out, 'different actors and agents often operate (sometimes craftily) across different scales' (2000: 79). Castree *et al.* elaborate on this:

> " The capacity to 'up-scale' actions from a place or places to larger spatial scales can be an enormous source of power for particular businesses or workers. For instance, transnational companies have the capacity to search the globe for suitable locations for certain of their production facilities. Likewise, the capacity to 'contain' actions – like a workers' strike – within a certain scale (such as the local) can be a powerful weapon for (or against) employers or labourers in pursuit of their respective objectives. (2004: xiii)

We would point particularly to the role of organisations in being able to span the boundaries of different scales. It is this that makes the analysis of organisation key to understanding both the personal and the political, because this is how the two are interwoven.

It is interesting, then, from our point of view, that Harvey sees these spatial scales as related to different modes of organising: 'Human beings have typically produced a nested hierarchy of spatial scales within which to organize their activities and understand their world. Households, communities, and nations are obvious examples of contemporary organizational forms that exist at different scales' (2000: 75). However, it is noticeable that in this account of different scales of organising, he does not include the actual organisational form (and here we do not solely mean for-profit organisations, but also the multitude of state, quasi-governmental, public sector, voluntary, social interest and social movement groups that make up the organisational patchwork quilt of modern western societies). This, for us, is a key omission[3] in the scalar analysis of interconnections between space and place and between the global and the body. Organisation, we would argue, mediates the construction of the social-spatial practices that go to make up all aspects of these social scales, as we hope to demonstrate in this book. We draw in Chapters 4 and 5 on Lefebvre's idea of a 'political economy of space', which uses an approach that cuts across the static idea of 'level of analysis' to consider how space is organised at different scales, with powerful social and material consequences.

Another important aspect that we need to consider in the analysis of 'abstract space' is that of time. Time has tended to be treated as an abstract category, separated from space and embodiment. Harvey comments that Marx and Engels did not manage to sufficiently analyse globalisation and uneven development because they 'got lost in a rhetorical mode that in the last instance privileges time and history over space and geography' (2000: 24). To some extent he sees this as a consequence of a 'Hegelian teleology' (p. 32) which formulates history as the active process and space as the passive recipient. Yet, as Lefebvre argues, 'Time *per se* is an absurdity; likewise space *per se*' (1991: 181).

> Let everyone look at the space around them. What do they see?
> Do they see time? They live time, after all; they are in time. Yet
> all anyone sees is movements. In nature, time is apprehended
> within space – in the very heart of space: the hour of the day, the

> season, the elevation of the sun above the horizon, the position
> of the moon and stars in the heavens, the cold and the heat, the
> age of each natural being, and so on. (1991: 95)

Thus we turn now to consider how time can be understood in relation to specific social, spatial and material relations, and also the relationship between time and the development of 'abstract space'. 'Time' has often been treated as a natural phenomena, which is 'linear, chronological (i.e. clock-based), objective, universal, independent, homogeneous, quantifiable, divisible' (Kavanaugh and Araujo 1995: 105). However, many social and historical studies indicate that diverse ways of understanding time are practised that are embedded in place and lived experience. Even where these focus specifically on time, the thrust of their analyses are that the experience of time is very much located in everyday lived practices, and cannot be dissociated from them.

Recognising, then, that time is embedded in social, spatial and embodied experience, also involves recognising the multiple experiences of time. Burrell (1992b) compares 'chronos' (clock-time) with 'kiros' (subjective time). Clark considers a greater multiplicity of 'chronological codes' and particularly draws a distinction between 'heterogeneous codes' derived from natural and social events and 'homogeneous codes' based upon the clock (1990: 142). 'Heterogeneous' codes recognise the impossibility of dissociating time from natural and social space. Heterogeneous codes may be characterised by different sequences, whether the trajectory of a phenomena is regular or less predictable, and how it is marked by key signifiers, for example, how to judge the times of planting and harvesting in different places and climates involves both a knowledge of the regularity of seasons and a sensitivity to changing or unpredictable elements of weather forecasting to detect more random storms, droughts, frosts and so on. Other elements include the duration of activities or phases and pace. Thus time may be continuing or rupturist, regular, cyclical or erratic, delayed, waiting, alternating; pushing forward to bring the future into the present, or explosive being discontinuous and unpredictable. Heterogeneous codes contain shared, socially constructed interpretations of time.

The dominance of 'homogeneous' time is also one which is linked with a devaluation of space and embodiment. It is time divided off from the social and natural world of which it is an intimate part, such that it becomes an abstract concept. It fits with an approach to science as universal, objective and 'outside' the observer, scientist or researcher. It also fits with a worldview that emphasises the standardised, measurable and increasingly machine-like (cf. Dale 2001). Homogeneous time can be objectively measured through its ordered constituent parts: seconds, minutes, hours, days, weeks, months, years. Universalism allows domination, whether by colonialism, cultural imperialism, conquest or globalisation. An abstract treatment of time leads to a unitary and uni-directional mode of social theory, where history can be seen as development, progress, enlightenment, civilisation or modernity (Burrell 1998). 'History' itself becomes universal and an idealist category, beyond specific and multiple social and material conditions. It is perhaps no accident that Lefebvre, whilst drawing on Hegel through his Marxist perspective, also considers Hegel to be the source of the loss of a unitary theory of space and time (Dear 1997: 50). This is the conception of time, therefore, embedded in terms such as 'advanced capitalism', 'less developed countries' or the 'first/third world' classification. Post-modernity may to some extent break apart this linear progression, but it tends to do so by further fragmentation and dissociation of time from space and from embodiment, for example through the use of 'pastiche' of different historical styles none of which relate to the social, material and political context within which they are manipulated by architects, writers and artists.

These different experiences of time, though, should not be taken as dichotomous or mutually exclusive. As Adam comments,

> despite this temporal separation of culture from nature through the creation of clock time, there is no before-and-after, no either-or condition. Rather, embodied time is lived and experienced alongside, despite of, and in conflict with the culturally constituted social relations of time. Our lives continue to be bounded by birth and death, growth and decay, night and day. In our daily lives we weave in and out of these different kinds of time without giving much thought to the matter. The entanglement and mutual implication of the times of nature and culture are

> taken for granted and disattended until, that is, the strains and
> stresses of the industrial temporal logic begin to produce anoma-
> lies that can no longer be contained within the boundaries of its
> logic. (2003: 61)

However, as Adam implies, although 'chronological codes' are experienced concurrently, the mechanised clock-time characteristic of modern
capitalist societies has a dominant social role. As such it becomes natu-
ralised, and infuses all other social relations (2003: 62). We will therefore
examine the development of this clock-time and its relationship to
'abstract space' in more detail.

E. P. Thompson's classic paper on 'Time, Work-Discipline and Industrial Capitalism' (1967) was perhaps one of the first to make an explicit
argument about how control of time and the 'time as money' perspective
came together in capitalism. Widely influential and equally widely criticised, his argument is seen as too rupturist in only seeing time discipline
located in industrialism and ignoring its longer history, and only locating
control in measured time.

In criticising Thompson's account for seeing the construction and
domination of measured time as only stemming directly from the Industrial Revolution and only related to the fulfilment of capitalist relations of
production, Thrift (1996, chapter 5) provides a very convincing account
of the development of time consciousness in medieval times that is bound
up with everyday social and spatial relations. He links systems of time
discipline to monastic routine (discussed in chapter 2) and the early
beginnings of urban industry and trade, and he shows that time (and
space) consciousness developed through a multiplicity of time markers
well before the development of the clock with its more exact measurements. Far from being unaware of the passage of time, medieval societies
had a 'rich temporal patchwork' (1996: 180) consisting of the rhythms
of the year and seasons, overlaid by the ecclesiastical calendar, that were
brought together through a knowledge of these rituals from year to year:
that 'lambs conceived at Michaelmas would be born before Candlemas;
that the ploughing should be over by Andrewmas' (Thomas 1971: 738).
The marking of time was known by a mixture of natural signs such as
the cycle of the moon and basic sundials, and human signals such as the

ringing of bells, which combined religious and secular meanings, such as the curfew bell instigated by William I and largely continued throughout the twelfth and thirteenth centuries.

This is certainly persuasive in showing that time consciousness did not suddenly develop in response to industrialisation. However, there are other aspects about the relationship of clock-time to the abstract space of capitalism that also need to be considered. Clark (1990) argues that 'homogeneous codes' are dependent on three elements: technological inventions to measure, standardise and compare timescales; the extended metaphor of clockwork as a guiding image; and the commodification of time, that 'time is money' and can be bought and sold. Adam (2003) links the development of clock-time with that of linear perspective in art, so we start to see a social and spatial context of distanciation and standardisation within which these developments are embedded. She also, following Weber (1930), sees the development of a standardisation of time and the idea that it was a gift or resource not to be squandered as set in train in the monasteries. Technologies for measurement of time evolved so that monks could structure their days and prevent time wasting in their service to God, part of their discipline that was intended to overcome the impulses of nature. These accounts give an appreciation that experiences of time are located within particular social and material relations, and also that the mechanisation, standardisation and commodification of time and space are interrelated, and inherent to 'abstract space'.

We turn now to the specific organisational form that is central to the production of social spaces and places: the profession and the practice of architecture.

Architecture: the negotiation of art and organisation

In the social production of space, at least in non-nomadic societies, architecture and architects hold a privileged position:

> It is the building, whose presence is usually mysteriously absent in every kind of social or cultural theoretical discourse (King 1990), in which the ideology of all 'imagined communities' (Anderson 1983) and 'imagined environments' is contained,

> materialized and symbolized. It is within the space and form of the building in which the social is most frequently constituted, in which its visual image announces its presence – in the city, in the nation, and in various distinct worlds. (King 2004: 5)

Thus, architecture is the place where space and organisation meet face to face. However, assumptions about the nature of architecture, and often the dominant beliefs of those who practice it, tend to obscure this confluence of space and organisation.

Architecture is a fusion of different skills and perspectives, from the highly ideological, even visionary, perspective on art and construction of society to the highly practical aspects of design, with all its necessary understanding of loads and pressures, and the technical aspects of using various materials, often in innovative ways. It is crystal clear from the outset that, whatever our interests, we are not experts in architecture. There is no attempt here to provide a textbook or a chronological study of the architecture of organisations. In relation to architecture we are more concerned with how the built forms of organisations relate to particular processes and structures as produced through diverse social spaces, as well as the impact of the organisation of architecture itself. Below we consider some aspects of the relationship between architecture and organisation, and how this is partially obscured by the dominant view of architecture as an aesthetic rather than an organisational practice, and some of the contradictions and tensions this produces.

In many circles, architecture is associated overwhelmingly with the external appearance of a building, rather than its function or use. One of us has a family tale about an architect cousin who designed a particular set of housing plans for a Gosforth firm that arrived in the hands of the bricklayers to include a central room with no doors and windows! This may be apocryphal, given that its source is as trusty as one's brother (a builder by trade, and hence this may also be a tale of competing occupational identities), but the implications for the perception of architects as preoccupied with external artistic merit and little common practical sense of use, tells one story about the profession. It is this preoccupation with external representation that links architectural definition with 'Art', and through this to a set of values and ideas about the nature of art as an aesthetic practice, not sullied by too obvious a functionality. Pevsner began his *Outline of European Architecture* (1943) with a statement that encapsulates this element of architecture's (self-) identification: 'a bicycle shed is a building; Lincoln Cathedral is a piece of architecture' (quoted in Sutton 1999: 7). This judgement makes a distinction not only between types and forms of buildings (architecture and non-architecture) but also between 'good' and 'bad' architecture. At the heart of architecture, then, lies this notion of superior aesthetic discrimination.

Art is often seen as autonomous. In being implicitly associated with aesthetic judgement, individual creativity and beauty over use, it can stand above the concerns of society, not be limited by cultural norms, beyond the dirty everydayness of business or organisation or function. Although it is apparent that architecture in practice will have a more ambivalent relationship with these assumptions. Yet, even whilst recognising some of this context, architects may self-define themselves as reaching for transcendence. Thus the architect Richard Rogers argues that

> Architecture has developed from man's need to order the world in space and time, which is a precondition to its being accessible to our understanding. It is problem solving in the environmental field where logic is transposed into form by art, combining science with art, the practical with the abstract, the measurable with the immeasurable. The science of architecture constantly progresses: science which proves more efficient supplements outdated science. Art in architecture, however, does not make linear progress; it is dependent on symbolism, and develops more randomly through philosophical and visual analysis. Art encompasses our hopes and beliefs beyond the limit of the immediate. (Campbell Cole and Elias Rogers 1985: 8)

And further, art is associated with the production of works of beauty by artists, which conjures up the image of the lone genius, and their art as the outward expression of an inward individual creativity. Although architecture is a highly diversified profession, it remains the case that specific high-profile buildings become associated with the name of a high-profile architect – the 'signature architect' – even where a large organisational practice is 'behind' that name and crucial to bringing these buildings into being.

As the aesthetic narrative about architecture individualises the artist it also individualises the work of art. Each building is therefore seen as an expression of a particular creative impulse, a separate masterpiece. Yet buildings are rarely isolated, but are linked together in various forms of networks. Even isolated farmsteads require their material networks to take animals and crops to market, and these in turn require another set of material, spatial relationships to turn them into food or other products. So in our consideration of the architecture of organisation, it is not sufficient to look at individual buildings (although that is a necessary part of our analysis). We need to go further and look at the multiplicity of interconnections and intersections that architecture provides for an understanding of the built environment.

In these ways, the association of architecture with art and aesthetics serves to obscure broader social and economic relations. Sociologically informed studies have, of course, always pointed to the social conditions and influences on the production of both architecture and art (e.g. Wolff 1981). Many architectural historians and theoreticians do not, explicitly at least, accept these connotations uncritically. They relate architecture, as with art, to the historical and social periods and conditions that have shaped them. Thus Sutton says of Pevsner's opening statement that 'in the event, no sentence in the book proved to be more controversial. Today, nobody would dare say such a thing. Architecture is no longer seen as a series of isolated great buildings, monuments, works of art: it is the totality of the built environment' (1999: 7). Thus, most contemporary commentators will recognise architecture not as autonomous art, but as a cultural and social practice located within systems of power and patronage. Architecture tells us about the ideas of a particular time and space, expressed materially. But this is not in a pre-determined or homogeneous way. It can also show the diversity, the contradictions and tensions of times and spaces.

Thus it is important to consider the wider economic-political conditions within which architecture is practiced and also which it influences. The issue of land ownership and control has to be fundamental to the original practice of architecture. For example, in the early days of the United States, the Virginia Company in 1610 came to a method of land apportionment that allowed individuals to accumulate large holdings. In this way we get the spreading characteristics of New England towns (Handlin 1985: 15). In contrast we see the very different relationship between land and people of many indigenous peoples. Architecture can very easily be used as a political tool, as for example in the very well known case of Haussmann and the Parisian boulevards which were driven through the working class and riotous areas of central Paris in order to facilitate social control (Harvey 2003).

It is in recognition of the web of power relations that surrounds the practice of architecture that prompts Glancey to quote the architect Phillip Johnson in describing architects as 'whores':

> as members of one of the world's oldest professions, they get paid for doing what other people want. And that means the design of banal office blocks and brainless shopping malls as well as beautiful private houses and churches that have the power to reduce the noisiest citizen to silence. (1998: 6)

Architecture as a practice is mediated through its relation to its clients, who are predominantly those individuals and especially organisations in society who have the resources and the power to produce the buildings and spaces that they think fit. The architect, Glancey continues, has been 'on the whole, a willing collaborator with governments, property developers and the moving spirit of the times' (p. 6). Similarly Eero Saarinen, following a visit to General Motors in 1958, commented that architecture was the only one of the arts that was not at war with society (Peter 2000: 81). The clear implication is that architecture cannot be understood in isolation from organisation. Sometimes the association of architecture with artistic endeavour, endowed with liberal credentials and individual key figures serves to mask the closely knit relationship between architecture and big business (Figure 1). Architects' clients are predominantly large business organisations along with a multitude of other bureaucratic organisations that shape the built environment: local and national governments and their diverse agencies, charities, housing corporations and all manner of leisure and retail industries. Rarely do we discern the organisational impact these have on us and on social space, except for the occasional public outcry to specific building projects, often overturned through circuitous organisational processes.

Figure 1 **Swiss-Re and Lloyd's Buildings. The City of London has been a concentration of financial and organisational power, indicated symbolically in the work of 'signature architects'. The most recent is the so-called 'erotic gherkin' from Norman Foster, here framed by Richard Roger's Lloyd's Building. Both buildings received much architectural attention, but the artistic discourse serves to obscure the relationship between architecture and finance capitalism.**

But just as architects have needed their clients to provide resources, these clients have needed architecture to provide them with the right façade in an increasingly image-obsessed world. Glancey (1998) argues that this role of imagemaker came from the need of architects to fulfil a distinctive function in the competitive construction industry. Often the architect could be marginalised, as society wanted more buildings but for less. Many early industrial buildings did not involve architects at all, but were designed and constructed by engineers and industrialists themselves (e.g. Jones 1985: 55). 'In order to preserve their role, architects had to become "imagineers", shaping and guiding the look of buildings and the way they related to their settings,' thus, 'architects try in their different ways to create order and would-be perfection from an imperfect world' (Glancey 1998: 7).

This image-creation became much valued by powerful patrons of architecture, with the elision between the external image of the building and the image of the organisation appropriated even within industrial architecture from early in the Industrial Revolution, where classical architectural forms could be used for the exterior of industrial buildings to convey a sense of rationality and order even where the interior might be more akin to the associations of the gothic imagination of the horrors of a chaotic Hell! Jones notes that early industrial architecture was rarely innovative, content to follow the trends of the time, but that industrialists did become aware that their buildings were highly visible to the public and thus that they might need to 'add an architectural gloss to their factories to advertise or raise the status of their businesses' (1985: 53). In the case of new train stations, such as those at Euston and Curzon Street built in the 1830s, he suggests that the classical style might have been used in part to dispel the fears of travellers on the novel and untried railways (p. 68). This concern for image persists in the use made of architecture as part of the 'image management' of a company, such as the unmistakable four-cylinder form of the BMW HQ in Munich or the IBM facility in New York State shaped like a typewriter or of the ANZ bank in Sydney shaped imaginatively like a gold bar.

Here we can see that the aesthetic preoccupations of architects, rather than being somehow autonomous from or above social and economic relations, stem from a particular set of historical and cultural locations. Worthington argues that

> " The architectural profession has grown out of a continuous tension between the role of the 'organiser' and that of the 'artist'. As early as 1788, John Soane clearly captured this balance when he stated that, 'the business of the architect is to make designs and estimates to direct the works and to measure and value

> the different parts; he is the intermediate agent between the employer, whose honour and interest he is to study and the mechanic whose rights he is to define'. (2005: 6)

In studies of the professional identity and organisational practices of architects themselves, these tensions are evident (e.g. Blau 1984; Cohen *et al.* 2005; Winch and Schneider 1993). Pinnington and Morris (2002: 197) point to how the business and the aesthetic elements of architecture are brought together through the use of 'competitions' and design awards to allocate business for particular projects, a professional twist to the practice of winning business contracts that seeks to elevate the creativity and originality in the process. These studies show that architects' organisational strategies are rarely straightforwardly focused on maximising business goals: 'financial success, size and market share and how to achieve them are not always the goals of partners in architectural practice, and, indeed, may at times be in conflict with success on the aesthetic dimension' (Winch and Schneider 1993: 934).

The structure of architecture as an economic and organisational sector is diverse. Architecture as a profession is made up of different levels of practitioner, and types of organisation and professional organisation, although it is the few elite 'signature' names that become well known to the public through the media. Ashly Pinnington and Tim Morris's work (2000, 1996; Morris and Pinnington 1998) does show clearly the heterogeneity and segmentation of architectural practices, from the 'art-architects' to the 'design and build' corporations. Worthington notes that

> " The architectural profession is composed of a small number of large practices and a myriad of small firms. A recent analysis of the shape and size of the UK architectural fee market (Wisam Kamleh-Chapman report submitted for MBA at Tanaka Business School, Imperial College, London) concluded that over 85% of firms have fewer than 10 employees and contribute 25% of the total turnover. Medium to large sized architectural firms provide a wider range of services in order to achieve growth and profitability. These can range from product design to city planning, can encompass different disciplines (engineering, management, landscape and planning), and may be selling services internationally. (2005: 3–4)

So it is that architects through their organisational relations and practices come to shape the spaces within which we spend much of our
everyday life. Yet architects themselves would seem to have a somewhat
ambivalent relation to 'space'. Frank Lloyd Wright claimed that the
'reality of a building is not the container but the space within'. And in
his account of his own architectural career, Nathaniel Owings, one of
the founders of an extremely powerful architectural organisation, Skid-
more, Owings and Merrill (SOM), makes a plea for 'non-architecture'
(1973: ix). He calls towards the end of his life for open spaces within
the city and the 'joy of living in the spaces in between' (1973). This
places architecture and space almost into opposition one against the
other. Perhaps one of the reasons behind this is another tension within
the practice of architecture, pointed to by Dovey:

> Architecture and urban design are the most contradictory
> of practices – torn between a radically optimistic belief in
> the creation of the new, and a conservative acceptance of
> the prevailing order. Architects and urban designers engage
> with the articulation of dreams – imagining and constructing
> a 'better' future in someone's interest. . . . Yet architecture is also
> the most conservative of practices. This conservatism stems
> from the fundamental inertia of built form as it 'fixes' and
> 'stabilizes' the world – space is deployed to stabilize time. It
> is this antinomous quality – coupling imaginative innovation
> with a stabilizing conservatism – that makes the interpretation
> of place so interesting yet problematic. (1999: xii)

But despite the ambivalence expressed by architects, it is this relationship between built form and space that produces significant elements
of social space. Architecture forms the production of boundaries and
connections, separations and conjunctions, a hierarchy or a levelling of
spaces and places, places that may be 'front stage' or 'back stage' in
analysing the processes involved in social 'presentation of self', to borrow
Goffman's (1969) terms. They develop spaces that bring people together
(processes that can be described as 'centripetal') or move them on with
limited interaction (processes that can be described as 'centrifugal'). And
we must not forget that architects have often used their skills to go
beyond buildings towards a more total envisioning of different social and
material environments. On the one hand they have concerned themselves

with the design and placing of the minutiae of everyday life such as furniture and decoration, thus involving in their construction of social-spatial aspects of bodily comportment, aestheticised ways of experiencing specific surroundings and the cultural understanding of particular modes of life. On the other hand, they have worked outwards to the development of whole towns, cities and even societies through both argumentation[4] and involvement in committees and institutions that shape the wider spatial society. Thus we return to the pivotal role of architects and architecture in constructing meanings, social spaces and organisations, in both material and interpretative forms.

Space for organisation

Perhaps we should try at this point to explain why two organisation theorists decided to write about architecture and space, and this centres on the key role we see 'organisation' playing in the construction of the places and spaces that form the experience of everyday life. Before we turn to some analysis of this term 'organisation', we consider some of the political issues involved in the bringing together of material from different disciplinary spaces that we attempt to do in this book. To those architects, geographers and planners who are experts in these areas, we are likely to be seen as interlopers or, at best, tourists into their hard won intellectual terrain. 'Fields' are usually fenced to keep the good in and the bad out. Space permits and yet constrains our movement within it. Intellectual space is no different. Either we are invading territory about which we have no professional knowledge or we are dilettante transients, come simply to admire the view. To denizens of our own field of organisation theory we might look equally suspect. Our interest might easily be perceived as self-indulgent, shirking the 'real' issues of organisation from either a business or a sociological perspective. Our undisciplined work, therefore, requires an explanation, although, no doubt in the way of these things, there will be people from either side of the bridge upon which we now stand who remain sceptical about our commitments.

In this book, we argue that 'organisation' is central to the constitution of social space. The political response to this may well be that we are bound to argue that particular point as organisation theorists, and therefore this move constitutes a protection of, even an extension of, our own disciplinary territory. The number of disciplines which claim centrality to the social science enterprise is a very long one. But we are not here to stake another claim for core status. On the contrary, we seek to adopt an approach which takes organisation out into the world, rather than seeking to bring the world to 'organisation'. Our lack of discipline, expressed as a movement outwards, is purposeful rather than a mere casual detour. Not only do we draw our material for analysis from a range of sources outside the particular theoretical and empirical spaces usually defined as 'organisation studies', but we hope to contribute to discussions that are both within and without that particular confined and ordered space.

Looking 'inwards' towards contemporary organisation studies, we want in this book to prompt recognition of the significance of space and architecture for understanding organisation. So let us acknowledge that 'organisation' is not an innocent term. It will already have become apparent to some readers that our use of it thus far has allowed the play of multiple meanings, both between 'the organisation' as a social form or institution that facilitates collective action, and 'organisation' as an ordering process that facilitates meaning and structure. From here on in, we shall use the term 'organisation' to cover both of these approaches. These understandings underpin different perspectives within the discipline of organisation theory. We, perhaps overly ambitiously or optimistically, wish to speak inclusively across these various complexions, as well as to have something of interest to say about space and organisation beyond the bounds of the discipline of organisation studies.

In considering the relevance of space and architecture for organisation, there is a danger that we might be simply viewed by some as simply adding in another set of variables to improve the task of a more complete organisation analysis. This ploy lies within the ever-popular 'contingency theory' where contingent variables vie with each other for significance, whether statistical or semantic, within the positivistic mode. There is a reluctance to prioritise which of the variables of size or structure or leadership or strategy or culture or 'x' have significance, so adding them into the explanatory mélange is seen as an improvement. However, we believe that the importance of thinking of organisations as having a built, spatial and material dimension goes further than any 'variable' might. We argue that organisations and organising are as embedded within the material world as they are within the social. This is an aspect of organisation that is, at best, taken for granted. We do not see it as yet one more contingent variable to consider alongside the rest: for space and materiality construct organisation as organisation constructs them.

However, looking towards non-positivistic approaches to space and the material can unfortunately produce its own problems. In some of the more recent theorisings about organisations, influenced by post-modernism and the linguistic turn, we would argue that organisation has become ever more abstract and representational. In the same way that Massey (2005) argues that space has become devalued through being reduced to representation, organisation has also experienced this tendency towards abstraction. The philosophically informed ideational work carried out under postmodernism's influence has effectively moved organisation and social theory away from grounded and rooted elements in the simultaneously material and social world. We seek then throughout the book to *re-materialise* organisation and organisation theory.

Looking out beyond organisation studies, we locate what we are trying to do within a broader social theory. There are a number of reasons for this. The concern for organisation has become located, as we have mentioned, in some very confined spaces, despite the often-cited (some-times lamented) diversity of paradigms within the discipline (Pfeffer 1993). Organisation theory is most frequently found in the business or management school within the modern university, and sometimes in the sociology department under the guise of a sub-field of 'industrial' sociology. For those readers who do not think that the spatial and insti-tutional location is of particular relevance for an academic subject, on the basis that true knowledge transcends such local features, we ask you not to give up on us just yet. The 'place' of theory is important. Both of these disciplinary locations have their effects in circumscribing the relevance that 'organisation' is seen to have in modern society. Within business and management, the subject area of organisation studies becomes limited to the teaching of 'organisational behaviour' – that textbook mixture of psychology and sociology that seeks to explain to budding managers why people in their companies behave so strangely. Sometimes organisation studies is subsumed so completely that it becomes indistinguishable from other areas of 'management'.[5] The pressures on 'business schools' mean that academic disciplines are seen as handmaidens of the goals of management and business, that 'relevance' is key, and that 'organisation' itself as a phenomenon of interest is limited to that of the specific historical and social entity of the profit-oriented business organisation. And then, only in relation to issues of work and production. Even within 'business and management' much work in the fields of marketing, accountancy and finance does not recognise the organisation as a theoretical construct of importance. The source of these pressures often comes from the primary place of business and management within the university's own organisational context to act as a 'breadwinner' for other departments/disciplines, a situation which often symbolically produces 'management' as 'dirty work', tainted with the commercial as opposed to 'pure' knowledge for its own sake (Ackroyd and Crowdy 1990; Douglas 1966). It is but a short – and oft-taken – move for it to be perceived as a lesser discipline in academic terms. Thus, organisation theory partakes in that abjection, where business and management is a necessary but debased element of academe. Meanwhile, within sociology, 'industrial sociology' is quite unfashionable, and the descriptor 'industrial' limits the scope of organisation. More generally, the title of the deservedly prominent 1987 text by Lash and Urry, *The End of Organized Capitalism*, suggested that, in a global world, 'organisation' was no longer as relevant to understanding society. We argue strongly in this book that this is not the case – capitalism is *differently* organised, but to understand it we need to develop a wider conceptualisation of 'organisation' than the one that is currently dominant in the mainstream locations of organisation studies.

We are not saying here that interesting and theoretically informed academic work is not being undertaken in these university settings: of course it is. It would be very easy to go on at length about this, but this takes us away from our current concern with space and organisation (but see for example, Grey 2001; Parker 2004). The point that we wish to make is that 'organisation' in its widest sense provides much more insight into society and social theory than its circumscribed institutional and disciplinary location appears to suggest. It is perhaps works of popular political investigation or of popular culture that continue to demonstrate the significance of organisation. Films as diverse as *Disclosure*, *Blade Runner* and *Glengarry Glen Ross* and television programmes such as *The Office* illustrate how we should take the personal and political effects of organisations just as seriously as did Kafka and Dickens in understanding our present and future. More importantly, investigations such as Klein's widely read and highly influential *No Logo* (2001) are quick to show the significance of the corporation in shaping the political economy of global movements in capital, as well as in recognising the centrality of spatial politics to the organised nature of both production and consumption. But in academic analyses of society, the pivotal particularity of 'organisation' often slips out of sight, with analysis continuing at the macro level of society or culture or the economy, or at the micro level of the individual.

So, what do we mean by 'organisation' and what is its relationship to space and architecture? As indicated by the quotation from Etzioni at the head of this chapter, we believe that organisations as specific social collective arrangements are a highly influential and pervasive character-istic of modern societies. Following Etzioni we are not solely interested in the 'work' organisations that form the dominant subject of organisa-tion studies. 'Organisation' is frequently taken to mean the organisation of production of either goods or services, predominantly for-profit, and epitomised by the factory and the office. Organisations of production are important, but a predominantly economic or managerial view of them can obscure both the relationship of organisation to the personal, to the self and its relations with others on the one hand, and to the wider political issues of power and social structures on the other. And organisations are also central to other aspects of social life as well as production, including, as we have tried to show, the domestic or so-called 'private' sphere. Tradi-tionally viewed as separate, the spheres of production or reproduction or consumption, have been treated as both analytically and spatially distinct (Slater 1998: 138–50 provides a useful discussion of the changing nature and contradictions of these dichotomies). However, one of the recurring themes of this book is that the boundaries between the categories and social spaces of these different spheres are often blurred. Furthermore, organisations are often analysed as social entities, without regard for how they are constructed spatially and materially. In this book, we shall try to build an analysis of organisations that understands the social and the material as mutually enacting and fundamentally 'entangled'.

We also see 'organisation' as indicating those social processes that produce social structure and meaning. Organisation is an important ordering process that produces particular knowledge and understandings of the world, but this is not simply a cognitive process that produces discourses. Organisation is also accomplished through spatial, embodied and material relations which can construct and reproduce certain power effects, as we shall see in more specific ways in the next chapter. The ordering and meanings that are produced through spatial organisation are often hidden through being taken-for-granted aspects of everyday life that seem 'normal'. Thus, it is as both an academic and as a political project that we seek to bring organisation and space together into the place of social theory.

The organisation of the book

Before proceeding to the rest of the book, we should pause and say a few words about the perspective taken. We are passionate about the arguments that we make on the need to reconsider social relations as irreducibly spatial, embodied and material. We are equally convinced that there is a need to recognise the organisational and organised nature of social life and the political effects of this on the possibilities and constraints of social relations in spatial, embodied and material terms.

However, although these are strongly held convictions, we also recognise that the stories we tell about the interconnections between space and organisation are only some of the multiple stories that could be told. We speak from a certain set of perspectives that are not drawn solely from academic theoretical research but from the social relations within which we live and write. As Stanley and Wise so tellingly put it, there is no research that has not gone through the medium of the researcher (1993). Thrift (1996: xi) adds that 'theory is situated and recast as a set of narrative sketches'. Our stories about space and organisation inevitably derive from our own social and spatial positions: from working-class coal-mining communities (though from the geographically different areas of

South Wales and Northumberland), from the cultural and social experiences of the relatively prosperous and peaceful capitalist post-World War II UK (albeit from two areas that experience a certain marginality), and now from family and professional relations set in 'middle England', so 'middling' in so many ways that it forms a key locus for political focus groups! We do not believe that any theory-building can 'stand outside' the conditions of its own making.

What is presented here is intended to be one contribution to a set of stories and conversations about space and organisation, not an end point. The 'empirical' examples are not intended as universal cases, but as intellectual springboards through which we can explore some interactions of space and organisation. We hope in this to reach for the integrity to which Williams refers when he says,

> " Having integrity, then, is being able to speak in a way which allows of answers. Honest discourse permits response and continuation; it invites collaboration by showing that it does not claim to be, in and of itself, final. It does not seek to prescribe the tone, the direction, or even the vocabulary of a response. And it does all this by showing in its own working a critical self-perception, displaying the axioms to which it believes itself accountable; that is to say, it makes it clear that it accepts, even within its own terms of reference, that there are ways in which it may be questioned and criticized. (2000: 5)

In telling our own stories in this way, we have tried to avoid the academic mode of 'making space' for one's own account by pointing out the shortcomings of existing narratives: the theoretical equivalent of using one's elbows to create a path through a crowd![6]

Another reason for this approach is the inter-disciplinary nature of this book. In order to construct our own edifice we have built upon diverse and rich materials from many places. We hope, then, that what we have created is of interest to readers across different fields. It is in this spirit that we try to refrain from fencing ourselves into our own field of organisation studies, and solely engaging with ongoing debates within that domain, yet still offer a focus on 'organisation' as a key social dynamic.

From this point of orientation, the rest of the book follows a broad movement from 'the spaces of organisation' towards the 'organisation of space'. In doing this it develops from a perspective that is more concerned with the empirical spaces of organisations, taken in the broadest sense to cover production, reproduction and consumption, and how they produce 'organisation', as a social dynamic. Later chapters move towards a more theoretical orientation that has at its heart a critique of that organisation theory and social theory which ignores the material, spatial and embodied characteristics of social processes and practices. The final section considers the possibilities of changing both theoretical and empirical spaces of organisation.

Lefebvre's analysis of social space is taken as the starting point for exploring some of the characteristics of organisational spaces. Chapter 2 can be seen as developing an analysis of 'representations of space' – what we characterise as 'organised space'. These are the spaces deliberately developed for the practices of organisation, and the forms of power embedded within them, often overlooked because of the taken-for-granted nature of space. The following chapter starts from the idea of 'representational space': the imaginary and lived spaces of organisation. In this, we look at how social, organised spaces are lived through the embodied subject. The second focus is on representations of space as connected with constructing identity and categories of subject.

Chapters 4 and 5 form Part II of the book, looking at the 'organisation of space'. Chapter 4 examines Lefebvre's conceptualisation of 'spatial practices'. This is something that can be described as 'the political economy of space and organisation'. It is about the 'routes and networks' (Lefebvre 1991: 38) of spaces, how they may be constructed, connected and separated within different economies and societies. We are concerned to understand the organisational practices that constitute and are constituted by these wider social-spatial practices. This theme is continued in Chapter 5, which considers how boundaries, both spatial and theoretical are constructed and sustained, and with what political consequences. It takes the notion of 'private space', the home, and considers how this too is an organised space.

The final part of the book attempts to construct a re-theorisation of social and organisational theory that is materialised, embodied and spatialised, through looking at the possibilities for 'alternative' spaces and organisations, and through building a conceptualisation of the mutual enactment of the social and the material.

Notes

[1] He wrote over 60 books and 300 articles (Shields 1999: 2), hence we cannot hope to do justice to the extent and development of his thought. It is also worth adding that his style can be difficult to follow, in part, according to Shields, because of his method of dictating his texts to a 'typist', often his female partner, and the works thus constructed include clarifications and discussions that take place with the unseen and unacknowledged amanuensis (1999: 6).

[2] Lefebvre does not explicitly define 'imaginary spaces' in *The Production of Space*, but perhaps the use of 'imaginary' used by Gatens (1996) in her discussion of embodiment can provide some delineation. She defines imaginary as not being simply the product of the imagination, but as 'those images, symbols, metaphors and representations which help construct various forms of subjectivity. In this sense, I am concerned with the (often unconscious) imaginaries of a specific culture: those ready-made images and symbols through which we make sense...' (1996: viii). Both Gatens and Lefebvre are careful to point out that the imaginary should not be put into a dichotomous relationship with some idea of 'reality' nor divorced from lived experiences of embodiment and social space.

[3] Although we will see that elsewhere Harvey does include the organisation in his analyses, as, for example, the Baltimore housing case discussed in Chapter 4.

[4] The two examples that spring to mind are Richard Rogers' books *Cities for a Smaller Planet*, from the Reith Lectures, and (with Anne Power) *Cities for a Smaller Country*, stemming from work with the Urban Task Force in the UK. Perhaps more controversial is the second, Will Alsop's *Supercities*, including his series of programmes for Channel 4 in Autumn 2003, advocating joined-up swathes of cities across the UK.

[5] One of us had the discomforting experience on being appointed to a university position in 'management' of being asked if we could teach 'operations management'! No doubt this crossover of management disciplines is assumed and even necessary to some, particularly smaller, management departments.

[6] We are indebted to Martin Parker for this lovely spatial and embodied image!

Part I

The Space of Organisation

INTRODUCTION: THE SPACES OF ORGANISATION AND THE ORGANISATION OF SPACE
• BUILDING ORGANISATION: SECURING AND OBSCURING POWER • BUILDING PEOPLE:
IDENTITIES AND SPACES • A POLITICAL ECONOMY OF ORGANISED SPACE • BOUNDARY
CROSSINGS: THE FRONTIERS OF ORGANISED SPACE • BUILDING A SOCIAL MATERIALITY:
SPATIAL AND EMBODIED POLITICS IN ORGANISATION • ALTERNATIVE SPACES:
THE RADICAL ORGANISATION OF SPACE? • CONCLUSIONS: DISORGANISING SPACE

2 building organisation: securing and obscuring power

The most successful ideological effects are those that have no words, and ask no more than complicitous silence.

(Dovey 1999: 2)

Introduction

Buildings are frequently associated with power in the most explicit ways. In *The Edifice Complex*, Sudjec examines precisely this notion that 'architecture is used by political leaders to seduce, to impress, and to intimidate' (2005: 2). He starts with Saddam Hussein's programme of monument building, quickly followed by those of Hitler, Stalin, Mussolini and both Maoist and modern China. But spatial power is not solely the province of leaders or states, and it is not even necessarily at its most potent in the overt form of the monument. Places and spaces shape our actions, interactions and sense of meaning, emotions and identity. The built world we inhabit tells us narratives, stories about ourselves and the societies that we live in, and it simultaneously influences what we do or do not do through structures that can be described by the most mundane of terms: 'walls', 'doors', 'windows', 'corridors' and 'steps'.

Organisations, too, are characteristically associated with the production of power (e.g. Bradley 1999; Clegg 1975; 1979; 1989; Etzioni 1964; Halford and Leonard 2001; Pfeffer 1981; Mintzberg 1983). In this chapter, we start to explore how the spaces and places of organisation – encompassing production, consumption and leisure organisations – are part and parcel of power relations. The built fabric and the very materials of organisation are usually seen as neutral in terms of power, indeed, in terms of social relations altogether. This in itself is one of the most significant ways in which buildings produce power effects: because they are almost invisible as social constructs. Framing of places through the construction of boundaries, connections, order and shape tends to be taken for granted. Debate about building tends to concentrate on the most efficient and functional use of space, but this is not necessarily seen as a function of power, and rarely are these spaces understood as constructing a particular phenomenological set of experiences, individual or collective. Some spaces may be bemoaned as not being as functional as they could be – witness any group of women queuing for the toilets in the interval at the theatre! However, the links between spatial form and practices of power are rarely made. So, for example, little attention may be given to the way that *Men's* and *Ladies'* lavatories are places that remain very heavily encoded and protected, hence any 'mistakes' over the use of these spaces is experienced through embarrassment and humour. This is a form of spatial control that surfaces most clearly through an ambivalence about the codification and use of space. Thus transsexuals face huge dilemmas about into which toilet they should go. Often the *Disabled* toilet is chosen because it avoids the clash with other users and the identity dangers that accompany this (Holliday and Hassard 2001; Munt 2001). In this chapter, we borrow a phrase from Burawoy (1979, 1985; Burrell and Dale 2004) that, we think, captures the workings of spatial power, although we deploy it in a different manner from Burawoy who used it to refer to the simultaneously achieved and hidden nature of surplus value through the labour process. The 'securing and obscuring' of power is about how power is concurrently maintained and its origins and processes hidden. It is at its most salient when it is embedded, embodied and thus taken as natural and inevitable.

A useful exploration of the relationship between power and built form can be found in Kim Dovey's *Framing Places: Mediating Power in Built Form*. Here he states that 'placemaking is an inherently elite practice. This does not suggest that built form is inherently oppressive. However, it does suggest that places are necessarily programmed and designed in accord with certain interests – primarily the pursuit of amenity, profit, status and political power' (1999: 1). In most modern societies, these interests do not stem directly from the will of individual power-holders but are mediated through organisations of all sorts. These include the state, and from the state, local government and quasi-governmental agencies; and corporate capitalist companies, and, more and more frequently, those organisations that stand between the two, with a foot in both state and corporate camps, such as agencies involved with Public Finance Initiative (PFI) building projects in the UK (Cohen *et al.* 2005; Monbiot 2001). We can see here connections with Lefebvre's discussions about the dominance of 'conceived' or 'organised' spaces, and the 'abstract space' of capitalism, described in the previous chapter.

Dovey analyses the different forms that spatial power can take, arguing power is not 'lodged inertly in built form' but is found in the everyday practices which are inherently mediated by built form (1999: 15). The power of built form may not necessarily be directly causal, but is a possibility; it is latent. He argues that built form can be coercive, where architecture or space can incorporate the inherent threat of power, and suggests three forms of this. The first is 'domination' or 'intimidation', which he equates with military parades, public monuments and the deliberate use of exaggerated scale or an imposing location (p. 10). However, in many ways spatial power is not so overt, though no less coercive, and here, for this more subtle reading, he evokes the Latin root of *'coercere'* – 'to surround'. Thus the second form of coercion in built form is that of 'manipulation'. Manipulation of space is achieved through keeping occupants ignorant of the sources and the operation of power: 'The subject is "framed" in a situation which may resemble free choice, but there is a concealment of intent' (p. 11). The third form of coercion as described by Dovey is 'seduction'. At once subtle and sophisticated, seduction of behaviour through space is achieved through the (apparent) articulation of the occupants' interests, desires and self-identity: 'The experience of place has the capacity to move us deeply, to "ground" our being, to open the question of "spirit". Yet the very potency of place experience renders it particularly vulnerable to the ideological appropriations of power' (p. 16).

Organisational spaces may sometimes use overt coercion, for example in the monumentality of tower blocks and expanses of glass. However, both manipulation and seduction can aid the achievement of the ordered behaviour that is embedded in everyday organisational life. These forms of spatial power are especially salient in understanding the current taste for restructuring the physical and aesthetic spaces of organisations. As Weinstein points out, 'Coercion consists in transforming private, communal, group or cultural spaces into organizational spaces in which people perform actions directed towards the fulfilment of another's plan, or refrain from performing actions subversive of the realization of another's plan' (1972: 69). This connects strongly with Lefebvre's (1991) analysis of the domination and appropriation of space by certain interests, especially under capitalism, as discussed in the previous chapter.

There are, of course, many cases where the built form is deliberately constructed so as to produce very intentional power effects. Two examples which immediately come to mind are Haussmann's driving of wide boulevards through central Paris as a deliberate act to make the barricades of a rebellious populace more difficult[1] and Le Corbusier's description, also thinking of French social unrest, of the high-rise block as 'the grave of the riot'. Other buildings and spaces are as powerful in their effects if less deliberately intended. The built environment can be constructed in such a way as to achieve 'programmed action', where we know that there will be consequences for 'acting otherwise'. Surveillance may be used to ensure that we follow these forms of behaviour and to alert us to the potential costs of not doing so. Although the use of terms such as 'coercion' and 'surveillance' seem to suggest a negative form of power, this is not necessarily so. For example, the programmed and monitored silence of a library may be found coercive by the student with a mobile phone call to make, but as a conducive environment by the academic with a paper to finish! Indeed, spatial organisation offers some possibilities and yet takes away others in routine ways. Dovey's analysis has the problematic tendency to see spatial power as embodying an intentional unidirectional 'power over'. He acknowledges this problem in relation to the argument that in being seduced by spatial forms of power, people do not recognise their own 'real' interests as being compromised. The difficulty with this is that it suggests that the pleasure and identity that they do experience are somehow not 'real' or 'authentic'. It is perhaps helpful here, then, to turn to Foucault's (1977, 1980, 1985) discussions on power which emphasise that power is not simply repressive but also productive: power itself can produce pleasure, desire, self-fulfilment and identity. Spatial power is therefore also productive.

Power, then, does not only operate in one-dimensional negative forms. Urban planners talk of 'desiring paths' for those routes that spring up in unintended ways and places, across courtyards and lawns, or through hedges, rather than following the designated paths. Yet the forms of acts of resistance are often produced by the very forms of power embedded in the spaces in which they take place. One of us has a nephew who manages a large city centre shopping mall. He recounts the frequency with which acts of sexual intimacy or obscenity are performed deliberately by members of the public in front of the security cameras: so much so that tapes of such acts are compiled by security staff for wider distribution. Since power is exercised over the shopper through visibility, resistance is also expressed through that visibility, rather than through finding, as one might expect, secret and secure spaces in which to enact defiance to control.

In this chapter, we start to look at the 'spaces of organisation'. The first section considers some of the ways in which buildings embody power. As we have already indicated, power is not just found in the external appearance of the buildings, but also in their construction of spaces and boundaries, inclusions and exclusions, places for meeting and those for segregation. Power is not solely in the creation of the monumental, the overt portrayal of power, but in how built forms embody different interests and identities. And power does not simply produce intentional effects, but also the taken-for-granted, the cultural assumptions and norms that become part of our spaces and hence our social relations. The second section of the chapter takes these aspects of spatial power and relates them to some key forms of organisation.

Space and power: enchantment, emplacement and enactment

In considering some of the links between space and power, three distinctions can be made in order to make the processes more analytically clear. The first is one that immediately springs to mind when space and power are discussed. This is the fusion of the material and the symbolic, and includes but is not exhausted by the sort of built expression of power that Sudjec concentrates upon in *The Edifice Complex* (2005). It may be described as an **enchantment** of space, of linking together matter and meaning in such a way as to produce various power effects. The second element can be described as **emplacement** in space, and refers to the construction of certain places for certain activities and certain people. It involves the processes of inclusion within and exclusion from specific spaces. The third element can be seen as **enactment** in space. Whereas emplacement implies that there are boundaries and compartments producing effects of fixity, enactment of spaces is about the ways that social spaces are lived, are processed through, are experienced through mobility and what power effects this brings about. Of course, as with all heuristic devices, these three elements are artificially separated for the purposes of analysis.

The power of buildings is most obviously seen in its monumental form. It is difficult to walk into a building such as the immense Cathedral at Seville or to stare at the lotus bud towers of the colossal Angkor Wat temple complex in Cambodia and not experience a sense of awe.[2] This may be to do with the sheer scale of these buildings, and an appreciation of the amount of dedication, not to mention resources, that went into their construction. It may be that in a secular society many will not have the same sense of awe as those who planned and built and carved for the glory of their gods, but even so something of the symbolic power of the architecture remains expressed through its materiality: it is this fusion of the material and the symbolic that produces such potent **enchantments**.

It is this experience of power that drove Hitler, with the architect Albert Speer, to design the Reich Chancellery in Berlin, inspired by Versailles: 'When one enters the Reich Chancellery, one should have the feeling that one is visiting the master of the world. One will arrive there along wide avenues containing the Triumphal arch, the Pantheon (the domed hall), the Square of the People—things to take your breath away' (Hitler quoted in Dovey 1999: 55).

Sudjec (2005) recounts the journey of the Czech president Hacha in 1939 through the ceremonial arches, past massive bronze statues, across a floodlit courtyard redolent of military strength, up the tall narrow steps to the entrance, and through a series of long halls designed to impress and intimidate, finally into the 4000 square feet of Hitler's 'study'. Hacha, with a weak heart, was to collapse twice under the pressure, having to be revived and forced to sign away Czechoslovakia into Nazi hands. As Dovey explains,

> This building needs to be understood as a form of symbolic choreography where the spatial structure operates to control the framing of a series of representational themes. Germany as a one-party state was signified in almost every space through the image of the eagle above the swastika, and naturalized through the oak and eagle icons. The narrative pathway constructed a myth of the progression of history through links to Greece, Rome and Paris, punctuated by a mounting of steps. The use of materials such as bronze, stone and marble evoked a sense of timeless immortality. The building also served to signify the controlled force of the nation state. The scale of both the vast and useless voids and the formal designs that enclosed them were designed to belittle the human subject. (1999: 59–61)

Thus the material–symbolic fusion is achieved to even greater intensity through the narrative enactment of the spaces.

Height, unsurprisingly, is an element of the symbolic–material fusion that organisations have particularly drawn upon. Companies struggle to build the world's highest building for they recognise that with height comes prestige; it is symbolic of potency (Dovey 1999; King 2004). Long before the collapse of the World Trade Center twin towers in New York on 11 September, 2001, and all that this revealed about the links between architectural symbolism and the nation state, corporations had vied with each other to dominate the New York skyline. In the 1930s, the Chrysler building, constructed largely from automobile funds, faced up to the Empire State Building, which was built in parallel by General Motors' money. Domination of the skyline is and has been equated to domination of markets and of the competition (King 2004). Part of this symbolic web of meaning comes from the equation of height with hierarchy.

'Hierarchy' means rule by the saintly priests who have a clear and obvious relationship of closeness to God. Dante's medieval texts written soon after 1300 are keen to elaborate on the relationship of hierarchy to height (and depth) where the vertical is an organisational dimension of the spaces and places of heaven, purgatory and hell. Hierarchy, heavenliness and height were inextricably linked. In 1300, Dante visited

San Gimignano, beloved of the tourist books as the 'Medieval Manhattan', as an ambassador from Florence. Two families of equal status lived in the town but belonged to two politically and ideologically distinct factions. The rivalry between the Ardinghellis and the Salvuccis first erupted in 1245 and the feud became constructively expressed in the skyline of competing towers. The local authorities at the end of that century decided it was time to step in and reduce this competition for social climbing and had built the municipal Commune Tower over which nothing would be allowed to be built taller. Because they were now capped at 54 metres high, architectural competition took the form of numbers of towers not their absolute height. Of the 72 towers built, 15 remain, the highest of which is the Torre Grossa, which had just been completed when Dante arrived in the town. For Dante, climbing to high places such as in San Gimignano was associated with 'delightful horror', the experience of the sublime, combining fear, terror and contemplation, hence the 'dreaming' spires. Tall places, whether architectural or natural, are meeting places of the earthly and the celestial and came to be seen as the work of the 'Sovereign Architect'. Height carries with it the association with the sky, the immensity of space, the dwelling place of the gods, the escape from the grounded nature of earthly travails and the sheer power of the vertical. All this points to the valorisation of the possessors of height and in part explains their ability to dominate.

But the symbolic does not have to be associated only with the monumental and elite. Indeed, it can be embedded very powerfully in the everyday. All aspects of life have seen a growing importance of image and 'aestheticisation' (Featherstone 1991), often associated with the development of consumption as a central activity and source of meaning in modern life.

Benjamin's (1999) major study of the Parisian Arcades captures an early stage in this particular symbolic and material fusion. In his first sketches for the Arcades Project in the early 1920s, Benjamin calls the arcades a 'Dialectical Fairyland'. Aesthetics is used by architects in creating these new palaces of crystal where the bourgeoisie could stroll in relative protection from the mob, by designers in laying out their shop windows to attract the attention of the buyer, and by owners in the training of the new breed of shop assistants who had artistic backgrounds and knowledge.

The Arcades are architectures of power in their disciplinary effects on producers and consumers, but more than this, they allow 'imaginary spaces', our hopes, dreams, desires and aspirations, to be appropriated. They facilitate the construction of the consumer through the fantasy experience of buying. The beautiful layout of the Arcades created a sense of them being 'phantasmagorical', as Benjamin expressed it: they formed the wish symbols or ideals, the 'century's magic images'. In his adoption of the idea of phantasmagoria to analyse the powerful fusion of symbolic and material, Benjamin expresses exactly the 'securing and obscuring' of power that pervades their spatial organisation. The phantasmagoria was a form of picture projection that became popular in the early nineteenth century.

> Painted slides were illuminated in such a way that a succession of ghosts ('phantasms') was paraded before a startled audience.... [I]t used back-projection to ensure that the audience remained largely unaware of the source of the image: Its flickering creations thus appeared to be endowed 'with a spectral reality of their own'. Benjamin used the phantasmagoria as an allegory of modern culture, which explains both his insistence on seeing commodity culture as a projection – not a reflection – of the economy, as its mediated (even mediatized) representation, and also his interest in the visual, optical, 'spectacular' inscriptions of modernity. (Gregory 1994: 231–3)

The technology of the phantasmagoria hid the production of its images, as aestheticised aspects of consumer society hide the relations of production that drive it.

Benjamin and the Critical Theorists of the Frankfurt School with whom he was associated articulate the politics behind the aesthetics which blur and transform the conditions of commodification and exploitation that underlie the social organisation of production. Just as Lefebvre analyses how the power relations of capitalism are obscured in 'abstract space', so for the Critical Theorists art is used so that people are increasingly inured to these socioeconomic underpinnings of capitalism (Tiedemann 1999). The term 'phantasmagoria' is in *Das Kapital* but Benjamin brings it to bear on consumption, as a deceptive image designed to dazzle, in which use value is hidden behind exchange value. He recognises that such features may be deceptive yet promising of social change at the same time. He is interested in the surface 'lustre' of beautiful aesthetics used to sell and produce commodities in order to fabricate some transcendent element to capitalism. Part of this fantasy experience of space, we emphasise, is that whilst the phantasmagoria dazzles, it simultaneously desensitises. Benjamin recognises this 'deadening effect', and we can extend this into looking at the interwoven nature of 'aesthetics' and 'anaesthetics'.

This is the dialectical relationship by which the human subject is seen as desensitised to other events that are taking place at the very same time as she or he experiences aesthetics. To the extent that one of the human senses is highly stimulated, the others become under-stimulated. The phantasmagoria of modern life is the product of multiple forms of labour process. It is this set of social relations and spaces that is hidden in the aesthetic dazzle. Yet this production necessitates, to a greater or lesser extent, the desensitisation of those who labour to produce the dazzle. Importantly, the consumer's experience is often very different from that of the aesthetic or emotional labourer. These labourers often survive the 'switching on' of the spectacle by 'switching off' themselves (Hancock and Tyler 2000; Hochschild 1983). The relationship between these experiences of self and the aestheticisation of work are further discussed in the next chapter.

Aesthetics and anaesthetics are both a matter of the management of the senses and the construction of certain organised spaces. Bel Geddes' design for the General Motors stand 'Futurama' in 1939 seems to have some of these features. In what prefigures a lot of Disney-type rides, visitors (sometimes GM car workers) were placed in a travelling vehicle from which they were meant to see the freeways of 1960 and the ameliorating effects these were to have on city life. By all accounts, visitors were amazed and delighted by this diorama. It can be seen as a phantasamagoria which dazzled the consumer and allowed GM to press ahead for freeway expansion on a massive scale.

The processes of 'Disneyization' (Bryman 2004) or of 'theming' (Gottdiener 1997) illustrate the spatial power embedded in this confluence of the consumption of the symbolic as achieved through the manufacture of an aesthetic realm and the consumption of the material objects placed within this setting. It is perhaps a perfect example of Dovey's simultaneously coercive-seductive spatial power as seen in the original meaning of the word 'coerce' as 'to surround'. The control of space is seen as essential within Disney-owned property, and through the ever-growing number of theme parks and places of the heritage industry. Once inside this spatial envelope, European fairytales fused with pre-industrial America dominate the symbolic realm. As guests are processed through their rides, the queuing areas have become part of the experience and are designed to make long periods of time spent waiting for something to happen less irksome by suggesting that as you wait you are still having an enjoyable experience. Just as hospitals process one to behave as a patient, schools as a pupil and so on, Disney-holding areas before the rides process the 'guest' to behave as such. Of course the guest–host relationship is a combined social and spatial one. The guest is in a particular place at the invitation of the host. The host thus holds the power of the space: the guest enters to the extent and at a pace dictated by the host. The relationship draws on a cultural history of polite and disciplined behaviour. The spatial dominance implied in the host opening their door to the guest (who is a visitor and does not therefore belong there) is also, incidentally, the source of the feminist dislike of male door-holding behaviour! What appears to be a trivial ritual at which it might seem out of proportion to take offence is underpinned by the symbolic control of space. Where it occurs in the workplace the spatial relations being acted out are symbolically that the woman employee does not really belong there. The idea that there are rightful and wrongful places for different categories of people takes us to explore the social-spatial power of emplacement in space.

Emplacement implies control in space through fixing. It indicates a certain ordering or organisation: everything and everybody are put in their rightful places. Fixity is also associated with knowledge, with the achievement of a crucial 'grid of intelligibility' (Butler 2004: 42; Foucault 1981: 93). It is a central part of many disciplines. Geography (maps), geometry (co-ordinates), architecture (buildings), anatomy (the fixing and staining of tissue sections), surveying (triangulation) and many more are all fundamentally based in the fixing of knowledge through their techniques of emplacement.

In a famous chapter on 'docile bodies' in *Discipline and Punish* (1977), Foucault provides a detailed analysis of what Lefebvre means by 'representations of space'. Although prisons are the main focus of the study, here Foucault looks at the organised space of early factories. His analysis of the spatial micropolitics of factory workspaces shows them to consist of four elements: first, *enclosure*, which he links with the development of factories as specific defined spaces for labour; second, *partitioning*, which is to locate individuals so as to facilitate some communications and prevent others, and to keep their movements controlled and visible. Enclosure and partitioning mean that 'each individual has his own place; and each place its individual' (1977: 143). Third, there is *classification*, through the use of functional sites, whereby the individuals thus partitioned are grouped into like operations, so that supervision was 'both general and individual' (p. 145) ensuring that workers doing the same task could be compared and classified according to speed and skill, and this led to the fourth characteristic of *ranking*, or placing individuals into a 'hierarchy of knowledge or ability' arranged in space (p. 147). The elements are central to the processes of emplacement, so we will look at them in a little more detail.

Foucault argues that 'Discipline sometimes requires enclosure, the specification of a place heterogeneous to all others and closed in upon itself. It is the protected place of disciplinary monotony' (1977: 141). He sees enclosure and partitioning as central in the development of the monasteries, schools, military barracks and also the factory. However, it would be limiting to see enclosure as operating in the same way in all cases. Enclosure can produce potentially different social relations. It cannot be seen as one-dimensional in its effects, for it can have multiple meanings. Enclosure can be a physical boundary that gives shelter and definition or it can be seen as a restriction, a way of forming exclusions and inclusions. It creates mental and social enclosures or sets of distinctions as well as material ones. Enclosure can act as a 'container' which enhances sensory stimulation by providing a single focus. However, the limitation of variety through uniformity in space can also produce a deadening effect. Partitioning further develops this process of separating and dividing spaces, each homogeneous but differentiated from the others. Enclosure and partitioning can create an environment where the amount of information is restricted, thus 'increasing legibility' of that environment (Kaplan and Kaplan 1998). This can work in different ways. It can reduce conflicting information or interpretation of a setting or the social relations within this, with the result of reducing potential conflict, resistance or awareness of otherness. Or it may work to enhance and heighten the experience of the setting, with greater emotion or concentration, thus as a way to maximise creativity or innovation.

The 'ha-ha', a military-inspired ditch to keep cattle and livestock out of the garden, is an interesting instance of an enclosure that does not work through the visual, but through a hidden physical barrier. It is no less powerful for that. It was designed so that the gardens of the propertied classes in the eighteenth century (including the growing number of the wealthy merchant classes) appeared to be integrated into the wider country landscape. The latter was itself as artificially created as the gardens, through the forcible enclosure of farmland, the expulsion of peasants and importation of suitably arcadian-looking cattle, and even the wholesale movement of the estate village in the case of Sir Robert Walpole's Houghton Hall in Norfolk. His son, Horace Walpole, was to say 'the ha-ha permitted the gardener to leap the fence and find that nature is a garden' (van Zuylen 1995: 85). Houghton Hall established the eighteenth-century fashion for enclosure, and in its separation of farm labourer from gentleman owner it gave a physical expression to the separation of classes and their interests. It offered the protected enclosure with the emphasis being upon the view of the property that it offered from the main house. However, in Jane Austen's novel *Mansfield Park* the character of Maria Bertram, flirting with the attractive Mr Crawford whilst her fiancé is away finding the key for the gate, says, 'that iron gate, that ha-ha give me a feeling of restraint and hardship' (1983: 93). Finally, she climbs over the ha-ha with the man to walk away with him into the 'wilderness' with no other chaperone. By the end of the novel this woman, now married, is disgraced by her willingness to climb over social and moral boundaries to run off with Crawford. Thus, it is made clear by Austen that the boundary of the gentle-woman's world should be marked by remaining within this sunken 'fence', and that to move outside the protective enclosures of gender and class is to put oneself outside the comfort and protection of social and family relations.

Spatial boundaries and codes have been important in the establishment of gendered social relations in organisations too. Cohn (1981) compares female clerical labour in the British Post Office and the Great

Western Railway between 1857 and 1937. Resistance to the employment of women was strong, and spatial constraints were deployed as the key to defending the male terrain. During the First World War, the shortage of male staff in the London Sorting Office led to the consideration of employing women. At first, this was strenuously fought off by arguments based upon the difficulties of having men and women working together in the same space or alternatively the need to construct expensive new segregated offices, not to mention the need to provide restrooms and chairs for women. Men stood up to sort, but it was not considered that women would be able to undertake such strenuous activity. Instead, wages for men were increased under the rationale that pay rises to attract men would be cheaper than introducing women. When severe labour shortages demonstrated that this policy was not working, the employment of women became the only option to maintain the postal service. In the event, the spatial problems were quite easily overcome by giving the women a separate floor at the sorting office, thus providing segregated office space and lavatories, and amazingly it turned out that women were as able to work standing up as the men (1981: 62–3)! Other studies show that ideally women were to be kept out of the physical and economic space altogether as they were in the case of the printers (Cockburn 1983), but where this was not possible their segregation in different physical spaces could be used to produce hierarchical economic effects to their detriment (Philips and Taylor 1980; Collinson *et al.* 1990). Thus, enclosure provides protectionism in more than one form.

The segregation of social spaces, however, is only partly about economic rationality and protectionism. Fear of the Other, the unknown, is manifest through the fear of touching, of sharing the same bodily space. Entrances to children's schools often were single sex, as were those of offices and factories so that the lower orders might not face the temptations of the flesh. This physical separation of the sexes continues in Islamic architecture. For example, the Sultan Qaboos University in Oman has separate lower and upper walkways for men and women to access the building and separate seating in classrooms. The famous Larkin Building, designed by Frank Lloyd Wright in 1902 to sit on an industrial site surrounded by railroads, factories and a gasworks became a Buffalo monument to cleanliness through its soap products. The building was hermetically sealed off to keep its products clean before being shipped off from this vast mail order edifice. It enshrined the separation also of its staff in very clear ways reflective of Victorian concerns about uncontrolled (hetero-) sexuality. Injunctions to work hard were everywhere in the main packing hall and the rhetoric of cleanliness's proximity to God was an early attempt at manufacturing a corporate culture which 'improved' its workforce.

Protection might also be seen as being on behalf of those outside the enclosure rather than for those within. For centuries, Jews were forced to live in a separate part of the towns in which they worked and worshipped. These areas are usually described as the 'ghetto' following on from that part of Venice where their enclosure was first made most complete, aided by the physical barriers of the canals (Sennett 1994) (Figure 2). The Jews came to face confinement of this kind where 'inter-cultural osmosis' was precluded in space by spatial practices. As Sennett comments, the Venetians were simultaneously fascinated by and repelled by difference (1994: 215). By being fixed in space the place of Jews was known and subject to a greater control than if there had been free movement, but more importantly it prevented contact, mixing and thus contamination. Reminiscent of Mary Douglas's notion (1966) that dirt is matter out of place, the language of cleanliness is often used where fixity is being sought. Each group is fixed into its own apparent sameness and marked out as different from the others (cf. Kanter 1977; Tajfel 1982).

In these examples of the construction of enclosure and partitioning, it has become clear that Foucault's other two elements of spatial emplacement are also occurring, as groups and individuals are segregated and compared one with another. Markus (1989, 1993) argues that buildings are 'classifying devices'. They function to reproduce these groupings through social-spatial relations that are facilitated or obstructed, and they locate classes of similar status at a similar 'depth' within the building, in terms of distance from the entrance and access to the more private or prominent areas. As we have already said, status is often indicated by relative height and controllable spatial area so that location, as well as size, is reflective of relative status.

In early school systems, a spatial arrangement known as 'place-capturing' was popular (Markus 1993: 57). Here pupils' seats were

Figure 2 **The Ghetto in Venice. The original Ghetto Nuovo was a bounded area of Venice surrounded on all sides by water, connected by only two bridges which were closed at night. About 700 Jews were sent there in 1516. Although they carried out their business in the city during the day, at dusk they had to return to the ghetto where the drawbridges were raised and outward facing windows shuttered. With balconies not being allowed, the outside of the building appeared as a wall. Jews were forced to rent the buildings at extortionate prices, and buildings grew to six or seven storeys high to capitalise on this.**

arranged according to their academic ranking. When one pupil achieved a better grade than another they would physically change places and move to a 'superior' location. As Markus comments, this system 'gave competition *spatial* outcomes' (1993: 57). In the experience of one of us this was still used in 1960s English grammar schools, so that if one's surname was early in the alphabet and one was not good at oral French then one started in a 'superior' seat but ended up close to the last desk in the classroom on a regular basis. This 'place-capturing' was essentially giving a formalisation and precision to a mode of social stratification already to be seen in spaces where different classes of people might mix. It was the awareness of the ecclesiastical enclosures and hierarchical separation he found operant in the Church of England that first led Joseph Arch (1826–1919), a farm labourer from Warwickshire, to form his desire to set up a farm labourers' union to offer some protection from the degradations of an ossified class system where there was no hope of transgressing set boundaries (Harrison 1984: 281–2). As an agricultural labourer he was expected to stand at the back of the Church, whilst the lords of the manor, the squirarchy and the landowners all sat in regulation pews marking off position in the social hierarchy. Social inclusion and exclusion could be mapped on distance from the altar, and symbolically beyond to God and Monarch. In his work as a Methodist lay-preacher and union organiser, Arch sought other, more democratic, forms of organisation and space, meeting in barns and walking literally thousands of miles to reach out to people in their own locales.

The hierarchical emplacement of bodies in space is not necessarily an obsolete, historical example, however, as we discovered when a friend described the spatial arrangements of the open-plan office she was working in at the time. This was the metropolitan headquarters of a recently re-organised non-departmental government-funded body providing advice and services to the public and previously part of the UK Civil Service. Our friend had been working there for just long enough to have pieced together the organisational and hierarchical relationships between the people within the headquarters office when she described how she looked up from her desk to realise that individual workstations were arranged in such a way as to express the formal structure of the organisation in spatial form. The semicircular arrangement looked informal at first glance, but there was a hierarchical placing of senior officers nearest to the windows working towards junior officers next to a corridor.

As we have seen in a number of these examples, being 'out of place' is seen as being problematic. This is portrayed in *The Bonfire of the Vanities* (Wolfe 1988), where the whole of the downward spiral of fortune for the self-styled 'Master of the Universe' Sherman McCoy stems from him being morally out of place by being engaged in an extra-marital affair, and physically out of place by being in a part of New York he does not know. Whilst he believes himself to be Master of the Universe, the paradox is that he does not know this particular locality in which he finds himself, having taken the wrong exit from the freeway. It is unknown territory and frightens him because Wolfe portrays New York as a place of separate warring districts each marked by particular racial and religious identities and hostile to all Others. His fall follows from taking the wrong exit to a place unknown. Those who have no identification with a place at all fare even worse. From the Elizabethan development of poor laws to deal with 'vagabonds' to the Nazi treatment of the gypsies, a lack of fixity within properly defined geographical and cultural boundaries is nearly always seen as transgression and suitably punished.

Hence, emplacement often develops a moral and political dimension: the separation of the sheep and the goats. As such it leads to the need to make visible, to monitor whether things and people are in their correct places. Knowledge of emplacement becomes a source of power in itself, as with the development of the Global Positioning System (GPS) system which was designed and is controlled by the US military, though now widely used for a whole range of activities. Should any conflict arise in which US interests were threatened then the US military could switch off the access to the synchronised geo-stationary satellites orbiting the Earth and the GPS would become inoperable. The European counter to this is Galileo, a non-military and allegedly more accurate system to which permanent access is guaranteed by all subscribers. The publicity material for Galileo stresses the vulnerability to US whims of GPS and the reality of positioning to power is made abundantly clear (Hambling 2005: 42–4).

Emplacement in the early factories was hugely problematic. Agricultural labourers did not want to give up the freedom of the land with its seasonal activity and 33 Saints' days, for a life governed in the mill by a mere six bank holidays, the whistle and the clock (Thompson 1967). To seduce workers into factories, the land had to be made harsher and the factory more attractive. But once they were inside the 'seminaries of vice', emplacement-based control of the factory worker was developed fast. Key distinctions of roles in early manufactories indicate the importance of the function of monitoring and knowledge: 'overseer' and 'supervisor' both derive from the power invested in inspection. Architectural features to aid this visibility and monitoring are embedded in the majority of organisational spaces. As is well known, supervision took place through aerial walkways as in the Rowntree's chocolate factory, through works manager's desks being placed in lifts such as in the BATA shoe factory at Dagenham and through other forms of the 'Panopticon' (Darley 2003). Developed by the utilitarian philosopher Jeremy Bentham, this 'ultimate managerial tool' was a building designed to allow complete surveillance of the inmates, students, workers and prisoners or whoever lived their lives under total observation. It was designed with a central observation tower surrounded by cells. Each cell has windows at each end such that light can be shone throughout the cell, making it entirely visible. In contrast, the tower is in complete darkness, so that the inmates of the cell can be seen at all times, whilst they will never know when they are being observed from the obscured tower. The inmates thus have to assume that they are under constant surveillance, and adjust their behaviour accordingly. As Foucault comments, this visibility 'assures the automatic functioning of power…the surveillance is continuous in its effects, even if it is discontinuous in its action' (1977: 201). The panopticon is a concept whose resonance with the late twentieth and early twenty-first century attempts to increase supervisory control has made it very fashionable. It is not surprising that organisation theory became enamoured with the concept of the panopticon[3] for in organisational terms it brings together a number of interesting factors: the spatial, the social, the discursive and the subjective, although in many accounts the spatial itself is not analysed.

The monitoring process means that emplacement is also very closely related to the production of knowledge: for as things and people are placed, classified and ranked, they have to be known and compared. As Foucault says, 'discipline organizes an analytical space' (1977: 143). It is in this way that the spatial and forms of knowledge come to be combined, although at times the *representation* of the space – the knowledge of it – becomes pre-eminent over the material and lived space itself, a key characteristic of capitalist 'abstract space' (Lefebvre 1991). Thus mapping, as a form of spatial representation, the intellectual territory becomes central to knowledge. 'Command' of an intellectual 'field' is shown through the mapping of the existing landscape of scholarship in relation to new fieldwork or theoretical terrain. The metaphor of the map is self-consciously used by system builders to order, emplace and control understandings of the intellectual space. Mapping the terrain, of either location or knowledge, involves constructing a narrative, the 'legend' or key to the map's meaning.

A central element of the spatial-representational organisation of the map is the grid. Grids are crucial to codification, to visibility and to making this knowledge intelligible. In *The Order of Things* (1970) Foucault announced that 'An episteme is, very roughly, a conceptual grid that provides conception of order, sign and language that allow a sense of discursive practices to qualify as "knowledge"' (in Gregory 1994: 21). This relates to the grid as a key part of the construction of 'abstract space' (Lefebvre 1991). Foucault argues that in Renaissance Europe, 'words' and 'things' were understood as resembling each other. However, in the late seventeenth and eighteenth centuries he argues that a space opens between 'words' and 'things', so that what was resemblance now becomes 'representation'. It was in the need to bring together this gap that vision became key. Foucault concentrates on the development of natural history in all this. For example, the classificatory system of Linnaeus created a 'sort of "optics" of plant morphology where nature was tabulated and spatialized' (Gregory 1994: 22).

In the control of space, the grid also becomes a significant tool of power. Sennett, writing in *The Conscience of the Eye* (1990), speaks of the grid pattern of cities. In the Roman grid this was a way of filling in the space within a boundary; but in the modern American planning, this was a way of extending out indefinitely through the emphasis on homogeneity. He links this with economics – the selling of parcels of land, not for what they are, but as standardised commodities. Mumford also argues, 'The resurgent capitalism of the seventeenth century treated the individual lot and the block, the street and the avenue, as abstract units for buying and selling, without respect for historic uses, for topographic conditions or for social needs' (1961: 480). In this, the natural features of the land are ignored in the production of an urban grid system that reduces everything to the same. The gridding of space was undertaken by the Western imperial nations throughout the eighteenth and nineteenth centuries to allocate land dispossessed from others in the process of colonialism because it was an easy and rational method, thereby fitting in with Enlightenment thinking. Parcels of land within a grid system were allocated on a variety of bases but the key thing was the grid system arranged around cardinal points of the compass and right-angled alignments. In this way, all land became available for exchange and the extraction of value:

> the gridiron planner opened the way for fat pieces of 'honest' municipal jobbery, in the grading and filling and paving of streets....All this means, in the gridiron plan, as applied to the commercial city, no section or precinct was suitably planned for its specific function: instead the only function considered was the progressive intensification of use, for the purpose of meeting expanding business needs and raising land values. (Mumford 1961: 482–3)

Because the imperialist urge was to parcel out this land from a distance then the two-dimensional map was favoured because the peculiarities and particularities of the landscape are obscured. Linearity brings with it a blindness to form and complexity. The line leads to a reductive geometry (Burrell, 1998). Sennett (1990: 60) proceeds more provocatively when he claims, 'Gridded space does more than create a blank canvas for development. It subdues those who must live in the space, by disorienting their ability to see and to evaluate relationships. In that sense, the planning of neutral space is an act of dominating and subduing others.'

In Ezzamel's (2004) work on organisation in ancient Egypt, this 'subduing' of others relates to the hugely unrecognised importance of rationality's link to both rations and ratios. Rationality is concerned about size and proportions. The bigger the block of land the more important it was. Ratios, rations and rationality go hand in hand so that the parcelling up of land into particular patterns is done on the basis of size and proportions. In the ancient Egyptian world another leader, the foreman of the work gang, received a larger bread and beer allowance than the ordinary worker based on a certain ratio of portions. Thus his rations were ratio based. And the rationality of the Egyptians in building that most rational of edifices, the pyramid, comes from the importance attached to ratios of proportion and rations of portion.

As we have seen, emplacement as a spatial practice is based upon fixity and stability, yet this has its limitations. In order for social and economic processes to be carried through there has to be movement between spaces. The grid as a form of knowledge and control has its place here too. The development of the timetable is one grid form which provides a way of producing knowledge and control of movement through time and space. If there has to be movement between places, it has to be controlled, so that time and space are known and rational. For Michel Foucault, this confluence of fixed and transparent space and time is a tool of power overtly used to contain the individual. He traces it back to monastic communities, whose spatial organisation we will explore later. Foucault sees it as having three elements to it, to 'establish rhythms, impose particular occupations, regulate the cycles of repetition' (1977: 149). This technique was to be extended to many social organisations and spaces:

> The new disciplines had no difficulty in taking up their place in the old forms; the schools and poorhouses extended the life and the regularity of the monastic communities to which they were often attached. The rigours of the industrial period long retained a religious air; in the seventeenth century, the regulations of the great manufactories laid down the exercises that would divide up the working day ... but even in the nineteenth century, when the rural populations were needed in industry, they were sometimes formed into 'congregations', in an attempt to inure them to work in the workshops; the framework of the 'factory-monastery' was imposed upon the workers. (Foucault 1977: 149–50)

A similar technique for controlling movement in space and time is demonstrated by Carmona, Ezzamel and Gutierrez's (1997, 1998, 2002) study of the Royal Tobacco Factory of Spain. Their analysis examines the use of new accounting technologies not simply as a textual resource, but as a way of organising space, making visible in material form the very idea of 'adding value' and how this is embodied in particular groups of workers at particular stages and places in the production process. The Royal Tobacco Factory at Seville was probably the most important factory in Europe at its time, housed in the largest building built in Spain in the eighteenth century and with around 1400 workers (Sánchez-Matamoros *et al.* 2005: 199). It is perhaps better known as the background to Bizet's opera *Carmen*, and since 1953 has been one of the main buildings of Seville University. One of the main drivers for spatial control was the practice of tobacco smuggling that took place. Guards escorted the raw tobacco from the port to the factory, examined workers as they left the factory and guarded the finished products until they left the city. Nevertheless, the incentives for theft were high given the workers' low wages and an active black market in tobacco to avoid paying high taxes. Such was the problem that the factory buildings included a prison area. The building itself was designed to maximise control: it was surrounded by a moat, with only one entrance, a high visibility central patio over which the tobacco had to travel whenever it was moved from one department to another, and 'the workshops were formed by repetitions of modules consisting of four columns and a dome. The diaphanous space of this structure facilitated surveillance of workers from any place' (2005: 200). Lower level workers (who were hired and paid by the day, unlike the monthly paid contracted employees) had their spatial movements restricted. This was controlled by them having to wear a letter that indicated which department they worked for and by being searched in full view of everyone. The movement of tobacco was also tightly spatially controlled, this being achieved through the accounting systems. Each time tobacco was moved, the movement and its weight had to be entered into the audit books for both the department it had left and the one it was going to. These accounts would be compared against each other by the Accounting Office. The internal auditor was in charge of *physically* checking all these movements in space and time (pp. 200–3).

The possibilities for resistance to these forms of spatial control might be seen in a recent television drama *Hot Money* (Granada Television, 2001), which portrayed a group of workers at a plant for destroying banknotes that were to be taken out of circulation. The opportunities for workers to steal these banknotes rather than destroy them were restricted by the careful control of space: workers for certain parts of the process were emplaced and their movement from these places highly restricted. Any movement that had to be made was under constant surveillance. No one worker could have succeeded in obtaining notes from the plant, but by working together a group of workers from different spatial locations and those who were involved in moving the notes were able to bypass spatio-bureaucratic controls and become rich, until ultimately given away by their luxurious lifestyle!

So we turn to our final element of spatial power, **enactment**. This is a form of control that is perhaps particularly pertinent to modern forms of organisation, although as we shall see it also has long historical roots. Enactment is about the lived experience of social space. It is about the interaction of people as simultaneously social and embodied beings with the power embedded in specific spaces. The types of spatial control that we have looked at in relation to emplacement emphasise the static element of space: that control can be achieved by keeping people and resources in specific places. In relation to this fixity, mobility has the appearance of freedom. Yet as social actors move in and through spaces, as part of a complex web that is physical, human and cultural, those spaces are lived in particular ways. Through the development of habits and routines for inhabiting and creating those spaces, a whole set of power effects and relations are incorporated. There are three aspects to this incorporation that we wish to tease out in developing an understanding of how enactment operates as a form of socio-spatial power. The first is that the learnt and routinised ways in which we engage with many social spaces becomes sedimented. This relates to the concept of the *habitus*, our everyday bodily ways of engaging with the world, discussed in Chapter 1. The second is that by 'living through' various social spaces, the constructions of both physical and imaginary space embedded in them become linked to processes of identity construction. Our understandings of ourselves, our place in society and our relations of others are intimately bound up with our enactment of everyday social spaces. The third theme is to introduce a notion of the 'neo-baroque' as a way of understanding some contemporary aspects of spatial power achieved through enactment. This incorporates an understanding of how embodied spaces relate to identity production with a recognition of the way (post)modern spaces are often aestheticised, linked with narratives of consumption and choice, appear to present multiple perspectives and routes, but through these same elements serve to simultaneously 'secure and obscure' their inherent power relations.

We turn first, then, to consider the effects of the habitual encounter with social spaces. Bentham's 'panopticon', which we have already come across in looking at emplacement, was designed around this very notion. Although often presented as a tool for surveillance and monitoring, Bentham's goal was much more far-reaching. He wanted to produce a transformation in the inmates of his panopticon which would allow their rehabilitation into society. This was effectively to be achieved through the enactment of the enclosed and visible space of the panopticon, which would be internalised and incorporated into the way that the inmate lived their life, and hence carried out of the prison as part of their *habitus* back into society. Thus there is not such an easy separation between emplacement and enactment as forms of spatial power as might first appear. The very lived experience of emplacement may produce the enactment of those spaces such that the power becomes 'lived through' or 'known without being known'.

Foucault (1977) takes Bentham's physical design of the panopticon and utilises it as a critique of modern societies. He sees the principle of 'panopticism' as a central (self-) disciplinary mechanism that has become generalised and extended to multiple social spaces beyond the prison. It is the technique whereby an individual fits their behaviour to the gaze of society in its various forms, this behaviour ultimately becoming the norm. Another element of disciplinary technology that concerned Foucault was the dynamic or motile form of socio-spatial power that he described as 'dressage', or the training of the body in movement. He looks at the prescription of bodily movements in space in military training and in education. We can add to this the detailed calculations of the most efficient way to complete manual work tasks in Taylorism and its attendant practice of time-and-motion study. Foucault breaks this dressage down into four characteristics:

> it is cellular (by the play of spatial distribution), it is organic (by the coding of activities), it is genetic (by the accumulation of time), it is combinatory (by the composition of forces). And, in

doing so, it operates four great techniques: it draws up tables; it prescribes movements; it imposes exercises; lastly, in order to obtain the combination of forces, it arranges 'tactics'. (1977: 167)

Children continue to be instructed in the way of dressage. Nurseries and schools still value the social conformity involved in quiet lining up and being able to sit still. These qualities of controlling movement are hugely valued throughout middle-class life. Indeed they are basic to the pursuit of higher education (since despite criticisms the lecture remains common), and cultural pursuits such as attending concerts and the theatre. However, Foucault's formulation tends towards a relatively fixed and inflexible notion. It also suggests a highly intentional and overt process. In developing the idea of 'enactment' as a socio-spatial process, we want to consider rather the more embedded and taken-for-granted aspects of spatial power.

An important element to this that Foucault does not adequately address is that of the cultural meanings and interpretations rooted in social space and our embodied negotiation of these spaces. Part of the control embedded in the social enactment of space then, is that of the system of norms and expectations of differently coded spaces. For example, Stallybrass and White (1986) discuss how a social logic of bour-geois public spaces came about. Such institutions as literary societies, museums and coffee houses developed norms of behaviour that were distinguished from those spaces of popular culture like the tavern, market and fair. Thus spitting, swearing, dirty footwear, fighting, gambling and such behaviours were prohibited as representing the 'low-Other' (1986: 87). Although Elias does not explicitly talk of space, it is clear from his work on *The Civilising Process* (1994; originally published in 1939) that this process includes the development of differentiated and encoded spaces, with different behaviours becoming acceptable or unacceptable dependent on social and spatial context. Individuals thereby develop a sense of their identities in articulation with the 'normal' behaviours of the places they frequent. Thus it is that in 'living through' a certain set of spaces, social and cultural power is incorporated and embodied in the then taken-for-granted notions of these spaces. In other words, power relations are performed without being seen as a form of power.

There is an underlying drama and dimension to the movement which is unremarked as it becomes habituated.

A number of years ago one of us experienced a performance of a medieval mystery play in the ruins of Coventry Cathedral. It was 'staged' such that there was no seating or fixed single stage, the audience moved with the events of the play, stopping at each point along the way of the story of Jesus' life and death. The Greeks had the view that the theatre was a place of moral education, not just a spectacle external to the viewer, and that in observing tragedy the audience member would experience 'catharsis', a psychological and moral cleansing, through the experience of vicarious emotions. Coleridge argues that in order to emotionally and cognitively identify with the drama, there must be a 'suspension of disbelief'. In the Coventry mystery play this participation was wholly embodied. Not only was the member of the audience a part of the crowd who listened to the Sermon on the Mount as if for the first time, who shared the bread and fishes in wonder, but they were also forced to become part of a crowd who were calling for the death of an innocent man. To feel oneself as a member of a crowd, drawn along through the spatial pull of the action of the play, from welcoming gathering to murdering mob was an undoubtedly more powerful and visceral experience than watching a distant stage.

Similarly, Hoskin (1995) explains how the Parthenon, often taken as the most perfect image of classical proportion, was built to be experienced through the dynamic movement of the body, through a series of narrative settings, where the viewer themselves becomes a part of the relationship between divine and human. Yates' account of *The Art of Memory* (1966) shows how the Greeks and Romans connected body and mind as one, as they trained the memory to hold vast numbers of facts or detailed speeches through the practice of picturing a place that they were very familiar with, such as a house or public building, and imaging themselves moving round this space with the items of memory placed in specific spaces. Each item could be recalled as they visualised travelling through these spaces. However, modern architecture is often assumed to be a form of culture to be experienced from the outside, as it were, from standing and looking at it as an artefact from an external viewpoint. And Hoskin (1995: 149) points out that when the arts of memory were again taken up in the form of the medieval and Renaissance Memory Theatres, the viewer had become static in front of an elaborate visualisation of a theatre complete with the objects of memory. In this light it is perhaps possible to trace a route via Francis Bacon to Descartes, with his imagined geometry, that had, at its root, the linear perspective, and to the Cartesian downgrading of bodily experience in favour of abstract representation.

This is the route that Lefebvre also traces in his account of the development of capitalist 'abstract space', although it lies in gradual social and spatial changes that pre-date industrialism. Lefebvre sees the dominance of visual perspective as highly significant. He argues that perspective originates from a changing social production of space between town and country from the thirteenth century onwards, especially felt in Tuscany. Serfs who were intimately connected with the land were succeeded by *métayers* who received a share of what they produced, and therefore had an interest in producing larger amounts, which in turn supplied the growing markets required for needs of the urban bourgeoisie. New social spaces and relationships grew up around this form of production, which was neither of the town nor the country, where the houses (*poderi*) of the *métayers* were arranged in a circle around the mansions of the bourgeois owners and their stewards, where alleys of cypress trees 'sectioned and organised' the land between (Lefebvre 1991: 78). This new 'representation of space' is, he argues, first shown in the work of painters, then architects, then in geometry, and it consists of 'a homogeneous, clearly demarcated space complete with horizon and vanishing-point' (p. 79). Romanyshyn (1989) sees the change in artistic representation as being one from conveying the specific emotional and material context of that moment, that situation which is being communicated, to one which standardises representation, ensures that all parts are portrayed as being in proportion. Visual perspective is thus connected with rationalisation, in the sense discussed above of rationality being linked to proportionality. Linear perspective in art is, of course, commonly achieved by the use of a grid, which is, as we have seen, a key tool for linking space, power and knowledge. Thus again there is a process of separation and distancing from the scene represented, achieved through the standardisation inherent in perspective.

This separation of embodiment and representation would appear to be problematic for establishing enactment as an important form of social-spatial power. However, into this 'abstract space' enters another element which, perhaps ironically, will strengthen the process of enactment. This is where we turn to the second element of enactment, whereby the lived embodied experience of certain social spaces is yoked to a narrative form of self-awareness central to identity building. This is what Hoskin (1995) describes as the 'self-examining self', which can be seen as a key component in the process of modern identity construction.

Hoskin argues that in solving the 'problem' of linear perspective, its 'anatomically impossible puzzle', Alberti had to develop a 'split self' (1995: 153). This other self 'floats free of the immobilized first self, moves round to view from the side, measures and checks the viewing co-ordinates, and then returns whence it came' (p. 153). Thus the production of the apparently 'objective' view of perspective involves both distancing the self from what is seen (and experienced) and denying the body. As Hoskin goes on to say 'the effect was to change the relation of viewing self to viewed space' (p. 154). It was also to change the relation of the self to itself. This is a process that Hoskin traces back as far as Dante's *Vita Nuova*, written around 1300, where, Hoskin argues, the author became triple '– narrator, poet and scholar – and thus constructs a text where he can both write and read the self in multiple ways' (p. 151).

This self-examining self is closely related to the development of what Foucault describes as the need of 'Modern man...to face the task of producing himself' (1987a: 42; Hoskin 1995: 159; Rose 1989). This is perhaps why, despite the influences of objectification, distancing and denigration of the body that may be linked with perspectivalism, the experience of spatial narrative is still powerful and may even integrate body and mind, the material and the ideational. As we have seen, into the space of the modern self comes the idea of a *narrative* of the self. This is an idea explored by Kermode in his influential book *Sense of an Ending*. He writes of the need to make sense of existence by fictional-ising it, although despite his preoccupation with time he tends to see this as an essential need rooted in biology or psychology (1968: 43–4), rather than as a cultural and historical product. The idea of narrative is predominantly associated with texts and discourse. However, it is also possible to spatialise narrative, and it is to understanding this process that we now turn.

Bennett explores the forms of narrative power embedded in the spatial organisation of the museum, particularly from the nineteenth century with the new theory of evolution being used to put a cultural ideology of the relationship between the 'primitive' and the 'civilised' that centred around racial and gender interpretations. He comments that 'the evolutionary narratives it instantiated were realized spatially in the form of the routes that the visitor was expected – and often obliged – to complete' (1995: 179). A routing through exhibitions reflected a narrative account of the human march from savagery to civilisation, the latter reflected by the visitors themselves as they progressed through the displays. This 'organized walking' was a form of control that incorporates both body and mind. Such spatial organisation certainly produced a powerful 'pull' effect, although this led Alfred Wallace to complain that visitors to natural history museums were not learning enough because they wanted to progress to the next thing too quickly (p. 181)! Following Mitchell, Bennett sees the exhibitionary institutions as 'mechanisms of truth'. They produced a division between 'the world of socio-material relations and their conceptual plan' whereby the conception, through its narrative ideology, was presented as the Truth, and thereby designed to reorder the social and material world itself. The ordering of this 'truth' through the spatial and material reconstruction of the museum spaces produced 'regulative strategies aimed at both body and mind where regulating the environments in which bodies were located was envisioned as a means of promoting inner-directed practices of self-interrogation and self-shaping' (Mitchell 1988: 100). Through these combined spatial and narrative means the individual's sense of identity and place in the world was represented.

Bennett contrasts the externally directed route of 'organised walking' of the museum with the self-directed 'freedom' of the *flâneur*, that urban figure with 'the detached gaze of a detached stroller' (Bennett 1995: 186) who can progress at their own pace and change their route at their own whim. The *flâneur* has become a somewhat idealised figure in social and cultural theory, representative of an independent identity, and the exercise of 'free choice'. This narrative of 'free choice' has become ever more powerful in advanced capitalist societies throughout the twentieth century and continued into the twenty-first century. Individual freedom of choice has come to seem basic to a strong sense of identity, even a basic 'human right'. It is also closely intertwined with cultures of consumption: the narrative of who I am is often the story of what I have. Even ethical issues are most potently diffused through the medium of choice and consumption, as witnessed by the idea that the ethical consumer can change corporate activity more readily than government edict. Although consumers in the twenty-first century may not be passive followers of advertising, the romantic view of consumption as some form of free choice, expressive of identity and even of resistance, continues to be influential (de Certeau 1984; Gottdiener 1997). The process of consumption can be seen as a mediating relationship, where people develop various strategies towards goods and shopping whereby they fashion their own sense of identity. The control of space here is not through the single directed route as in the nineteenth-century museum, but through the logic of consumption which holds it all together. The very narratives of choice, desire and pleasure that construct the consuming self as supreme, simultaneously obscure the forms of power inherent in these narratives. The underlying logic is that in order to be a self, one has to consume, and to consume the right things on the right occasions. The logic of consumption contains within it a certain sort of social and material relations: the consumer will judge and be judged by their consumption; the material of consumption will require care (insurance, cleaning, putting away, servicing etc.) or they will become waste within society; desire will be sated only briefly and then further consumption must be undertaken; and the supposed boundless freedom of the consumer is limited by the availability and cost of those goods and services that they consume.

These themes of identity, apparent choice and the obscuring of power relations leads us to the third aspect of enactment, the notion of the 'neo-baroque'. In developing this idea, we draw together the spatial practices of the Baroque period and Jameson's (1991) discussions of post-modern spatial power, which he also links with the Baroque. Although we might urge caution over the use of these overarching terms,[4] there are themes

BOUNDARY CROSSINGS: REPRODUCING ORGANISED SPACE • BUILDING A SOCIAL MATERIALITY: SPATIAL AND EMBODIED
POLITICS IN ORGANISATION • ALTERNATIVE SPACES: THE RADICAL ORGANISATION OF SPACE? • CONCLUSIONS: DISORGANISING SPACE

2   73

in common that we believe have a congruence with characteristics of the recent organisational interest in space.

Baroque forms of spatial organising were fundamentally about securing power whilst obscuring its operations. Power and politics could be masked, apparently removed altogether, through the use of aesthetics. Indeed, the sensual, especially the visual, could be overloaded with a surplus of images and splendour. This spectacle was often theatricalised, and intended to seduce the observer. Visual tricks were employed, such as *trompe l'oeil*, distorting mirrors and *chiaroscuro*, the playing of lighted and shadowy areas against one another, often to suggest the visionary or miraculous (Hyde Minor 1999: 93). Space is 'played with', through illusions of scale, perspective and distance. There is the use of *quadratura*, or the painting of illusionistic architecture, which eliminates the difference between 'real' and 'fictive' spaces (1999: 26). The apparent openness and transparency of science were rejected. In obscuring their production, and being concerned with the power of effect, these aspects of Baroque spaces have much in common with the phantasmagoria, discussed earlier in relation to the enchantment of space. But whereas the phantasmagoria presented moving images to a static emplaced audience, Baroque spatial practices blur this distinction between image and observer, and are fundamentally about movement, embodiment, immersion, and even absorption, into the space. It is at once 'more ambiguous and more activated' (Anderson n/d). Thus the Baroque is not just about the visual, but attacks all the senses. And through the senses, often through the disorientation of the senses through structures such as labyrinths, grottos and mazes, the body and mind were to be taken out of normal, everyday experience and self-hood.

Harbison argues that 'The Baroque is set apart from what precedes it by an interest in movement above all, movement which is a frank exhibition of energy and escape from classical restraint' (2000: 1). Thus one of the most important aspects of the Baroque was that it was to be experienced through movement, rather than from a static viewpoint. And this movement involved a problematisation of 'inside', 'outside' and the boundaries between. Ceilings and walls as material boundaries and closure were especially worked upon, made to look as if the roof did not exist and that space extended upwards or outwards, out of sight. Baroque principles of the movement within space emphasise not visibility from one point as in the panopticon, but visibility from multiple perspectives.

However, despite its playful appearance, its 'writhing forms and spatial tricks' (Glancey 2003), the Baroque is fundamentally about power. Indeed, it is not just about power is a general way, but about the authoritarian and absolute power of the God and the Monarch who ruled by Divine Right. Louis XIV especially used the Baroque as a form of power: 'as an important element in the machinery of propaganda' as Hyde Minor says (1999: 60). He believed in the power of absolute monarchy (he suspended the French parliament in the 1660s), he distrusted and feared the aristocracy and thus moved his court out of central Paris to Versailles. It became the centre of government and was continually enlarged every year between 1667 and 1710. He needed to demonstrate the status of the King as embodying the State through the divine right of the monarchy, and this he achieved through his appearance and surroundings. Despite the huge size and perspectival scales of Versailles, the King would appear from hidden entrances and disappear through concealed egresses. He loved grottoes and mazes. He had the command of what was open and what was hidden. The King's full plans for the fountains were never to be achieved, since resources had to be diverted into war, but through them he had intended to demonstrate his power over nature itself. Since he did not have sufficient water for all to be working at once, Louis had to deploy a complex sequence regulated by gardeners, timed through the use of boys with whistles (Harbison 2000: 131). Visitors thus had to follow a guided route: 'This was not nature in random order or at ease but something like a carefully calculated pageant' (2000: 131). Versailles is about the controlled movement of the aristocracy – a group which Louis XIV did not trust – and their physical participation in a demonstration of the King's awesome power. It is no accident that Hitler admired and sought to emulate the spatial strategies of Versailles (Sudjec 2005).

Turning to Jameson's (1991) discussions of (post)modern spatial practices in the contemporary world, there are a number of points of similarity with the spatial play of the Baroque. First, they further develop this idea of controlled movement so that movement through spaces has a narrative form and yet no single point of view is adequately descriptive. Jameson says that

> We know in any case that recent architectural theory has begun to borrow from narrative analysis in other fields and to attempt to see our physical trajectories through such buildings as virtual narratives or stories, as dynamic paths and narrative paradigms which we as visitors are asked to fulfil and to complete with our own bodies and movements. (1991: 42)

The crucial difference between the narrative forms and embodied responses of the Baroque and the present day is that Baroque spaces were oriented towards an experience of transcendence, the miraculous and the sublime, in doing so evoking awe of the all-powerful Other. Contemporary spaces that are built upon these spatial plays evoke an inward turning to the *self*.

Jameson (1991: 48–9) goes on to argue that in postmodern aesthetics 'critical distance' has been abolished. In other words, they aim for a conflation between the lived experience of the space and a cognitive view of it; in Lefebvre's terms the conceived-perceived-lived triad of social space would be collapsed into one. This is interesting in relation to workspaces, as it implies that by having to live and experience the spaces, there is no possibility of being 'outside' them, either spatially or reflexively. This reinforces the idea that such spaces are constructed so as to achieve a certain close psychological relation or identification between individual and organisation. This is achieved by the same spatial obscuring that is present in the Baroque, as Jameson says, 'a certain figural concealment or disguise is still at work here, most notably in the high-tech thematics in which the new spatial content is dramatized and articulated' (1991: 49).

It is as well at this juncture to point out that the neo-baroque is not total, despite appearances. These spatial strategies may be constructed to produce different political and power effects. Movement through a multiplicity of perspectives can produce the consumerist detachment of the tourist or the shopper, who can pick and choose for their own amusement and desires, or can decide to be entirely disengaged. This is the space of the fleeting look, the snapshot. It is the effect of multiple perspectives translated into distance between self and objects of view, the indifference or ambivalence that Bauman (1991) delineates as a key characteristic of contemporary times. Thus Featherstone characterises the modern museum as 'sites of spectacles, sensation, illusion and montage; places where one has an experience, rather than where knowledge of the canon and established symbolic hierarchies are inculcated' (1991: 70).

On the other hand, the power of the enactment of the body in space may at its best be used to produce a deeper understanding of the Other, through a physical and representational 'walking in the other's shoes'. Such an encounter may be seen in the accounts people have given of their experiences of Libeskind's Jewish extension to the Berlin Museum, with its final blank concrete wall representing 'the memory void' and intervening maze-like *cul-de-sacs*. Libeskind says that he sat for hours looking at photographs of people in the Alexanderplatz in the 1930s before embarking on its design. Politically speaking, this is a very different variety of the directed walking rhetorics of the nineteenth-century museum described by Bennett (1995) earlier.

The significance of enactment as a socio-spatial form of power is the simultaneous taken-for-granted nature of the power relations as 'lived through' embodied and cultural spaces, and the processes of identity construction that may be facilitated by the narrative opportunities of these spaces. We will particularly draw upon the process of enactment in Chapter 3, in looking at current spatial strategies in organisations.

In the remainder of this chapter, we turn to more specific spaces of organisation to consider how spatial power is mediated through organisational practices.

Organisational space and power: the military, the monastery and the manufactory

Having discussed three forms of spatial power, namely enchantment, emplacement and enactment, we now start to look at how these socio-spatial practices are incorporated into organisations. In this section, we consider the spatial practices of three institutions that have come to form the very notion and form of social organisation. We need to be very clear in looking at the buildings of the Roman army, the medieval monasteries and even the pre-industrial factories, that we are not searching for the unattainable point of origin of the coalescence of buildings, organisation and power. However, in the development of these social spaces can be seen significant 'representations of space', as developed in the organisational principles and practices of those large organisations of army, church and state that can be argued to have put their imprint on diverse features of modern organisational life, even though from a very different set of goals and assumptions. We also need to be careful that in looking at historical forms of organisational spaces we do not 'read' them simply from the assumptions of current organisational forms. For example, James (1999: 38) argues that the term 'the Roman army' is an anachronistic reification, since it was not seen as an institution or entity at the time. However, the significance of it as an organisational form comes from the self-identity of the soldiers themselves, as a social grouping within Roman society, and from the replication of its organisational practices in the construction of the Empire.

The past is both connected to us *and* separated from us. Foucault explicitly compares monastery discipline to the development of the factory (1977: 142), and certainly in looking at the development of monastic organisation there are many commonalities with modern forms of collective social life, to developments as diverse as hospitals, schools and even in theatre staging (Burton 1994: 136), originally developed as part of the liturgy. However, it is also important to bear in mind differences at the very heart of what it meant to be a society, a religious community, an individual in this particular organisation. As Lawrence comments,

> It is hard to recapture the experience and atmosphere of daily life in a medieval cloister. Our documents can conjure up for us the exterior acts of the monastic routine; but, at the end, the inwardness of it eludes us. Our sources cannot penetrate the interior experience of the individual that energised and gave meaning to a pattern of life built around a belief in the omnipresence of the supernatural and the power and necessity of constant prayer, and to whom the modern secular world offer us no key. (1989: 111)

In searching for spaces of organisation, we start with the Roman army, the organisation of which led to one of the world's most enduring dominations of social space. The Roman army was not always the ordered,

professionalised body it is recognised to be at the peak of Roman imperialism. It began as a regular citizen's army; only propertied citizens
of Rome were members, and these only for specific campaigns. It was
Augustus (around 27 BC) who recognised the centrality of the army and
the need to have it loyal to the Emperor first and foremost. He brought
in regular payment of soldiers (three times a year), organised their retirement handouts of money or land, and, understandably, as both of the
former were paid from his own resources, he insisted on an annual oath
of allegiance. He regularised length of service, making it essentially into
a lifetime vocation, he also appointed commanders and organised the
campaigns, the successes of which brought the soldiers more wealth and
status within the Roman state. Augustus actually pared down the number
of legions that he inherited, not only for the sake of his purse, but also for
political security. For this reason, too, he distributed the soldiers carefully
across the Empire. The soldiers were arranged in legions of about 5000
fighting men, organised into 10 cohorts, and then divided into centuries
(which were in practice about 80 men each). These were in turn divided
into *contuberniums* of eight men who shared a tent whilst on campaign,
and a pair of barrack rooms in a more permanent fortress. Along with
the fighting men, the army also consisted of intelligence officers, administration and other necessary services. There were also auxiliary troops,
who were made up of men who were not Roman citizens and were from
the newly won provinces. These were highly significant as they brought
skills not found in the Roman army itself: the cavalry, including scouts
and messengers, sling shots, archers and bargemen. These allied units
were incorporated through also being paid by Augustus, and the promise
of Roman citizenship with all the advantages this entailed.

Nothing in the building of the fort[5] was left to chance. Roman
surveyors, engineers and architects were central to the process of Empire-
building. When the surveyors had found a suitable site, related to strategic
importance, availability of water and other resources, the site for the
commander's tent (*praetorium*) would be set in the centre, containing
the senior officer's living area and the headquarters of the unit or legion
(*principia*). This latter was the administrative centre, a complex of buildings with a covered courtyard. As forts became more administrative
and permanent than combative, the commander's quarters were moved

BOUNDARY CROSSINGS: REPRODUCING ORGANISED SPACE • BUILDING A SOCIAL MATERIALITY: SPATIAL AND EMBODIED
POLITICS IN ORGANISATION • ALTERNATIVE SPACES: THE RADICAL ORGANISATION OF SPACE? • CONCLUSIONS: DISORGANISING SPACE

2   79

further from the centre affording some privacy. From this centre two roads would be marked off. The one across the front of the principia was the *via principalis* and the one at right angles to this the *via praetorian*. These were long straight streets that divided the fort into four areas, and which led from the centre to four gates in the defensive outer structures. Even temporary camps did not fail to form some enclosure. These included various types of ditches, palisade stakes and ramparts sometimes made of standardized size turfs which could easily withstand battering rams and were fireproof, and sometimes made of stone. The granaries were also fairly central to the design, where the precious supplies could be protected from rot (on raised floors) and theft through ease of surveillance over them. The barracks were usually thin rectangular blocks arranged in facing pairs, another means of maximising visibility, and the *contubernium* of eight men would have a pair of rooms, one for sleeping and one for storing equipment. A centurion would be attached to each block, and his rooms would be more elaborate.

The Romans built different sorts of spaces for different sorts of task and social encounter. Thus there are clear distinctions between the buildings and spaces used for barracks, baths, storage, hospital, parade and the collective hearing of orders. There seems to be a distinction between stratified spaces such as houses (and by extension, the commander's house in the army fortress) where social relations were governed by ritual, ceremony and status. Other buildings were more utilitarian and less differentiated. The Roman military establishments, then, can be seen as essentially bounded, exclusive and restrictive spaces (Le Bohec 2000; Lefebvre 1991: 244–6).

Yet, the planning and setting out of the Roman military camp, as the town, was not simply a matter of good location in terms of roads, water and other resources and internal organisation, as with a modern town. Roman religious and imperial beliefs were fundamentally incorporated into the spatial arrangements. The military camp was related to the augural *templum* – a place set apart for functions of state and religion, and the general's tent was called *auguraculum*, after the tent used by the augur, the Roman religious official who foretold the future (Rykwert 1988: 45–8). Like the *templum*, the camp had boundaries and was oriented (sometimes it is said that the main gate faced the enemy, sometimes the orientation was the south–north line as with towns) from the central *praetorium*, the camp's staff headquarters (1988: 48). Near to this was the general's *auguraculum*, from where he read the omens. To the left of this was the *tribune*, from which he addressed the soldiers on the will of the gods. Thus right at the centre of the military camp was the incorporation of religious rites to determine the will of the gods. The Roman belief, as stated by Livy, was that 'It is by auspices, in peace as in war, within as abroad, that all things are governed: everyone knows this' (p. 68).

Rykwert says that the conventional view is that Roman towns echo the form of the military camp, but he argues the inverse: 'the Roman military camp was a diagrammatic evocation of the city of Rome, an *anamnesis* of *imperium*' (1988: 68). So spatially, the camp also spoke to the army of the empire that they were a part of. 'The Romans did not treat the setting up of the camp as a makeshift for a night's sleep: it was part of the daily military routine that no army was permitted to settle down for the night without setting up camp ceremonially' (p. 68). The constant re-enactment of the supreme imperial city, in both temporary and permanent establishments, could be seen as a very powerful spatial reminder of the army's loyalty and connection to Rome, the mother city. This functioned as a form of simultaneous cultural and material control.

The Roman fort also conveyed the power of the state to the surrounding populace: its coercive function, to use Dovey's term. At Caerleon in Wales, for example, the remains of a huge amphitheatre have been found, that would have been able to hold 6000 people. It would probably have been used for parades, displays and exercises. The significance of this dominance of space is illustrated in the fact that it was rebuilt three times during the period of Roman occupation. The scale and luxury of the commander's house marked its use for the symbolic enact-ment of ritual and ceremony, and it would have been the place where local leaders were brought to impress on them the might of the Empire.

However, power over the subdued spaces of the expanding Roman Empire was by no means the only form of spatial power. Control of the army itself was also an essential element to Roman success, and some writers have argued that the fortification and surveillance mechanisms were as much to do with control of the soldiers within, as to protect them from the enemy without (James 1999). Oliveras comments that

> " Military camps supported spatial designs that allowed the stability, order and social security desired by the enlightened... the military camp is traditionally a space that sorts out, implants, and minimizes individual freedom. Through the ordered distribution of the tents and the streets that cross themselves vertically, done to give perspectives from the entries, drawn trying not to disturb visibility, but to improve it, it is possible to quantify and control the inhabitants (1998: 63 in Sánchez-Matamoros *et al.* 2005: 189)

Part of the value of the spatial-bodily discipline brought about by the organised nature of the military camp was the regularised behaviour developed through repetition of standardised tasks. In the letters and documents found at Vindolanda (Chesterholm) on Hadrian's Wall in the UK, the evidence of carefully organised life can be seen in duty rosters, personnel lists and accounts. This not only produced order in the ranks, but could save the day in terms of the conduct of war. In reflecting on a near disaster in 57 BC, Caesar wrote that he was saved by two things, the first of which was, 'the knowledge and experience of the soldiers, whose training in earlier battles enables them to decide for themselves what needed doing, without waiting to be told...' (Caesar 1984: II, 20, in Peddie 1994: 60). Thus the body was trained, with amphitheatres for combat practice and competitive sports; it was disciplined, through a codified series of punishments; and it was cared for in terms of health, with diet planned and hospitals provided. The soldier was literally incorporated into the army organisation through their enactment of the military spaces.

So although in many ways the spatial organisation of the Roman army looks like a study of emplacement, with its enclosures and partitioning, its segregated and codified spaces, it is also important to have a sense of the way that the individual was brought into a particular way of collective life and identity through the organisation of space. The imperial identity, both political and spiritual, was inscribed in the body-in-space of the Roman soldier and citizen. As we turn now to the development of collective religious organisation in the church and monastery of medieval times, we can see further facets of the power involved in the enactment of organisational spaces.

The spatial arrangement of churches and monasteries is interesting because it attempts to combine the spiritual and transcendent with the functional needs of a living community, an organisation. To many people studying modern organisations this will be perceived as a question only of interest in certain narrowly defined quarters. However, the Christian Church and its institutions have been a pervasive influence in the development of western societies and cultures, and have shaped the development of both organisational practices and their analysis. Weber (1930) is obviously a central figure in this. To him we owe the application of the hierarchy, as derived from the rule of saints, to secular bureaucracy; charismatic forms of power; and the Protestant work ethic. The modes of control and discipline developed most fully by the church houses, including the process of 'desexualisation' and the regulation of the body, have also been argued to be significant for modern organisation (Burrell 1984). In more recent years, analogies have been drawn between ideas of the sacred and the appropriation of notions of 'spirituality' within organisational discourse (e.g. Bell and Taylor 2003, 2004). However, the influence of the spatial practices of churches and monasteries have not been widely considered as significant for understanding organisation, yet here we see the development of a wide range of practices and arrangements that have diffused into other institutional settings, related to the spatial arrangement of control and discipline, and the locus of hierarchical status and task division. In particular, we can see in monastery life the importance of the embodied and spatialised enactment of individual and collective identity.

The spatial form of churches and monasteries drew first from the Roman basilica. This itself was of Greek origin, meaning 'royal', probably originally applied to royal halls. It was adapted in the Roman Empire for a variety of functions. It is classically the most basic building for communal meetings, a collective space: 'a place of encounter and of "commerce" in the broadest sense of the word' (Lefebvre 1991: 369). Importantly this was the space of participation, a 'socio-petal' form that fitted with the culture of the community. It was usually rectangular in shape, often with an opening, an apse or *exedra*, on one side as a point of authority which could be used for a throne or judge (Stalley 1999). The adaptation of this building form for the Christian church, as it became institutionalised through first the Roman Empire and then through the great monastic tradition of the medieval period, is not surprising. It provided a space where the whole community could gather, and the '*cathedra*' or seat of the presiding bishop took the place of the *exedra*.

This initial form is largely undifferentiated both in relation to spatial functions and to aesthetic adornment. As the liturgy developed, and the church grew more complex as an organisation, so did the spatial form expand and become more elaborate. The symbol of the cross was incorporated through the cross-axis of the transepts (although some commentators dispute its development as a deliberate symbolic feature). In some ways this echoes the cross-axis of the Roman fort and town, but it also marks the need to differentiate space for different groups of people. The choir was the place of the monks themselves, the inner community. This was distinct from the nave, which was the place of the public. The difference between religious Orders who were primarily a community for the performance of the liturgy and those who saw their role as preaching the gospel can be seen in the relative size of the nave. The crypt was developed as a place where pilgrims could visit the shrine of saints without disturbing the performance of the liturgy. In the newly built Norman cathedral at Canterbury this division of the interior became paramount. The whole choir and Trinity Chapel were surrounded by an 'ambulatory', so that pilgrims could move around without disturbing the monks. Thus simple differentiation for emplacement develops into a more complex ordering of circulation, the control of body and activity in space and time. Time and timetables also are important here originating in the regimes that governed the religious institutional day (Corbett 2003). 'Clocks enabled regular intervals to be sounded by the monastic, and then secular, church bells, soon to be translated into the continuous visual analogue of fingers moving over the clock face'. It has been argued that this later translates to the regularisation of space and time for the purposes of maximising profit (Markus 1993: 249).

As the communities grew, the spatial arrangements of necessity came to be more complex, and more differentiated to provide a system of emplacements to accommodate a larger number of different functions and different roles and hierarchies. Monasteries became the centre of local economies that were dependent on the monasteries at the same time as the monks were dependent on this external labour and production of resources. Thus Platt tells us that some two-thirds of the community at Rievaulx in the medieval period were lay brethren and similarly Fountains Abbey became the centre of a network of 'home farms' or 'granges' (1984: 48–9). New buildings were needed to maintain this division: there were lay brothers' dormitories and refectories, and the church became more subdivided by screens between the presbytery for the monks and the nave for the lay brothers. The infirmary was developed to provide medical care for sick and old lay brethren as well as monks. This had its own refectory, the misericord, which was the only place in the monastery where meat could be eaten. By the 1300s dispensations were frequently given to share in the meat of the infirm, and even rotas to eat there were instigated! The acquisition of lands and labourers also led to the growth of administration, with a growing number of monks having to spend time in what were essentially managerial tasks and the development of an elaborate command chain. This again led to further refinements of space for different sorts of tasks, also indicating a differentiation of levels. Some monasteries developed separate quarters for the abbots, together with their own refectories and studies (Burton 1994: 144–6).

Markus (1993: 250) comments on the spatial arrangement of St Gall monastery in Switzerland, the pattern of which was used across Europe, by saying that 'The ninth century plan of St Gall (Horn and Born 1979) uses a standard module. It both looks backward to the land grids of the Roman *agrimensores* and forward to the graph paper planning of Durand in 1800. Its grid enabled corridors, passages and stairs designed for quick and easy circulation to penetrate the plan'. So we can see again the effectiveness of the grid in providing a transparency of knowledge and intelligibility. Economy of time was gained through regularity of space. The plan shows that by the time of Charlemagne (742–814), the Benedictine monastic order had become a big departmentalised institution.

Monastic living was based upon a series of sets of 'rules' that we can see being made material in the development of the institution. The most well known of these is the Rule of St Benedict, written between 530 and 540. This includes seven chapters on the aims of the ascetic life, 13 on daily ritual, 41 on constitutional matters and 12 on penalties for breaches of discipline: probably one of the earliest texts on organisational life! All

BOUNDARY CROSSINGS: REPRODUCING ORGANISED SPACE • BUILDING A SOCIAL MATERIALITY: SPATIAL AND EMBODIED POLITICS IN ORGANISATION • ALTERNATIVE SPACES: THE RADICAL ORGANISATION OF SPACE? • CONCLUSIONS: DISORGANISING SPACE

2   85

aspects of collective life are covered within these rules. It effectively lays down a timetable, a set of job descriptions for different roles (from the abbot to the cellarer and the doorkeeper) and a way of accounting for the material life of the monastery in clothing, food and drink (private possessions to be forbidden). Lawrence argues that the figure of the abbot is derived from the Roman paternal role, based on unquestioning obedience within a context of mutual love, and that the Benedictine abbeys of the middle ages were based upon the plan of the Roman country villa (Lawrence 1989: 25–6).

Although in functional terms the monastery had become, borrowing from Le Corbusier, a 'machine for worship', its spatial development was also very much bound up with the aesthetic expression of the sacred. Thus the plain form of the basilica becomes the monumental gothic cathedral, with its play of space, light and height, all soaring spires, expanses of glass and intricate carvings. The objective of this confluence of the material and the symbolic is to connect the individual and collective experiences of spirituality within an institutionalised and spatialised setting. 'The celestial vision depicted is to make us forget that we stand in a building of stone and mortar' (von Simson 1952: 6).

Yet this is not meant to be an externalised set of symbols to be viewed from a distance, but a way of life, a negotiation of embodied spatialised living with the sacred. Thus the fundamental purpose of the spatial organisation of the church was the enactment of the liturgy, the living out of the religious experience that came from an ongoing relationship with God. It can be quite difficult in these times of sophisticated multiple 'readings' of culture and postmodern irony to capture the integration of body, mind and soul that was materially expressed in the buildings of the medieval church. An expression of the close identification sought, such that the separation between self and Other disappeared, can be seen in the phenomena of the stigmata: the physical manifestation of Christ's wounds on the body of the most faithful follower.

The Church developed multiple ways of bringing together embodied space and imaginary space. The senses were incorporated into the liturgy. Art, in the form of stained glass, icons and paintings, brought the experience to the eye; incense to the nose; music, bells, silences to the ear; the dressage of procession, standing, sitting, kneeling to the touch. The

Eucharist itself as central to the liturgy, forms a re-enactment of the Last Supper and incorporates the bodily experience of taste. This appeal to all the senses is made explicit in the teachings of Loyola that form the basis of the Jesuit movement, as an attempt to use somatic appeal in preventing the flight of Catholics to Protestantism. Loyola wished Catholics to move through each church and find afresh new sensory excitements at every turn. This holistic appeal to all of the senses can be seen in current (secular) organisational practices where the aim is that the sensorium be turned to the close identification between self and organisation, as we will explore further in Chapter 3.

Although, like the Roman fort, the monastery included within its area specialised buildings for different functions, these divided spaces were also linked together as a fluid and sensual space, being unified through the liturgy, which forms the basis for the organisation of the life of the community. Procession was a key aspect of the liturgy, producing an enactment of faith, so in those houses that emphasised it modifications would be made in the shape of processional doorways into the cloister from the south transept and back into the church from the western end (Burton 1994: 139). Developments in the liturgy were to contribute to western culture through art, music and theatrical staging. The refectory was more than just a building for eating in. Its layout and the conduct of the meal formed a re-enactment of the Last Supper. The spiritual dimension was brought home by the required silence, in contrast to the sociability of most communal meals, with the sole voice heard being that of the reader of scripture (Bruce 2000). Within the meal, the bread is the 'body', but so too is the church itself the corporate 'body'.

The collective experience of life as worship was embodied in even trivial details of the daily routine. The monks slept in their habits. When they were woken by the bell they made their beds, put on their cowl and night-shoes. They must not enter the lavatory, at the far end of the dormitory, with their head uncovered. They left the dormitory by the night-stairs, which led directly to the church, hence spatially enacting the significance of their devotions above all other activities. Even shaving and taking baths were supervised communal activities. The razors and bowls were passed around the monks in the cloisters. When not in use they were kept in a communal cupboard at the entrance to the dormitory. Bathing took place three times a year. Monks were called in groups to the bathhouse, they undressed and entered a cubicle shielded with a curtain, and washed in silence (Lawrence 1989: 119).

This spatial negotiation of the individual and the collective is also expressed through the development of sign language. The development of sign language specifically to deal with the practicalities of communal life, despite the institutional requirement of silence, might appear to be a form of resistance from control. Yet, apparently it was not developed as an idiosyncratic 'private' language. It was accepted by the church authorities as a collective form of communication. Bruce (2000) traces how the signing used at Cluny in France became part of the disciplinary technologies to safeguard the observance of silence, how it was adopted at other monasteries and how it went on to influence the development of education for deaf people in Spain. It has been argued that silence would have helped to ameliorate the lack of privacy (Lawrence 1989: 119) which many monks might have felt, whilst still facilitating living in community.

The need to combine the mundane aspects of community with the transcendent and sublime of spiritual experience continues into the twenty-first century. The architect John Pawson was recently commissioned to build a modern Cistercian monastery at Novy Dvur, in the Czech Republic. He comments on the most important aspects of this:

> The success of monastic architecture rests as much on the way it accommodates the rituals of life – eating, sleeping, bathing, dressing – as it does the rituals of religion, a fact reflected in a brief the size of a telephone directory which included specifications for temperatures in different parts of the monastery and a request for measures to address the problem of snoring brothers. (2003)

For having spent some time in the Mother monastery at Burgundy:

> I came to understand that it was not simply knowledge of a particular set of religious rituals which I had to acquire. Monastic life takes the everyday rituals of life and formalises them, harnessing the potential for gravitas in the simplest of actions. It was crucial that the details of the architecture would support these details of behaviour. (2003)

Architecture critic Deyan Sudjec accompanied him on one visit, and comments on the profound effects of living the liturgy on both mind and body: 'Your sense of time stops and somehow speeds up all at the same time. It clears your mind; ritual expands to fill every available synapse' (2004).

However, as Lefebvre (1991) argues, spaces can be dominated or appropriated for other purposes and by other powers at different points in time. The political significance of the monasteries was not lost on William I after the Norman invasion of Britain, and he sought to extend and use them for his own ends rather than suppress them. Societal and cultural changes are also reflected in the changing architecture of the religious houses, some of which may be analogous to Elias' (1994) theory of the 'civilising process'. Thus, for example, at Cleeve in the 1530s the dormitories were remodelled with separate bedchambers now providing privacy. More hearths were added for comfort. In some monasteries private possessions were tolerated, and monks kept these in their own studies (carrels) in the cloister (Lawrence 1989). The notion of the self-controlled 'individual' with a separate sense of identity meant monasteries were changing places of organised space.

The military and monasteries illustrate some key developments in the ways that organisation and power can be brought together spatially. We now turn to those spaces that are more commonly associated with organisation, and especially with the development of pervasive, large-scale organisations through the growth of industrialism, capitalism and mass production (Thompson and McHugh 2002). They are by no means a world away from the buildings already considered, though. As Markus comments, many forms of military discipline were incorporated into industrial organisation, and when the 'factory system gets going, camps, barracks and prisons are not far below the surface' (1993: 261). However, factories did not spring into perfect being with the advent of the Industrial Revolution. Production by regularised means and of large quantities had long been required by the state for military or revenue purposes. The development of ship and weapon production was often highly organised using specialist workers within a high level of division of labour. The Roman army organised ironworks and weapon and armour 'factories' in order to ensure supplies of a design and standard required. By 1300 Dante incorporates an image of the Venetian *Arsenale*, Europe's largest munitions factory, into his vision of Hell in his *La Divina Commedia*.

Markus notes how workers in royal manufactories possessed valued, and often highly secret, craft skills (1993: 250). The spatial arrangements of the factories embody this. They would be enclosed, gated and with restricted access. The workers' homes were within these boundaries, which ensured that time was not wasted, but also that the knowledge was protected. These homes would be well provided for, demonstrating the status and worth of the workers – whilst they were physically part of the factory organisation at least. As with the Roman fortress, there would be a range of buildings included, such as workshops, chapel, school and offices, ordered by task, but also symbolically and socially within the confines of the manufactory. Not surprisingly elements of surveillance were incorporated into the spatial design. For example, Toufaire, the chief engineer of the Royal Port of Rochelle, also designed the Le Creusot Foundary in France. This was based around a long axis with a narrower avenue crossing it at right angles, similar to the central streets in the Roman fort. At one end of the axis was placed the Director's house, at the other end were the furnaces and workshops. In between, on either side of the central axis, were the workers' houses. The central courtyard and axis provide an open space for surveillance. Markus states that 'formal devices underline the spatial strategy: the long axis unites control and investment, and the houses of those with least power become lateral sentinels' (p. 251).

Yet it is interesting to see that although control through surveillance was a usual plan of the design of manufactories and other organisational spaces, it was not followed through to the letter in a strictly rationalistic manner. It is known how Bentham complained that the principles of the panopticon had been seriously undermined in the building of the Bridewell prison in Edinburgh because the prisoners' day rooms had been placed between the central observation tower and the cells (Markus 1993: 252). Similarly, six years previous to this, the designer of the Royal Silk Mills in Budapest protested that the architect overseeing the building had moved the pillars to fit a classical architectural form whereas they had been deliberately designed off-centre so that the supervisor was able to see every worker clearly. Neither objection was successfully upheld, indicating that principles of control through line of sight were not enshrined as totally natural and inevitable.

As demand for production increased through mercantilism rather than directly from the state, other spatial forms were adapted or developed. Textiles especially, often associated with luxury goods, required the development of workshops. These were initially within or an extension of the domestic space. For example, houses were adapted by the Huguenot silk weavers of Spitalfields in London, with the addition of long upper rooms and horizontal weavers' windows, also seen in the weavers' houses of Lancashire, where cellar loom shops beneath weavers' cottages were also common.

There has been much discussion in industrial and economic history as to the key drivers of the factory system: the development of new power sources that could drive faster and more advanced machinery, and ultimately be linked together, or the need to control both workers and materials in the same time and space (e.g. Berg 1985; Landes 1969, 1986; Lazonick 1978, 1979; Marglin 1974). The adaptations of the Coventry ribbon makers' houses show an alternative to factory organisation that illustrates Berg's (1985) point that multiple production modes were maintained simultaneously. Markus (1993: 284–5) describes how the houses became differentiated in function within themselves with rooms specifically for meeting with customers and so on. Then he shows how they dealt with competition from early factories by joining together to share their technology and sources of energy, often having joint drive belts running through each others' houses. Wherever individual artisan workers could fight off the large factory owned by someone else, they almost certainly did so. However, Markus (p. 275) maintains that the weaving shed exerted a great influence on new sorts of social relations because of being a vast undifferentiated space for multiple large machines. These were alleged to be economically, technically and organisationally 'superior' to the putting out or neighbourhood based collective/independent approaches that in many places for many years, artisans hung on to (Marglin 1974).

Whatever the deliberate intentions behind the development of the factory system, the effects were certainly to incorporate control of the workforce through specific spatial arrangements, specific spatial practices and the embodied subjectivity of organisational members. Here, we concentrate on mass production because in some senses this is a defining impellor of the twentieth century. The processes within the factory have been widely studied but little has been said about the architectural framework in which these take place. Factory spaces are easy to take for granted but these had to be achieved as revolutionary edifices in the face of many extant practices within 'prior' yet commercially aware workforces. Thus, the innovative factory designs discussed below open up significant possibilities in the building of the relations of capitalism and for the construction of the mass-produced mass producer, a specific new category of worker (Jacques 1996).

In Pevsner's (1976) account of the development of the factory as a building type, he spends the majority of his time on nineteenth-century developments. When he turns to the twentieth-century factories of mass production he moves swiftly from Albert Kahn to the more architecturally notable factories of Behrens and Gropius. We, however, believe it is worth looking at the work of Kahn in more detail. In his collaborations with many well-known industrialists, most especially with Henry Ford over a 30-year period, he is responsible for giving Fordism and Scientific Management their spatial form. In the organisation of his own architectural practice, Kahn Associates (founded in 1895 and still in existence), he mirrored many of these business and managerial forms, which contributed hugely to his success.

Albert Kahn was born in Germany in 1869, emigrated to Detroit with his parents in 1880, and died in New York in 1942, but his influence was to become global. The United States of America, from the late nineteenth century, was undergoing an industrial transformation, especially with the growing importance of the automobile and aeronautics industries. This also transformed the industrial geography of the United States, with a much broader regional range of industrial centres. Detroit, where the automobile industry originated, was key to this, bringing with it a whole new organisation of work and of the employment relationship (Jacques 1996). Kahn's first factory work was in Detroit for the Packard Motor Company. In this project he used reinforced concrete, rather than bricks, for its cheapness, standardisation, clear lighting, fireproofing and ventilation. More than anything else, though, the relative lightness and strength of the concrete allowed him to produce a more open factory floor suitable for the needs of car production, unencumbered by so many load-bearing supports. In Packard Building No. 10, the interior columns were spaced 30 feet (9.1 metres) apart, which was an unusually large span at the time. It also allowed for larger windows, so the usable space could afford to be larger and still not be too dark for working. He followed this with a single storey, top-lit modular design for the George N. Pierce Plant in Buffalo, New York. Designed to produce uniform lighting and physical flexibility, it rapidly became the prototype for American factory design. Previously factories had been dark, overcrowded, dirty and inefficient. Kahn worked together with the industrialists to concentrate on the rational arrangement of the interior of the building. He considered what workers there were, what they did and where the materials should be in order to achieve a workflow. The more flexible space made it possible to experiment with new ways to organise the production process. As Curtis (1996: 81) tells us, concrete 'recommended itself for the design of wide-span factories to accommodate the new techniques of "Taylorization" whereby all steps of fabrication were submitted to a scientific rationalization for the mass production of goods'.

The success of these innovative buildings soon led to Kahn's association with Henry Ford. Although Ford was not the inventor of the mass-produced car,[6] he was the man with the vision to see the advantages of mass producing a cheap but technologically advanced standardised model (Bergoneron and Maiullari-Pontois 2000). Kahn was to become the architect of the Ford Highland Park site which was built in 1909, and is generally regarded as the first locus of the mass production of cars with the iconic Model T. Kahn designed it as a straight-forward rectangle, 228 metres by 22.5 metres in dimension on four floors. Staircases, lifts and lavatories were all placed on the corners of the building whilst the narrowness of the building and its large windows allowed maximum lighting. Deliveries of components and raw materials were to all four floors by lifts. The main production line was a continuous process running vertically through all four floors, cleverly exploiting gravity. In or around 1913, the production line was mechanised and the motive force of gravity was replaced by mechanical power (Ackermann 1991: 49).

'But Highland Park had its shortcomings. Production did not flow; it moved between floors, sometimes through windows, and even between buildings. So soon after, in his 1917 design of the landmark half-mile-long, glass-walled Ford Rouge plant, Kahn created Henry Ford's vision: an efficient plant where automated assembly lines flowed uninterrupted, all on one level, from raw materials to the finished car': a model provided in reverse by the Chicago meat-processing industry. 'The Rouge grew into the largest manufacturing complex in the United States covering 1100 acres, with a labour force that peaked at 120,000 workers'. The large-scale single-storey factory illuminated by saw-tooth roofs became his trademark 'daylight factory' (Ackermann 1991; www.albertkahn.com).

River Rouge was originally used for the production of submarine chasers for the US Navy, given the needs of the First World War. Indeed, Kahn's practice designed the majority of US airfields and many naval bases during the First World War and received over $200 million in defence contracts in the first three years of the Second World War, the last three years of Kahn's life (www.albertkahn.com). He built the Willow Run complex for Ford in Ypsilanti, near Detroit, which became known as the 'Arsenal of Democracy' and which in 1943 was the largest war factory in the world (Bergoneron and Maiullari-Pontois 2000). Even during this period of frenetic large-scale building for the needs of the Second World War, he developed the innovation of a blacked out building with electric lighting and air conditioning for the Ford plant, which made B-24 Liberator bombers, but became a model for future peace-time production.[7] Without the use of these spaces of mass production, the Second World War would have been very different. Here is an indication of the inextricable links between organisation, space and war that we explore more fully in Chapter 4.

By the late 1930s, Kahn employed over 600 people and Gossel and Leuthauser (1991: 404) calculate that Kahn controlled and was responsible for 19 per cent of all US industrial construction: an incredible influence at a time of great industrial growth and change. In all, Kahn probably built about 2000 factories between 1900 and 1940 (Bergoneron and Maiullari-Pontois 2000). He was also closely involved in the building of the large offices newly required to service a mass production economy, including the General Motors Building, banks, insurance and media buildings. This massive production of architecture involved a process of standardisation that mirrored that of his industrialist clients and hence he rationalised the whole of the architectural and building process, right from the design and supply of materials. He also followed a system of employment relations that was mimetic of the demands of capitalism in the same way as SOM were to echo the practices of large bureau-cratic corporations in the 1950s. Darley comments that 'his office was a place for technicians, not designers' (2003: 85). In fact he did not employ architectural graduates, believing that they would prioritise art above qualities such as 'team co-operation' (Saint 1983: 80). Kahn was known for saying that 'architecture is 90 percent business and 10% art' (Bergoneron and Maiullari-Pontois 2000). Interestingly, another two Kahn brothers, Moritz and Julius, were centrally involved in the patenting and production of reinforced concrete (Darley 2003: 82), and they, too, were skilled in the promotion of their business and techniques.

Perhaps even more staggering than his influence in the USA was the fact that Kahn was entrusted with *all* industrial building projects in the Soviet Union until the mid-1930s.[8] On the strength of a huge $40 million contract with Stalin, he set up office in Moscow in 1929. Thus we see that the organisation of 'abstract space' (Lefebvre 1991) is not constrained to capitalist countries, but becomes involved in wider attempts in the dominance of space, what Harvey describes as capitalism's 'spatial fix' (2000: 26–30).

In his factory design and close collaboration with industrialists, Kahn turned his back on the aesthetic imagination associated with architecture. This is seen by some as a defining moment in twentieth-century archi-tecture. The Packard Building has been described as 'zero architecture'. In *A Concrete Atlantis,* Banham says it was,

 a zero term in architecture, and hardly any other architect or builder with a professional conscience could have done it. Few could have brought themselves down (or up?) to this level of cheese paring economy – or ruthless rationality, if you

> prefer – even if they had to affect such an attitude to keep the attention of profit-oriented entrepreneurs whom they had hoped would commission buildings for their offices. (1986: 86)

Kahn's factory buildings predominantly excluded any decoration, although some factories with public frontages had to be given some semblance of architectural normality for the sake of company image. Although this form of design has been claimed by some to have influenced the development of European modernism, the economic and organisational context within which these forms came about should not be neglected. Architecture was no longer for art's sake but for industry's sake. With it came the 'anaesthetisation' of the factory worker in what Kamata was later to describe as the 'automobile factories of despair' (1974). What he offered to Ford, the US Department of Defense and to Stalin was a brilliant 'phantasmagoria' in which the image consumed by the hierarchs was of huge populations of industrial labourers producing almost limitless amounts of goods under one roof and one central controlling command structure. He allowed a material appropriation of this centrally planned imaginary whether it was by democrat, communist or industrialist. These are the key imaginary spaces of the twentieth century which recur again and again in critical cultural productions such as Chaplin's *Modern Times*, Sillitoe's *Saturday Night and Sunday Morning* and Fritz Lang's *Metropolis*.

Although in some ways the vast flexible undifferentiated spaces of the Kahnian paradigm appear to allow openness and transparency, what they produce is very much the grid of control so characteristic of 'abstract space' as we have seen in Chapter 1. The concrete structures certainly resemble this grid, as Curtis, from a more aesthetic perspective points out: 'A characteristic morphology of grid plans and simple rectangular elevations of pleasing proportions resulted' (1996: 81). But it within this apparent openness that the homogeneity and standardisation that is mass production was to form not only a diverse range of materials into a replicated product, but also the diverse workforce who entered the gates. Undifferentiated replication is a major instrument of social order and control (Dale 2001), as can be seen in Huxley's portentous critique of Fordism in *Brave New World* where it brings 'Community,

Identity, Stability' (1994: 5). These elements were important in the new representational spaces of that epoch, for it is important to realise that many of the new entrants to the plants of Detroit and Stalingrad came straight from agrarian roots, may not have spoken the language of the metropolis and were unused to the rhythms of the factory day. The control of their workspace allowed the efficient socialisation of the worker in programmes of re-education: they were constructed as a new category of industrial employee (Jacques 1996).

Kahn's designs, then, represented the archetypical structure of the industrial factory and have contributed, through this phantasmagoria of docile, undifferentiated workers, to the employers' appreciation of how to control large groups of people under one roof. The dazzling apparition he conjured up was a mirror to their corporate desire for huge controlled productive spaces of mythic proportions. For us, it is a clear example of the securing of production and power through architectural design. It produces protection and enclosure; positioning and codification; control and boundary maintenance, all within the assertion of the need for harmony and control.

Leach has claimed, 'power is no longer linked to space, and architectural forms have little control over human behaviour' (1999: 80). In a world fascinated by the possibilities of virtual reality and distributed technologies that challenge the idea that humans are limited by the place and time they occupy bodily it is easy to see why that argument might be made. However, we hope in this chapter that we have demonstrated the lie to this, and shown some of the multiple ways in which human social, spatial and organisational relations are inextricably linked. Spaces and places are not merely containers for habitation. There is a recursive enfolding of the spatial and the social. As humans construct places to occupy those places come to construct us. Thus even whilst working at a computer or playing in some virtual reality arcade, the materiality of those spaces – even through their phantasmagoric appearance of liberation from place and the body – form the sites of multiple power effects.

In the following chapter we consider how spatial, social and organisational interconnections influence how people experience their own identities, their relations with other people and their identification or otherwise with organisations.

Notes

1 Although Harvey makes clear that Haussmann's reconstruction of Paris cannot be reduced to a single type of intervention nor be simply accredited to the vision of one individual (2003).

2 Seville (1402–1519) is the largest Gothic Cathedral, while Angkor Wat (twelfth century) represents the cosmic Indian mountain, Meru (Glancey 1998).

3 We are mindful of the comment of our colleague and friend Colin Williams, who lamented that management students could identify a panopticon from a mile away but did not understand fundamental management processes!

4 The Baroque may be defined as covering a significant time span, during which it did not have a single, homogeneous expression. It also differs across countries and cultures (Harbison 2000: vii–x). As with the 'postmodern', there is considerable debate as to whether the Baroque is a reaction to or a fulfilment of what went before.

5 Webster (1998: 167) suggests that 'camp' should be used for temporary campaign and marching sites; 'fort' for the more permanent site for a single unit; and 'fortress' for the establishment of a whole legion. He also delineates the variations between these over time during the Empire. However, it is sufficient for our purposes to point to the fact that there was not a complete homogeneity, but enough in common for us to make these general observations as to the links between power, space and organisation.

6 This was Ransom Olds, who sold his first car in New York in 1893.

7 Willow Run was but one plant of one company. General Motors and Chrysler also did their part. Former automobile plants built everything from tanks to bombs to guns. In just the first 18 months after Pearl Harbor, 350,000 people came to the city of Detroit to work in defense plants. Automakers and their suppliers produced $30 billion worth of military equipment from 1942 to 1945. It is claimed that 'Detroit truly was the Arsenal of Democracy. As Walter Reuther had predicted, "Like England's battles were won on the playing fields of Eton, America's were won on the assembly lines of Detroit."'

8 These too were to be converted to the large-scale production of armaments during the war.

3   building people: identities and spaces

BUILDING ORGANISATION: SECURING AND OBSCURING POWER • BUILDING PEOPLE: IDENTITIES AND SPACES • A POLITICAL ECONOMY OF ORGANISED SPACE • BOUNDARY CROSSINGS: REPRODUCING ORGANISED SPACE • BUILDING A SOCIAL MATERIALITY: SPATIAL AND EMBODIED POLITICS IN ORGANISATION • ALTERNATIVE SPACES: THE RADICAL ORGANISATION OF SPACE? • CONCLUSIONS: DISORGANISING SPACE

> *The task of the architect is not to build houses. It is also not his[1] task to create houses for people as they are. His actual task is rather to consist in creating new people – who would then suit the architectures which one intends to build.*

> (Welsch 1997)

> *The architect is a molder of men, whether or not he consciously assumes the responsibility.*

> (Frank Lloyd Wright 1999)

> *The most important Manhattan Projects of the future will be vast government-sponsored inquiries into what the politicians and the participating scientists will call 'the problem of happiness' – in other words, the problem of making people love their servitude.*

> (Huxley 1994 unnumbered)

In this chapter, we examine further the relationship between the spaces and places of organisation and the social production of subjectivity and intersubjectivity, a person's conceptualisation of themselves and their relations with others. Here we develop the interconnections between space and power, especially those of enchantment, emplacement and enactment, through a consideration of the relationship between self and organisation. In particular, we look at recent moves by organisations to physically reshape the workplace in order to better achieve institutional objectives, especially where the intention is to incorporate employees into the organisation such as to 'capture hearts and minds'; that is, to encourage individuals to *identify* themselves with the organisation. A number of design consultancies have been at the forefront of these initiatives, and we examine the work of one of the most influential of these companies, DEGW. Such design consultancies are active in producing an array of organised spaces, being 'conceived' or 'representations of space' in

Lefebvre's terms (1991: 39). Their principles and models for spatial arrangements are used not only for workplaces, but also for places as diverse as arts complexes, housing estates, national and local government buildings, heritage sites and retail outlets. Thus, although we focus in detail in this chapter on workspaces, the relation between spatial practices and identity has a much wider resonance. Indeed, our argument in this chapter, as throughout the book, centres on the idea that 'places are always already hybrid' (Massey 1995a: 183).

Modern conceived workspaces draw on shifting identities which are shaped by the dynamic nature of social and cultural relations across space, and which can also be seen in relation to 'imaginary' spaces. Yet when we think of workplaces, the tendency is to treat them as bounded and different from other spaces such as home or leisure spaces. However, modern forms of life have led to the blurring of these boundaries. This can be seen literally through the construction of new 'mixed use' spaces and buildings, such as the Mailbox in Birmingham or the Docklands area in London. Here work, play, sport, consumption and accommodation are deliberately combined with greater or lesser success. On a smaller scale this can be seen in a number of workplaces, such as the BBC Media Village and St Lukes Advertising Agency with their spaces for table football, pool or other games, the British Airways HQ 'street' with its shops, or the gym and wetlands areas at EnergyCo discussed in Chapter 6. Of course we have to be careful that we do not fall unwittingly into an acceptance that organised space is deterministic. Just because designers, architects and managers have particular ideas about the relations of employees, consumers or householders with the spaces they have conceived, does not mean that either identity or social relations are influenced in such a direct or straightforward fashion.

Nevertheless, the development of mixed or hybrid spaces indicates, for us, a changing set of possible relations between self and workplace. Across a number of different facets of these redesigned organisational spaces, we discern a theme that may be characterised as the 'disappearing workplace'. On the one hand, this refers to the changing physical characteristics of work as less bounded within a certain place and time. Dealt with in more detail in Chapter 5, the concept of 'separate spheres' has always been somewhat chimerical. However, recent trends accelerate the dispersal of paid work, as Felstead *et al.* (2005) show in detail. There are various aspects to this, for example, in the technological facilitation of mobile work that they describe as the 'electronic envelope', within which the employee travels and works regardless of their physical location. There is also the growing recognition that workplaces are physical assets that might be managed more economically and efficiently. Real estate and facilities management perspectives on achieving maximum occupancy levels, optimum densities and time-space usage have increased in importance and predominance in organisations. Additionally, in a growing service economy, spaces are never solely 'work' spaces: they are simultaneously spaces of consumption, retail, leisure and education. One sometimes glimpses a little of this 'backstage' (Goffman 1969) employment relationship in a shop or restaurant, through instructions displayed on walls to employees about how they should conduct customer service. To some extent, this overt declaration of a relationship mediated by organisational rules disrupts the construction of a space dedicated to the seemingly free choice and pleasures of the consumer, so the hybrid space faces its own particular challenges.

Ironically, at a time when work is less physically bounded and defined, the spaces and places of the organisation have been drawn into a 'battle for hearts and minds' in more and more consciously planned and explicit ways. Thrift (1996) argues persuasively that the increase in speed, electronic transactions and trans-national business relations does not lessen the need for face-to-face relations. Indeed, he demonstrates that there is a correspondingly greater move towards the establishment of embodied networks and physical meetings. Similarly, within the organisation there is a greater need for the commitment, involvement and identification of the employee with company goals and culture. And we would argue that it is in fact partly because of the very openness of the spaces of work and the extension of work beyond the physical boundaries of the company, that there is a greater need for the identification of the employee with the organisation – a powerful identification that is strongly bound up with individual identity, an identity that they then ideally carry with them 'outside' the entity of the organisation, even external to the formal time and place of work. Although the employee may be frequently 'outside' the workspace, it is through the spatial practices of the organisation that the identity-identification links are often aimed towards internalisation. Yet again, it seems contradictory that the 'tie-ins' between self and organisation are increasingly focused through appeals to aspects of social identity other than that of 'the employee'. Thus in some ways the workplace is also disappearing psychically, as organisations appeal to employees' sense of identity and desires as consumers, citizens or aesthetes.

The development of organisational spaces and employee identities

We begin by taking a brief look at the changing and diverse relations between organisational spaces and employee identities. The relationship between identity, work and space is multiple, ambiguous and shifting. Social relations did not simply convert from an identity with land and feudal lord to one with employer through the wage nexus. During the early period of industrialisation in the UK, as Littler (1982: 64–72) points out, even where work was found in one physical space, relations to employment and control were frequently indirect. Instead they were mediated through a multiplicity of traditional social forms such as gang work systems in the docks and the 'butty' system in mining; the master craftsman in areas such as ironworking who, when he moved to a different iron-works, took his own workers, whom he recruited and paid; the familial systems in cotton spinning and other textiles; and the skills hierarchies in other subcontracted groups such as the work team or 'chair' in the flint-glass industry.

In the USA, Jacques gives an account of how the very category of 'the employee' came into being at the end of the nineteenth century, with a new continuing form of relationship between individual and organisation that had not existed before. Indeed, the idea of being a 'hireling' had previously been associated with the lowest form of social relationship. The American ideal was rather one of self-sufficiency and opportunities for workers to raise themselves out of the temporary state of the employment relationship to become self-employed, and able to take on their own labourers (1996: 48). The new contractual relationship eventually led to a qualitatively different form of identity relations: of employee and employer. It is this nascent employment relationship that Albert Kahn and Henry Ford concretised spatially, as we explored in Chapter 2, and that is now taken for granted as being embedded in everyday life for the majority of people in capitalist societies.

The development in spatial terms of the identity of 'the employee' takes some quite different paths. Although the factories of Kahn and others brought about the creation of a mass class of employees, and constructed the direct relationship of the individual to the organisation in terms of tight spatial control, the idea of the identification of the worker with the employer was in its earliest stages. However, capitalists were only too aware that workers had started to identify collectively with each other, across different occupations but through the same shared experience of the social relations of employment. So industrialists worked hard to try to prevent the self-identification and collective organisation of labour. Henry Ford was keen to outlaw labour organisation, but also to encourage workers to identify themselves as consumers of mass production (and thus his products). To inculcate workers into a worldview that normalised the economic and cultural power of the capitalist organisation, he produced (with Samuel Crowther) a series of books of what can only be described as propaganda (e.g. *Moving Forward* (1931) and *Today and Tomorrow* (1926)). He also wished his workers to live their non-working lives 'outside' the organisation, in such a way that production could be maximised, hence his development of the activities of the infamous 'sociological department' to monitor workers' private lives (Beynon 1973; Corbett 1994). But in terms of the work itself, of course, Fordism and scientific management meant that the worker's subjectivity and even knowledge were rendered unimportant. The 'unemployed self' was the term used by Gouldner (1969) to express this notion. Once the routine of production and the predictable traction of assembly line or clerical work had cut in, then huge areas of the creative consciousness of employees was left to its own devices. 'Thoughtful' employees entertained themselves once they knew their work routines forwards and backwards. Output levels could be easily attained (Sillitoe 1960). If freed of economic attachment to the workstation, workers could make the space an expression of their oppositional identity through sequestering of completed output or 'goldbricking' (Roy 1952) and appear to be busy whilst not, a behaviour sometimes called 'soldiering' (Taylor 1911). Thereby, measurements of output were easily circumvented and trips to the toilet for a quiet read and a smoke became commonplace. There are stories at the Longbridge car factory in Birmingham of the night shift enjoying a nightclub atmosphere where drinking and sex were regular occurrences amongst the enclosed rafters of the assembly-shed roof. If production can be delivered in a certain time within the parameters of the workday then space is found for the unemployed self. Self-reflection and self-identity took place 'away' from the workstation – if not physically, then certainly mentally.

But aspects of the selfhood of the worker were becoming significant in some areas of management and management research. The Hawthorne Studies and resultant Human Relations School uncovered the social and psychological identity of the worker. Although the research had its origin in the physical conditions of the workplace, by the time of its dissemination and popularisation through the work of Roethlisberger and Dickson (1939), and Mayo (1949), the spatial and material aspects of the study had been effectively consigned to the dustbin. But just because there was a comparative lack of awareness of the social production of space after Hawthorne, this does not mean that historically the work*place* has not been influential in how employees daily construct themselves and their relations. Hofbauer (2000) makes this clear in her study of *burolandschaft* – the spatial organisation of different office designs. Following Duffy (1992), she distinguishes between 'open-plan offices' which line up individuals and make them transparent to supervision; 'single-cell offices' which organise individuals in separate enclosures; and the more recent forms of 'office landscape'. These latter arrangements emphasise 'the co-operative effort' ('emphasis is on "communications" rather than on work flow', Duffy 1992: 82).

Contemporary management, then, has recognised that there is more to effective organisation than the mere economic control of resources and the direct control of employees. Modern management has been described as centrally about the 'management of meaning' (Gowler and Legge 1983) and the 'management of identity' (e.g. Collinson 1992; Watson 1994). This is often expressed as the battle for 'hearts and minds', and tends to involve the requirement of an identification of the individual with the organisation and its goals. Ethnographic studies show the inter-action of individual identity construction in relation to organisational practices. For example, Watson's (1994) work illustrates 'managers in search of themselves', where managers' roles include working on the identities of their subordinates so that they are personally committed to the company whilst simultaneously working on their own identities as managers. Similarly Grey's (1994) study of trainee accountants illus-trates the twin pressures of the individual and the organisation in the undertaking of the 'project of self'.

In these studies of worker, manager and professional, the physical environment has been just that – an environment or a context. It is an empty container in which social relations take place (cf. Lefebvre 1991: 15). Yet if we look at the detail in these studies, we can see that the spatial and material dimensions are highly relevant. For example, Collinson's (1992) shop-floor workers use the 'alternative' spaces of the washroom to appropriate space and time, thus creating themselves as oppositional to organisational culture attempts to make them identify with the company. On the other hand, Grey's (1994) accountants have to extend their 'work identity' into ever-greater spaces and time beyond the strictly organisational, such as golf courses, pubs, dinner parties. The pressure to close the potential gap between individual identity and iden-tification with work or the organisation only grows with hierarchical progression, with those unable to perform this elision being weeded out. In Chapter 6 we try to develop an approach that brings the signifi-cance of material relations into the analysis of organisation. For now, we turn to look at the development of research about identity, and consider how this is linked to how identity might be seen to be spatially performed.

The spatial performance of identity

Over the last twenty years or so there has been a sea change in theories of the social actor. From seeing the individual as a pre-given personality formed through a confluence of biological determinism and early expe-rience, and subsequently fixed in this self-hood, subjectivity has come to be seen as 'a specific, historical product that is ambiguous, fragmentary, discontinuous, multiple, sometimes fundamentally non-rational and often contradictory' (Collinson 1992: 28). The idea that people come into the workplace with their identities already fixed and determined has given way to a much more processual view of identity as an ongoing negotiation between the social actor and their social relationships. In this, the situation and relations of the workplace have been seen as the most significant site of identity construction in late capitalist societies. There are a number of reasons for this. First, the sheer amount of working time that makes up the typical adult life. Second, work and employment are seen as so central because of the need, in capitalist economies, to sell one's labour power in order to achieve economic survival and social status. This has led to a close identification between an individual and their employment relations that transcends the basic 'wage nexus' to become a key component of self-definition and intersubjective relations. The most common initial question on being introduced to a new acquaintance is to ask 'what do you do', meaning 'what is your employment?', and thence to a means to start to understand what sort of person they are, what education they are likely to have achieved, and where they stand in the social hierarchy. Consumption is another site of social identity construction that has come to be seen as of equal, sometimes of more importance to identity than that of the relations of production. Bauman (1998: 1) sees a movement to 'a society of consumers, in which life-projects are built around consumer choice rather than work, professional skills, or jobs'. In acquiring, using and displaying certain goods and services in certain ways (or not), it is argued, a particular presentation of self can be achieved (Gabriel and Lang 1995: 81–99). However, since consumption depends on earning power, production and consumption can never be truly separated.

The elaboration of theories of production or consumption identities tends to be from within different academic fields. For example, an emphasis on work relations tends to be found in management and industrial sociology, whilst a focus on consumption tends to be found in cultural studies and marketing. However, some commentators have explicitly drawn connections between production and consumption in considering modern forms of identity construction (e.g. Campbell 1983,

1987; du Gay 1996; Rose 1996, 1999). Our discussion below as to the connections between the spatial and identity practices of the redesigned organisation depends on cutting across these boundaries between social 'spheres' such as production, consumption, leisure and reproduction.

Perhaps one of the most important aspects of modern identity, one which cuts across social relations of production and consumption, is its *self-reflexivity*. This is the aspect of the modern self that can be related back to the development of the 'self-examining self', discussed in the previous chapter. Contemporary individuals, argues Rose, are encouraged to 'live as if running a project of themselves; they are to work on their emotional world, their domestic and conjugal arrangements, their relations of employment and the techniques of sexual pleasure, to develop a style of being that will maximise the worth of their existence to themselves' (1996: 157). There is in this 'project' the assumption that the individual has autonomy and a high degree of choice over what they become, how they fashion themselves. What you make of yourself is presented as an imperative, and there is a social and moral judgement of those who 'make nothing of themselves'.

This stress on the individual 'project of self' downplays and obscures wider power relations, inequalities, differential resources that give opportunities or constraints for self-fulfilment. It all taps into a more generalised 'American Dream' where 'anyone can be anything they want to be'. This view of unfettered choice for an individual who is not restrained by societal structures such as class, gender or ethnicity, very much fits with the libertarian ethos of advanced capitalism. Thrift expresses this 'unfettering' powerfully:

> For quite a few people, capitalism is not just hard graft. It is also fun. People get stuff from it — and not just more commodities. Capitalism has a kind of crazy vitality. It doesn't just line its pockets. It also appeals to gut feelings. It gets involved in all kinds of extravagant symbioses. It adds to the world as well as subtracts". (2005: 1)

It is this ethos of self-fulfilment, pleasure and desire that links in the possibilities of advanced capitalism with the project of identity. Indeed, Campbell (1987) argues that production and consumption identities are characterised by the same social forces; that 'the psycho-cultural forces that drive a pleasure-orientated consumption also account for the broad range of work attitudes' (Gabriel and Lang 1995: 103). Here we see an expression of the confluence of identity with self-fulfilment and pleasure, directly related to social and material relations produced by capitalism. It is a very telling demonstration of the way that we as individuals, rather than being unfettered, are tied into these social and material relations in the most intimate fashion.

Furthermore, techniques, programmes and experts spring up to 'help' the individual in their quest for self. 'Evidence from the United States, Europe and the UK suggests that the implantation of such "identity projects", characteristic of advanced democracies, is constitutively linked to the rise of a breed of new spiritual directors, "engineers of the human soul"' (Rose 1996: 157). We would like to suggest that the designers and architects of organisational and organised spaces can be included in this category of 'engineers of the human soul', as we will illustrate in the discussion of spatial design below.

Much emphasis has been put on the influence of 'discourse' in how individuals construct their subjectivity (Casey 1995; Collinson 1992; Henriques *et al.* 1984; Hollway 1991; Shotter and Gergen 1989). Here discourses are seen as 'texts' or 'storytelling', where the individual constructs a narrative of the self that holds a consistency between events and across time, thus creating a coherent subjectivity. These are not narratives that are constructed in an individual vacuum, but can only be developed in relation to the availability of certain *socially legitimated* discourses of identity; for example, a professional ethos (Grey 1994), a 'good' mother (Rossiter 1988), the oppositional anti-authoritarian identity of 'the lads' (Willis 1977) or the sexualised masculinity of the shop floor (Collinson 1992).

Thus far we have considered a number of ideas about the production of modern identities. Now we want to consider how these can be incorporated with a social view of subjectivity that recognises the social actor as also a *spatial and embodied actor*, not just as a discursive construction. The lack of attention to spatial and embodied forms of identity in the social science literature indicates that the Cartesian influence is alive and well, despite a great deal of rhetoric to the contrary. As we argued in

Chapter 2, the *enactment* of organisational and organised space is a key mode of the production and reproduction of power relations that is often overlooked.[2] Enactment, or the lived experience of social spaces, is also central to the negotiation of identity.

One of the difficulties in using the word 'enactment' in relation to spatial-social relations is its resonance with the theatrical metaphor. When an actor takes on a theatrical role, it is still assumed that there is a 'real' identity to the actor underneath the 'performance' identity that is being presented. An actor has also taken on the role they play consciously, intentionally and through choice. Distinctions have been made between 'surface' acting, which is as it suggests a superficial change of appearance and demeanour to fit the required social role, and 'deep' acting, where people work to deliberately change their feelings, attitudes or values (Aldridge 2003; Hochschild 1983). We want to try to avoid these ambiguities between surface/depth and conscious/unmindful aspects of identity that stem from the theatrical metaphor and focus on using the concept of 'enactment' for the spatial and embodied 'living through' of social relations, spaces and identity. The approach that we have taken to the spatial production of identity derives in part from Judith Butler's conceptualisation of 'performativity'. Although this sounds as if it is closely related to the theatrical, Butler very clearly points out that 'performativity is neither free play nor theatrical self presentation' (Butler 1993: 95). Rather it is 'the forced reiteration of norms' (1993: 94), a repetition of 'regulatory fictions' that constitute the subject (p. 95). Again, though the idea of 'fictions' hints at a discursive performativity, Butler's work centres on the production of the sexed *body*.

Whilst this is not explicitly spatial it can be related to spatial practices, and particularly to the routes and routines that form the *habitus* of everyday life. It can also be developed through de Certeau's notion of 'walking rhetorics' (1984: 100–3). In his exposition of walking in the city in *The Practice of Everyday Life*, de Certeau links the activity of the pedestrian with that of creating a narrative, through the spatial practices of choosing and improvising routes and crossings which 'organises an ensemble of possibilities' (1984: 98). That de Certeau chooses this account of spatial self-formation in the city is particularly resonant with the rhetorics used by the design consultancy we consider below.

However, as we shall discuss later, we do have reservations over de Certeau's assumption of the autonomous self and the notion of the free choice of spatial practice.

Our point here is that we wish to develop the concept of enactment to show that identity is not simply a discourse but needs to be enacted by human bodies in social spaces on a daily basis. In seeking a way that may help us see the interconnections between spatial practices, organised spaces and identity more clearly, we turn to Ricoeur's (1988) theory of narrative. Although Ricoeur relates narrative specifically to time, thus appearing to disregard space, he connects the development of narrative to lived experience: he argues that narrative starts 'from our experience of being in the world and in time, and proceeding from this ontological condition towards its expression in language' (1984: 78). He also sees narrative as formed by both historical action and imagination, which, following Lefebvre (1991), we could link to both lived and imaginary spaces as being significant in the development of narrative identity. This point is developed by Ezzy (1998):

> While a narrative configures lived experience, it is not determined by it. Narratives give lived experience a clearer, richer meaning. However, self-narratives are not free fictions: 'Humanity, we have said with Marx, only makes its history in circumstances it has not made' (Ricoeur 1988, p. 216). The plots of narrative identities are formed in a complex interaction between events, imagination, significant others, routines and habits, and the structure of the soliloquy that forms a person's self-narrative.

Although we might have a narrative of identity, it is not only a series of discourses that we hold in our heads; it is a series of practices that we live through.

As we have tried to demonstrate throughout this book, we see social life as intimately bound up with organisational life, and social space with organised space, and not simply in relation to the supposed confines of the work organisation. We develop a perspective below that recognises how the concepts of 'performativity' and 'walking rhetorics' can be used to develop the idea of the 'enactment' of spatial power and politics that we discussed in the previous chapter. The walking performances that go to make up the subject identity are a negotiation, in Lefebvre's terms, of the spaces of representation (conceived and organised spaces) with representational spaces (lived spaces).

With this concept of spatial enactment of identity in mind, we consider the work of the 'engineers of the human soul' in the form of one of the most influential design consultancy firms, DEGW, and their involvement in the production of organised spaces as a set of potential embodied narratives or 'walking rhetorics'. The design companies provide exactly the wherewithal to support this process of daily enactment of one's identity.

The redesign of workspaces: the example of DEGW

The design of space is big business. All aspects of space are open to the transformation of expertise, from urban development and planning through to the interior design of intimate domestic space. Workplace redesign is no exception to this. There are a large number of design companies, consultancies and networks of practitioners who offer cradle to grave spatial solutions to companies. Well-known architectural practices, such as Foster and Partners, put the redesign of workspaces in prominent places on their websites. What particularly characterises the most significant of these is their claim to integrate key organisational decisions and strategies into spatial, architectural and material form. In the project examples put forward by the Space for Business Consulting network (www.spaceforbiz.com), for example, spatial reconfiguration is used to integrate company cultures after merger, to achieve organisational change and to facilitate new work patterns having evaluated the impact of alternative spatial arrangements.

In order to explore some of the main characteristics of this deliberate reshaping of workplaces, we consider in more detail the influential work of design consultancy DEGW, probably the foremost of those which concentrate predominantly on the workplace (Myerson 1998). DEGW was formed in 1973, its letters being taken from the initials of its four founders: Frank Duffy, Peter Eley, Luigi Giffone and John Worthington. It is a multi-professional group involving ergonomics, psychology, planning and architecture. It has over 100 staff in the UK and about 250 worldwide, having 12 offices across Europe, North America and Asia-Pacific. A list of its clients (www.degw.com) indicates the extent of its involvement across the public sector, education, financial services, pharmaceuticals, media and professional services. DEGW provides a service that is specifically tailored to the client, rather than off-the-shelf generic solutions. Its comprehensive range of services includes detailed in-company research, developing spatial strategies for companies and all aspects of design. It uses detailed 'Time Utilisation Surveys', which are copyrighted materials, to understand how and when each space is utilised. These surveys allow businesses to relate their internal spatial arrangements and flows to managerial and organisational goals. It also conducts 'post-occupancy' studies. These measure how efficiently reordered space is being used, and whether goals are being achieved. Its founder members and key personnel are actively involved in the production of knowledge about space and organisation. They have produced a number of influential books (e.g. Duffy 1992, 1997; Worthington 1997), have been involved in government and quasi-government projects on design (e.g. researching the links between building design and business performance for UK's Commission on Architecture and the Built Environment in 2004) and run a 'Workplace Forum' network which brings together practitioners, managers and academics to explore current design issues.

Frank Duffy, one of the founders of DEGW and past RIBA president, argues that space is often neglected by managers seeking organisational change: 'clients have sophisticated discussions about IT, and perfectly sophisticated discussions about organisational issues, but elementary discussions about building. And these people never talk to each other: it's a silo mentality'. In contrast, he sees buildings as 'agents of change. Buildings have a catalytic effect. They can express new ideas and push possibilities forward' (13 November 1996; www.vnunet.com/articles/print/2076131). A key aspect of this organisational change, which is not solely about reducing fixed building costs or improved operations in a simply technical sense, is the integration of spatial reordering with how employees perceive themselves and their role in the organisation: it is intimately connected with issues of the management of meaning and identity as discussed earlier. DEGW's website declares that 'Space is beginning to be perceived as a tool and as an enabler for increased productivity through collaboration, strengthened cultural values and knowledge sharing' (www.degw.com).

The primary aim in all this is to 'deliver measurable business benefits' for clients. Andrew Harrison, Director of Research at DEGW, identifies four elements of value that may be maximised by companies through their buildings. The first of these is 'image value', associated with the semiotics of the structure and its aesthetic cachet. The image value may enhance the second element, the 'exchange value', or how much the building might be sold for when the time comes for its disposal, especially if it is associated with the work of a popular 'signature architect'. Alternatively it may detract from this exchange value if it is so idiosyncratic that it can only be connected to a particular company or if it conflicts with the third element, 'user value', which concerns itself with flexibility for the owner and the continued capacity of a building to change what goes on within it over time. However, it is the fourth element, 'business value', that underlines the predominant view of organisations of their buildings, since the idea of this, as mediated of course by design consultancies, is to incorporate and hence capitalise on all these forms of value in one package. The phrase 'Less space, better used', the focus of GlaxoSmithKline's global 'Space Program', could be used to encapsulate the synthesis of economics and human relations management characteristic of DEGW. We will look briefly at several recent examples of DEGW's role in the redesign of workplaces to illustrate some trends in the conscious reshaping of organisational spaces.

Perhaps one of the key aspects is the openness of recent workplace redesign. Arguably, the most high profile work done by DEGW to date has been for the British Treasury. The Treasury is at the apex of the British Civil Service and is said to be the most powerful of all departments. Its entry requirements are the hardest to achieve and once in post its staff are least likely to shift departments of state. Its power is of considerable concern to government and in this major reshaping an attempt has been made at cultural engineering through changes to architecture and work design. Out went the miles of panelled corridors – the original corridors of power. Out went the privatised cubicles in these corridors. In came atriums and open-plan offices. A reception area was constructed to be 130 feet high with a clear roof, like a shopping mall.

Glass lifts increased the sense of transparency and openness and even the Permanent Secretary moved into full visibility of his or her staff. Of course, they were now also in full visibility. In all, seven and a half miles of corridor was demolished to make way for this brave new world. Work practices changed dramatically too. Collaboration was enhanced, with shared PC networks and networking encouraged. The bike-shed area became a highly utilised café (Allen *et al.* 2004). These sorts of physical changes signal that many organisations are interested in better communications and participation, that they want to break down bureaucratic divisions and create a more holistic understanding of the organisation for both customers and employees. In JWT (formerly known as the advertising giant J Walter Thompson), DEGW helped to develop 'a more open culture that encourages the enhancement of skills through sharing knowledge and ideas. The design has created a transparency that goes right through the building, helping internal communication and welcoming visitors into the company' (www.degw.com). In the design on the Google Headquarters in California, the plan of 'neighbourhoods' joined by a 'street' is based upon the idea of facilitating 'circulation': of individual, workgroups, air and light.

As we can start to see from this description of Google, another central element in DEGW's recent spatial designs is the use of ideas and images drawn from urban design. These form a recurrent feature. For example, at the HQ of a call centre of a major insurance company in the UK, staff retention in the 18–23 age group who form the majority of the workforce was an issue. DEGW saw the problem as one of building motivation and used a 'townscape design' with novelty designs for the interior and 'sanctuaries' for protection from the high-pressure job of dealing with difficult customers. At the Boots the Chemist headquarters in Nottingham, the goals were greater communication and flexibility which DEGW helped to encourage through 'using neighbourhoods and home-bases'. Similarly in MLC Sydney they created a 'vertical village', in Apicorp (Saudi Arabia) 'an office-village' and at Capital One's European Headquarters in Nottingham a 'townscape' that was both stimulating and provided humanising landscapes to break up the large scale of the building (www.degw.com). The 'campus' design has also become prevalent. DEGW have worked with both Philips in Bangalore and Microsoft in Hyderabad to develop campus-style workplaces. These are often located near to academic institutions, as well as modelled upon them. At a DEGW workshop in Hong Kong in 2005 (www.degw.com), one of their Asia-Pacific Directors, Peter Andrew, provided a typology of campus designs that also illustrates their confluence with urban inspirations: the campus in a park (sometimes degenerating to a campus in a car park); the street campus (illustrated by Philips' Bangalore site); the vertical campus (or vertical 'street' such as MLC Sydney); the high-rise campus in the sky and the virtual campus. The aspect which brings them together is the desire to create a culture which maximises opportunities for 'ad hoc and serendipitous' interaction (www.degw.com).

Another key element to the redesign of workspace is that of aesthetic pleasure. Workplaces are designed as bright, colourful spaces that are intended to be as attractive for employees to spend time in as for customers. This elision between different types of spaces and activities is also shown in the provision for employees' needs beyond the direct work environment through workplace nurseries and gyms (see also EnergyCo in Chapter 6). For JWT, DEGW placed 'inspiration' zones around an integration hub and when staff were asked if they wanted a gym they argued and won the case for an 'S' shaped bar instead. Staff satisfaction is a key component of DEGW's approach, particularly at places such as JWT where staff retention in a competitive labour market was a major concern. At the BBC Media Village each team was allocated a budget for artwork, with at least one group even coming into work at weekends to complete their own canvasses. At the Egg Headquarters, lighting was changed to affect the mood of the staff and dynamic background projections were thrown onto the wall also to impel mood shifts.

There of course remains much research to be done on the 'rhetorics and realities' (Legge 1995) of these spatial reorganising processes. In regard to the links between spatial reordering and attempts by organisations to enrol the identity of employees in ever closer ways, we turn now to a number of aspects that we see as relevant to this production of the 'disappearing workplace': liquidity, aestheticisation, identity through 'community' and 'the consuming self'.

BOUNDARY CROSSINGS: REPRODUCING ORGANISED SPACE • BUILDING A SOCIAL MATERIALITY: SPATIAL AND EMBODIED
POLITICS IN ORGANISATION • ALTERNATIVE SPACES: THE RADICAL ORGANISATION OF SPACE? • CONCLUSIONS: DISORGANISING SPACE

3   115

The disappearing workplace

In the spatial designs and the accompanying rhetorics of many modern organisations, we discern a trend towards the 'disappearing workplace'. A bounded and specified 'place' of work is disappearing. Whereas, a key phase in the development of the industrial revolution was the location of work in a defined space and time, in today's advanced capitalist societies, this bounded structure has been blown apart by globalisation, technologies, economic shifts and the diversification and dispersal of organisations. 'Within' the organisation itself, 'placings' have gone: the spatial markers of function, section and hierarchy are rarely present. The stasis of having a 'workstation', an office, even a permanent desk has been swept away by many organisations. Workers are expected to be mobile, to work in multiple physical environments including the train or plane, the café or the home (Felstead *et al.* 2005). This is not to suggest, however, that work or its place, even though changing and mobile, is decreasing in saliency. Indeed, one of the effects of the disappearing workplace is to extend the times and spaces of work into ever more aspects of everyday life, whilst simultaneously attempting to obscure this colonisation (Massey 1995b).

We argue that what is probably more significant than the physical disappearance of the workplace is its psychic disappearance. The traditional associations and constructions of 'work' are being disassembled, to be replaced with symbols and resonances from other social arenas: those of the community (village-pumps, neighbourhoods, townscapes), the domestic (an imagery of the family), leisure (fun, art, workplace gyms) and consumption ('streets', employee shareholding). The dismantling of these trappings of the 'workplace' leaves the individual as the free-play of the mobile identity. If the concern for 'hands' has been replaced by the battle for 'hearts and minds' in the rhetoric of management, this is mirrored in many of their spatial practices too. The physical and the psychic disappearance of the workplace operate 'hand in hand', such that identity construction is something that may be taken with the employee through whatever spaces in which they are working – and, indeed, into spaces and relationships in their lives where 'work' defined as employment would not usually accompany them.

In the early 1990s, the energetic consultant Tom Peters demanded of practising managers: 'How is it that you have the most enthusiastic, most committed, most talented group of employees – except for the eight hours a day they work for you?' His aim was to harness the identity and self-fulfilment that employees might be supposed to have in their lives 'outside' work, and to bring these into the sphere of management control. Pleasure was to be managed to maximise business returns (Burrell 1992a). But this new confluence of work and identity was not solely to remain in the workplace, but was to extend the workplace out into the rest of the individual's life. Thus the desire expressed by such as Tom Peters is that employees will be working for the interests of the company 24 hours a day, 7 days a week, 52 weeks a year. By these means capitalism gains the highest possible return for its 'investment in people' and maximises extraction of surplus value. And this was how the positive and pleasurable aspects of capitalism described above by Thrift and Campbell were to become internalised into people's 'gut feelings' (Thrift 2005: 1).

A first, perhaps necessary, element of this 'disappearing workplace' is a valorisation of **liquidity**. In the workplaces of the contemporary epoch, the ideology of de-sedentarisation seems to be fashionable. 'We have taken the logic of passing through to its logical extreme and created smooth, frictionless spaces that hurry the postmodern subject onward like a slippery slope. It is "geared to keep you mobile"' (Buchanan 2005: 19). The theme of 'movement' is very strong in the design literature because there has been much effort expended by management and their consultants in identifying the weaknesses of typical business practices. 'Thinking within the box', 'silo mentalities', 'organisational chimneys' and so on all suggest a previous era when bureaucracy represented 'an iron cage'. In other words, organisational life was seen as frozen into rigidity and a stasis born of imprisonment in old structures. Indeed, Duffy (1980: 268) has a beautiful example of the desks designed for the Larkin Building, the exemplary large-scale office building of architect Frank Lloyd Wright (Buffalo, New York, 1905). These rationally designed desks incorporated a hinged chair, which as well as saving space, restricted the movement of the clerk. In contrast, the new emphasis is on movement, on flow, on serendipitous interaction and on communication. It is on an organicism where smooth edges, fluid transitions and a lack of straight lines come to the fore. The rise of 'liquidity' as a key metaphor of the moment reflects a celebration of the 'management of change'. Work practices are now meant to be flexible, untied to the desk or the clock or the calendar or the country.

In this rhetoric of liquefaction, the very physical structures of the organisation, such as the towering office block which in its modernist design represented a bureaucratic headquarters, have been deemed to be in need of major attention. Indeed, 'all that is solid melts into air' as the physical constraints of time and space are overcome (Harvey 1989), and the organisation itself circulates nomadically through multiple places and virtual spaces searching the capitalist nirvana of cheap labour, ideal financial and product markets.

The fluidity of spaces is also integral to the formation of organisational identities. The breakdown of physical separations and enclosures is echoed in the dismantling of the (potentially protective) separation between public and private selves and roles. In securing compliance through workplace design, the fixities of organisation structures and power relations are hidden in favour of the movement and interaction of staff. Through the design of openness and transparency into the material fabric of the organisation, the employee too is opened up to the holistic meaning and identity of the company.

Rather than the emplacement of employees into fixed places in the organisation, they are now 'free' to enact organisational relations of power and identity. Thus this liquidity of organisation may be seen as linked to the neo-baroque forms of spatial control that we introduced in Chapter 2, whereby the sources and effects of power are obscured beneath an apparent choice of routes and places. This facet of changing workplaces is also linked with the following two rhetorics: community and consumption, which we explore in more depth below.

However, as we will see later in this chapter and in the case study in Chapter 6, there is a tension between keeping employees mobile and in engendering commitment through community; a contradiction between speed and engagement. This can be seen in an amusing example from the workplace redesign researched by Warren (2002) when the provision of a micro-scooter to speed up movement around the large-scale office was used by employees for the creation of informal games and competitions, but was confiscated by management and health and safety personnel due to the likelihood of it obstructing efficient work through accidents.

There is also, as Dovey points out with acuity, a tension between the openness of the physical space and an assumption of a corresponding freedom of choice: 'The deterministic conflation of physical enclosure with social constraint, or of open space with liberty, is a dangerous move. An open syntax can operate as a powerful signifier of solidarity and democracy in the absence of the practice' (Dovey 1999: 24). It is to these rhetorical signifiers of solidarity and the way that they, too, are spatialised, that we turn now.

We can describe a repeated theme in the imagery of workplace design as being a **spatial rhetoric of community**, derived from that of social structures external to employment. Hence the valorised metaphors in DEGW's work are village, town or city. As Hofbauer comments,

> Open design is said to lead to 'greater teamworking, interpersonal familiarity and spontaneous interaction among those who are mutually accessible' (Steele, in Hatch 1990: 131). The underlying assumption of this design type is that affective bonds rather than management hold organization together (cf. Duffy 1992: 82). On the other hand, it implies concepts of peer review and self-discipline. (2000: 174)

The point of using 'community' as a spatial rhetoric is to emphasise the social bonds which exist between people more than the cash nexus that binds the employment relation. The attachment to the organisation as a 'second home' comes about by making it equivalent to one's home community. This seeks to invoke what we might term 'emotional memories' (Stanilavsky in Berg and Kreiner 1990: 47) of a time when the home was located in an active community and was positively viewed as a place of love, retreat and comfort. By obscuring the boundaries between office and home through clever design, it is as if the office can become the second home with all the attendant emotions that domestic bliss in a bucolic village conjures up.

The emphasis on community as a way of obscuring the realities of organisational life is very strong. Hofbauer (2000: 183) notes that the 'immediate association is not with the pre-planned city district, built from scratch, but rather a village developed over the years and generations, with social territories, recreation zones, pathways and gangways leading to and fro'. These design techniques seem to focus upon the rebuilding of a valorised notion of community into the organisation, occluding the organisation as the unit of analysis.

The attempt to define the workplace as a community is not new. Even before the wide-ranging influence of the Human Relations School advocated seeing the employee as a person with social needs and the importance of co-operative activity to both the organisation and to society (Mayo 1949), the Larkin Building, opened in 1905, had communal values emblazoned upon its very walls:

> " Inscribed on the red sandstone walls of the building's interior and adorning the sculptures displayed outside were inspirational messages, written largely by William Heath, that extolled the importance and virtues of work and "declared the aspirations and identity of the Larkin Company". The messages were most evident in the main building's light court, which provided a setting bathed in diffused light. This atmospheric setting highlighted the company's conflicting impulses toward employee welfare on the one hand and workplace efficiency on the other. Inscriptions from the Sermon on the Mount were juxtaposed with fourteen trios of inspirational words, including "Co-operation, Economy, Industry," "Generosity, Altruism, Sacrifice," and "Integrity, Loyalty, Fidelity." Wright spoke eloquently about the ideal of domesticity he tried to build into the corporate structure, which he called "this family home": "the family-gathering under conditions ideal for body and mind counts for lessened errors, cheerful alacrity and quickened and sustained intelligence in duties to be performed … " (Stanger 2000)

However, as has been described above, the materiality of the Larkin Building was designed for highly static and prescribed actions and roles. Despite Lloyd Wright's rhetoric, the office building was intended to facilitate a Taylorised labour process, 'routinised and factory-like' (Duffy 1980: 265). Duffy links the rationalised furniture to 'the degradation of the clerk' (1980: 268), in a workforce that is deskilled and dehumanised. The spatial organisation of the Larkin Building holds all the characteristics of the *emplacement* of bodies in space, inserted into the capitalist machine:

> " the office, to some extent, should be an expression in physical form of the organisation of the business... that is, it should show the lines of authority, the separation of functions, and the direction of work through the different departments. (Schulze, 1919, in Duffy 1980: 269)

This, we would suggest, is quite different from the appeal to community within modern workplace design. Rather than the discursive exhortations to community displayed in the Larkin Building, today one finds the *enactment* of communal relations incorporated into modern workplaces, so that employees have to actually live through them bodily. The organisational team player is not only asked to feel part of a village community, but to move through the buildings and spaces in such a way as to act out this communal identity day by day.

To achieve this, one of the favourite metaphorical devices of the office and factory builders of the early twenty-first century is the 'street'. This inevitably suggests, indeed produces, movement. The street is a place of neighbourliness, of spontaneous interaction and chance encounter, it is a place of consumption and shopping opportunity, it is a locale for those who know you to pass the time of day and appear to care about you and yours. It is not the anonymous organisation of routinised workstations and fixity but the personalised world of movement and constant interaction. The urban image, then, is useful for the designers in evoking a multiple set of associations that are the converse of the traditional images of the workplace and the worker as controlled, directed, limited in what they can do. However, looking beneath the surface, we can see it is not a traditional view of community but one that is based upon the individuated yet collective, social 'community' of consumption. This is the shopping street more than the residential street of neighbours.

So we turn now to another aspect of modern identity that plays a key role in workplace redesign: that of the individual as a **consuming self**. Gabriel and Lang describe the process since around the 1920s whereby 'consumption moved from a means towards an end – living – to being an end in its own right. Living life to the full became increasingly synonymous with consumption' (1995: 7). As we have already discussed, the primary characteristic of consumption is choice. Choice is associated with the good. It is seen as good for the economy (it drives efficiency and growth), good for individuals, good for social systems. And individuals have come to believe that they have choices, and that this is a fundamental aspect of 'freedom' and something that they would even fight for. This new discourse of choice is even manifest within the British Welfare State, for example in health care, education and the sale of council housing. The Welfare State itself is now discussed in terms of 'public services', which emphasises choice rather than paternalism, market rather than state. Yet exercising choice in consumption in modern times actually involves the consumer in a great deal of 'work' (Bourdieu 1984). One is supposed to know or to find out about the 'best' products, about how to exercise that consumer choice wisely, whether it is in knowing the characteristics of different products in able to make an informed choice between them (one only has to think about the amount of knowledge of the financial markets required in making a 'choice' of mortgage) or even simply to know where to obtain the best price for a product that one has chosen (one can spend hours 'researching' through consumer magazines and websites such as 'kelkoo' or 'pricegrabber'). The same magazines, along with television programmes, tell cautionary tales of those unfortunates who have been taken in by the likes of second-hand car dealers or financial services advisors: those who have not internalised consumption norms sufficiently to become an intelligent consumer. Alternatively, one can express a different identity by being a 'green' or 'ethical' consumer (although not consuming is much less visible as a positive option).

Gabriel and Lang (1995) suggest a number of different images of the consumer, many of which present the consumer as a positive identification: chooser, communicator, explorer, identity-seeker, hedonist, rebel, activist and citizen. For them, only one of these images, the consumer as victim, has a dystopic view of consumption (although the image of consumer as identity-seeker contains elements of anxiety). What all these images apart from that of victim have in common, though, is that the consumer is active, a social agent. Thus when the organisation taps spatially into the identity of the individual as consumer, this is a positive image of choice, agency, autonomy, desire, pleasure and self-fulfilment.

Brueggemann (1999: 22) traces back this modern ideal, one celebrated by Luther, Descartes, Locke, Kant and Freud, as ' "a turn to the subject", which celebrated unmitigated freedom requiring the rejection of every authoritative tradition'. Yet we can see in a capitalist society that ideal position is inevitably going to be compromised on a daily basis by the relations of production, precisely requiring that the individual subject relinquishes their freedom and submits to authority if they wish to be able to sell their labour power in order to live. This contradiction between freedom and the relations of production may be said to have been mitigated in the long run by the appeal to consumption. This is a very useful outcome also for the longevity of the capitalist system that requires its products and services to be widely and continuously consumed in order for the cycle of capital to turn (Legge 2000). Thus, into the process of consumption has been poured all the ideals of the autonomous subject, who is free to satisfy themselves in a realm of plentiful stimulation and choice. Brueggemann goes on to say that the autonomous subject finds their fulfilment in

> 'the therapeutic culture'.... in which the subject is endlessly fasci-
> nated with self without any reference points outside the self. The
> outcome of this programmatic development course has been a
> self-indulgent society in which the disciplines of neighbourli-
> ness, that is, attention to the other, have disappeared. In place
> of neighbourhood has come mall. (1999)

Thus in bringing the shopping mall into the very centre of the space of organisation, architects and designers are drawing on a range of positive associations, but that also reach into the heart of the paradoxical situation of the supposedly autonomous self in capitalism. Consumption is ambiguous in that it stands somewhere between 'workplace' and 'home', between 'work' and 'leisure'. As Lehtonen and Maenpaa (1997) argue, it hovers between privacy and sociability, and between rationality and impulse, between a 'pleasurable social form' and a necessary maintenance activity. Shopping malls themselves, becoming more a feature of workplaces such as British Airways and GlaxoSmithKline, could be described as 'public-private liminal spaces' (Zukin 1988: 431).

On a recent visit to Canary Wharf in London, we were struck by this continuity between work and consumption spaces, and the continuity of the control of space. At lunchtime, the lifts from the corporate skyscrapers above ground disgorged their employees down into the subterranean shopping mall, which during the morning had appeared almost too empty and silent for comfort. Once outside the corporate elevators, it would appear that workers have an hour of freedom, a worship of choice in the 'cathedrals of consumption'. However, security guards, in enormous numbers, ensured that no one sat down or ate in public places outside of permitted areas. They appeared to be on the look out for the young, the old, the overall wearers. Sitting is OK for these groups on the specifically provided seats but not on low walls or steps; eating is OK as long as one is patronising the cafes or restaurants. Otherwise, one is moved on – politely but firmly. In this way the imaginary experience of freedom of movement and choice was disrupted by the lived experience, yet the celebration of consumption as autonomy still goes on.

Yet Giddens argues that the mall provides a reassuring sense of place in a globalising world:

> The reassurance of the familiar, so important to a sense of ontological security, is coupled with the realization that what is comfortable and nearby is actually an expression of distant events and was 'placed into' the local environment rather than forming any organic development within it. The local shopping mall is a milieu in which a sense of ease and security is cultivated.... Yet everyone who shops there is aware that most of the shops are chain stores. (Giddens 1990: 140–1)

In the mall there is a form of 'street sociability' – being both interested and yet also indifferent, anonymous; there is the sharing of a public space, of 'being present together' yet fundamentally not involved (Lehtonen and Maenpaa 1997: 156). This may perhaps be a difficulty with the designers' emphasis on communication and interaction as seen through the lens of the consuming self. How can an atomised consumption experience, focused on individual self-gratification, be reconciled with a fostering of the workplace as community, and how can the alignment of employee interests be reconciled with organisational interests?

However, in linking the above workplace designs to identity, it is useful to draw parallels with what Falk and Campbell (1997) write about the shopping process and identity construction. They argue that it is not solely the actual purchase and ownership of goods that constructs social identity, but also the process of self-reflection that accompanies the activity of shopping, even where no purchase is made or even intended to be made as in window-shopping. The negotiation of self-reflection in the engagement with the material goods of potential consumption involves asking the self questions such as 'Am I like that?', 'Could I be like that?', 'Do I want to be like that?'. These are acts of self-formation whether they relate to purchase or not (1997: 4). Even without this being a cognitive self-reflection, there is a self-relatedness about the experience that 'articulates the "feeling" of one's self – both as an emotional state and as a physical (sensory) experience' (p. 4).

We would suggest that a similar process of identity construction goes on in the designed and aestheticised workplace, built around the material trappings of a particular company, its culture and way of life made concrete. For an employee in such a setting, engaging with the organisation may be similar in some senses to the modern experience of shopping. Falk and Campbell say that the self-reflection that accompanies shopping is always 'interested not disinterested' (1997: 6) because it holds the potential of possession. Ownership in advanced capitalism is not simply related to need, but to the 'project of self', expressed through the consumption of objects, experiences and the overall construction of a 'lifestyle'. The same is often true of the modern relation with an organisation: it also can be related to this ideology of choice and self-determination, as an expression of oneself. Thus the appeal of corporate spaces to the consuming self is the appeal of being able to spatially construct a positive and self-fulfilling embodied narrative of self.

This ideology of the consuming self obscures the underlying need in capitalist societies to sell one's labour power; the emphasis on the individual and on choice obfuscates the extraction of surplus value. In this section, we focus upon the creation of explicitly **aestheticised spaces** which contribute to this obfuscation: we are stunned by the spectacle of the organisation into being unaware of the underpinning relations of power and control.

Featherstone (1991) argues that the 'aestheticisation of everyday life' is upon us in the postmodern world where appearance is deemed to be crucial wherever one goes. It has come to be seen uncontentiously as a neutral managerial tool. Practitioner books such as Olins (1989) Schmitt *et al.* (1995) and Dickinson and Svenson (2000) attempt to use

BOUNDARY CROSSINGS: REPRODUCING ORGANISED SPACE • BUILDING A SOCIAL MATERIALITY: SPATIAL AND EMBODIED POLITICS IN ORGANISATION • ALTERNATIVE SPACES: THE RADICAL ORGANISATION OF SPACE? • CONCLUSIONS: DISORGANISING SPACE

3   125

aesthetics to sell the organisation and its products and to manipulate its employees. In *Beautiful Corporations: Corporate Style in Action* Dickinson and Svenson explicitly reveal the desired effect of their consultancy advice in producing employees 'that would have such confidence and satisfaction in the organisation that they would, if you met them at a party on a Saturday night, want to press a business card in your hand' (p. 41). This encouragement of a somewhat off-putting enthusiasm is a more up-to-date expression of the advice that Tom Peters was giving a decade earlier that the pleasure of the employees was a huge unexploited resource that should be targeted by big business. And pleasure and aesthetics are seen as intimately related. Aestheticisation may be seen as a process of transfer whereby the organisational goals and the organisational 'identity' are transferred to the employee by the inculcation of the values of creativity and pleasurable employment in stretching and demanding activity. A positive feedback loop is engendered by an organisational emphasis on aestheticisation of the workplace, stimulating good sensations, thereby in turn rendering creativity and innovation pleasurable.

Schmitt *et al.* (1995: 83) argue that their field of corporate aesthetics refers to 'a company's visual...output in the form of packaging, logos, trade names, business cards, company uniforms, buildings, advertise-ments, and other corporate elements that have the potential of providing aesthetic gratification'. However, it is not only the visual that has been targeted, but the whole range of senses – the sensorium (Corbett 2003, 2006). In the BOX building at the London School of Economics, for example, a recording of springtime bird song is played via hidden loud-speakers. This is meant to contribute to concentration, stimulation and mood enhancement. Conversely, as we shall see in Chapter 6, white noise is pumped into EnergyCo's atrium to dampen background noise levels within the void, making an environment more conducive to calm and concentrated work.

Thus what is sought through aesthetics is some control of the sensual. Aestheticisation has been used in a variety of ways, for example, in companies like St Lukes Advertising Agency in London where style and aesthetics are perceived to offer competitive advantage to the firm. Other companies have tried to aestheticise facilities in order to increase serendipity, or increase participation, or increase movement of customers.

Labour has been also aestheticised, so as to make the bodies and appearances of employees part of the image of the organisation itself (Hancock and Tyler 2000). DEGW talk of their methods being used 'to enable clients to make more efficient, more effective and *more expressive* use of workspace' (www.degw.com; emphasis added).

But this managerial encouragement to appear and perceive in a certain way also brings with it an accompanying process of what might be described as 'anaestheticisation' (Dale and Burrell 2003; Welsch 1997). In Chapter 2, we have discussed how Benjamin's use of the concept of 'phantasmagoria' illustrates how heightened aesthetic experience can obscure the power relations behind the spectacle. We also linked this to the conceptualisation of a process of 'anaesthetics'. Here we examine this theme further in relation to the spatial enactment of identity. Welsch (1997) argues that continued excitement leads to indifference. Over-stimulus gives way to the nervous system shutting down, nothing seems beautiful anymore and the sensuous gives way to desensitisation. The globalisation of the aesthetic means that ubiquitous beauty loses its appeal and its meaning. For, to the extent that one or more of the senses is stimulated through an aestheticised stimulus, it is implied that one or more of the remaining senses is anaesthetised. It is very clear that in the experience of aestheticised labour, the aesthetic experience of the customer is achieved by a level of anaestheticisation for the employees (Hochschild 1983). Thus, in the aestheticised organisation, the idea of 'anaestheticisation' may help to explore the politicised use of aestheticised space and its lived experience. Here there is a difference between the 'conceived' space of aesthetics (Lefebvre 1991) – what we might describe as the managed or organised space of aesthetics – on one hand and the 'lived' aesthetics of an organisation, the phenomenological experience of it, on the other. Aesthetics can be used to mask and de-politicise (Dale and Burrell 2003). One example of this is the use of dazzle patterns derived from vorticist principles in the display on one of the entrances to the BBC Media Village (Figure 3). Since these were originally employed by ships in the First World War in order to camouflage themselves from German submarines, the visitor is forced perhaps to ask 'what is being camouflaged?'. For at the other entrance there is a huge display of the BBC values, pronounced to all staff and visitors.

Figure 3 **Dazzle Wall at the BBC Media Village. Similar 'dazzle' patterns were painted on ships in the First World War in order to disrupt the enemy eye, breaking up the outline of the ship so that its movement and shape could not be accurately perceived. We might ask what the dazzle obscures in the modern aestheticised workplace.**

The link between organisational control and aesthetics is quite clearly made in a bank in Melbourne, Australia, which we visited. This was a highly planned and designed building, with a range of different spaces for different activities. It was maintained and run very actively by a Facilities Management company. Throughout the building were placed little cartoons, drawn by the numerous and visible facilities management staff, reminding bank staff of their responsibilities in putting back seats and tables if these had been moved in a spirit of flexibility. Some depicted employees as children fighting over the furniture, as toys that should be shared. They were, to our mind, condescending and close to suggesting infantilism amongst staff, but their stated intentions were to be a fun way of communicating spatial rules.

The use of aesthetics resonates with ideas of play and leisure, rather than of work. These are again more positive and pleasurable aspects of identity, which workplace design is seeking to appropriate. Play has often been an element advocated in radical accounts of organisation or social relations (e.g. Burrell 1984; Kane 2004), as a transformative approach opposed to conventional power relations and exposing the exploitative and instrumental nature of capitalism. However, play – the ludic – has become co-opted into workplace redesign with very definite organisational goals in mind. At a Workplace Forum meeting in February 2006, John Holm of DEGW, described workplaces as moving 'from dark satanic mills to holidaying at work'. A number of workplaces, including St Lukes Advertising Agency, the BBC Media Village and JWT have facilities that overlap these distinctions. Providing table tennis or table football tables and the like are connected with tapping into the sort of spontaneous creativity that people have in aspects of their lives 'outside' work, and harnessing this in the service of the organisation. The idea is that work starts to look very much like productive play.

Lefebvre prefigures a critique of this, in his recognition that spaces of leisure and play cannot be solely seen as 'free' or 'outside' the relations of power and production:

> Certain deviant or diverted spaces, though initially subordinate, show distinct evidence of a true productive capacity. Among these are spaces devoted to leisure activity. Such spaces appear on first inspection to have escaped the control of the established order, and thus, inasmuch as they are spaces of play, to constitute a vast 'counter-space'. This is a complete illusion. The case against leisure is quite simply closed – and the verdict is irreversible: leisure is as alienated and alienating as labour; as much an agent of co-optation as it is itself co-opted; and both an assimilative and an assimilated part of the 'system' (mode of production). Once a conquest of the working class, in the shape of paid days' off, holidays, weekends, and so on, leisure has been transformed into an industry, into a victory of neocapitalism and an extension of bourgeois hegemony to the whole of space. (1991: 383–4)

The involvement of dominance and appropriation in the design of the workplace supposedly centred on play and aesthetics is illustrated well by Alferoff and Knights in their study of call centre work. Here,

> work is presented as play and heroes and champions are winners in games of skill and dexterity. Seasons are celebrated with decorations. Masks and fancy dress are worn, managers can appear in the nude on calendars, thus reversing authoritative roles and

> playing the 'fool'. Treats in the form of food and alcoholic drinks, weekend holidays and trips to concerts are to be won. Boxes of 'party fun' are stored on top of metal cupboards for the next celebration, or campaign. (2003: 88)

Yet, employees did not regard this ludic and sensory play as fitting in with the espoused corporate objectives of profit making and profit taking and therefore felt it was illegitimate to expect them to participate fully. Some saw this sort of aestheticisation as a direct threat to their own identity. Some believed the 'lightheartedness' of corporate sponsored play to be in direct contradiction to the plethora of control and disciplinary techniques available to management. In other words, the 'conceived aesthetics' and the 'lived aesthetics' were not in conjunction with one other.

The difficulty is that true 'play' perhaps needs to be autonomous and spontaneous. This is an issue that Warren (2002) points to in her study of the deliberate aestheticisation of the web-design department of a large IT firm. The designers *did* feel that they needed creative freedom and play to produce innovative work, but the managerial manipulation of the workspace through such manifestations as massive Russian dolls, a pool table, a micro-scooter and a 'think tank' brainstorming room were seen as artificial. In comparison, for these designers the

> true aesthetic experiences (from which many of them believed their creativity flowed) were to be had away from the office, in amongst the trees and the fields surrounding the company's buildings. For these people, the idea of freedom in various guises was what they prized above all else: freedom to work as they chose, freedom to play, freedom to express themselves as they wanted to be recognised. (Warren 2002: 16)

The manipulative dimension to the process of aestheticisation then is often grasped by those exposed to attempts to change the built environment. On the first day after nationalisation of the British coal industry in 1947 new signs appeared throughout the pitheads and whitewash was used on the major mine walkways underground. The response amongst the coal miners to such cosmeticisation was a generalised utterance of an underlying exploitative continuity – 'Same bloody gaffers'. Even where the aesthetic effort is a 'stunning' one where the entrant to the space is 'bedazzled', its manufacture eventually shows itself. The projector behind the phantasmagoria somehow, sometime is revealed.

Conclusion

We have explored a number of spatial devices that are used in the redesign of workspace in the attempt to convert employees' identities into tools fit for the organisation. However, we have also seen that there are many contradictions and paradoxes in these spatial rhetorics, which mean that spatial practices are always in negotiation between the conceived, the perceived and the lived.

In developing our ideas on how organisational practices relate to the spatial performance of identity, we placed de Certeau's 'walking rhetorics' after Butler's 'performativity'. Now we turn the order around. De Certeau takes quite a romanticised, self-determined view of the pedestrian as an actor with choice, with possibility, who constructs their narrative of identity as they construct walking routes. And yet when we take a critical view of the urban space, we know that the pedestrian does not have unlimited choice. There are multiple no-go areas; there are fears, there are class-, gender- and race-based exclusions (Sibley 1995). The Romantic notion of the *flâneur* as free agent, walking where 'he' chooses, taking in the sights and sounds of the city, became a popular image in social and cultural theory. However, this image ignores the embodied individual as part of the social-spatial world. Underlying the Romantic notion is a disembodied, all-seeing eye and brain, detached from the anonymous crowd (Featherstone 1991: 75). Yet, as Wolff (1985) points out, the *flâneur* is 'an embodied human being whose appearance and demeanour give off readable impressions and signs to those around him' (Featherstone 1991: 75–6). This explains why the *flâneur* is inevitably a 'he' given the spatial constraints on lone women walking aimlessly in the city and the way in which these actions would be differently read of a woman. Thus the performance of 'walking rhetorics' is much more like Butler's 'forced reiterations'. But the interesting thing about identities – including employee identities – constructed around a predominant ideology of autonomy, pleasure and self-fulfilment is that these rhetorics hide the way that the routes are repetitious and pre-designed. Literally then we are 'incorporated', even whilst we 'choose' our spatial narratives of self.

Nevertheless, we would like to end this section with an account that shows that the negotiation of identity through spatial practices is not determined, but is dynamic, and often contradictory. The final episode of a recent political comedy in the UK shows the relations between a government minister and his staff as they move to an open-plan building that is uncannily similar to the revamped Treasury building described earlier. It is a production entitled 'The Thick of It', shown first on BBC4 in 2005, written by Armando Iannucci. The building chosen to represent the new government offices is in fact the BBC Media Village. The characters in Iannucci's comedy hate the building's open-plan aspect. 'Everyone will be able to see us shooting up,' jokes the minister to his clerical staff, who are not amused. Throughout, the characters enact a set of oppositional relations in their negotiation with the building. The writer puts discomfort with the corporate landscape into the words and actions of the protagonists. Whereas the design is intended to give visibility, the bullying figure of Malcolm Tucker, the 'Policy Co-ordinator (Enforcer) from Number 10', seems still able to come up behind people unannounced. Here, the open plan aids the power of the bully to overhear and wrong-foot his subordinates, even major figures in the government: 'he'll love this place. Four ministers in one building. Its his wet dream'. As the Minister for Social Affairs comments, 'I don't know what's worse, watching him slowly rumble towards you like prostate cancer, or him appearing suddenly out of nowhere like a severe stroke'. The arrangement of floors around an atrium becomes the setting for a discussion of 'organisational suicide', playing on the spatial/career linkages. It also encourages a new organisational spectator sport where staff are asked, 'who wants to go and watch bollock vision?' This is the public humiliation of staff who are subjected within the resonant atrium to 'a bollocking'. This BBC-produced episode using brand new BBC facilities is a highly enjoyable overt exposure of the manipulations involved in corporate building designs, and shows that organisational identity may turn to oppositional identity. Furthermore spaces, however carefully conceived, contain their own contradictions.

In this chapter, we have sought to explore how spatial practices influence subjectivity, and especially to consider how work spaces are being explicitly drawn into organisational attempts to 'win hearts and minds'. Throughout this first part of the book, we have focussed on 'the spaces of organisation': on how the social production of space is constructed and reproduced within organisations. In the next part of the book, we turn to consider 'the organisation of space'. Here the crux of our argument is that social space is in multiple and significant ways bound up with organising processes and practices. This takes us beyond the boundaries of particular organisations and particular social spaces in an attempt to understand the organisings that, through a construction of social-spatial connections and separations, produce what Lefebvre (1991) describes as a 'political economy of space'.

Notes

[1] One might mischievously point to the specifically male desire to change people to fit their buildings. It may be the architectural equivalent of the impulse to usurp reproduction discussed by Easlea (1983). Lloyd Wright's war against the housewife is discussed in Chapter 5.

[2] These spatial power relations are thus doubly obscured: first, by the taken-for-granted nature of them by the people who 'live through' these relations and second by the failure of linguistically obsessed analysis to perceive them.

BOUNDARY CROSSINGS: REPRODUCING ORGANISED SPACE • BUILDING A SOCIAL MATERIALITY: SPATIAL AND EMBODIED POLITICS IN ORGANISATION • ALTERNATIVE SPACES: THE RADICAL ORGANISATION OF SPACE? • CONCLUSIONS: DISORGANISING SPACE

3   133

Part II

The Organisation of Space

4   a political economy of organised space

BUILDING ORGANISATION: SECURING AND OBSCURING POWER • BUILDING PEOPLE:
IDENTITIES AND SPACES • A POLITICAL ECONOMY OF ORGANISED SPACE • BOUNDARY
CROSSINGS: REPRODUCING ORGANISED SPACE • BUILDING A SOCIAL MATERIALITY:
SPATIAL AND EMBODIED POLITICS IN ORGANISATION • ALTERNATIVE SPACES:
THE RADICAL ORGANISATION OF SPACE? • CONCLUSIONS: DISORGANISING SPACE

> *The anatomy of civil society is to be found in political economy.*

> (Marx 1990)

> *Capitalism has found itself able to attenuate (if not resolve) its internal contra-*
> *dictions for a century, and consequently in the hundred years since the writing*
> *of Capital, it has succeeded in achieving 'growth'. We cannot calculate at what*
> *price, but we do know the means: by occupying space, by producing a space.*

> (Lefebvre 1976: 21)

A 'political economy of space'

In this chapter, we start to explore in more detail 'the organisation of space'. This also entails a movement from concentrating on 'the organisation' as an entity, towards considering the implications of how 'organisation' more widely colonises the social and spatial world. In this first section, we will explore what Lefebvre described as a 'political economy of space' and how this both builds upon and yet is a critique of Marxian 'political economy'. In order to illustrate some of the ways in which this 'political economy of space' is organised we draw on two examples. First, the creation of the Vasari Corridor in Florence illustrates how space may be organised such as to produce a political economy of boundaries and connections, and hence inclusions and exclusions in social space which stem from and reproduce certain power relations. The second example is drawn from David Harvey's work on the housing markets in Baltimore in the United States. Here we can see how coalescences of different organisations can produce differentiated social spaces, and further produce differentiated social relations of class and ethnicity. The rest of the chapter moves on to use three key examples to demonstrate how 'political economies of space' have come to make up the 'abstract space' of capitalism (Lefebvre 1991). The first two of these relate to significant 'moments' in the development of the spatial relations of capitalism. We clearly do not literally mean moments in time here, but rather processes of momentum which come to fundamentally produce and change the social spaces of capitalism. These are the changing relations of people to land and locality, and the development of Fordism as a societywide structuring impeller. The third example is not historically specific, but rather provides a pervasive influence on 'abstract space' across time and space: this is the organisation of warfare.

The term 'political economy' is a contested one. It can be generally taken to mean the interaction of political and economic activity, and thus the production and distribution of goods, ideas and services within an identifiable political and economic system constituted by the state, corporations, political institutions and the media. From the work of Marx onwards it has come to take on a particular slant in relation to the analysis of capitalism. The political economy of advanced capitalist societies is based on its logics of capitalist accumulation and commodification. In *Capital*, Marx made a distinction between political economy and 'vulgar economy'. The former looked at the 'real' relations of production whilst the latter only considered 'appearances' (1990: 174–5 n. 34). As we recover from this somewhat Platonic sounding distinction, we can draw out two relevant points from the Marxian approach to political economy. The first, which Marx is referring to, is that it is about the *material relations* which underpin a society, rather than a set of abstract theoretical categories. The second is that it is concerned with *power relations*. This in turn relates to the significance of the operation of various institutions or organisations. It also develops into a consideration of questions of exploitation and equality, including relations of class, gender and ethnicity amongst others.

Yet we need to be careful in our use of 'political economy'. Throughout *The Production of Space* Lefebvre castigates the Marxian conception of political economy as a pseudo-science. He argues that only a re-conceptualisation of it as a 'political economy *of space*' could 'rescue it from bankruptcy' (1991: 104). Lefebvre tends to demonstrate this in his discussions rather than elucidating explicitly what this might entail. However, he argues that this re-conceptualisation should not be about things *in space*, but a political economy of the production *of space* (p. 299). A political economy of space, then, considers not only the economic relations between the various types of institution, but looks at them in relation to the way they produce, sustain or destroy various sorts of social space. It also considers how these institutions are interconnected in social space, and conversely the ways they produce separations, distances and exclusions. As we described in Chapter 1, Lefebvre argues (1991: 53) that capitalism has produced 'abstract space'. This encompasses ' "the world of commodities", its "logic" and its worldwide strategies, as well as the power of money and that of the political state. This space is founded on the vast network of banks, business centres and major productive entities, as also motorways, airports and information lattices'. Lefebvre is also concerned with the 'spatial practices' of capitalism, which, he argues, bring together 'daily reality (daily routine) and urban reality (the routes and networks which link up the places set aside for work, "private" life and leisure). This association is a paradoxical one, because it includes the most extreme spatial separation between the places it links together' (p. 38). Thus a political economy of the abstract spaces of capitalism incorporates production, consumption and reproduction.

Effectively in modern capitalism there has been a 'de-territorialisation' in the realisation of surplus value (Lefebvre 1991: 347) which is now global, compared to the time when Marx was writing when capitalist industry was 'an isolated island encircled by a sea of independent farmers and handicraftsmen' (Mandel 1990: 11). Thus capitalist relations have produced an extended and yet interrelated social space. Lefebvre points to the way that the relations of capitalism are not simply located in specific points such as the factory or the stock exchange, but are articulated together into links which produce both local and global social spaces in particular ways, for example the relations of uneven development between nations and regions. He recognises that 'the division of labour affects the whole of space – not just the "space of work", not just the factory floor. And the whole of space is an object of productive consumption, just like factory buildings and plant, machinery, raw materials and labour power itself' (1991: 347).

Lefebvre is astute in pointing to how closely our social, political and spatial relations are intertwined. Yet these 'spatial practices' produce a social and physical landscape that we routinely take for granted. It is perhaps only in times of disruption of these spaces that the networked, organised nature of our spatial localities are shown in all their interconnectedness. Two examples serve to demonstrate this. First, in the UK, the demonstrations against the rising price of fuel in 2001 showed in a fairly short time the interdependence of diverse aspects of socioeconomic life. The blockades at oil refineries and the prevention of road tankers distributing fuel, quickly affected the whole infrastructure of the country. Work in all businesses was disrupted, as workers and materials could not be gathered in the same location. Delivery of goods for retail could not continue, with the prospect of food shortages looming due to the dependence of the majority of people on bought foodstuffs. Emergency services such as ambulances and fire engines were threatened. Spatial relations of power are shown to be far more complex and interwoven than the idea of a sovereign territory ruled over by monarch or state government.

The second example is the effect of Hurricane Katrina upon New Orleans in 2005. The state of Louisiana and the United States were shown to be unprepared for a natural transformation of the spatial and material landscape. Warnings were not heeded at municipal, state nor national level of the likely effect on the levees of such a storm. Prisoners were left in gaol as the guards fled. The armed forces attended white middle-class areas first, yet non-white areas were the most vulnerable to the inundation. Media pictures still penetrated outwards, but nothing else seemed to be able to enter. The outside world metaphorically gasped to see the 'civilised' veneer of capitalist society so quickly stripped bare. The breakdown of space was met with a breakdown in custom and practices. When everyday routes and routines were disrupted, even the might of the armed forces seemed unable to reassert themselves for days.

Thus, compared to subsistence economies, the distributed spatial practices of capitalist societies obscure the much greater interdependence there is in an organised network of social and material relations. The relationship between the individual and the production of even the most basic goods such as food, clothing and fuel for cooking or warmth is mediated by organisation. As Durkheim (1972) noted, the move from mechanical solidarity to organic solidarity places the societal member in a much-changed relationship with others, because of a much greater interdependence with strangers. In this theoretical move, Durkheim was reflecting the views of Saint Simon who saw 'organisation' as the key integrating concept to arise out of the French Revolution (Heilbron 1995: 184–9). Organisation thus is central to this move to interdependent organic solidarity and its spatial practices, which go to make up the characteristic political economy of the spaces of modernity.

It is important to reiterate here rather than seeing 'organisation' as an individual economic unit, we must see 'organisation' in this context as about social processes that produce social and material ordering, and in doing so produce cultural and historical meaning. For the treatment of 'the' organisation as an isolated and bounded entity has political consequences. It obscures the effects that 'organisation' on a wider scale has on the construction of particular forms of society. Even where the relations between organisations are analysed, business interests and arrangements tend to be treated as natural, thus vertical or horizontal integration or supplier networks might be the focus of analysis. The political economy of space changes this perspective and politicises it.

Lefebvre looks to understand the social production of space through how it is organised and interwoven. He considers the flows and networks that produce social space, but he is careful to provide a critique of the notion of abstract flows that have been 'mistakenly generalised by some philosophers' (1991: 350) and instead develops a useful spatially and materially embedded view of flows and networks:

> The economy may be defined, practically speaking, as the linkage between flows and networks, a linkage guaranteed in a more or less rational way by institutions and programmed to work within the spatial framework where these institutions exercise operational influence. Each flow is of course defined by its origin, its endpoint and its path. But, while it may thus be defined separately, a flow is only effective to the extent that it enters into relationship with others; the use of an energy flow, for instance, is meaningless without a corresponding flow of raw materials. The co-ordination of such flows occurs within a space. As for the distribution of surplus value, this too is achieved spatially – territorially – as a function of the forces in play (countries, economic sectors) and as a function of the strategies and know-how of managers. (1991: 347)

There are two points at which we would wish to critique and extend Lefebvre's analysis. The first is a fixation on urban routes and routines. Here Lefebvre shares with other Marxist commentators such as Castells, Harvey and the Situationists an overriding emphasis on the 'urban revolution' as the key to understanding the capitalist spatial economy. He develops a dichotomised relation between declining countryside and rising urban importance (Lefebvre 1991: 268), into which the social and physical space of capitalism is inserted. We hope below to provide a more historically and politically situated consideration of the socio-spatial relations of land and locality. The second issue is the association of separate spaces for different activities. Rather, we would say that there has been a growing flexibility in spatial use, and a tendency to blur spatial categories, thus recognising the hybridity of spaces (Massey 1995a: 183). This will be further discussed in the next chapter.

In order to look in more detail at how a political economy of the 'organisation of space' is produced we will first consider two examples that illustrate the ways in which space can be organised. The first example is the construction of the Vasari Corridor in Florence. The Vasari Corridor in Florence is an architecture of power which, although it dates from the sixteenth century, illustrates these themes and provides links to characteristics of more modern organisational forms we will talk about later. The Vasari Corridor links the Uffizi Galleries to the church of Santa Felicia, the Palazzo Pitti and on to the Boboli Gardens via an elevated passageway that leads out of the first floor of the Uffizi, down the street and turns a corner to become the upper storey of the Ponte Vecchio across the Arno River. These days it forms part of the cultural experience of the tourist to Florence – although the inside of the corridor is only available to those few who know to arrange a visit in advance, not to the masses who queue to peruse the works of art in the Uffizi Gallery. The significance of the Uffizi itself is that it was not built as an art gallery but as the administrative and judicial centre of the Dukes of Medici: the highly influential rulers of Tuscany, widely credited as important patrons of the arts, influential in creating the context for the Renaissance blossoming of culture. However, it did not take long for art and administration to meet, when 20 years after it was built the Grand Duke Francesco I turned the top floor into a place for 'walking with paintings, statues and other precious things' (Fossi 1999: 8).

It was Vasari, predominantly known as the biographer of the Renaissance artists, who designed the Uffizi in 1560, and who was requested five years later to develop the elevated gallery and thus create 'a unique urban relationship' which 'unites the nerve centres of the city' (Fossi 1999: 8). Of course, this unification is only for the aristocracy: the powerful few of Florence could perambulate from the Uffizi all the way – almost a kilometre – to their trans-fluvial gardens thereby integrating mind, body and soul in the form of home, work, river crossing, prayer and leisure pursuits.

As well as creating unifications, the corridor creates distances, both physical and symbolic. The Vasari Corridor separated those in power from those who were not, and provided views where the Court could look down on their inferiors. The separation was further produced by the forced ejection of the original butchers who traded on the Ponte Vecchio to the more refined (and less smelly!) trade of the jewellers who retain their position there today. The separation was also marked by the presentation of high art along the walls of the corridor, so that the powerful could avoid any reminder of the world outside their own ranks and concerns. Indeed, the art works consisted primarily of portraits of the aristocrats so the whole effect is one of reflection of the powerful back to themselves: a sealed off and closed existence. Today, the Corridor contains around 800 works of art, and the section over the Ponte Vecchio contains 'the most famous collection of self-portraits in the world' (Fossi 1999: 180). In terms of representational space, the corridor symbolises hierarchy and cloistering, high art for those high in the sky, a superior access to church for those closer to God, interests and pursuits that are not base and an aesthetic sensibility that would go over the heads of the Florentine mob. It is the ultimate creation of the fantasy of unfettered power.

Florence was a city state of considerable power both within Italy and beyond. It traded with the world within what was emerging as a capitalist set of relations based on profit. It was within Renaissance Italy that double entry bookkeeping (Hoskin and Macve 1986) and a panoply of techniques and technologies for capitalist accumulation started to form. Not far away from Florence, the Venetian *Arsenale* is probably the oldest and at times the largest site of mass production of ships and weapons. Early forms of factory production could also be seen in Venice in areas such as glass and mirror manufacture and printing (Burke 1986; Gerulaitis 1976; Rapp 1976). The political economy which came to dominate the world in some measure started in the North Italian plain and Italian analysis of its features continues to this day in, for example, the work of Tony Negri (2005a, 2005b; Hardt and Negri 2001, 2005).

The Vasari Corridor is a useful example of the how spatial and social modes of connections and boundaries can be constructed in a concentrated area. In the rest of the chapter, we are more concerned with how much wider distributed spatial economies are constructed, but the illustration of the confluence of social, economic, cultural and spatial connections and separations is one that remains important throughout.

The second example is David Harvey's (1983) study of some aspects of the development of segmentation in the housing markets in Baltimore, USA. This looks at how multiple organisations are involved in the construction of differently 'zoned' urban residential areas, and with this, the identity of the 'house-owner' expressed through the habitation of these locales, along with differentiated class and ethnic identities.

Harvey develops for the reader a complex case of intersecting organisations, spatial constructions and segregations, and the influence of both of these on how people come to see their place in society, how they come to define themselves and see where they belong, spatially and socially. Harvey argues that in the USA the social discontent of the 1930s, and again that of black and urban poor in the 1960s, was diffused to some large extent through a government policy of the creation of house-owners with financial loans or mortgages, who thus become 'debt-encumbered' and less likely to rock the social boat.[1] It is worth adding at this point, that most mortgaged house-owners do not tend to define this relationship in terms of 'control', but rather as an 'opportunity', even in some cases as a 'necessity' because it is becoming more difficult for young people in the UK to achieve this status given how the average price of houses has risen. House ownership has become associated with successful transition to the adult world, a sign of independence, and indeed one of freedom of expression that is furthered by multiple television shows and magazines on interior design. Many, because of these processes, have become habituated to home ownership. To return to Harvey and Baltimore, he asks the question, 'How are these national policies transmitted to the locality and how do individuals come to incorporate them in their decisions?' (1983: 343).

The answer is through the co-ordination of multiple organisations. These organisations are not necessarily interested in, or even cognisant of, national policy on home ownership and its relation to social stability. They are indeed diverse in their own interests and objectives. For example, Harvey argues that in the US a key to this co-ordinating mechanism is the highly complex and hierarchical structure of financial institutions. These can include state and federal chartered savings and loans institutions that operate in the housing sector. Some of these are community based, depositer controlled and operate on a non-profit basis. There are also the commercial mortgage and savings banks. All are affected by money markets and government regulation. Another aspect of the organisation is the Federal Housing Administration, which administers government programmes, but which has multiple autonomous state and local level organisations. A third facet of the organisational coalescence around housing issues is local government and its agencies. Harvey draws a distinction, for example, between Baltimore County and Baltimore City. The former was the largest US local government administration and long-dominated by the interests of speculator-developers who were able to manipulate zoning laws to maximise their returns, through investment in the county and not in the declining city. Hence local government was active in encouraging people to migrate into what was defined as an improved lifestyle and advantageous investment.

Meanwhile, in Baltimore City, Harvey distinguishes 13 sub-markets that were constructed through differential practices by the local government, housing and financial organisations. One, West Baltimore, is worth looking at in more depth to consider the effects of the organisation of space on a particular group of people:

> West Baltimore was essentially a creation of the 1960s. Low- to moderate-income blacks did not possess local savings and loan associations, were regarded with suspicion by all other financial institutions, and in the early 1960s were discriminated against

> by the FHA. The only way in which this group could become homeowners was by way of something called a 'land-investment contract' which works as follows. A speculator purchases a house for, say, $7000, adds a purchase and sales commission, various financing charges and overhead costs, renovates and redecorates the property and finally adds a gross profit margin of, say, 20 percent. The house is then sold for, say, $13000. To finance the transaction, the speculator interposes his credit rating between that of the purchaser and the financial institutions, takes out a conventional mortgage up to the appraised value of the house (say $9000) borrows another $4000 and then packages a $13000 loan for the buyer. The speculator retains title to the property to secure the risk but permits the 'buyer' immediate possession. The monthly payments cover the interest charges on the $13000 plus the administrative charges, and a small part is put to redeeming the principle. When the purchaser has redeemed $4000 (after, say, 10 or 15 years) a conventional mortgage at the appraised value of $9000 may be obtained. At that juncture, the purchaser will get title and can start to build equity in the house. (Harvey 1983: 347)

This form of loan was legal, and it was the only way that many black people could become homeowners at this time. However, it obviously cost black people considerably more than white people with equivalent income to enter the housing market, and black people recognised themselves as being exploited by this 'black tax'. The fact that many took up these loans is perhaps a testament to the strength of the cultural norms and social status bound up in the identity of being a homeowner. The use of the law here created particular effects at the level of the political economy. It also created a very different local area. Housing was improved by speculation and homeownership and it had a very different identity from inner city low-income rental areas, but there were strong social pressures for white people to move out of the area (and often to Baltimore County where the speculator developers would benefit from the migration) thus leaving it as a segregated community. Thus spatial relations are intimately bound up with class and ethnic identities.

We continue to analyse 'the organisation of space' through looking at three key nodes of spatial practices that have come to make up the 'abstract space' of capitalism all around us and that we take so much for granted in every day life. We first consider the changing spatial and social relations of early capitalism, through the development of the abstract and place-less social relation of contract and through the construction of land as an abstract productive resource rather than as a locality in the long-run formation of the 'enclosures'. Next we turn to the particular organisation of space generated by Fordism and the automobile as a space for mass production and mass consumption. At the time of completing this book, we travel 28 miles each way by car from our home to our work institution. The 'choices' we made in this were governed by good and available schooling, childcare and family relations taking priority over proximity to work. This would have been a set of decisions that made no sense a hundred years ago, yet it is a set of spatial relations that we and many others hardly consider. It is also a spatial arrangement that has been made even easier over only the last ten years or so by personal computing and Internet technologies. The organisation of space behind these characteristics of everyday life is a significant one, if hidden through its very pervasiveness, as we hope to show. Finally, we turn to an organisation of space that is usually seen as marginal and periodic within society, and yet that, we argue, underpins a great many social, spatial and organisational practices: that of war.

Place, property and power

Over time, the social-spatial landscapes within which we are habitually located become incorporated into our lived *habitus* and thus become taken for granted. We live today within well-accepted notions of the sanctity of personal property and the contractual relationships that govern the major aspects of social life such as employment, consumption and property ownership. So everyday are these that perhaps we can conceptualise no alternatives to this configuration. However, it is useful to trace how these socio-spatial characteristics became organised and embedded, since they mark a significant transition to the 'abstract spaces' of capitalism. The interaction of changes that we will consider is the material process of the 'enclosure' of the common lands and accompanying shift to large-scale farming, the associated 'closing in' of the idea of property and its greater privatisation, and the abstraction of social relations from being local and place-bounded to becoming universal and standardised in the form of the contract. Thus we look at the change in *conceived* space, as the gentry plan out their new large farms and landscape gardens; in *lived* space as labourers are uprooted and displaced; and *perceived* space as the way space is seen becomes more extended, neutral and disembedded from place.

Before capitalism social relations were place-bounded first and foremost. It was a paternalistic system 'rooted in a society in which everyone was presumed to belong some*where*, and the greatest parameters of belonging were kinship, locality, religion, occupation, and social class' (Selznick 1969: 123, emphasis added). But society was shifting in hugely significant ways, threatening this conjunction of the social and the spatial. Whilst it might be expected that in rural areas traditional patterns would continue the longest, there is evidence that it was in the countryside that these social changes were originally precipitated. Despite the way that capitalism, industrialism and urbanism become conflated, the evidence is that capitalism develops first in the rural sector, and well before industrialism. In the West Country of England, for example, by the early sixteenth century, agriculture was dominated in parts by large-scale capitalist farming (Neale 1975: 92). This different orientation towards 'place' in the form of land transformed it from a locality, a social rootedness, to a commercial activity centred on profit. Neale (1975: 94) tells us that 'on the land there was a massive shift away from a feudal and paternalist relationship between landlord and tenant, towards one more exclusively based on the maximisation of profits in a market economy'.

This process of the capitalisation of agriculture involved a significant change in social relations in rural areas. Landowners achieved their large-scale enterprises by evicting small-scale farmers and 'enclosing', or privatising, the 'common lands' that peasant labourers had previously had the use of for their subsistence. We happen to live three miles from a place called Newton in Northamptonshire which, in 1607, saw the killing of 50 local people as part of the suppression of an uprising by agricultural labourers across the English Midlands. The Newton Rebellion was part of the so-called Midlands Revolt in which labourers from Northamptonshire, Warwickshire and Leicestershire rose up against food prices after a bad harvest, but more importantly against enclosure of the common land. The local landlord for the people of Newton was Sir

Thomas Tresham, whose son had been involved in the Gunpowder Plot of two years before.[2] In late 1606, enclosure of the common land around Newton began and was met in June 1607 by the uprising. Sir Thomas confronted the rioters with a heavily armed gang of supporters and magistrates and killed around 50 of the crowd. The bodies of the dead were buried in communal graves and other rioters were publicly hanged and their bodies quartered for display in local market towns. Survivors had to make amends by signing a declaration of apology at nearby Boughton House. The document shows that these people made their mark rather than use a signature, but remains a catalogue of surrender to the forces of enclosure. The Newton Rioters made little mark on history, though, and it is Tresham after whom local colleges and civic buildings are named.

There were successive waves of enclosure in the UK so that it should not be seen as a brief period of intense social unrest but as a recurrent strategy to commodify the land and those who lived on it. Enclosure might be considered to be capitalism's first 'spatial fix'. Wealthy English landowners began to noticeably re-conceptualise the 'countryside' in the mid-eighteenth century (Hill 1969: 146–8). A series of Parliamentary Acts led to the enclosure of huge tracts of formerly common land. The Black Act of 1723 (Fox 1985) defined 50 additional offences against the property of the landowner, all punishable by death, and these included deer stalking, the taking of hare and pheasants, rick lighting and the mutilation of cattle. This made explicit the process of peasant resistance and landowner discipline that was part and parcel of the alteration of the social space of the countryside. Thompson (1968: 245) tells us that 'Game laws, with their paraphernalia of gamekeepers, spring guns, mantraps and (after 1816) sentences of transportation... all served directly or indirectly to tighten the screw upon the labourer'. The mutilation of cattle is a strange act which requires explanation. At the same time that landowners were reshaping their farms into large-scale commercial enterprises, they were also reshaping their country homes and gardens. An illusion of bucolic idyll was central to the fashionable gentry at this time, in contrast to the social and spatial upheaval they were creating in material terms. In the cause of painting this picture of rural harmony, the landowners 'went as far as to import cattle not for any economic reason but purely to provide a "living landscape"' (Hamilton 1995: 21). Whilst the commons had been the 'poor man's heritage for ages past', they became conceptualised as 'a dangerous centre of indiscipline', as a 'breeding ground for barbarians, nursing up a mischievous race of people' (Thompson 1968: 242). In other words, there was an attempt to alter the 'imaginary space' of the commons so that enclosure appeared to be necessary to social civilisation rather than an act of greed. Cottages and gardens were often systematically destroyed to prevent the possibility of any self-sufficiency and survival after enclosure. Some paternalistic landowners moved their remaining estate workers to highly visible sites at the edge of the enclosure such as model villages like Blaize Hamlet, near Bristol. Others, such as Sir Robert Walpole at Houghton Hall in Norfolk, erased an entire village so that it would not block the view from the main house of the re-engineered 'natural' landscaping (Schama 2001). Marx quotes from a landowner at Holkham Hall, just down the road from Walpole, where the Earl of Leicester, another successful capitalist farmer, said, 'I look around and not a house is to be seen but mine. I am the giant of Giant Castle, and have eat up all my neighbours' (1990: 849)!

These conflicts and changing relations illustrate an example of the contrasting form of social control that Fox (1985) identifies as 'market individualism', based upon the contractual relationship. Here, individualism is assumed as a principle of belief. Rather than economic behaviour being seen as based upon social obligation and, we might add, on 'a rootedness of place', individual interest was now seen as best served by contract behaviour. This was a condition of 'supposedly free, equal and self-determining individuals, each seeking to maximise his [sic] own interests in the open market' (1985: 5). This form of relation, at least by those who advocated it, is evoked by the language of 'a free and open arena' (p. 6). It is a very different sort of 'space' than the 'place' of feudal, paternalistic and even guild-based relations. It relies upon a sense of private property rights which agricultural labourers would have found quite alien. 'Alien' has these combined spatial and social connotations, which are carried into the development of the term in social analysis.

The concept of 'alienation' is well known to social scientists and has a wide range of interpretations arising from its centrality to the young Marx. It most likely comes from 'lien', which is Old French for a bond, a tie, which holds by right. Thus 'a-lien' refers to the act of untying a bond and having a right undone. Later the term comes to mean the transfer of ownership or title of a particular piece of property. After this, the social philosophers get their hands on it. The untying of bonds to the places that generations have known is a useful extension of 'alienation' for our present purposes. It carries with it the creation of an 'abstract space', freed from sentiment and opened up for business.

Thus a parallel process had been taking place alongside the material changes of the enclosures. This was a process that involved the restructuring of definitions and norms of social roles and connections. It involved a reorientation of the individual's 'place' in society and the basis of their relations with others. The reconceptualisation very much incorporated a shift from the notion of local place with all its specificity to one of open space which is homogeneous and extended, the logico-mathematical space that Lefebvre sees as being divorced from embodied and embedded socio-spatial relations.

This process was not a simplistic and straightforward one, but as fraught with contradictions and conflicts as the spatial changes of the enclosures. From the sixteenth century, there were a number of state interventions trying to extend a traditional social order into a different spatial order. In 1563, the Statute of Artificers was enacted, which applied on a national level the sort of local rules and regulations governing craftwork that had been traditionally applied in local guilds, by local magistrates. This is an indication that place-boundedness was becoming more problematic. A series of laws and provisions for paupers and vagabonds also illustrates the unease and ambivalence about those who were both socially and spatially dislocated. These culminated in a social division between deserving poor who were effectively to be rehabilitated through the local actions and relief of the Parish, and the 'wandering' vagabonds whose mobility saw them defined as a danger to civil order to be controlled through a very different programme of local fixity, the Houses of Correction. From a different side of the fence, so to speak, the property-owning classes too were seen to be pulling the reins on the 'open space' of contract relations, which did not necessarily benefit them. The free movement of labour might put up wages and disadvantage property owners. So, by tying employment relations more firmly into more traditional notions of 'master and servant' with their localised notions of (hierarchical) place and obligation (Fox 1985: 6), a supply of docile labour might be maintained. But this resort to paternalism was by no means the only strategy adopted, as the notion of the 'free market' was beginning to be developed. Often the open market principle meant that no responsibility whatsoever was felt towards employees and the free market meant the freedom of labour to wander unemployed and dislocated.

The development of free market principles is necessarily based upon a disjuncture between 'market' and 'place'. Yet the marketplace has a long history as a social and material space of consequence. As Zukin says,

> At its origins, a market was both a literal place and a symbolic threshold, a 'socially constructed space' and 'a culturally inscribed limit' that nonetheless involved a crossing of boundaries by long-distance trade and socially marginal traders. But markets were also inextricably bound up with local communities. In feudal times and beyond, local markets occupied a specific place and time, usually in front of the church on festival days. The denseness of interactions and the goods that were exchanged offered local communities the material and cultural means for their social reproduction – that is, their survival as communities. (1991: 6)

In the market towns, those places so often lost when a simple rural/urban division is made, employers had seen the guild system also as determinedly local and place bound. To be a member of a guild was often the only way to gain the 'freedom' of the town and therefore be able to trade there (Fox 1985: 8). Guilds provided a tight system of social control, controlling entry to a craft or trade and thus creating a monopoly within a particular town. They also had a comprehensive system of controls through rewards, and status, or punishments such as fines or even imprisonment, administered through their own institutions of courts and executives (1985: 6). The changing social-spatial relations affected the guilds, based so firmly upon their place-bound organisation, with their decline dating from the early sixteenth century.

Thus we have seen that in the development of the 'abstract spaces' of capitalism, there is a movement, consonant with the Durkheimian approach to changes in 'social solidarity' (Lukes 1973), away from a strong human connection to 'place' to less tying abstract contract relations.

For Durkheim, this change from 'common ideas and sentiments' to economic-based relations led to a shift in the nature of morality, and this was best traced through looking at the law. Lukes (1973: 140) argues that Durkheim was highly influenced by Maine's (1878) theory of the movement of the legal basis of society from Status to Contract. The law of contract is crucial here because it plays a central role in shifting rights of occupation and usage away from the peasant and towards the property rights of the growing bourgeoisie. The growth away from the near universal acceptance in law of the obligations of 'the nobility' to those for whom they are responsible, gives way to a near universal commitment to law based on written rights of personal property. Such a move plays into the hands of the 'Gentleman' because within this 'class' both 'writing' and a concept of the 'personal' are fully entrenched, whereas in the peasantry neither is well established. The bourgeoisie embrace modernity for what it delivers – new spaces, new landscapes.

What we see clearly in this 'political economy of space' of the enclosures is the transformation of both material and social in articulation one with another. There is an enrolment of power relations that transcends locality, in the process weakening the very bonds of locality. A similar (re)organisation of space that cuts across different spatial scales can be seen in the next example.

How Fordism won the West – and the rest

In this second example, we consider the processes which stemmed from the mass production of the motor car and came to organise and reconstitute the 'abstract spaces' of capitalism. Henry Ford was not satisfied with having developed mass production techniques for the automobile. He was determined to push forward a set of spatial practices that construct quite deliberately new interdependencies between employer and employed, buyer and supplier, and manufacturer and customer. In a series of books in the 1920s and 1930s, Henry Ford produced an apologia for big business, the Ford way. In *Today and Tomorrow* (1926) we see a glimpse of his vision for the spatial transformation of America and beyond, through the car:

> From a mere handful of men employed in a shop, we have grown into a large industry directly employing more than two hundred thousand men.... Our dealers and service stations employ another two hundred thousand men. But by no means do we manufacture all that we use. Roughly, we buy twice as much as we manufacture, and it is safe to say that two hundred thousand men are employed on our work in outside factories.... And this does not take into account the great number of people who in some way or another assist in the distribution or the maintenance of these cars.... These people require food, clothing, shoes, houses, and so on.... (Ford 1926: 1–2)

That there is an impetus for spatial transformation alongside the mass production ideology is seen more clearly in the propaganda he claims to have exported to the Russians:

> When the representatives of Russia came to buy tractors for their state farms, we told them: 'No, you first ought to buy automobiles and get your people used to machinery and power and to moving about with some freedom. The motor cars will bring roads, and then it will be possible to get the products of your farms to the cities'. They followed the advice and bought some thousands of automobiles. Now, after several years, they have bought some thousands of tractors. (Ford 1926: 7–8)

In *Moving Forward*, he devotes two chapters to explaining how Ford has been 'taking the methods overseas' (chapter 16) and 'the work abroad' (chapter 17). The spatial dominance is also catalogued in detail in *Today and Tomorrow* (1926: 40–4). Here, he lists the 28 plants that the Ford family own outside of the 68 in the USA and Canada. They range from Manchester, England, to Geelong, Australia; Sao Paulo to Port Elizabeth, South Africa. Ford also lists the different related industries they own: including mining, foundries, tool making, glass manufacture, electric power, railroads, even grocers. They produce ammonium sulphate and benzol, the latter sold in 88 stations and also on to aeroplanes.

The 'other' side of this spatial control is illustrated in *Moving Forward*, where he states that

> We abandoned our Highland Park Plant – which was in its day the largest automobile plant in the world – and moved to the River Rouge plant because in the new plant there could

> be less handling of materials and consequently a saving. We frequently scrap whole divisions of our business – and as a routine affair. And then one has to be prepared against the day when a complete change may be necessary and an entirely new plant constructed to make a new product. We have gone through all of this. (Ford 1931: 29)

This is a clear and unequivocal example of Marx and Engels' famous statement from the *Communist Manifesto* that 'all that is solid melts into air', describing the flexibility of capital to adapt its situation by tearing down and rebuilding spaces in its own likeness. The 'abstract space' that Ford inhabits in writing makes it plain that this is a space for exploitation.

This abstract space is, ironically, eased into being by the very specific place of a small group of like-minded industrialists who sought collectively to construct a world that was laid wide open to capitalism. This was the coalescence of interests to be found at Fort Myers in Florida (Figure 4). Thomas Edison, not just an inventor but an astute and energetic businessman, bought his home at Fort Myers in 1885, although he did not

Figure 4 **The Ford and Edison compounds at Fort Myers, Florida. The juxtaposition of the vacation homes of these key figures in American industrialisation suggests a place from which the domination of space by mass-produced goods for a mass market might be planned and executed.**

occupy it regularly until 1906. Ford bought an adjacent estate in 1916. These winter homes were visited seasonally to avoid the northern cold and can still be seen today. There is a well-known photograph of Edison, Ford and Goodyear, the tyre magnate, taken at Edison's estate in Fort Myers. Henry Ford worked on the development of his automobiles here, until they went into production in Dearborn, Illinois. Every Christmas, in Fort Myers, these industrialists met and discussed problems they were facing in finding markets for their products. A set of decisions was taken which amounted to a project for colonising the space of the USA – and beyond – for the motor car. What was required was a national system of tarmacked roads, the provision of reliable gasoline supplies at requisite points, garages to service the vehicles, reliable road maintenance, signs and maps, the removal of competition especially that offered by the railways and a population with a disposable income large enough to buy automobiles.

The story of the competition over the provision of tyres to the car industry between Goodyear and Firestone, along with the need to source the raw rubber for this, shows very clearly the significance of space and place. Ford had struck a deal with Firestone in 1906. In 1910, Harvey Firestone bought 23 acres of farmland in South Akron as the site for the first major expansion of his company. It was a four-storey factory of steel and glass, modelled on Highland Park. Using this facility, he undercut Goodyear in supplying tyres to Ford. Not to be outdone by the attractive, planned community, Goodyear Heights, Firestone also bought a 1000-acre tract of land and designated it for low-cost employee housing. By 1916 there were over 600 workers who had moved in. Its winding streets were arranged in the shape of the company logo (Firestone and Crowther 1926). However, the migration of workers to Akron during the First World War, led to a shortage of housing that manufacturers dealt with by creating 'tent cities' that looked like they were military encampments. In 1918–1919 Firestone went on camping trips with Ford and Edison which were important public relations triumphs. In the face of the competition from Firestone, Goodyear's company went into receivership in 1921.

However, the dominance of space and spatial practices is far more extensive than this control over both the specific place of production and thence over the US rubber industry. Firestone's influence extends to cultural and wider international spatial practices. Firestone became a major proponent of 'Americanization Programmes' which involved corporate classes to teach immigrant workers English and the rudiments of American culture. Ford mimicked these, where the culmination of the classes was made into a theatrical production where non-American labour, dressed in traditional costume, entered a large 'mixing pot' and after a moment or two exited wearing standard American dress. The audience were encouraged to make as much noise as they could as the celebration of the completion of the process of Americanisation was a crucial moment in everyone's lives.

This cultural domination of space within the USA reflected wider colonial relations of dominance and appropriation. The actual requisition of raw rubber had proved to represent a huge difficulty, for it reflected international power over spatial resources. By 1914 the USA imported over 50 per cent of the world's crude rubber. Here the spatial politics of colonialism becomes central because rubber can only be grown successfully in certain conditions and these were in the control of colonial powers, mainly Britain. The combination of business and colonialism was seen starkly in the First World War by a voracious American industry. By 1915 it had become clear that motor vehicles had a huge military value over trains and horses. Great Britain lifted its embargo on American rubber imports on the condition that the USA did not supply Germany with rubber exports. The German military was therefore highly disadvantaged in moving troops and supplies to the front by the shortage of replacement tyres.

The USA and Great Britain continued to struggle over access to supplies of crude rubber and to the price charged during the 1920s. New innovations concerning tyre manufacture meant that in 1922 longer lasting 'balloon' tyres were launched. These were fitted for free to car owners, whilst improved roads at this time meant car sales continued to increase. At Christmas 1922, Firestone persuaded Ford and Edison to explore the possibility of creating an American rubber company by which to offer competition to Britain's predominance of rubber sourcing and control of tyre manufacture. The search for synthetic rubber was thereby launched by an inter-organisational network. The role of multinational corporations is key in creating a world fit for capitalism, but their part in dominating and constructing spaces that recreate the material and social worlds in their interests is perhaps less appreciated.

The organisation of society through large business and state organisations has created 'abstract spaces' of exploitation. Massey (2005: 65) argues that

> What was evolved within the project of modernity, in other words, was the establishment and (attempted) universalisation of a way of imagining space (and the space/society relation) which underpinned the material enforcement of certain ways of organising space and the relationship between society and space. And it is still with us today.

We can see this demonstrated in both the relations of land and property, and in the dominance of Fordist mass production and consumption. Another form of this abstract space can be seen through the organisation of space in war and the 'warfare state'.

War and its organisation

The organisation of warfare has a significant role in a 'political economy of space'. Its influence is ubiquitous and pervasive, although not often remarked, except in actual periods of war which tend to be bracketed as exceptional times despite their frequency. Defeat in war has hugely serious spatial consequences and so it is little surprise that many societies prepare for war constantly and its warriors are given high status. Over the ages war has been seen in most societies as a constant, universal fact of life and death. Above the gates of the Venetian *Arsenale*, according to Robert Burton in 1621, was the inscription: 'Happy is that city which in time of peace thinks of war'. One of the consequences of this normalisation of the organisation of war is its part in the construction of abstract space.

As we discussed in Chapter 1, abstract space has three elements: the geometric format, the optical or visual format and the phallic format (Lefebvre 1991: 285–91). The first creates the plan, the second develops anaetheticisation, the third symbolises masculine violence. In relation to the organisation of war, the first and second may be connected to the planning of war and its representation. The conduct of warfare often involves war planners dealing with abstract space, a neutral medium into which disjointed material and objects might be introduced. The terrain upon which war is fought becomes seen through the reductive lens of a diagrammatic plan; it is conceptualised as a container into which personnel and weaponry are 'inserted' and then 'extracted'. The hairlines of the targeting array are aligned on a distant object to create an icy cold image of that most abstracted of spaces, 'ground zero', the point at which the bomb explodes. As ordinary citizens we also become inured to the organisation of war through this abstraction. As well as the multitude of electronic games involving war-games, television has also cashed in, with, for example, the BBC showing *Time Commanders*. Teams use computer-generated graphics to re-enact famous historical battles, along with advice and feedback from military experts. These illustrate the distanciation effect of the 'optical or visual format' of abstract space, since we are immune to the visual representation of war, and do not have to be immersed bodily in its smells, movement and brutal tactile experience. The phallic format of the organisation of war clearly requires less explication, since war is where the symbolism of masculine violence merges with its material actuality. However, it can be seen that the phallic also allows for abstraction. For example, Easlea (1983) shows how the first plutonium and uranium bombs were given names like 'big boy' to reflect their potency, but also as a way of distancing the scientists from focusing on their destructive potential.

The organisation of and for war has had a substantial influence on both urban and industrial organisation. The development of army barracks within most of the capital cities of Europe was of immense significance. Because standing armies were developed on the basis of permanent warfare, the state had to solve the problem of creating special forms of housing where members of the general populace were not required to quarter the military. According to Mumford (1961: 415) 'the army barracks had almost the same place in the baroque order that the monastery had in the medieval one'. On the Champs du Mars in Paris and equally in Berlin, turning out the guard, drilling and parading became great mass spectacles. With the presence of armed might within the city walls, the population became more cowed and more used to the martial trumpet than the church bells. In Berlin in 1740, 25 per cent of the population were troops and their mechanised obedience affected all of the population to a greater or lesser extent. This tradition continued. Schama describes Prussia as 'the barrack house kingdom' (2001: 381). Hitler, too, drew on the ways that the dominance of social space by military organisation had been incorporated within the general *habitus*.

> " In planning his mass meetings, Hitler's architectural skills gave him a sophisticated appreciation of the importance of the physical ambience of a site. His principles were strict. The space itself was ideally to be rectangular. It was to be isolated from the outside world. The participants were to be formed with military exactitude into solid blocks. (Spotts 2002: 59)

Across Europe for centuries, the army supplied the civil as well as military codes of conduct by its ubiquity in the garrison town. In Ireland there is a widespread antipathy to 'garrison sports' like football and rugby with the more Gaelic originals being preferred for political and historical reasons.[3] Army dominance of social space continues to be utilised by states when disruption or dissent appears, and this does not only apply to explicitly militarised states. The role of the army was key to the re-appropriation of the spaces of dissent in the UK in labour strikes of the early twentieth century. Although media attention has made this less overt and more carefully managed, there has been much opinion that the army was used surreptitiously in the Miners' Strike of 1984–1985, and they were used for emergency cover in the petrol blockades of 2000 and the Firefighters' Strike (2002–2003).

Thus we start to see that there is a huge degree of overlap between the organisation of war and the organisation of capitalism, which together come to dominate social space in numerous ways. Autobiographies of industry leaders are replete with metaphors of battle, indicating that the organisation of war dominates the imaginary spaces of capitalism as well. The material interaction is made explicit by Weber, who argues that 'no special proof is necessary to show that military discipline is the ideal model for the modern capitalist factory, as it was for the ancient plantation' (Gerth and Mills 1968: 261). Spatial forms of organisation, where different functions are involved at different points on the surface of the Earth, often involve the 'military' option where discipline, obedience and regimentation are valorised. For example, Kamata describes what it was like to work for Toyota as a seasonal worker. He is plagued by injuries received in speeded up work practices, for, as Dore notes in the introduction to the book:

> It is all like nothing so much as an army camp.... The firm has very close connections with the Self Defense forces and makes a strenuous effort to recruit former soldiers and NCOs. 2,500 of its workers and a tenth of its foremen are ex-soldiers. It is primarily a matter of ideological affinity no doubt. (Kamata 1983: xiii)

Toyota sprang into existence some 50 years before this to fulfil Japanese military contracts, its original supervisory staff sometimes being samurai who refused to commit suicide despite their loss of face. Its corporate word for labour turnover was 'escape'. In the first years of the twenty-first century, it is perhaps in other Asian countries that militarisation and life in barracks is more evident. This is especially so in the organisation of the 'export processing zones' which stand in an independent relation to the nation state within which they are physically located, as relatively autonomous capitalist enclaves. Klein describes the Cavite Export Processing Zone in Manila, for example, as 'a miniature military state inside a democracy'. The workers tend to be migrants, far from home, requiring shelter and basic amenities, but they confront a management style derived from the military.

The arsenal is of particular importance as a site of confluence between the organisation of war and capitalism, indeed, very often organisational techniques still central to capitalism were derived from the arsenals. In the sixteenth century a huge number of such buildings were constructed and it is here where we shall focus some attention. The 'geometric, visual, phallic' abstract space of capitalism is to some extent laid out on the floors of the arsenal. Our concern is to show that the arsenal as an organising device for the conduct of war has large implications for the rest of society and the ways in which life became organised for civilians. It becomes a 'representational space' of major significance in that it seeks to universalise spatial practices from inside the arsenal and to place them on the outside. It will be our argument in this section that arsenals are key spaces from and in which socio-technical innovations arise. Since they tend to be government sponsored they have access to vast resources and are the focus of huge attention by those charged with running the government. They act as test beds for ideas on new forms of social and technical organisation and are seen as offering large efficiency rewards for certain rationalistic modes of organising.

The Venetian *Arsenale* is supposedly the oldest arsenal in existence although there is clear evidence of the simultaneous growth of the arsenal at Constantinople. The word itself comes from Arabic and is variously translated as manufactuary, factory or building place. Founded by the Doge in 1104, the original *Arsenale* was a munitions store and place of ship construction. It was surrounded by stout walls and security was extremely tight. When Dante described it in *Inferno* (canto xx1, 11.7–18) in around 1300 it had been enlarged to four times its original size. Two hundred years after that, it employed 15,000 carpenters alone and had become the largest complex of skilled labour ever seen. It saw the birth of the production line system. It is famously said that when King Henri III of France visited, he was shown before a banquet an unprepossessing pile of pre-assembled galley parts. On leaving the dinner he was presented with those same bits, now a duly completed galley, ready to sail and full of provisions. A century later, in 1570, when the Turks invaded Cyprus one hundred galleys were completed within two months. All this was made possible by using the techniques of mass production, namely standardisation of parts, quality control, functional specialisation of labour and the good treatment of the skilled workforce including jobs for life and retirement pensions. The enterprise was governed by a Council of Three who took turns to act as night watchman and guard the keys, but the Magnificent Admiral controlled the operations of a highly complex organisational form involving hundreds of different trades and requiring a vast array of resources and raw materials.

From Venice the arsenal form of military organisation spread around the Western world. It is often forgotten, for example, that Ford's River Rouge Plant was developed upon a river site because its first function was to build the First World War destroyers for the US Navy. The 'representational' role in particular that these arsenals took can be seen by just some of the examples below. Arsenals were central to accounting procedures and the development of ways of the state understanding how its money was being spent. It has been calculated that medieval states spent about three-quarters of their public purse directly on the military. In 1977, at then prices the USA and USSR were spending jointly $430 million per day on weaponry. In the light of this, it is understandable that arsenals have been a focus of interest of professional accountants. Hoskin and Macve (1994) have shown how accounting at the Springfield Armoury in the New England area of the USA led to changes in the ways the costs of general engineering were accounted for and then spread 'out' into industry in general.

Additionally, arsenals were centres of interest in manufacturing techniques. Taylor and his relationship with Watertown Arsenal in 1911 are worthy of note. Used by General Crozier, Controller of Ordinance, since 1906, Taylor's ideas had been worked upon in the arsenal but their use and the problems they caused came to a head when the moulders went on strike five years later. The notion of 'soldiering' used by Taylor to reflect bad practice is not an innocent one here since it refers to these workers paid directly by the Secretary for War. They were highly skilled and well paid. They believed that the commercial speed up was not for them because they were of and for the military. Taylor's interest in the Watertown Arsenal was driven by the centrality of the rise of mass production techniques where skill was seen as an issue of control. As is well known, in 1801 Eli Whitney had developed 'the American system of manufacture', by emphasising the mass production of locks, stocks and barrels in order to defeat the British army with its sensitive customised bespoke weaponry. Production was undertaken by less skilled workers of necessity in the absence of British apprenticed staff and so the American system emphasised how in the absence of the highly skilled, production of a French model of musket might still be undertaken. And Taylor was clearly hoping that this sort of opportunity in the Watertown Arsenal might lead to a similar breakthrough. But the Hearings of 1911 on Senate Hill led not to the embracing of Taylorism but to its banning from all government establishments until 1947. The assistant secretary for the navy in 1911 was one F. D. Roosevelt and he recognised that the skill levels required in production of naval weaponry meant that this 'knowledge base' needed to be preserved as a craft form rather than trusted to the vagaries of scientific management. It was he who banned Taylorism and its threat to the equipment of the armed forces of the USA for 35 years. And in a nice continuation of the knowledge base perhaps, in July 2001, the site of now closed Watertown Arsenal was sold to Harvard University for $125 million.

However, arsenals have also been the target of standardisation, in order to increase production, both in terms of their systems and their products. As we have seen, Eli Whitney undertook this in the early years of the nineteenth century but the sword works in Toledo, Spain, underwent standardisation in 1761. Prior to that, the manufacture of arms had typically been undertaken by workshops in private households for private soldiers. Hand to hand combat was the ordering of warfare, and weapons were often customised for the gentleman wearers operating within private armies. But changes in warfare drove the Spanish authorities to centralise standardised production in the Royal Sword Factory. The arsenal thus shaped the demise of the small 'houses' in which bespoke sword manufacture had been undertaken. In 1761, it produced about 10,000 to 12,000 units per year. By the mid-nineteenth century this rose to 40,000 per annum but without the bespoke work for gentlemen adventurers. Swords were now produced in mass production ways to a standard. This led to the development of similar processes in the Royal Tobacco Factory at Seville where cigars now became controlled and standardised as swords had been. The model of the 'standard', produced in standard ways in standard spatial arrangements was winning through.

Since arsenal workers have been central to the state in most places at most points in time, they have been the target of many attempts to control their labour and its quality in space and time. In the Second World War, the Ministry of Supply was the country's largest employer and was responsible for 42 Royal Ordnance factories and 300,000 workers. To ensure their satisfaction with their work, 600 labour officers and 5500 welfare officers were employed in arsenals, there were 46 new Whitley councils established and there were 2000 joint production committees taking their lead from the ordinance factories. Legislation and policies on industrial relations have often been led by concerns for the performance and welfare of workers within the arsenal. The need to control and motivate workers in space and time also spilt out of the arsenals into wider social space. When there was perceived to be a problem with the quality of the shells in the First World War, it was blamed on the alcohol consumption of munitions workers on the Scottish/English border just north of Carlisle. The British government nationalised the public houses around Carlisle (where the Temperance Movement had traditionally been strong) and introduced closing times and restricted opening hours for all pubs. The decision was taken by Seebohm Rowntree, the well-known Quaker, who headed up the 'Health of Munitions Worker Committee' in a year when three million rounds of artillery ammunition were deemed necessary for the British Army on the Somme alone. The leakage of spatial implications here from Jutland, back to the Arsenal, thence to Parliament and back to the town of Carlisle create out of this quadrilateral a Lefebvrian, dominated space, transformed by technology and practice.

Yet it must also be recognised that it is also in the twentieth century that the 'imaginary space' of privatised capitalism comes to effect the military. With the industrialisation of warfare and weapons production, a number of armaments manufacturers arise who are not part of the state apparatus – at least in ownership terms. Companies such as Krupps, Armstrongs and Scheidners undertake much development work on new weapons. A weapons race then ensued in which these companies and their logic of capitalist accumulation played a major role, not least in exporting lethal hardware around the world. The admixture of arsenals where the state controlled routine weapon production, alongside private companies undertaking research and development of new, expensive weaponry became the norm. It was this integration of public and private, state and corporation which Eisenhower had identified as being crucially different.

The hybridity of these state arsenals and private companies started to fully develop during the years of Vietnam, and the Military–Industrial Complex became very well established. For example, Monsanto made the defoliant Agent Orange and the Rand Corporation, (standing for R and D) calculated the cost of the war in terms of deaths per $1000. Rationality of a sort was evident in their very footsteps. Just as it had been perhaps for the German firm, IG Farben, 30 years earlier in its manufacture of the Zylon B to be used in the gas chambers of the concentration camps. In 2002, the Rand Corporation, still active in military circles, produced a document for discussion on the future of US

BOUNDARY CROSSINGS: REPRODUCING ORGANISED SPACE • BUILDING A SOCIAL MATERIALITY: SPATIAL AND EMBODIED POLITICS IN ORGANISATION • ALTERNATIVE SPACES: THE RADICAL ORGANISATION OF SPACE? • CONCLUSIONS: DISORGANISING SPACE

4   165

arsenals. It recommended that the 11 contractor-operated arsenals in the USA in 2001 all be privatised and that the two government-controlled arsenals move towards this status by 2007. The largest US arsenal and therefore the biggest probably in the world is the Redstone site in the Tennessee Valley.

The Tennessee Valley Authority (TVA) has been analysed in the context of its state-corporate relationships, and the idea of close state – private organisation relationships in the 1940s has attracted the interest of organisation theorists (Selznick 1953). However, its organisational practices have rarely been connected to it as the development of a region, and its domination by the military–industrial complex. Roosevelt himself saw it as 'a corporation clothed with the power of government but possessed of the flexibility and initiative of private enterprise' (1953: 3). During the First World War, two nitrate plants had been set up by which to manufacture explosives and the Wilson Dam had been constructed. The combined cost was $100 million. All three facilities were deemed to have been failures and over the next 15 years there was contention over their future and that of mixed government–private sector collaboration. There were two presidential commissions on the topic. The TVA had been set up by Congress in May 1933 as an example of public ownership and the expansion of the whole scheme for the Tennessee River system. The concept here of a 'region' with a river valley as the integral unit was very new. There was to be much more production of electricity and dams to control floods and allow navigation (p. 4). We can see clearly here that the material space is to be reshaped and dominated, at the same time that the space of hybrid state–private organisation is also be reconstituted. The huge amounts of electricity produced from the damming of the river made it attractive to those involved in weapons manufacture. Oak Ridge played a significant role in the development of the atom bomb and was a top-secret site. Elsewhere within the Authority not one but two other large arsenals were built. One at Huntsville was famous for its women workers whose output and quality levels bettered those of the predominantly male workers elsewhere. Whilst this achievement was vaunted in the mid-1940s it was, in fact, the first American arsenal to close in the post-war period. In ways which are highly predictable, the sexist agenda of the Department of Defense moved rapidly to reflect the dawning of a new age of men returning home from war to reclaim their public spaces from women. The other site at Redstone today consists of 2000 buildings covering 38,000 acres and employing 24,000 people. It has become the site for the Strategic Star Wars activity and is ensured of huge government investment. The site is also open to a large number of private contractors who see the arsenal as ripe for takeover.

The privatisation of the arsenals of the Western world is associated with a broader privatisation of its military and the rise of Private Armies. Private Military Companies (PMCs) have received $300 billion from the Pentagon in the last ten years. Some of the larger PMCs include Blackwater USA, Vinnell, Brown and Root; MPRI (Military Professional Resources Inc.) and Sandline International but numerous others exist. It was reckoned that in Africa, primarily in Angola in the 1990s over 90 such companies were operating. Although they have 'ceased to trade' (one description of such armies is that they are 'non-lethal service providers') Executive Outcomes and Sandline spawned other offshoots. Such activity is legal and there are serious attempts being made to relax international law regulating the use of mercenaries or 'civilians authorised to accompany a force in the field'. However, 'the US government has no idea of exact numbers, let alone individual names, of persons performing extra-territorial contracts outside of the US on behalf of the US' for the Department of Defense does 'not keep a record but such assignments are part of a growing trend' (*Military Law Review* 2003, fn. 425). Naturally, however, there are huge concerns about the use of such forces, including questions of their motivation, their loyalty, their efficiency and their humanitarian stance. Their role in warfare and changing the face of nation states through the medium of their hybridity implies that research upon them is well overdue.

The 'barracks' and the 'arsenal' are key metonyms of the organised world. Arsenals are key buildings within capitalist structures. Whilst they might appear to predate capitalism, and in some cases do, they become sites of inter-organisational expertise used to generate profit, maintain property rights and defend capitalism from its enemies. Because of the ubiquity of war, arsenals are key universalising spaces, configuring complexes of the military and the industrial, where the state and the large business corporation meet.

BOUNDARY CROSSINGS: REPRODUCING ORGANISED SPACE • BUILDING A SOCIAL MATERIALITY: SPATIAL AND EMBODIED
POLITICS IN ORGANISATION • ALTERNATIVE SPACES: THE RADICAL ORGANISATION OF SPACE? • CONCLUSIONS: DISORGANISING SPACE

4   167

We believe it is time that studies of organisation recognised the political nature of how organised spaces are constructed, and a 'political economy of space' allows for these routes and routines, networks and flows to be traced. In the next chapter, we follow form of these interconnections that links the personal and political through the social and the material. At a very different spatial scale, a confluence of state and business, culture and identity meet right in the heart of the home. Therefore we look in more detail at how domestic spaces are simultaneously private and organisational, and thus how the traditional boundaries of social science between spheres of reproduction, production and consumption, and between identity and structure, are hybrid and permeable.

Notes

[1] Under Thatcherism in the UK, it is clear that the privatisation of council houses was motivated by a similar belief that those with a stake in property have more invested in the status quo.

[2] As a devout Catholic, Sir Thomas Tresham spent many years in prison for his faith. During this time he designed an architectural expression of his faith, which he later built as a gatehouse. It expresses all the (suppressed) symbols of the Catholic religion in material form, particularly the centrality of the Trinity which it incorporates as three floors, three windows on each side, triangular chimneys and of course the whole building is an equilateral triangle. It can still be visited.

[3] Croke Park in Dublin, a stadium that was the site of a massacre by the British Black and Tan forces in November 1920, had banned the playing of any 'foreign' games until 2007 when a rugby union game between Ireland and England was played amidst much controversy.

5 boundary crossings: reproducing organised space

LDING ORGANISATION: SECURING AND OBSCURING POWER • BUILDING PEOPLE: TITIES AND SPACES • A POLITICAL ECONOMY OF ORGANISED SPACE • BOUNDARY CROSSINGS: REPRODUCING ORGANISED SPACE • BUILDING A SOCIAL MATERIALITY: SPATIAL AND EMBODIED POLITICS IN ORGANISATION • ALTERNATIVE SPACES: THE RADICAL ORGANISATION OF SPACE? • CONCLUSIONS: DISORGANISING SPACE

> *Modernity prides itself on the fragmentation of the world as its foremost achievement. Fragmentation is the prime source of its strength. The world that falls into a plethora of problems is a manageable world. Or, rather, since the problems are manageable – the question of the manageability of the world may never appear on the agenda, or at least be indefinitely postponed. The territorial and functional autonomy which the fragmentation of powers brings in its wake consists first and foremost in the right not to look beyond the fence and not to be looked at from outside of the fence.*

(Bauman 1991: 12)

Separate spheres?

In the last chapter, we attempted to demonstrate the connections between political economy and 'the organisation of space'. There, we showed some of the routes and routines that cross spatial and social scales to produce certain forms of taken-for-granted social spaces. In this chapter, we continue to utilise Lefebvre's (1991) ideas about spatial practices. Here we explore routes and routines across the 'social spheres' of production, consumption and reproduction, to see the organisation of their spaces and the boundaries and links made – and sometimes hidden – between them (Figure 5). These social spaces and the routes between them are lived through the habituation of the body and become sedimented, appearing as natural and unquestionable. Thus these spaces reflect daily routine as well as being gradually developed through a society's history (Lefebvre 1991: 33–8). The routes and the barriers between the social spheres of home, employment, leisure, retail and so on are not only social and material, but are also conceptual and imaginary. For example, a physical path provides a short cut through a certain housing estate, but the imagined space of

Figure 5 The Vasari Corridor in Florence at one and the same time spatially connects yet divides. It provides a superior route between office, church, garden and home for the powerful, whilst separating them physically and symbolically from the general populace below.

that estate is one of danger; the local library may be very central and accessible, but it is not necessarily part of a 'mental map' of places to take the children in the holidays. As Lefebvre's work on space shows, the physical and the theoretical and the imaginary are not separable, but are brought together through the medium of the embodied social subject who mediates both the material and the conceptual. The conceptual and the imaginary in research and theory-building about society are also related to these boundaries and connections. Within this chapter, we will see how the material, embodied places and the abstract, conceptual spaces of production, reproduction and consumption also map onto each other. We begin by considering the construction of the idea of separate social spheres and spaces, and go on to look at the spatial construction of the home and especially the kitchen as hybrid spaces where production, reproduction and consumption meet.

Drawing boundaries is a political act. To include and thus exclude, to join and still separate, to draw lines of demarcation and yet homogenise that which is within, all function to exercise power. These 'grids of intelligibility' form modes of knowledge that produce certain possibilities and norms, particular actions and ideas in and about different spaces and places. The separation then of 'public' from 'private', of 'work' from 'leisure' and of the 'individual' from the 'collective' both obscures and secures the political acts that are being undertaken in the production of each social space as well as their conceptualisation as separate social spheres. Only certain binaries have been privileged. Only certain values and power arrangements have been valorised. In looking at how these spatial and conceptual boundaries have been drawn and with what consequences, it is possible to understand more clearly the organised and organisational nature of social space. In this chapter, we consider these spatial and conceptual boundaries in relation to notions of spheres of the 'home' and 'work' that have predominated in those economies characterised by industrial capitalism. Between these economies, of course, there are important differences of culture and tradition. Our focus here is concentrated on material from the UK and the USA in order to draw a picture of the changing spatial and organisational boundaries around these social spheres.

It has become widely accepted that since the Industrial Revolution in the West, two spheres of human activity have become separated. These are sometimes labelled 'work' and 'home' and are conceptualised as mutually exclusive and hierarchically ordered. In other words, one 'leaves' one sphere to 'enter' the other and in 'normal' (i.e. taken-for-granted) circumstances the world of work predominates. This is because the capitalist economy requires the selling of labour power in order to live, and this compliance brings with it more intangible social rewards such as status and acceptance. As many social scientists have pointed out, the reproduction of the labour force – both its maintenance as fit to work on a day-to-day basis and its reproduction over the generations – is an essential underpinning to the operation of capitalism. It is also a highly gendered one. Yet it is ultimately an incalculable benefit to the system compared with the economic certainties (as they appear) that can be expressed through GDP and productivity rates. However, the home takes its part in the ideological construction of the capitalist society as well, often as the necessary consolation for employment. Thus there are 'ideal types' of the (Western) home and workplace that are placed in opposition to one another. The 'ideal home' is a constant theme in Hollywood movies, which focus upon the home understood in terms of a 'family'. Moreover, it is a myth that valorises a long list of elements which differentiate the 'home' from 'work'. The home is a place of a personalised nature in which humans enjoy rest and recuperation from the world of work. The household is small and is non-hierarchical. Leisure time predominates and is carried out without surveillance, constraint or interference. It is a place of hyper-affectivity in which emotion and pleasure predominate. The family members may feel they are 'individual' human beings known intimately by those in the home. The fellow members of the home will generally be small in number and highly localised in their movements. The activities within the home will be seen as private and not subject to checks from external agencies. There is no overt concept of career progression and no sense of belonging to an 'organisation'; indeed it is a haven of respite in the organised world (Hayden 2002: 87). In contrast, the world of 'work' is a depersonalised space in which humans labour in large, hierarchically run organisations. This work is done in the face of surveillance, constraint and interference.

It is a space of hypo-affectivity in which rationality predominates and the worker may feel they are an 'anonymous number' within a 'massified' labour force. This labour force may be large and in some cases will be global in spread. The member of the organisation will feel they are constantly on show and subject to public checks on their performance. The concept of 'career' and progression may have some effect on their organisational behaviour, and also their sense of self and social status.

As industrialism grew in the nineteenth century, the ideology of the family was seen as the bulwark against the problems caused by industrial society and 'the house with feeling' (rather than one 'without feeling') was encouraged by Andrew Jackson Downing in extolling the virtue of family life. Wajcman argues that

> The split between public and private meant that the home was expected to provide a haven from the alienated, stressful technological order of the workplace and was expected to provide entertainment, emotional support, and sexual gratification.... With home and housework acquiring heightened emotional significance, it became impossible to rationalise household production along the lines of industrial production. (1991: 85–6)

Just as the home-as-haven is an ideological construct, so too is the idea of paid work as unrelieved drudgery. In contrast, the workplace may be experienced as a place of pleasure, self-fulfilment and social relationships. For some it may be an escape from the home, just as the home is a place of escape from employment for others.

The separation between these spheres and the power involved in these divisions has been explored by social scientists. This is perhaps the case especially of feminists who have pointed to the circumscribed experience of women in space, especially in relation to the boundaries between different spheres. For example, women are seen as putting themselves in danger if they 'step out of line' by entering various 'public' spaces. There are a set of implicit norms that govern the behaviour of women in these 'no-go' areas, including those of dress, time of day, the protection of a male and so on. If a woman transgresses these norms, she receives the opprobrium due to someone who has moved, physically and symbolically, outside society's sanctioned spatial divisions. Should she come to harm, she may be defined as responsible or to blame. Even so, a greater proportion of attacks on women occur in the supposed 'safety' of the home. Yet the home is defined as the appropriate sphere for women, and therefore there has been a tendency for society to filter out these uncomfortable facts. Since, ideologically, the home is a haven, a whole range of behaviours that conflict with this dearly held concept become well-nigh invisible, including violence towards men, and between same sex partners, which have maintained their taboo status even longer than domestic violence against women and children. Instead, the biggest societal anger is expressed towards actions that violate the sense of the home-as-haven emanating *from the outside*. These may be against property and its boundaries as much as violence towards the person, but both slice through the spatial and the symbolic separation of spheres.

Social scientists have also pointed to the power effects of the conceptual divisions: thus 'work' is associated with the societally valued activity of 'paid employment', and that 'work' which is related to the maintenance of home and family disappears from sight. This devaluation of activities in the 'domestic' sphere is carried with the woman worker even when physically she has crossed the boundary to 'real' work in the sphere of production. Davies and Rosser's (1986) study of women working in particular administrative jobs in the National Health Service in the UK demonstrated how these jobs required skills of communication and mediation with a wide range of people including patients, families, diverse medical and ancillary staff; co-ordination of tasks and people; and an ability to multi-task across these demands. The women who undertook these roles were perceived as invaluable and irreplaceable by the management of the Health Service because they possessed these skills. Yet analysis of the background and age profile of these women administrators found that they were all 'women-returners', who had had a period 'away' from the workplace to care for dependent children. The study showed that these valued skills were ones that had been developed within the home, during the period of time when the women had supposedly 'not been in work'. Since these were skills that were not recognised within the production sphere as developed through work experience or qualification, their value was not rewarded, and the women themselves were not perceived as promotion material: they could be happily kept in the roles where the skills they derived from the gendered nature of their life cycle were of so much benefit, but not crowd out the career ladder for the bright young things whose full commitment, measured in time and space, was for the production sphere.

Despite the ideological constructions, and their material effects, the separation between 'home' and 'work' has never been spatially complete, but always overlapping. As well as the domestic work carried out in the home, much paid work has continued to be done there too. Home-working cannot be treated as a single type of work, since it covers a wide range and levels of tasks, from low to high levels of technological use, both within the formal and the alternative economies. Suffice it to say here that the construction of the home/work divide tends to obscure its presence. Yet it may form one of those facets of the capitalist 'spatial fix' that Harvey (2000) discusses. Whatever form it takes, it throws certain costs of production back onto the household. Massey (1995b) describes how paid employment colonises the space and time of high technology professionals in her research into science parks. These workers (predominantly men) tend to 'take their work home' with them. This is at least partly because they are engaged with their work. As we discussed in Chapter 3, the coalescence of pleasure and identity with work mediates the employment relation so that it is carried as part of the employee through multiple spaces. From their research in a number of locations, including the home, Felstead et al. (2005: 177) have also made this point when they say that 'Work has broken out of the constraints of specialised locations and fixed hours. It is not just extending its grip on time and space; it is conquering time and space. Hence, wherever we look, drawing a line between work and non-work becomes ever more difficult'.

The denigration of reproduction as being 'outside' the economic and political spheres has also been challenged. Feminists have taken the lead in seeing domestic production and reproduction as being crucial to the economy, rather than reliant on it. Other studies explore the definition and boundaries of what is legitimised as part of 'economy', and have also demonstrated the significance of the sphere defined as 'reproduction'. Some estimates of the value of the 'alternative economy' place it is as equivalent to that of the conventional market economy. This ratio of 1:1 in monetary value terms, if true costing was undertaken, shows that what happens in the home is not a separate sphere from the political economy but contributes to it in an equivalent way. By reversal of this argument, the political economy of the industrialised society interacts with the domestic household in a very intimate way (Leyshon *et al.* 2003; Williams 2005).

What we are interested in at this point is the material construction of space and how it has been produced by ideas from within the organisation of production. Unlike Wajcman, whom we quoted above, we do not accept that it became 'impossible to rationalise household production along the lines of industrial production'. Far from it. As Hayden (2002) shows, it is a prime strategy for home construction. Our argument is that the domestic is not a separate realm to be 'penetrated' by cultural and social influences, including 'consumerism', that have been primarily 'pumped in' through the media. The concept of the boundary around the home, between 'public' and 'private', needs to be problematised. The domestic 'sphere' is already constructed by social and organisational influences from the very outset. It exists within an inter-organisational field (Chapman and Hockey 1999; Morley 2000). Indeed, the very ideas and structures of what constitute the 'domestic' or the 'home' are shaped by organisational discourses and knowledges oriented towards consumption, even if these social-organisational processes are largely hidden behind the very nature of the symbolic 'sanctity' of the private dwelling. Home dwellers are acculturated to specific forms of consumption concretely locked into the design and building of houses, the setting up of services connected into the home (e.g. plumbing, gas, telecommunications and electricity) and the mass-produced design of room layout. Many organisations, paralleling the media, are involved in pre-organising the home for consumption through its material and ideological construction. This construction emerges out of inter-organisational processes of negotiation, power and conflict across business, public sector, consumer and political interests. Discourses make 'truth' claims about the world, realised in and through processes of enactment. The 'materiality of ideas' (Braidotti 1994: 126) means that discourse is already constituted in action and in the concrete world (Foucault 1970): in other words, discourse is integral, not external to, the social production of space.

For many writers, including us, then, the binary construction of spaces is not enough. It does not reflect the complexity of spatial orderings, nor how they have come to be constructed. It is argued here that the organisation of the space described as 'home' is no less visible to organisation, no less tangible, no less influenced, no less material than the organisation of the 'work' place. By considering the entwining of the organisation of production, reproduction and consumption, we wish to look at how organisation itself is produced and reproduced as a social practice. The (apparently) personal is also the political, economic and organisational.

Building the home

In this section, we look at the organisation of the domestic space, and its construction in relation to production and consumption. First, we consider the production of spatial divisions within the house itself. Second, we consider how the house comes to be constructed as a separate and isolated sphere. Third, we explore how the supposedly private space of the modern home is traversed with organisational power.

It is useful to take a further look at the development of the home-as-haven, and its physical and ideological separations, both within itself and from the 'wider' world of community and economics. In Chapter 2, we have already pointed to the division of spaces within the Roman Commander's house, separated between those that were public, ceremonial and hierarchically marked, and the private, less-delineated spaces. We have also there alluded to the divisions within the home of many workers, including the silk workers of Spitalfields and the ribbon-makers of Coventry. Yet in many domestic dwellings over much of history, spaces, inhabitants and functions were not divided in ways that tend to be seen as 'normal' today. A visit to Flag Fen, near Peterborough in the UK, provides an insight into the experience of dwelling during the Iron and Bronze Ages. These round houses centred on a chimneyless fire. The hearth is key to the frequent valorisation of the traditional home: 'A central fire is more efficient than a fire on an outside wall and you can get twice as many people around it' (Rivers 1992: 9). So we can see the development of the house as a socio-petal space, a space of bringing people together, of gathering.[1] Interestingly, the word 'focus' is Latin for hearth, and, despite the attempts of some modern developers and the greater effectiveness of central heating, preference still tends towards the fireplace as the focus of a family living room. The later 'Hall House', derived from the Anglo-Saxons and adapted by the Normans, retained this central fire, with the wall-chimney not becoming common until the thirteenth century (1992: 9). Although the Hall House was rectangular, it also retained the essential communality of domestic life. The central fire in the hall house is associated with the communal sleeping, eating and living of all the inhabitants together within an extended family- or clan-based system. The Anglo-Saxon poem *Beowulf* describes such forms of living conceivable in terms of routes and routines: it is described as 'mead-hall', place of feasting and celebration that Heaney (1999) trans- lates as 'hall-session'; 'war-hall' and the group of kinsmen and warriors are called 'hall-troop' and servants 'hall-serf'; it is also called the 'gift hall' after the giving of gifts from the chieftain to reward followers and tie them in through reciprocal relations. It is to the magnificent hall, Heorot, which the monster Grendel comes, and is slain by Beowulf. The hall house is often associated with a communal kitchen outside of the hall to ensure the risk of fire was reduced. Similarly, laundry and washing were done away from the hall because of the need for access to running water. But in the hall everyone lived together. It is this 'hall' that in the modern house has become merely the entrance to the house:

> " a corridor, insulation against strangers, mere circulation space, an intercession between rooms to render them all the more private...the hall has shrunk; it has been de-developed. It is the opposite of what it was. Now it is a barrier; once it was byre and bur, an expression of tribalism, of a lost communality. (Rivers 1992: 8–9)

The division of rooms not only by function, but also by class of people to be included and excluded becomes more common. Rivers quotes the poet William Langland from the fourteenth century: 'The hall has come to a pretty pass when the lord and lady avoid it at mealtimes, dining every day in a private parlour to get away from the poor people' (Rivers 1992: 12). A dairy and a bakehouse might be attached to the hall but other rooms were now to be found upstairs where the owners lived, leaving the hall for the servants. Four-poster beds with curtains not only kept out draughts, but were increasingly useful for ensuring privacy, since it was usual for rooms to contain more than one bed. Large houses required large numbers of servants to run them. With this number of people running around within enclosed spaces, privacy was difficult. During the sixteenth century, Cruickshank (1992: 65) tells us, privacy became more valued, and seen as a sign of greater social distinction. Greater spatial organisation and differentiation had to take place to try to achieve these aspirations. Rooms were developed for different purposes, such as the study for the growing pastime of reading. The bedroom had moved upstairs and was becoming a private domain, although some elements of communal living continued, so that bedroom sharing was accepted between non-family members. As Samuel Pepys tells us, his bedroom was shared by himself, Mrs Pepys and the serving 'wench' named Willett, so that she could wait upon their needs at all times of the day and night. Dr Johnson was to say that servants would get themselves into positions where they could 'govern or betray' their employers and the tension of sharing the same room with 'wenches' brought about a technical fix in the late eighteenth century. The wire bell pull was developed as a technological solution so that servants might live at a distance from their employers but nevertheless be summoned for help when necessary, without too much delay. Architectural solutions such as servants' staircases also provided differentiated circulation routes around the house. The period of separation was upon the British home so that masters and servants came to live apart, children and parents began to live in separate spaces and eventually so did husbands and wives. The closed door came to predominate in aristocratic places where the open vista of the *enfilade*[2] plan had previously been found. In the vertical plane, the ground floor was 'dedicated to hunters, hospitality, noise, dirt and business. The first floor ... was the storey dedicated to taste, expense, state and parade' (quoted in Cruickshank 1992: 83). This history so far then is the story of a developing separation and enclosure. In *1984* Orwell describes Winston Smith's nostalgia for the pre-Big Brother world where,

> It seemed to him that he knew exactly what it felt like to sit in a room like this, in an armchair beside an open fire with your feet on the fender and a kettle on the hob; utterly alone, utterly secure, with nobody watching you, no voice pursuing you, no sound except the singing of the kettle and the friendly ticking of the clock. (1948: 117)

Orwell's valorisation of this world of individualised privacy would have been shared by many post-war Britons. The organisation of domestic space has profound influence over the lived experience of space: whether it is experienced as isolating or communal, multi-functional or task-specific, expressive of hierarchical or egalitarian relations.

The space of the house, therefore, became more divided and delineated within itself. It also became more separate and isolated as solely the place of family life, divided from production – although this distinction has often been more ideological than factual. In crossing the boundaries and making the connections between the spheres of production, reproduction and consumption, we need to extend beyond the dichotomy of 'home' and 'work', and consider the multiple threads of organisation that come to make up these spaces. Thus we turn to the 'neighbourhood' as a hybrid spatial form that gives some indication as to boundaries and connections. Houses are not isolated pockets, despite the emphasis on privacy illustrated in the sentiment that 'the Englishman's [sic] home is his castle'. Houses are part of complex social, spatial and inter-organisational networks.

In *Redesigning the American Dream* (2002), Hayden compares two new towns built in the USA in the 1940s. Vanport City, Oregon, otherwise known as 'Kaiserville' after its industrialist owner, was built in 1943. It was wartime and demand for the products of its shipyards was at its height, but traditional male labour for the engineering business, as well as building materials and energy resources were scarce. The town was built to house the necessary labour, and considerable thought was given as to how best to achieve the spatial structures required for the 40,000 people of diverse ethnic and social groups who would populate it. Female labour in particular had to be sought: the image of Rosie the Riveter, filling the shoes of male workers in the national time of need, was to the fore. However, through the design of the town the accommodation of women went far further than just advertising for recruiting and training them. The integrated design provided schools and nurseries (and their staff), and moreover placed the affordable housing close to these facilities, with the explicit aim that parents did not have to deal with long journeys to childcare at the beginning and end of their working day. To achieve the easiest routes for making journeys to the different places of this community life, the roads were straight. Integrated public transport was also provided. The six large nurseries were open for 24 hours a day, seven days a week, to cover the continuous shift patterns of the shipyards. Childcare was affordable for normal working parents, rather than the expensive luxury it predominantly was at this time. The nurseries even included healthcare services, bathing facilities and catering services, so that parents were aided in these other aspects of their domestic life too. This was not a homogeneous community though, and a variety of housing was designed to meet the needs of diverse living arrangements: for single people, single-parent families, and non-family groups as well as the nuclear family.

The second new town that Hayden describes is Levittown, Long Island, designed for 75,000 people. Its first houses went up for sale in March 1949 and $11 million worth of them were sold in three and half hours. Here all the houses were identical, each 'designed to be a self-contained world' (2002: 21). The curves of the roads, leading to more of the same, were the only feature to break up the replication. The interior of the house was built for the stereotypical family of working male, housewife and children, with built-in televisions and washing machines. Neither energy conservation nor low maintenance were design issues, since the image was of the 'haven strategy' for housing where homes were 'retreats for male workers and workplaces for their wives' (p. 24). This 'Cape Cod' model house became a famous success. The community was not integrated, but a privatised residential suburbia. The houses were not close to employment opportunities or social facilities. It was homogeneous in terms of race and class. Levitt claimed he was not prejudiced, merely concerned with business, when he stated, 'I have come to know that if we sell one house to a Negro family, then 90–95 percent of our white customers will not buy into the community' (p. 23). Mortgages were also not available to single mothers. This reflects the same processes in the organisation of social and spatial exclusions and inclusions that were at work in the Baltimore housing market (Harvey 1983) described in the previous chapter, down to Levitt's declaration that 'no man who owns his own house and lot can be a Communist. He has too much to do' (Hayden 2002: 23).

This was the beginning of the heyday of mass-produced standardised housing, placed in neighbourhoods to match. 'Kaiserville' was dismantled

BOUNDARY CROSSINGS: REPRODUCING ORGANISED SPACE • BUILDING A SOCIAL MATERIALITY: SPATIAL AND EMBODIED
POLITICS IN ORGANISATION • ALTERNATIVE SPACES: THE RADICAL ORGANISATION OF SPACE? • CONCLUSIONS: DISORGANISING SPACE

5   181

whilst Levittown and the suburban detached house designed for the nuclear family became the standard model for government subsidised housing schemes for the next 60 years. Replicant 'Levittowns' were constructed in Pennsylvania (1952), New Jersey (1955) and Puerto Rico (1965). Levitt built his suburban towns on the same basis as the assembly line. The design of the house was simplified so that load-bearing walls were all lined up and door and window sizes were standardised. Each operation was broken down into its constituent tasks, and then workers would carry out the same task on each house in a lot, being paid on a piecework basis (Eichler 1982). The effects of the political economy, expressed through the institution of the large corporation, upon the home are obvious. This is precisely where the 'industrial strategy' for housing production (Hayden 2002) comes to the fore. The success of these residential suburbs, of course, relies on the domination of the motor car and the proliferation of roads that was developed to accommodate it: this is the Fordist domination of space we discussed in the previous chapter. The Highway Acts of 1944 and 1956 were designed to connect all metropolitan areas with a network of 'freeways'. This was 90 per cent funded by the US government and 10 per cent by state governments (mainly from petrol taxes). The Acts had made millions of acres of suburban land available and accessible: a prime resource for new building projects (Eichler 1982).

The spatial production of the 'American Dream' was a land built by developers who act through organisations using the industrial model, and this production of social space led to particular social consequences. People flocked to Levitt's houses: they were cheaply priced with low down payments, so they were widely accessible to workers who could not afford more traditional housing, and they appealed to those same workers' dreams of owning their own homes. Although so identical that stories circulated about how new owners had to telephone for directions to their own houses, Gorringe (2002: 102–3) comments that this critique contains the taint of class snobbery. Their design echoed traditional colonial housing, and thus Levitt's houses had much more immediate appeal, for example, than the rented 'housing project' appearance of Kaiserville.

However, the standardised model could not provide for social change, and the ideology of the ideal home became a barrier to the production of more appropriate social spaces:

> Single-family houses have been getting larger and larger in each decade since World War II. Yet households have been getting smaller. Married-couple families with children under 18 constitute less than a quarter of all households in 2000, and most of these were two-earner families. Almost a third of all households consisted of one person living alone. (Hayden 2002: 29)

Suburban residential areas make it even more difficult for these diverse residents to commute to employment and find social support facilities.

The clean-living suburban community appearance also hid severe prejudices. When one black couple bought a house in Levittown, Pennsylvania in 1957, they received racist abuse, bomb threats and stones thrown at them. In 1963, Levitt's 'all-white' policy led to civil rights demonstrations at one of the company's subdivisions in Maryland.

Even within the interior of the ideology and the space of the suburban home, the consequences of the gendered domination of space were felt. These consequences were described by Betty Friedan as 'the problem with no name':

> Each suburban wife struggled with it alone. As she made the beds, shopped for groceries, matched slipcover material, ate peanut butter sandwiches with her children, chauffered Cub Scouts and Brownies, lay beside her husband at night – she was afraid to ask even the silent question – 'Is this all?'. (1963: 11)

It was a picture that was to be explicitly connected to Levittown when Gans (1967) wrote of the listlessness and boredom shared by the women who were tied to their isolated homes.

Thus the home has become differentiated, individualised and isolated in terms of being a lived and perceived space. Yet as a conceived space it is an increasingly open and transparent one, as we have started to see in relation to state and corporate organisations. So we turn now to explore further the role of organisations and inter-organisational networks in the constitution of the domestic sphere. The most significant opening-up of the home to organisation occurs through the process of consumption, although of course this constitutes the production sphere for the organisations who seek to reconstitute the space of the home and is part of the process of reproduction for those who inhabit the home. In this way the supposedly separated spheres of capitalism are closely intertwined.

In earlier times, it may have been only the aristocracy who had access to the services of architects and interior designers, and whose homes were subject to the requirements of following fashion and the dictates of 'taste', but the growth of mass production and the needs of mass consumption to some extent democratised, certainly accelerated, these impulses, opening up the organisation of domestic space to more and more mediation by the space of the organisation. A multitude of magazines, television programmes and experts combine to produce a set of discourses about the home as an expression of identity, and thus the need to spend time, energy and money on it.

However, the construction of the home through an ideal blueprint of consumption goes much deeper into its material production than just 'changing rooms'.[3] The modern family home is meshed in a web of interventions by the state and its agencies, developers and builders, public utilities and private corporations. Property developers have obviously been central. Although they would maintain that they were reflective of fashion, large building firms create markets as well as responding to them. Rivers demonstrates these interconnections in the typical house originating in the 1930s boom in British housing. These were predominantly semi-detached, with three bedrooms one of which was a 'box', a bathroom, and with a garage designed to fit an Austin 5. They were placed in 'suburbia', often a long way from railway or public transport connections. The use of the garaged car was thereby greatly encouraged. The kitchen was generally designed to be large enough to house the consumer durables pouring into homes. To accommodate the increasing influx of consumer goods into the house through the 1960s and 1970s, walls came down to produce larger 'open-plan' spaces (1992: 29–30). In expensive houses, very large picture windows appeared and even some copper chimneyless flues rose above a centrally placed fire. Central heating and fitted carpets also arrived, as did staircases in the middle of rooms. The developers now assaulted clientele with 'aesthetics management' so that by 1990 a complex semiology was available to those selling property. Rivers (1992: 36) does an analysis of Britain's best-selling type of house in the early 1990s, 'the Cunningham' (Barratt Homes), and concludes that, because of its drawing upon diverse cultural and historical cues to make itself into a sales pitch: 'If the history of architecture were copyrightable this house would be arrested for plagiarism'.

As well as the developers, governments have had a hand in constructing the home around consumption norms. In 1922 Herbert Hoover,[4] the then Secretary of Commerce in the US, set up the organisation 'Better Homes in America'. This comprised manufacturers, real estate owners, bankers and advertisers and had thousands of 'chapters' all over America. Its aim was to sell domestic products, mainly electrical, to the post-war country. A decade later, in the face of the Depression, the now President Hoover set up a Commission which later became the New Deal. A key part of this was to popularise homeownership, through the construction of single-family dwellings. In this he appealed to the ideology of the home-as-haven, but only where this was the privately owned home: 'Those immortal ballads, Home Sweet Home, My Old Kentucky Home and The Little Gray Home in the West were not written about tenements or apartments.... They never sing songs about a pile of rent receipts' (quoted in Hayden 2002: 33). Simultaneously, Hoover promulgated national schemes for cheap and plentiful electricity production, as in the Tennessee Valley Authority (TVA) experiment discussed in Chapter 4, with the objective that this would be eagerly bought by homeowners to run the ever-growing number of consumer appliances. The Commission popularised the idea of cooking in the private space of the home using electricity produced by such public utility organisations as the TVA, which was in the face of collective, solid-fuel cooking then typical of many American working-class families. Its membership included Mrs Lillian Gilbreth, who with her husband Frank was a pioneer in the field of industrial efficiency, especially time and motion study, and who was to revolutionise the kitchen, as we shall see later. It was thus a Commission charged with developing demand for the services of the large public utilities whose creation Hoover had sanctioned in a national attempt to use Keynesian notions of how to achieve economic recovery.

Therefore, gas, water and electricity companies, whether public or private, also came to play key roles in the construction of private space. The taken for grantedness of these services constitutes 'a knowing without knowing' built into the very fabric of the home and into the *habitus* of those who live through the space. Access for monitoring of consumption, safety of usage, ease of reach to their services offered by the home and so on have all affected the shape of where and how we live. Thus it is useful to examine the organisation of space produced through the wide-scale provision of these infrastructures. By 'infrastructure' we also mean the ways in which the material, physical constitution of the home presupposes certain sorts of social relationships presented discursively as the ideal family, home, neighbourhood and community. Such ideational aspects of interpretation and construction come to influence how space is and should be used (Attfield and Kirkham 1995) in a very material sense. The access to private homes offered to the utility companies in the UK is superior to that of the police and only marginally less than that granted to customs officers. In 1812, the London Gas Light and Coke Company was chartered and there were many British cities that had similar corporations as the century moved on, but progress in developing the technologies for use in the home was slow. A gas geyser for heating water was on sale in the late 1850s but lethal explosions were a regular event. Technical fixes were sought. By the late 1880s, recognisable competition in the gas and electricity sectors was becoming well developed in the UK. The Electrical Association for Women, founded in 1924, did sterling work in selling power to the people in the tradition of a 'Mrs Lancaster' who could say in 1914 that electricity 'never wants a day off, never answers back, is never laid up, never asks for a rise' (quoted in Darley 1992: 127). In other words, electrical power was the ideal servant!

In the United States, the process of reconstituting the home as a vehicle for the consumption of energy was transformed by the work of the English-born and aptly named Samuel Insull. Insull worked for Thomas Edison, and his aim was to make America fit for the Edison Company and then its successor, General Electric (GE). And this was to be done by mimicking the gas companies. According to Platt (1991: 13) in *The Electric City* 'gaslight was the first form of energy that was delivered directly and automatically into building interiors' but its take up was limited. Insull, however, wished to penetrate every home. New routes into the homes were identified as were new routines that consumers might be encouraged to follow. In the 1890s he moved to Chicago which was a world centre of industrialisation. Insull believed this world was to be transformed by the encouragement of consumption. He began by offering attractive incentives to customers in Chicago to install electric service in their homes. Free wiring, reduced rates and other giveaways saw increased demand from the middle classes. He instituted sophisticated statistical analyses of consumption patterns over the day and the year. The Edison researchers found that electric lights were switched off for long parts of the waking dark hours and very few customers used all the relevant lights that could be switched on. But when visitors arrived, consumers appeared to switch on all their lights. Electricity consumption was a luxury good. It was also discovered that electric irons were becoming increasingly popular in the summer but not in the winter for flat irons were still used more in the colder months when the fire was lit. In 1912 about 17 per cent of Chicago homes had electricity within them. By 1918 it was closer to one-third. The encouragement of consumption in the home was close to being ubiquitous. In *The Ladies Home Journal* of 1918, an article called 'I am glad my Servant left' explained that now the maid had moved on, the woman was free to buy all sorts of exciting new electrical equipment like a vacuum cleaner, a dishwasher and a washing machine. Helpful books appeared around this time like *The Servantless House* of 1920. Forty (1986), however, argues that the replacement of the servant directly by technology was a myth of the advertisers but it does show nevertheless the construction (which was largely successful) of the desire for these household objects by 'Mrs Consumer' (Scanlon 1995) within the advertising sections of the mass media. Insull's gospel of unlimited consumption of electricity driven by the rise of household appliances (made by GE) only came to an end in the oil crisis of 1974 – and then only briefly. During the Depression, electricity consumption actually grew by 45 per cent, fuelled by radio listening and the growth in use of refrigerators, both of which consumers refused to switch off.

People do not passively accept the organisation of (domestic) space. There is also the potential for tensions between the ideologies of privatisation and consumption. For example, developers at Harlow New Town in the UK designed large, 'picture windows' onto the street, as a vehicle for selling the smart modern houses. However, residents rejected this construction, covering them with net curtains to take back control of their privacy and maintain a clear boundary between private and public (Morley 2000: 62–3). Le Corbusier was also to see himself as engaged in a symbolic battle with the housewife. He was opposed to the 'sentimental hysteria surrounding the cult of the home', which distracted architects from designing 'healthy and virile, active and useful' machines for living in. 'The knick knacks on the shelves, the anti-macassars on the armchairs, the filmy curtains on the windows, the screen before the fireplace' were quite opposed to the modernist aesthetic of openness and transparency (Le Corbusier quoted in Morley 2000: 61).

In contrast to the mass-produced houses and their desiring-spaces of mass consumption is Buckminster Fuller's revolutionary Dymaxion House of the 1930s. He came close to rethinking every part of the house with efficiency as the ultimate goal. It was to be a mass-produced house, using factory methods particularly drawn from the car industry, with the purpose of reducing all drudgery. But within its structure it sliced apart mass production from its necessary other, mass consumption. The Dymaxion House used very little water, recycling all it needed through an atomiser. Laundry was automatically washed, dried, ironed and placed in storage units. There were no walls, only air filled mattresses for bedding and movable storage units. It hung from a mast which held its utility core and was supported from guy ropes. It was never built – perhaps because it was seen as a 'house without feeling'. Architectural commentators such as Lampugnani (1988: 112) describe the Dymaxion as not 'an object for aesthetic contemplation but is more correctly viewed as an assemblage of mechanical services in conjunction with living areas'. The real problem with the Dymaxion, however, may well have been that because it was environmentally aware, it did not consume enough. The Keynesianism inherent in much thinking in the 1930s emphasised consumption as the way to increasing production, and thus escape from economic difficulties.

However, what we mostly see is the increased privatisation and individualism going hand in hand with the increase in domestic consumption. Ross notes that 'privatisation, or losing oneself in the repetitions and routines of "keeping house", meant an increasing density in individual use of commodities and a notable impoverishment of interpersonal relations' (1996: 108). Thus this privatisation can be seen to indicate a widespread change in social space, with

> the withdrawal of the new middle classes to their newly comfortable domestic interiors, to the electric kitchen, to the enclosure of private automobiles, to the interior of a new vision of conjugality and an ideology of happiness built around the new unit of

> middle class consumption, the couple, and to depoliticization as a response to the increase in bureaucratic control of everyday life. (1996: 11)

Pawley perhaps goes even further in linking the confluence between the domestic sphere and consumption with social atomisation and dysfunction:

> " do we all secretly want to live alone? .... One hundred and fifty years ago the average Victorian household numbered 5.8 persons; the average household today comprises 2.1. Soon it will dip below 1.9 and we shall begin to understand the true anti-social purpose of all the labour-saving technology with which we have filled our houses and our lives. We shall begin to suspect the hidden agenda of the car that frees us from public transport only to tie us up alone in traffic jams; the meaning of the super-market that saves us from having to cook; the washer-dryer that frees us from the laundrette.... (1992: 150–1)

The 'social destination of all consumer durables', he argues, is to offer 'a level of privacy and isolation that previous generations would have considered pathological'. In the final section of this chapter, we examine one particular domestic space whose vicissitudes demonstrate the conflicts and contradictions in the production of a social space where reproduction, production and consumption meet: the kitchen.

The battle for the kitchen, or the meeting place of reproduction, production and consumption

The kitchen is frequently asserted as 'the heart of the home' in a way that places it as a collective and emotional focal space. We argue here that it is also the heart of a social space that brings together reproduction, consumption and production. As we write, there is an impetus in new house building and renovations towards an enlarged kitchen that incorporates dining and sitting areas ('family rooms'). Indeed, this is a form of open-plan living we ourselves have adopted in reshaping our 1930s house, and it does constitute the place where the family spends most of its time together. However, this ideal must be thwarted in much of the housing stock in the UK by the relatively small, bounded kitchens that characterise the majority of house developers' designs over the last century. Thus the *idea* of the kitchen, as an 'imaginary space', must be as powerful as its actual physical construction. Even so, the actual physical aspect of the kitchen is very big business; indeed many estate agents would claim that it is a kitchen that sells a house. Freeman (2004: 55) calculates spending on kitchen furniture in the UK ran at over one and a half billion pounds a year in 2000. This did not include appliances or floors or tiles. Of the sample of 74 kitchen buyers that comprises her research, the lowest spend on a kitchen was £800, the highest £30,000. Even this does not hit the current top end of the UK market, where a kitchen from designer Jonny Grey, for example, might average £60,000. A number of magazines are devoted to the planning and selling of kitchens (for example, in the UK, *25 Beautiful Kitchens*; *Kitchens, Bathrooms and Bedrooms*). In a multitude of ways the kitchen is a significant social space.

The kitchen has been the site where social and cultural changes have become material and spatial over a long historical period. It is also a key site of the economics of household production and consumption on an ongoing basis. Today there is a tendency to take these social and economic characteristics of the kitchen for granted, as if they are somehow natural. However, by looking at some of the developments that have taken place in the construction of this space, it is possible to see how it relates to broader aspects of the social organisation of space. Darley (1992: 108–9) suggests that the medieval kitchen of monasteries or large houses was set apart from the rest of the house because of fear of fire, and that it was most likely to be staffed by men due to the heavy jobs such as preparing animal carcasses and carrying water and wood over large distances. In comparison, in smaller dwellings, probably until Victorian times, cooking did not take place in a separate room, but over the hearth. There would also often be a communal village oven or bakery (p. 111). Laundry, too, was a collective activity, taking place in washhouses, or even by a stream or well. In Glucksmann's oral history of women workers in Lancashire between the wars, interviewees give a vivid picture of the communal use of the wash-house, and how this transcended separated spaces and times for housework and leisure:

> Mind you if I say I was with Annie, we used to go in the bath and one would watch the washing because they used to nick it if you didn't watch it. And you watched my washing while I'd go and have a bath and we used to watch their washing while they went to have a bath. (2000: 59–60)[5]

Thus the kitchen as a site of predominantly women's labour, carried out individually and privately in the home, is a relatively recent construction.

Within the context of this privatisation, one of the major influences on the modern kitchen was 'scientific management', thus entering the kitchen from the realm of production. There had been earlier advocates of the rationalisation[6] of housework in the shape of the American Charlotte Beecher, who saw good kitchen organisation as being an expression of religious and moral duty, and Isabella Beeton in the UK. The latter's household management included costed recipes, instructions for cleaning including formulas for cleaning solutions and cleaning schedules, all based on a model of the well-managed kitchen for the bourgeoisie, with appropriate segregation and hierarchy. The demographics of who lives in house are crucial of course. Mrs Beeton thought that at the top of the social scale a complement of 12 male and 13 female servants in each household was the norm. At the lower end of her continuum, the mistress and master of the house could probably not afford a 'man' at all but would have to do with three maids. To some extent, this also shows how under capitalist employment conditions where the norm is that male wages are higher, housework became a more feminised occupation. However, it is not until the effects of the industrial efficiency movement were felt in the private domestic sphere, via the work of Christine Frederick and Lillian Gilbreth, that the shaping of the modern kitchen as a particular social space is seen.

Christine Frederick (1883–1970) was effectively a frustrated housewife who managed to reinvent herself as a writer and consultant through her application to the home of the industrial efficiency methods she heard about from her businessman husband, an executive in the nascent advertising industry. Hearing how 'scientific management' was transforming industry, she decided to apply it to reducing the time and waste involved in housework. With enormous energy and enthusiasm she subjected even the smallest chores to time and motion studies, photography and detailed analysis. Frederick advocated a reorganisation of the physical space of the kitchen to achieve this efficiency through the correct height of furniture, correct lighting and the correct tools in the space available and by minimising the number of steps to be taken in that space by how it was ordered (1919). She achieved a huge influence through her articles in *The Ladies Home Journal* and her book had a preface written by Frank Gilbreth. His partner, Lillian Gilbreth (1927), who we have mentioned in relation to Hoover's 'Better Homes' Commission, also argued that time and motion studies of the kitchen, which she undertook for the first time, showed how efficiency might be dramatically improved. Together these writers promoted a vision of housework which was centred on the drive to standardise around the same homogenised routine in the same spatially organised and well-routed workspace by the same worker inhabiting the same standardised body. The 'One Best Way' was to triumph. This is just as clearly still the case, as demonstrated by a myriad articles in contemporary magazines devoted to the kitchen which still advocate the reduction of unnecessary steps through planning the kitchen around 'the work triangle'.

The 'work triangle' as dominant leitmotiv of efficiency had to be created and defended. Today the specific configuration of the triangle has been questioned because new technology means there are more than three focal points to kitchen tasks, but the underpinning principle of efficiency based on layout of space and technology is so well entrenched that it is perceived to be a self-evident truth. Spatial practices create routinised social arrangements which become habituated, and vice versa. The impetus to reduce unnecessary steps is made on the assumption that there is one worker who traverses between the three elements of work, sink-cooker-work area. In Germany, efficient kitchen design was taken further by the architect Grete Lihotsky, influenced by Frederick. Using a time and motion study she defined the optimum size of a kitchen as 1.9 x 3.44 m. This only allowed one person at a time to be working in the kitchen. Lihotsky's classic 'Frankfurt Kitchen' moves the design much closer to the modern 'fitted kitchen'. Even Frederick and Gilbreth had still been working with the traditional discrete pieces of furniture. Lihotsky's designs heralded the 'continuous kitchen' with continuous worksurfaces of the same height and banks of cupboards above and below these surfaces. Between 1926 and 1930, Lihotsky's kitchens were installed in 10,000 housing project flats (Freeman 2004: 41). In 1989 when she was 92, Lihotsky commented that she had designed the kitchens for women who worked, to minimise their household chores. In many ways this is a much more liberal approach than that of Frederick and Gilbreth, who aimed to professionalise housewives to give them pride in their allotted role in the domestic sphere. Indeed, Freeman (p. 100) argues that because Christine Frederick was 'politically super-ficial, her ideas were vulnerable to conservative appropriation'. Thus they became used as part of a campaign to limit women's opportuni-ties for paid employment in favour of stressing that their role was in the domestic sphere. However, Freeman also discerns a middle-class bias in Lihotsky's assumptions that is demonstrated in the cost of the basic equipment that these kitchens required for their efficient functioning (p. 100).

The enduring outcome of these spatial arrangements that are derived from production models is the isolated domestic labourer. The separation of the kitchen and its reduced accessibility to family members can be on the basis of size of area made available for it. The implication is that only one person is able to be in the cooking area at any one time. So, the development of the 'galley kitchen' was to individualise and personalise tight physical space on the assumed efficiency for the lone housewife who must shoulder the role and responsibility for domestic work.[7] Cowan (1979: 59) shows how these spatial arrangements transform the social and economic landscape: 'Several million American women cook supper each night in several million separate homes over several million separate stoves'. So the battle has been lost and efficiency standards are the dominant rhetoric behind contemporary kitchen designs. And once this battle with the home-dweller has been won then the reconstituted 'home', now often privately owned (by the mortgage lender!), becomes a place as well as a space fit for capitalism to exploit.

As well as ideas and methods from production, the modern kitchen is thoroughly infused with an ethos of consumption, and its increased privatisation has massively extended it as a potential market. Glucks-mann's study of women workers in the interwar period makes very clear the interconnections between the changes in production, reproduction and consumption:

> " Putting it crudely, working-class women were the producers and middle-class women the main consumers of most of the new goods. But even these empirical facts were connected in a complex spiral of links: one of the reasons why middle-class women became the main consumers was because they could not find domestic servants and so bought domestic appliances and processed food instead of paying servants to do the work involved; domestic servants were no longer available precisely because young working-class women much preferred working in factories to being domestic servants and avoided such work whenever they could. Consequently, those very women who might have gone into service in an earlier period now worked in assembly industries making the goods which middle-class women bought to aid domestic labour because they could no longer get servants. And quite apart from this chain of connected developments, and in addition to it, the higher wages which working-class women earned in factory work enabled them too to ease the burden of their domestic labour in the home by purchasing some of the new labour saving goods. Domestic labour was thus undergoing enormous changes in both middle- and working-class households. (1990: 228–9)

The type of consumer goods available to both classes included ready-made food and off-the-shelf clothes, which reduced time spent in food preparation, sewing and laundering considerably. The cost of the growing number and variety of domestic appliances, though, meant that they were only initially available to the higher earning middle-class families, but become significant 'objects of desire' that women from all classes were willing to save up for. Of course, this was not all a straightforward linear process. There was sometimes considerable suspicion and resistance to newfangled technologies, and often a continued belief that the tasks would not and could not be done so well by machine as by hand (Horsfield 1997: 134). In addition, although the technologies could in theory reduce the time spent on household tasks, often they did not, either because they brought along new needs of their own or because women increased the frequency with which they cleaned or laundered. Cowan (1983) points out that the one key thing that domestic appliances enabled was that the work could be done by one isolated individual alone in a house. This certainly indicates how the domestic space has been constructed around the centrality of consumption demands.

The consumption of new technologies continues to proliferate in the big business of kitchen design. Recent developments involve the networking of these technologies throughout the home and to the wider information and communication technologies of the Internet. For example, the Whirlpool 'web tablet', which works like a fridge magnet but allows 'smart' technology to control the maintenance of the home, uses 'always on' Broadband connection. Through the web tablet there is instant access to a myriad of networked appliances. Access is provided to what we might describe as 'management information' for the home: new recipes, best forms of stain removal, a shopping list that tells you what is running low inside and so on. It also forms a centralised means of managing actual tasks at a distance. It can be used for preheating the oven: 'Cooking need not confine you to the kitchen' because it can be programmed from other parts of the house. It has an interactive calendar, address book, lists. Connects to mobile phones, work PC, detects gas leaks and electricity cuts, alerts you to intruders' (*Smart Homes*, 2000: 87). Whilst the high-tech fridge proliferates, 'the empty fridge' is an imported metonym from the United States. It signifies that the kitchen is not a place for food preparation, because eating out is commonplace. About half of all US meals are eaten outside the home today and the proportion is growing rapidly. Thus the material space (as indicated through expensive kitchen design and appliances) and the social space (as indicated by its use) are often dissociated, the physical space of the kitchen becoming more of a status symbol through its presentation of a possible lifestyle and conspicuous consumption.

In the early twentieth century, the drive for domestic efficiency was thoroughly imbued with this ethos of consumption from the first. This centred on the creation of 'Mrs Consumer' (Hayden 1981; Scanlon 1995), who was trained to consume new technology, new kitchen furniture and products. Christine Frederick's book of 1929 entitled 'Selling Mrs Consumer' was a landmark in this commercialisation, for she argued for the segmentation of the market and the use of images, not text, in selling products to women (Gottdiener 1997: 61). Idealised images of lifestyle are what Frederick thought would sell best, and she was very successful through this. Frederick was enamoured of 'consumptionism', and advocated the industrial strategy of 'progressive obsolescence' (Horsfield 1997: 148). Hayden (1981) comments that 'housing units did not imply shelter to her but rather endless possibilities for sales'. Frederick was rather good at selling herself, too, becoming a 'consultant' who endorsed the products of a number of companies. Rutherford points to the ambiguity in her position, in that 'As an expert on the home, Frederick encouraged advertisers and manufacturers to appeal to women as homemakers. Disingenuously representing herself as a typical housewife, she appeared to remain in the domestic sphere while working in the public one' (2000). Lillian Gilbreth's work also transcended the production–consumption spheres. Her first foray into kitchen design was sponsored by the Brooklyn Gas Company. She found it straightforward to use time and motion concepts to rearrange the kitchen to be more efficient, but found that appliances were not designed to help efficiency. The involvement of Gilbreth and others provided a feedback into the manufacturing process, through which ultimately, of course, women consumers would therefore stimulate sales of better-designed products (Freeman 2004: 33).

An important part of this combined drive for more efficient production and greater consumption in the kitchen was the reconstitution of the imaginary space of the kitchen and the role of the housewife within it. Frederick and Gilbreth promoted the kitchen as the workplace of the professionalised housewife, which Gottdiener argues was instrumental in creating a new sensibility for exploitation (1997: 67). The kitchen was raised to a higher status by the evocation of science and technology. Tarbell in 1913 said,

> Housekeeping is a many sided business calling for training in theory and practice for scientific management. It needs as varied qualities as any business known to human beings, and yet as things are now girls and women are getting only the most superficial and artificial training in it. It needs to be formulated and professionalised and every working girl rich or poor should be taught at least its principles: at the same time she should be taught its relation to all economic and social problems and in particular to the cost of living. (Tarbell 1913)

Additionally, housework became ideologically constructed as pleasurable (especially as aided by exciting new technologies), meaningful and socially worthwhile (Glucksmann 1990: 238). As Cowan says,

> Laundering had once been just laundering; now it was an expression of love.... Feeding the family had once been just feeding the family; now it was a way to communicate deep-seated emotions.... Diapering was no longer just diapering, but a time to build the baby's sense of security; cleaning the bathroom sink was not just cleaning, but an exercise for the maternal instincts, protecting the family from disease. (1976: 151)

Thus far in this chapter we have considered the involvement of organisational forces within the construction, both material and symbolic, of the home. This has suggested an increasing attempt to commodify and privatise the home and to stave off economic depression through the encouragement of consumption within the home. Whilst privatisation might mean a thousand people every night in a village each need a cooker whereas a few large ones might do, it was precisely for this reason that some saw the importance of maintaining communal facilities which the collective might share.

In order to understand just how taken-for-granted is the social space of the modern kitchen, we end this section by looking at the Material Feminists, and the attempts of them and others to revolutionise social and gender relations by transforming the key spaces in which these relations were acted out. Material Feminists were active between the American Civil War and the Great Depression. They advocated payment for housework and proposed 'a complete transformation of the spatial design and material culture of American homes, neighborhoods, and cities' (Hayden 1981: 5). They challenged industrial capitalism through contesting 'the physical separation of household space from public space'. To do this 'they developed new forms of neighborhood organisations... new building types, including the kitchen-less house and the day care center' (1981: 5). Similarly, for social reformers in Victorian times in the UK, the kitchen-less house had been very attractive. A co-operative home for professional ladies in London was announced in 1874 and it was designed around a communal dining room. The wife of Ebenezer Howard, 'father' of the Garden City movement, was treated to a kitchenless flat in Letchworth, where his ideas found fruition. Of course, this often meant that it was communal servants who were actually undertaking the cooking duties for the young professional women: changing gender relations did not necessarily translate to class.

Some similar alternatives to privatised domestic spaces also emerged from a different quarter in the 1850s with the rise of industrialisation. Great efforts were made to design more healthy homes with a sound physical environment using more rational methods of construction. This was the great age of organisations and organising. It is the birthplace of what Hayden (2002: 88) calls the 'industrial strategy', best exemplified in the ideology of the socialist state in which the domestic sphere was abolished. It is well expressed, argues Hayden (p. 89), in the ideas of the Marxist writer August Bebel whose 'spatial container for this interchangeable, industrial nurturing was to be the apartment house composed of industrial components and equipped with large mess halls, recreation clubs, child-care centers and kitchenless apartments'. This was a centralised approach to the domestic sphere. More recently, for 20 years in Denmark, the Co-Housing Movement has sought to develop shared communal facilities, whilst keeping sleeping accommodation private.

These experiments in communal kitchens and childcare failed and by the 1970s had been forgotten by the second wave of feminists. 'Wages for housework' were discussed, but the possibilities for spatial and material changes facilitating social and gender changes appears to have been lost. Sometimes this 'failure' is expressed as the result of the privatisation of the home, with the 'invasion' of white goods and scientific management into domestic space creating total exclusion zones for pre-existing communal ideas. The confirmation of the ideology of the nuclear family and its private space had been so successful that history appears to have forgotten the alternatives.

However, it is important not to forget that the eventual 'victory' of the private domestic kitchen, as we now understand it, over the communal kitchen and dining room, was achieved in the face of a plethora of alternatives. Hayden (1976, 1981) shows us a plurality of organising spaces that were neither 'public' nor 'private' because they were, and are, communal forms of organising. These are attempts to 'build better worlds' and it is often forgotten how these alternative ideologies about how society could be constructed based on neighbourliness were not just ideas and theories, but were also materially and spatially constructed. It is important to emphasise the diversity of these, because there are so many attempts to constrain and contain organisational options. The experiments of the Material Feminists are now often forgotten; the day-to-day reality of the municipal wash-houses is now lost, in architects' and designers' taken-for-granted assumptions about the construction of the nuclear family home (Hayden 2002).

Conclusions

The 'domestic' is an organised space greatly influenced by large business organisations. The home is a product of state and business interventions – in post code differentiation, in safety, utility provision, white goods' availability, advertising and 'lifestyle' encouragement. Analysis of the changing material and imaginary space of the kitchen makes clear that it is an ideological space, just as the home is. It can be conceptualised very widely indeed with all sorts of alternative modes of preparing food being theoretically possible. But the (physical *and* conceptual) closure of the kitchen to other forms of thinking and doing has not been achieved without huge social choices. Despite the predominance of male professional chefs in the media, the gendering of kitchens continues to press on unabated. Very few publications specifically for men mention the kitchen at all, whereas women's magazines are replete with relevant articles and advertisements. Other forces for conservatism are the identification of conventional house ownership with the widespread availability of mortgages. Try getting a standard 'home' mortgage for an unconventional spatial arrangement involving no kitchen and shared communal facilities.

The construction of the social and spatial worlds of Western capitalism as being separated into different spheres of the 'domestic' – (productive) work, and leisure and consumption – allows the fragmentation of which Bauman speaks in the quotation at the beginning of this chapter. This fragmentation allows these spaces to be more manageable, to be more open to the logic of capitalism. As we have seen in this chapter, the apparent separation of social spheres facilitates the greater integration of the circuit of capital through a confluence of reproduction, production and consumption, all of which are centred on the supposedly private and individualised space of the home. Ironically, the more this became distanced from wider social and spatial relations and bounded within itself, the more open it became to the 'abstract space' of capitalism.

In the final section of the book, we look in more detail at attempts to differently organise space, often cutting across connections and boundaries of the dominant and dominated social spaces of production, reproduction and consumption. In the following chapter we consider an alternative theoretical approach to understanding organised space through the lens of 'social materiality' and then we move on from that to look at the diversity of possible alternative 'spaces of organisation' and 'organisation of space'.

Notes

[1] Heidegger (1971), in the essay 'Building, Dwelling, Thinking', draws a very clear relationship between 'building' and 'gathering'.

[2] Rooms running into each other, providing an expansive vista through each grand space, rather than the use of corridors between rooms.

[3] The name of an incredibly popular and long-lasting television makeover programme in the UK. Teams had two days to decorate a room in their neighbours' house, while the same process was happening to a room in theirs. Both had the use of an interior design 'expert' who designed the makeover and provided the necessary materials. Given the limited time and resources involved, the transformations were purely cosmetic, but still involved the mass media production of current fashion and taste in homestyle, and normalised the idea that changes could and should be regularly and easily effected.

[4] Hoover himself had started as a mining engineer and was driven by the quest for efficiency. He headed the 'Waste in Industry' survey which blamed much of the extant inefficiency upon management and, as we have already pointed out, was Secretary for Commerce in the 1920s when he revolutionised the department in favour of corporate industry. It might be said, then, that Hoover was highly motivated to change the routes and routines of American industry, not necessarily an accepted idea at the time given there were also a number of militant workers groups who were avowedly anti-big business.

[5] The rise of the private bathroom, within the house and preferably located upstairs in the most private area, and thence the multiplication of bathrooms and en suites, indicate the growing importance in the labour attached to the aestheticisation of the body, as well as the increased privatisation of life. We would like to thank Karen Legge for this insight.

[6] Rationalisation is often associated with industrial mass production. However, rationalisation of the kitchen does not necessarily imply mass production, as this would suggest that large-scale factory-type communal kitchens would form the most efficient model. Yet within the circuit of capital as a whole rationalisation and mass production are intensely connected. If mass consumption is the necessary other of mass production, then the privatisation of the kitchen worked along with its rationalisation to further mass consumption, as will be seen later in this chapter.

[7] Based on the idea of the woman's control of the kitchen, Dennis Wrong (1968) wrote that the American home, like the American polity, was a pluralist structure of power, with the woman having control of the kitchen and the man control over financial resources. As has been subsequently pointed out (Burrell 1980; Giddens 1974), this formulation is based upon a much skewed notion of the relative power of each issue and how they interact.

Part III

Changing Spaces, Changing Organisation

BUILDING ORGANISATION: SECURING AND OBSCURING POWER • BUILDING PEOPLE: IDENTITIES AND SPACES • A POLITICAL ECONOMY OF ORGANISED SPACE • BOUNDARY CROSSINGS AND EMBODIED WORK • BUILDING A SOCIAL MATERIALITY: SPATIAL AND EMBODIED POLITICS IN ORGANISATION • ALTERNATIVE SPACES: THE RADICAL ORGANISATION OF SPACE? • CONCLUSIONS: DISORGANISING SPACE

6 building a social materiality: spatial and embodied politics in organisation

The emphasis on hypermobility, global communications and the neutralisation of place and distance in the mainstream account about economic globalisation needs to be balanced with a focus on the work behind command functions, on the actual production process in the leading information industries, finance and specialised services, and on global marketplaces. . . . We [need to] recover the material conditions, production sites and place boundedness.

(Sassen 2000: 168–9)

The whole of (social) space proceeds from the body, even though it so metamorphoses the body that it may forget it altogether . . .

(Lefebvre 1991: 405)

In the first part of this book we looked at the spaces of organisation. In the second part we considered the organisation of space. This final part is about changing spaces and changing organisation. In this chapter, we seek to explore the relevance of 'materiality' and 'embodiment' to understanding social organisational life and space. We do this in order to argue for a re-conceptualisation of organisation and social theory that takes seriously the recognition of human existence as irreducibly and simultaneously both 'social' and 'material'[1].

This chapter is organised into three sections. In the first, we look at why and how materiality and embodiment have been relatively neglected within social theory and organisation theory. Second, we examine the relevance of materiality and embodiment to a theory of the social production of space and a way of re-conceptualising them as part of the 'social'. From this, we move to a case study of the social and material production of one specific organisational space to try to bring together the threads of this argument.

The obscuring of materiality and the forgetting of the body

The relationship between materiality and organisations is one that is contested in recent accounts. On the one hand, processes of 'globalisation', along with new information and communication technologies, and the emphasis on organisational capabilities, brand and image, seem to indicate that organisations are no longer dependent on particular places nor material assets. Rather, so the argument goes, the world of electronic flows and intangible representations is much more central to organisational success. On the other hand, a corrective to this is the growing realisation that a growth in services, the culture industries and brand dominance in some areas of the economy still depends upon quite different material conditions of production, consumption and reproduction in other places (witness, for example, the reception of Klein's *No Logo*, (2001)). Some analyses do manage to avoid the pitfalls of both 'hype' and dichotomy. As mentioned earlier, Thrift (1996), provides a convincing account of how the very nature of global, technologically mediated finance capitalism simultaneously generates a greater need for specific meeting places, personal contacts and networks. In this, he shows the importance of *both* intangible flows *and* embodied experience, of the integration of social and material forces.

On the whole, the materiality of the world is only partially attended to within the social sciences. It could be argued that it constitutes an 'absent presence'. It is simultaneously taken for granted, but also regarded as incidental to the 'real' subject of social processes and interactions (Law and Hetherington 2000: 52). This marginalisation arises partly because the development of disciplinary boundaries separates out the subject matter of the world for different areas of study. The direct study of the material world is thus seen as the province of the 'natural' or 'physical' sciences. This indicates the prevailing tendency to see materiality as constituted by natural objects, mere matter. These can then become the object of knowledge by the active mind. In other words, the relative lack of attention to materiality in the social sciences is related to the prevalent influence of Cartesian dualistic thinking, whereby the indwelling mind is privileged. The mind is seen as distinct from the materials of the world, including even that of the human body: the separation of *res cogito* (that which thinks) from *res extensa* (that which is matter) has crucial significance for the study of the material (Dale 2001; Williams and Bendelow 1998).

Thus, within the widespread Cartesian tradition, the material, the spatial and the embodied tend to be leached out of social research. For example, although ethnographic descriptions continue to include the material world as the context of organisational life, these then tend to be analysed through the lens of conceptual tools that focus on a predominantly ideational level: discourse, culture and identity. There are aspects of materiality inherent in each of these concepts, of course. Discourse is linked not only to linguistic forms but to various forms of actual texts; culture has multiple material elements, as shown in its roots within anthropology; and much in recent work on identity has pointed to the body as a tool of identity construction and presentation, along with the significance of consumption of goods and services in the formation of self. With some key exceptions, including work on organisational symbolism (such as Gagliardi 1990; Turner 1990) and work in the Actor-Network Theory tradition (such as Law 1994; Woolgar 1991), both of which we look at in subsequent sections, materiality does not tend to feature much in accounts of organisations. This withdrawal from the contemplation of material objects is a form of 'abstraction' which needs to be addressed here.

One example of the abstraction of the social and material can be seen in how social concepts are forcibly extracted from the material and embodied processes in which they are embedded in the process of theory-building. This is a process that has also been commented upon in studies of the production of scientific knowledge (e.g. Gilbert and Mulkay 1984; Latour and Woolgar 1979). Latour and Woolgar (1979), for example, see the end product of scientific research as the 'inscription device' of the published scientific paper, which conforms to a conventional form that excludes all references to the social, organisational and embodied processes within which the laboratory work is conducted. Within the social sciences, many ethnographically grounded studies do express an experience of organisation that allows the sensory and sensual side of organisational life to speak. There are a number of instances in academic accounts where the inclusion of the phenomenological body provides insights that would be difficult to convey in a more abstract form. For example, Zuboff's (1988) ethnographically based accounts of the transition from physically based skills to intellective skills at a pulp and paper mill and her description of the workers physically prising apart the electronically controlled doors, conveys the embodied negotiation of this change much more powerfully than abstracted conceptualisation. However, her work is often reduced, through abstraction, to the concept of the 'information panopticon' and its possibilities of 'informating' compared to 'automating'. The changing embodied *habitus* of the workers which Zuboff describes is lost within a conceptualisation that draws instead on a Cartesian tradition of knowledge as rational and intentional. Theory-building frequently operates in this way, by abstracting 'social' constructs and ignoring a wider social-material embeddedness. This relates to another form of abstraction critiqued by Lefebvre (1991) where research treats space as an empty container that has no relevance to the social interactions that merely take place within it. In this move of separation, the material becomes taken for granted and thus effectively invisible to social science.

Before attempting to build a conceptualisation of 'social materiality', we will briefly consider three approaches to organisational studies that have taken materiality seriously. Labour process theory has a long history of shedding light on the multiple processes of power and resistance in the workplace (e.g. Jermier *et al.* 1994; Knights 1990; Thompson 1986). It is not surprising, given its marxist roots, that it has paid much more attention to the material conditions of production than most theoretical approaches to the study of organisations. In a recent contribution in this tradition (Thompson and Warhurst 1998), the physical environment of the labour process is studied directly in a chapter by Baldry *et al.* on call centre buildings. They explicitly argue for 'the reincorporation of the physical work environment into any analysis of the labour process' (1998: 163), and follow this through by examining how workers in three organisations experienced moving to new buildings. The findings focus on lack of control over the physical environment as a key aspect of discontent and discomfort. The types of job they study are data processing and other clerical tasks involving work mediated by the computer and telephone. The lack of control of the physical environment mirrors the lack of control in the jobs themselves, which centre around routinised and scripted tasks combined with intensification and a high level of monitoring. These organisations tap into certain aspects of new forms of control: they require flexibility from the workers (fragmented tasks have often been reintegrated), and this is reflected in the use of multi-functional teams, but these operate in such a way that Baldry *et al.* describe them as 'team Taylorism' (p. 168). The mutually reinforcing social and material conditions of the work are shown in the workers expressing their unhappiness with their material environment, and the lack of control is incorporated into their embodied experience, often through ill health. This is very much a physical environment explicitly alienated from the workers, designed by architects, designers and managers. In this account, the material is a physical extension of the 'them and us' conflictual control relations. Control here fits with the long-standing notion of spatial control as linked with territory where possession and power go together to create a material environment. There is no doubt that the material world can be experienced as powerfully alienating and alien: Sartre in *Nausea* expresses this existential sense of dissociation with the material particularly powerfully.

However, the labour process approach to the physicality of the workplace tends to fix it as yet another structure of control. This is akin to a long-standing perspective on matter that sees it as inert and passive, as opposed to that which is seen as the active and mobile. As we have already pointed out, this form of dichotomisation is closely related to the highly influential Cartesian split between mind and body, with the former as the agentic and the latter as passive, mere matter. Reincorporating the material within a labour process perspective, however laudable, seems to maintain this assumption of the material as something inert that can be manipulated by the action of those with social power, and that then becomes part of the structural conditions of organisational control for those who do not. This view, we would argue, limits appreciation of the less intentional and the more reciprocal elements of the ongoing social–material relationship. It also perpetuates the difficulty that labour process theory has had with subjectivity. Since the material is only treated as an external, objective reality, there is no space for understanding the embodied negotiation between self and materiality, as mutually constructed.

Another area of organisational analysis that has recognised the importance of the materiality of the workplace is organisational symbolism, perhaps best exemplified by the edited collections by Gagliardi (1990) and Turner (1990). In contrast to the labour process perspective, where the material is reduced to the physical, organisational symbolism constructs the material as fundamentally a vehicle for the expression of social, cultural and aesthetic values. In other words, the material comes merely to stand in for the social, its significance lying in what it communicates about the social relations going on around it, rather than for the activity and influence inherent in its very materiality and in the social interaction with it. Again, the relationship between social and material is portrayed as unidirectional, reinforcing the dichotomous separation of the two. It is on the perceptions of the subject rather than the materiality of the object that emphasis is placed. The active subject has to 'read off' the significance of passive objects in the context of the organisation and it is clear that the power of the 'reading' overshadows the power of that which is read. It is, however, possible for discourse to be more engaged with embodied, spatialised materiality. Foucault's work, for example, demonstrates very clearly the interaction of the social and the material, and his use of 'discourse' is not simply limited to language or text, as it is often presented by those commentators who would locate him in a poststructuralist box. Rather, as Braidotti puts it, 'what really interests Foucault is the materiality of ideas – the way that they exist in an in-between space caught in a network of material and symbolic conditions, between the text and history, between theory and practice, and never in any of these poles' (1994: 126).

A third theoretical approach that takes materiality seriously and has influenced organisational studies, although more associated with social studies of science and technology, is Actor-Network Theory (ANT). However, for us, ANT and ANT-inspired organisational research maintains an unremitting Cartesian dualism, whilst ostensibly arguing for a network of heterogeneous materials. It is clear from the language used that the human body is merely material, the same as other materials in the world. This is not a new approach but a re-emergence of Descartes' classic separation between mind and material. The human body is stripped of agency and fragmented into parts (Cooper 1993: 281–2; Lilley 1998: 92) in a way that echoes a long history of anatomisation as a means of creating knowledge (Dale 2001, 1997). In this process, the body as object is divided off from the social actor, the now disembodied mind, as exemplified below in the language used by Cooper: 'A major consequence of the body being able to represent itself in external artefacts is that the human agent can more easily control and modify the latter than it can its own body' (1993: 281). The social actor in ANT is in practice the same rational, intentioned *cogitas* of Descartes. Even where the very significance of materiality in interaction with the social is being argued, the tendency is to privilege abstractions such as texts, inscriptions and representations. A strange confusion can be unpicked from the language used, as with this statement of Callon: 'Our concern should be to read the many intermediaries that pass through our hands: to learn to read artefacts, texts, disciplined bodies, and cold money' (1991: 140). Here both 'our hands' and 'disciplined bodies' appear to be mere passive objects like money or artefacts; the active process must therefore be, it appears, a cognitive one of reading the (symbolic, representative not material) nature of these artefacts. Yet as social actors we do not sit passively as the world comes through our hands, and we do not only interact with the world through our eyes and brains but also our hands and the rest of our embodied beings create, remould, and are themselves shaped by the interaction we have with the social-and-material world. In the famous example often used by Latour (1992) of the automatic door closer, (sometimes called a 'groom') the view is expressed that the door closer prescribes a specific piece of behaviour. Here appears to be the point at which ANT envisages, indeed articulates, a role for the now active material world and that this article, in so doing, obviates our critique. But this beautifully balanced piece is a rare example in the ANT approach. As we have shown earlier, building in the activity of the material and the passivity of the human does not come easily to ANT and it is Latour alone, perhaps, who on occasion manages to achieve this. Dant argues that what ANT fails to do

> is to study closely the interaction or the lived relationship between human beings and material objects' and that 'it is noticeable that there are very few accounts of the perceptual or tactile interaction between humans and objects in the network, few detailed field observations, photographs or use of video to study the process of the network that would allow the material objects to have a presence in the accounts. (2005: 81)

Whilst it is recognised in a footnote that Latour has produced pictures of relevance in the Aramis project, Dant (2005: 81) proceeds to argue that it is the sociologist who is in control of the interaction and the play of interpretations and it is the reader who is kept at a safe distance from the lived workings of the network. So, while ANT may talk of the importance of heterogeneous materials, these materials themselves all too often remain curiously inert.

In the above section, we have tried to analyse the neglect of the material, embodied world in relation to organisational structures and processes and to suggest some of the dimensions on which this might be rethought. However, so far, the exercise has been limited to the 'add-in' variety: how might the material be brought back into an understanding of organisational life to provide a richer, deeper analysis? In the next section, we aim to go further than this in developing the concept of 'social materiality' – that the social and the material are mutually interacting and therefore not separable.

Building blocks: materiality, embodiment, space

We have seen earlier how the physical world, including material objects and even the human body, have been seen as not social, almost the opposite of social, in that they are just inert matter. But materiality is not simply things, 'the stuff of the world' (Law and Hetherington 2000: 52). Materiality is imbued with culture, language, imagination and memory; it cannot be reduced to mere object or objectivity. And, even further, it is not just that materiality has taken on social meanings, but that humans enact social agency through a materiality which simultaneously shapes the nature of that social agency. For humans are part of the material world, not transcendent gods or magicians able to manipulate the material without being incorporated or changed by it. Therefore, to examine the relevance of materiality to the production of organisational and social space, an approach to materiality is required that navigates between the Scylla of realist material determinism that presents the physical world as a natural given, and the Charybdis of a strong social constructionism that only recognises the social and cultural as meaningful. The very depiction of these twin hazards however indicates the tendency to separate out the 'material' and the 'social' (themselves not innocent terms) as mutually exclusive realms of analysis.

A useful starting point for this conceptualisation of social and material as entwined is the body of work within the field of 'material culture'. This work largely stems from an anthropological perspective, although Miller (1987: 110–1) describes how materiality even became marginalised within this discipline. Miller's work is important because he argues that material objects are constitutive, not simply a reflection, of social relations (p. 112). He demands that we recognise their 'active participation in a process of social self-creation in which they are directly constitutive of our understanding of ourselves and others' (p. 215). Miller also points to the diversity of the relationship between humans and objects (p. 115). Beyond their utility or even relatively straightforward symbolic value, objects have an ability to stand in for or mediate a variety of social relations through, for example, the reciprocity of the 'gift', fetishism, monetary exchange, commodification, performativity and incorporation into self-image.

The cognate notion, developed within archaeology, is of 'material engagement', a term derived from the debate between Hodder (1998) and Renfrew (2004) in particular. In this strand of theorising, the 'life histories of things' are asserted to have a social dimension and thence to take on the role of subjects. Things become parts of 'external symbolic storage systems' with which humans have to interact. In the attempt to avoid the 'insubstantial', the 'material' is given the status of an 'indissolvable reality of substance'. It is the substance which archaeologists have to confront in their excavations which perhaps encourages them to see these materials as permitting of a material engagement with the society that produced them. Studies of material culture also demonstrate how social relations are produced and reproduced on a very everyday, embedded level. Indeed, it is this level of triviality, of taken-for-grantedness, that makes the significance of materiality both hidden and powerful. Here is where the concept of **entanglement** comes in. In archaeology, there has been great concern to explain the very long time period between the rise of *Homo sapiens* and the development of a sedentary lifestyle with a modicum of technological development. The favoured response today appears to be that the everyday struggle for survival, with the need to find food, shelter, protection and social support entangles the tribal peoples in a material world of drudgery and inescapable commitment. The need to survive drives an unrelenting pressure to satisfy crucial material wants and that constraint admits of almost nothing else. Humans are 'entangled' unto death. As we pointed out in Chapter 4, it is only at a point of discontinuous change, and sometimes not even then, that the binding effects of materiality within social relations become apparent. It is the level of triviality, of taken-for-grantedness, that makes the significance of materiality both hidden and powerful.

Valuable as these studies of material culture are, there are some difficulties in linking them directly to an analysis of organisational and organised space. First, they tend to focus on discrete objects, although embedded in a social context. In organisational life, it is less specific objects in themselves that are of significance in the combined social and material construction of the built environment. The integration of the social and material is much more embedded in the ongoing everyday construction of organisational life and cannot be reduced to discrete objects, as will become clearer in the case study discussion below. Second, the analysis of these discrete objects often focuses on their place in exchange processes, whether these are of 'the gift' or commodity exchanges in capitalist societies. Writers such as Appadurai (1986), however, have pointed to commonalities between these forms of exchange, rather than the tendency to romanticise the 'gift' alone. Appadurai takes this further in recognising that material objects have a lifecycle, and that they can move in and out of the commodification process, gaining other meanings as they are incorporated into people's lives. Third, in relating objects to consumption, writers tend to emphasise, positively or negatively, the place of consumer choice in the self-making relations between object and individual (e.g. de Certeau 1984; Miller 1995). However, we do not conceptualise 'choice' as an autonomous agentic process, but one that is embedded in relations of power, identity and culture, as well as materially constituted. We also see the relations of consumption, production and reproduction as highly interrelated, as will have been apparent throughout this book. Dant (1999: 70) comments that in comparison with the material expression of lifestyle and identity involved in home building, 'at our place of work we manipulate the material world in routine ways regulated and specified by someone else'. However, in Chapter 5 we sought to demonstrate the organised nature of the most private spaces. Although in the following case study we focus on one organisational space, we hope to develop an approach to 'social materiality' that is useful for analysing the whole diversity of 'spaces of organisation' and the 'organisation of space'.

Social materiality: a riparian metaphor

The first step to negotiate a way of understanding the combined social–material world that is not reductive, that does not isolate the two aspects but recognises the mutual enacting of both, is to try to re-conceptualise a relationship that does not institutionalise the material as fixed and inert structure, while leaving the social as active and dynamic. Here the metaphor of the relationship between the river and the riverbanks may be of some use. The everyday picture of the 'river' is of an active, potent force which has the power to change the landscape it moves through. This capacity for alteration may be through the active cutting away of rock over millennia and thus the creation of the banks and beds as it goes. In contrast, the riverbanks are seen as passive, as being inscribed by the river's movement: they are the fixed structures, the matter that is acted upon. At this point, the metaphor appears to fit in with the treatment of the social (the river) as active and dynamic and the material (the banks) as fixed and passive. This relationship of activity/passivity is expressed in the notion of embankments as flood 'defences'. However, a closer look at the relationship between the river and its banks reveals a different story. Hydrodynamics suggests that the very formation of the river itself is created by the shape and configuration of the landscape; as it moves over different forms of structure, over different types of rock, it is also shaped and changed. For example, if a river runs over permeable limestone it will be taken underground until it reaches a deeper impermeable layer of rock. Similarly gorges are created by the action of the movement of river water but in turn channel that water is a particular way. The structure of the material itself appears to be influential, although not as obviously so as the moving power of the river because of the differing time scales of human perception. This metaphor here seems akin to debates within sociology over social structure and agency as to how they shape each other.

Yet the metaphor is still not a subtle enough one to counteract the assumption that the material equates simply with fixed structure – even though it is now seen that this too is active in changing and shaping – and the social being linked with activity and agency, although the agent is now muddied by showing how it is influenced by structure. To look back again at the river and the banks the following should be noted. As the river cuts through the banks it erodes the rocks. Not only this but it picks up the rocks and tosses them together as part of the river itself. Now, there is no easy distinction between river-and-banks: they are held together as a solution, a suspension or emulsion. The river and banks can be seen as the mutual exchange of molecules, of fixity and motion, of solid and liquid, mutually shaping and reshaping. Together they pass on down the course of the river. The fragments of rock and silt from the river bed themselves create something new out of the river, as the oxbow lakes and meanderings come out of this mutual enactment of river and banks. Notoriously, the eddies and movements of the river and its banks cannot easily be analysed by scientific models. Little has changed since Mark Twain pronounced the Mississippi River as unknowable. Despite the attempts of hydrodynamics and even chaos theory to map these relationships, they retain a level of unpredictability that we can appreciate at a basic level in the unexpected floods of recent years in the UK or in the Mississippi delta itself. It is the river bank as much as the river that in combination create phenomena that surface in embodied human consciousness.

The choice of this particular metaphor as a means of thinking through the material–social relation also owes something to the very noticeable prevalence of flows and fluidities in recent social theory (e.g. Bauman 2000, 2001; Castells 1989: 171; Luke 1996; Virilio 1997). The riparian image, with its recourse to thinking about flows in a more complex way than that often proffered to us by theorists of liquidity, is intended to suggest a reconsideration of the use of these ideas. Thus, this riparian metaphor is not just about social flows and structures, as seen for example in structuration theory or figurational sociology, but it seeks to bring in materiality. But the material is not simply the fixed and inert. In the employment of this metaphor, the material has both structures and flows, as does the social, and all are intertwined, entangled, within the social-and-material. It is this perspective that we have tried to utilise in examining the development of networks that constitute 'abstract space' in Chapter 4 and that construct the hybrid domestic space in Chapter 5.

Social materiality through embodiment

Another way of rethinking the dualistic relationship between the social and the material is to consider human embodiment. Traditionally, as we have noted in several places, there has been a dualism between 'material body' and 'thinking mind'. As Lefebvre frequently reminds us in *The Production of Space*, developing a sociological and phenomenological understanding of 'embodiment' is key to understanding social space. We have already explored in previous chapters how it is the social-and-material embodied actor who enacts social and organisation control and identity. 'Embodiment' is a more helpful term to use here, rather than 'the body'. 'The body' tends to be associated with the Cartesian split between 'mind' and 'body', with all its associated assumptions, where the body is seen as a container for the active mind, as a natural material object and as an object of knowledge and control by biology and the medical sciences. 'The body' also points to a generalised, normal body, a fixed and finished entity, and thus obscures the diversity of bodies along with their processual being. 'Embodiment' is much more active, indicating the negotiation of everyday life in relation to the material world and to the creation of social life. Embodiment is irreducibly both corporeal and social. Embodied experience is developed in relation to self and others, social representations, psychological projections and cultural images. It is also important to acknowledge the specificity of embodiment, which challenges the idea of 'the body' as a universal natural object (masking a white male able-bodied 'norm'), so recognising a multiplicity of differences and allowing that these are socially and culturally mediated. As we go through these reasons it becomes clear that this view of embodiment has much in common with the perspective on social space that has been developed through the book following Lefebvre.

The writer who has had the most influence on this view of embodiment, and who for Williams and Bendelow (1998) provides the most radical critique of Cartesianism, is the French phenomenologist Merleau-Ponty. He argues that 'to be a body is to be tied to a certain world' (1962: 148), for perception of the world is always embodied perception, since 'the perceiving mind is an incarnated mind' (1989: 3). He sees embodiment as 'reversible', which emphasises the body as sentient and sensible, sees and is seen, hears and is heard, touches and is touched. In this conceptualisation the 'material' and the 'social', the 'object' and the 'subject', 'nature' and 'culture', and the 'body' and the 'mind' are not dichotomised but entwined (Dale 2001; Williams and Bendelow 1998: 51). In his writings, Merleau-Ponty recognises the historical and social bases of the embodied subject, expressed through specific acquired and socialised skills, gestures and bodily techniques (Mauss 1973). Thus embodiment, what Merleau-Ponty (1962, 1973) describes as our lived 'being-in-the-world', is neither ideas nor matter, subject or object, but both at the same time. Merleau-Ponty 'identifies social, embodied action with the production of meaning. Meaning is not produced by a transcendental or constituting consciousness but by an engaged body-subject' (Crossley 1996: 101).

One example of this notion may suffice. In the production of meaning for the ancient Greeks, justice was a perfect cube, symmetrical and therefore aesthetically beautiful (Boyle 2003: 51). But cubes have their own problems for the engaged body-subject. It is not for nothing that 'cubism' in art challenges conventional ways of viewing the world. The nature of the human body and embodied sight is such that we cannot see all sides of a cube simultaneously. Throw a dice on a table and not all sides are visible at any one time. Even if the observer rotates around the dice in space, the downward face of the dice cannot be seen. Both the perspectival view (as discussed in Chapter 2) and the abstract 'logico-mathematical' cognitive space (Lefebvre 1991) take an approach that denies the embodied experience of sight and increases our distance from understanding how the materiality of the world influences and shapes us as irreducibly embodied and spatial social beings, as we shape the material world around us.

Thus out of this conceptualisation of the embodied subject, we can fashion a tool for understanding the negotiation of the material and the social, and the organisational and the subjective. With these building blocks of a 'social materiality' now in place we turn back to organisational space.

Social materiality and control in a privatised utility

In this section, a specific organisational example will be discussed to illustrate the mutual enactment of the social and the material in organisational space. The organisation is one of the privatised utilities in the UK, an electricity company that at the time of its 2002 annual report employed over 6000 people worldwide. It has been acquired recently by a European energy giant. In this chapter it will be referred to as 'EnergyCo'. This empirical example is intended as an illustration of how spatial and organisational relations have interacted over a period of time. It relates to a number of the themes that have been developed throughout this book, including the idea of the enactment of organisational power, of the aestheticisation of organisational spaces and the connections of both of these with employee identity. We observed the changing material and social conditions unfolding over a period of eight years of informal contact with this company in a number of guises, but not from a formally set up and bounded piece of research. It is true to say that through observations of the changing spatial arrangements in this organisation our conceptualisation of organisation space and architecture became less static to appreciate more the fluid mutual interaction of changing material and social relations. There has been an element of serendipity to the case study, involving informal contact with employees as acquaintances and students, as well as a relationship where visits and discussions have been easy to access. Four major visits took place, with the first being in 1994, immediately after the company headquarters moved from a city centre location to a new, purpose-built structure on a business park on the

BOUNDARY CROSSINGS: REPRODUCING ORGANISED SPACE • BUILDING A SOCIAL MATERIALITY: SPATIAL AND EMBODIED
POLITICS IN ORGANISATION • ALTERNATIVE SPACES: THE RADICAL ORGANISATION OF SPACE? • CONCLUSIONS: DISORGANISING SPACE

6   217

edge of another city (with the usual local government support) three years after the completion of the privatisation process; the second was a year after this, with the third in 2001 and the fourth in 2002, in the period immediately preceding the takeover. The advantages of this have been the chance to observe closely longitudinal change and to engage in spontaneous and open discussions on the experience of this workspace without the pressure of respondents feeling that they were deliberately under observation or being subjects of research. The disadvantages are that it does not have the rigour of a planned project. There have not been structured interviews with a sample of employees from different organisational backgrounds. For example, discussions have been with all post-privatisation employees and all from HQ rather than from power stations or the growing number of regional and international offices, as the organisation has diversified and taken over smaller energy companies. Knowledge about the building, its design and day-to-day operation, stems from detailed conversations with the managers responsible for the buildings and facilities, and from published work on the building in the field of architecture and planning. Information of the human resources aspects of EnergyCo come from secondary research sources, company reports and documents, as well as discussions with employees. However, despite the limitations, we hope that it fits with Weir's notes on research practice as 'an ability to use language, to observe, and to empathise, above all to listen quietly, and to reflect over a long period of time' (1993: 22, in Watson 1994: 8).

Different aspects of EnergyCo's spatial organisation will be focused upon, and to a large extent these build upon Lefebvre's spatial dimensions, the conceived, the perceived and the lived, as discussed in Chapter 1. The case integrates the deliberately planned elements of the building (conceived space) with the physical arrangements and how these change over time (perceived space), along with the ongoing relationship between the social and the material (the lived experience of the space). The case looks at both the physical dimension of space and, perhaps crucially, the imaginary dimension, or how the lived experience of the space incorporates not only the physical actuality but also the imagined spaces of aspiration, achievement, teamworking, open communications and commitment. The placing of these deliberate, organised elements along with the spontaneous, enacted aspects produce a complex picture of the social and material enacting together to produce relations of power and identity, and contradictions within these.

The EnergyCo HQ was highly consciously designed, planned and ordered. In terms of Lefebvre's spatial triad, it is easy to relate the workspace to the concept of 'representations of space' (1991: 38), as the dominant mode of production of this social space by the organisation through the ideas and structures of architects, engineers and planners (Harvey 1989). The original decision to relocate to a purpose-built new HQ was bound up with a consciousness of the importance of spatial use in the development of a privatised company differentiated from its public sector past. It was not a decision about corporate image to be expressed through architectural form: indeed, the design team was specifically instructed to avoid corporate extravagance (*The Architect's Journal*, 2 March, 1995, p. 44). The new building is quite unassuming from the outside, eschewing any temptation to express its new status through conspicuous symbolism or grandiosity. However, in two important ways the design of the building is expressive of espoused corporate goals. First, it is designed to be highly energy efficient. It could have displayed a conspicuous consumption of its own product, but here a responsible outlook towards the guardianship of energy resources is demonstrated. In material terms, it is a 'smart' building, designed with the technology to monitor and adapt the internal environment to maximise responsiveness to changing conditions and minimise unnecessary energy use, and yet maintain comfortable working conditions (1995: 44). Second, the design of the building as a workspace was intended to facilitate specific business goals, notably the integration of what were quite disparate parts of the company, and to encourage networking, sharing of information and a more dynamic environment conducive to the competitive, profit-centred organisation it now had to become. The person at EnergyCo responsible for the new building project said, 'The company decided that a new, purpose built HQ would, among other things, help to improve internal communications and team working' (p. 44). To achieve this, the spatial design and the new human resource management policies and practices were formulated to work in tandem. Thus it is a very specific case, where the move to a new building created a discontinuity allowing new possibilities of spatial control (cf. Carmona *et al.* 2002: 242). Contrary to the idea of a form of labour process proceeding *despite* the building (cf. Thompson and Warhurst (1998) discussed earlier), the key here is the deliberate manipulation of social and spatial organisation in order to effect a certain vision of work and organisational form. In other words, the 'representation of space' in terms of the design, cannot be divorced from the 'imaginary' space bound up in it, as will become clear in the following account.

Entering the building for the first time one is confronted with an almost total open-plan space. There are three floors, built around a central atrium. The openness is thus not only across one floor level but also up and down across all three levels. The only physical barriers across this space are waist level banisters to prevent accidents: there are no internal glass walls or dividers. At one end of the top floor, above the entrance foyer, there is a restaurant. There is also a small directors' corridor of conventional rooms on this floor: the only area of the whole building to have separate and enclosed offices. All other managers have workstations on the open-plan floor spaces. The directors' area also boasts a greater use of polished wood and a display of art. These are not overly prominent but still function to mark off the status of those in this part of the building through the use of materials for their symbolic representation (Lefebvre's 'representational space', and again an expression of how the social space is dominated). Underneath the main floors of the building there is a purpose-built gym (run by an external company). This had to be expanded to meet demand, with 40 per cent of staff – over four times the target – becoming members (*Building*, 10 September, 1999). Outside, a wetlands area has been created with the aid of local environmental groups. This also provides some external area for employees to sit in the summer, given the building is on a business park, away from local amenities. The building has won awards for its innovative design and the company continues to be proud of it and keen to show visitors its successful characteristics. All of these aspects of the material environment contribute to the simultaneous construction of the specific imaginary space of high achieving professionals and managers.

The level of domination of the 'conceived space' of EnergyCo becomes even clearer when the second layer of deliberate design of its interior space is examined. In order to achieve effective design of the interior workspace, EnergyCo hired in the services of SpaceSyntax, a group of architects who specialise in the mapping of social interactions in a variety of urban, commercial and work environments. The techniques used by SpaceSyntax are based upon the work of Bill Hillier, Professor of Architectural and Urban Morphology at the Bartlett School of Architecture, University College London, and his texts *The Social Logic of Space* (1984, written with Julienne Hansen) and *Space Is the Machine* (1997). Hillier's orientation is anti-normative with regard to aesthetics, but is based upon computer analysis and modelling techniques for the 'complex interactions between spatial organisation and people' (www.spacesyntax.com/people/hillier).

SpaceSyntax argues that the most effective organisations provide more opportunities for people to interact, and not only the interactions that management expects, but also the more innovative and less predictable interactions. They believe that spatial design of the organisation can hinder or promote these interactions:

> As soon as you get up to go to a meeting, or the photocopier or whatever, you become 'available'. What the pattern of space does is to make people available for this type of interaction. If the plan of the building strictly reproduces the 'management' division of the organisation, and seeks to minimise 'interruption' or the need to move, by excluding people from other groups from passing through, then the conditions can be created in which that structure 'fossilises' and the building only helps to reproduce the existing 'view' of the nature of the problem. (SpaceSyntax 2003, www.spacesyntax.com/offices/offices.html, page2)

The methods that SpaceSyntax use to determine this spatial use are through computer modelling and scoring systems. The spatial design they devised for EnergyCo was intended to be the most successful so far (a score of 1.2 compared to the next successful one, the design for Scandinavian Airline Services in Stockholm at 1.1) (promotional brochure on the new EnergyCo HQ). This can be linked with Harvey's (1989) development of Lefebvre's spatial dimensions (see Chapter 1), in relation to the control of accessibility and reduction in the effects of distance.

Given this theory of organisational space, the most important factor was the design of circulation routes and meeting places, described as 'village pump' activities (*The Architect's Journal* 1995: 48). The terminology of this and its connection to an image of traditional community is significant, and fits with the discussion of how work relations are being obscured by other social forms that we made in Chapter 3 in relation to the work of design consultancy DEGW. Six 'towers' incorporating stairs and service facilities (toilets and coffee machines/kitchen areas; and photocopiers and stationery) were constructed to 'act as points of social contact, consciously arranged at constructed points in the plan alongside WC cores and IT rooms leaving the office floor plates free of obstructions' (1995: 46). There are two of these towers at each end of the building and two in the middle: the only structures to break up the incredible open-plan expanses.

The material openness could well have been perceived as threatening. Certainly our first impressions were that it formed a classic disciplinary panopticon! However, informal discussions with employees at the time of relocation indicated that this was not the predominant response to the new building and a survey conducted nearly five years after the move confirmed that 91 per cent of the sample found the layout acceptable, good or excellent (*Building*, 10 September, 1999). Communication of the ideas involved in the new building, and tours of employees prior to relocation had been part of the whole package. Indeed, the move was not from a totally differentiated, enclosed set of spaces but from a more traditional mixture of separate offices and open-plan spaces. However, another reason that the building was not perceived through the lens of negative surveillance was the congruence between these spatial material arrangements and the development of a series of Human Resource Management discourses and practices. In terms of Lefebvre, this shows the domination of the organisation both through the carefully conceived space, and through the construction of an imaginative space. This is a space created through both physical and discursive effects, such that the employee can understand themselves as a successful individual in relation to this organisation (Figure 6).

Figure 6 **BBC Media Village atrium. The atrium has become a somewhat dominant form for modern office buildings encapsulating the open-plan approach. Surveillance is enhanced in such designs, although often masked by the rhetoric of improved communications, empowerment and teamworking.**

This imaginary space is constructed in a number of ways, over a period of time, and is less totally consciously produced than the representations of space. In the process of transformation from public utility to private enterprise, EnergyCo sustained huge job losses (from nearly 8000 in 1992 to under 5000 in 1994 when the new building opened, rising

BOUNDARY CROSSINGS: REPRODUCING ORGANISED SPACE • BUILDING A SOCIAL MATERIALITY: SPATIAL AND EMBODIED POLITICS IN ORGANISATION • ALTERNATIVE SPACES: THE RADICAL ORGANISATION OF SPACE? • CONCLUSIONS: DISORGANISING SPACE

6 223

again later with new UK and international ventures, and then falling through rationalisation before their takeover). These figures, significant as they are, mask the full extent of personnel change, for at the same time as long-standing employees from the nationalised era were being made redundant, there was a recruitment drive of young graduates with a keen business interest (a number of recent MBAs were appointed and other new recruits have been routinely encouraged and supported to undertake MBAs, a clear pointer to the changing ethos of the company). The new jobs were different from the old, nationalised industry type of task. The organisation now has a wealth of people and skills to undertake competitor analysis, corporate strategy and strategic planning, used not only for the core business but for the growing internationalisation and diversification into related business areas.

One element of this is the increasingly individualised employment relationship, with national collective bargaining dropped after privatisation, and of individualised communication. EnergyCo operates three employee share ownership schemes. Employees are encouraged to see their relationship with the organisation in terms of their individual career interests, and these are built upon business acumen, knowledge of the whole business (as opposed to the specialised skills of a traditional bureaucracy) and thus networking across boundaries. These are all constructed into the spatial openness and lack of divisions in the building, helping to explain why the openness is predominantly experienced as a positive opportunity rather than as a negative disciplinary gaze, although of course, in practice the space can and does function as simultaneously control and opportunity for the individual. Foucault's formulation of power as productive is useful here: at the same time that the open spaces produce a self-disciplined labour force, they also help produce a sense of identity with the company's goals, an idea that we have explored in previous chapters.

Flexibility is a key aspect in both discursive and material forms in EnergyCo. It is even seen designed into the very chairs that employees sit on. The furniture was chosen before any employees moved into the new building, with the criteria that it was easily able to be re-configured with minimum disruption. Five work groups trialled different furniture arrangements for one-month periods before the furniture was finally chosen. Workgroups are able to select the furniture layouts they find most suitable. However, some areas of the arrangements are very tightly controlled: maximum partition heights are strictly fixed and maintained by the facilities management team. The information management systems were also redesigned for the building move. They too indicate this combination of control and opportunity. Whereas previously larger departments had provided their own IT applications and support, this was now all centrally designed as a common infrastructure. As well as the usual cost reductions involved in the simplification and economies of scale, the homogeneity of the system aims to facilitate communications and information sharing across the whole company (Promotional brochure, EnergyCo, n.d.).

In observations, employees were frequently seen to use a 'sign language' of their own formulation to communicate across the open spaces. In some senses they are resisting the explicit design of the space for meeting places and intersection, but in another way they are amply fulfilling this. We might compare this to the use of sign language developed in the medieval monasteries to overcome the practical difficulties of silence discussed in Chapter 2. This, too, might have appeared as resistance to control but actually constituted a fulfilment of the identification and commitment to the goals of the organisation. In both cases it is a creative use of embodiment. In EnergyCo, it functions to simultaneously overcome the distances and yet use the openness of the space to facilitate communication. Although the content of this communication was opaque to outside observers, what was clear was that it achieved its goal of conveying messages between people across large expanses of the offices and different parts of the formal organisational structure. In her analysis of changing employment relations in privatised utilities, Mulholland comments that 'In the absence of a visible career ladder, managers and the movers and shakers in particular seek other ways of achieving the attention of corporate agency' (1998: 196). In the material environment of EnergyCo's new head quarters this has been translated into the embodied agency of the employees. The use of sign language makes a highly visible statement of who the 'movers and shakers' are and how they are moving and shaking! Just as surely as in the specific content of their discourse, these employees signal their knowledge and interaction with other parts of the business through their embodiment. In many ways it does not matter what the actual content of the communication is – it may be to signal joining up for a coffee, although as we will see later even the organisation of the restaurant and coffee machines has significance. The signal still shows loud and clear that they have connections and networks across traditional organisational boundaries and teams, that they are known and taken notice of (signals are reciprocal). Here the social and material arrangements of EnergyCo seem to have come together to create and reinforce the enactment of a particular sort of organisational space. In some ways an analysis of this would suggest that there has been an appropriation of the space by employees, despite the dominant construction of the space through organisational design (cf. Lefebvre 1991; Harvey 1989). However, the domination of the social space is not only of the representation of space – the actual managed design. It is also achieved through the imaginary space – how employees see themselves as belonging to and part of that social space. Because both of these are stable and consistent with each other, it is difficult for the employees' appropriation of the space to become fully radical.

However, the mutual enactment of social and material is not fixed into a structure once and for all: the social production of space and embodied subjectivity is in continuous process. Thus, although EnergyCo's building was deliberately and consciously designed to produce particular organisational goals, the ongoing everyday social–material process is more unpredictable and spontaneous. In initial observations there was a definite air of calm quiet professionalism (partially achieved through the technological means of pumping white noise into the building to take the highs and lows off what would otherwise have been three floors' worth of sound). The contrasting conditions of observation just prior to the takeover of EnergyCo prompted much more awareness of the significance of changing and unpredictable use of space.

In later visits, the number of employees working in the building had increased by about half again, taking it well over its design capacity. Previously there was little overt demarcation between workspaces and workgroups, apart from small unobtrusive signs indicating each functional area as one walked along the length of the atrium edge of each floor. But with the move from spaciousness to cramped conditions, the huge influx of additional furniture had been placed so as to create clear divisions and enclosures, with a wall of filing cabinets around each team, thus tending to reassert traditional bureaucratic silos. Rather than the circulation routes and flow of networking and communication intended from the building, the social and the material now seemed to have become melded together as structure and mass. Although (presumably) functional in providing necessary documents, the particular grouping of cabinets into specific 'walls' around areas, seemed also a clear indication of a perceived need to create separate spaces, perhaps to personalise and privatise spaces, in a way that was very different from the previous arrangements. Conversation with the facilities manager indicated that these specific material arrangements were determined by the incoming teams, along with the now-displaced existing employees. The entire material and sensory experience of the building had changed at the time of our final visit. The calm sense of professionalism was replaced with a loud buzz of conversation (the technological deadening seemed to no longer work as effectively) and even the professional suits seemed to be exchanged for more colourful and casual clothing, with the influx of previously externally accommodated teams.

In this material reconstruction of the workspace, the consciously designed control-commitment system of the organisation with its goals of communication, openness and lack of boundaries was impeded. In creating these bounded enclaves the social and the material are again inextricably intertwined: on the one hand the agency of the employees is in play, and on the other there are the material constraints of (lack of) space, extra furniture and bodies. Neither of these can be seen as the determining factor and to analyse either the social as active and the material as inert, or vice versa, would be to diminish understanding of the processes of change going on. The combined material-social enactment leads to a different embodied relationship between employees and EnergyCo that cannot be reduced simply to social factors surrounding the impending takeover, along with uncertainty over jobs and management arrangements. In some senses, 'resistance' to organisational change and control has become embedded in the social and material reconstruction of the interior. The majority of approaches to resistance tend to locate resistance in a consciousness of conflictual relations and a deliberate opposition to organisational control. The activities of EnergyCo employees in reshaping their material surroundings would be difficult to fit into this cognitive, intentional view. Rather than themselves seeing their construction of an enclosed workplace as intentional acts of resistance, EnergyCo employees are negotiating physically with how they carry on working in an overcrowded building. In the process the conceived and organised space of the managers and designers is being appropriated by the employees through their lived experience of the changed, overcrowded space. Although there may be no deliberate or rational decision to impede organisational forms of control, the social restriction of interaction, networking and communication comes from an embodied subject developed in mutual enactment with the changing materiality of the workspace. This changing lived experience of the space also influences some changes in the dominant imaginative space.

Within the study of EnergyCo, it is also possible to see the elision between ideas of production and consumption identity that we discussed in Chapter 3. This especially relates to the idea that new forms of organisational control are tapping into broader discourses of self-fullfillment and aspiration, that span both production and consumption spheres (Rose 1989), and that social spaces are becoming more hybrid. The workplace gym and wetlands areas at EnergyCo already indicate the combination of work, play, sport and consumption within one space and time. Two further examples will help to demonstrate how values and norms associated with consumption are embodied in organisational activity in this particular case.

Right from the inception of the new building, the differences between a publicly owned utility and a profit-orientated business were embedded in the material. The restaurant, an inviting area with views from the top floor and subsidised meals, displays a constantly changing lit up display of the company's share-price performance. Even as employees relax from their specific tasks, the space constructs them as they construct themselves as simultaneously consumers (both of food and, as employee shareholders, of the company) and as producers (of wealth for themselves, as well as the company). Both emphasise the high status of the consumer (experienced in the subjectivity of the employee), the power of individual choice and self-gratification. The entwining of production and consumption through the construction of space and embodied subjectivity is even more powerfully conveyed on the 'trading floor'. This is an area that was not initially planned into the organisational space, but has developed with the developing confidence and diversification of EnergyCo. It certainly demonstrates in material form how the company has thrown off any remnant of the public sector utility. Part of the central floor has been transformed by large computer screens, giving constantly updated information on the changing electricity market. In the privatisation process a set of 'market' processes and institutions had to be artificially created. One of these is the Electricity Pool, a 'spot market' for trading electricity. The dealing area has been created despite the annual reports for EnergyCo indicating that less of its business is going through the Pool. Employees in this department stood rather than sat at desks; their attention was focused on the market information on screens and computers: they looked like the familiar image of city traders in their bodily 'dressage' (Foucault 1977; McDowell 1997). Organisational progression, and hence self-development, are enacted through their very embodiment of the control inherent in the 'marketization' of professional work (Scarbrough 1995) and the primacy of commercial values.

The second example of how consumption norms become habituated also demonstrates the potentially contradictory relationship between how organisational space may be managed and designed, and how it may be 'lived'. As we have seen, the massive increase in employees working in EnergyCo's HQ building had consequences for the design of the space to achieve specific organisational goals. One side effect of this, both trivial and telling, was the increased demand on the coffee machines. Deliberately designed and located as part of the 'circulation' flows of employees, pressure of numbers using these now caused queuing and thus dissatisfaction. The facilities management team took an interesting decision to spend approximately ten thousand pounds one weekend to double the voltage and thus speed up the machines (as an energy company this 'technological fix' was perhaps an obvious choice). The flow of electrons was increased in order to increase the flow of hot water, to increase the flow of people, to increase the flow of electricity, to increase the flow of profits: a mutual enacting of social and material flows (cf. Lefebvre 1991: 347, discussed in Chapter 4). In the original planning of the space, these meeting places were seen as key to creating organisational opportunities and innovation; in the individualised world of the employee as consumer, the immediacy of need satisfaction has primacy. In a traditional labour process account, the decision to speed up the machines would be seen as direct managerial control over workers' time and space. However, in this case the locus of control is much more difficult to see, because the ideology of 'individual choice' is embedded and embodied throughout the organisation. In this context of individual career opportunity, chatting to others whilst waiting for coffee may be experienced by some as a waste of time and slowing down the adrenalin highs of work. There are of course both elements of choice and control here simultaneously: control is both 'secured and obscured' (Burawoy 1979), as we discussed in Chapter 2, in the interwoven nature of the social and the material, the enacted and the embodied.

We need to take seriously the interwoven nature of materiality, social relations and organisation. The coffee machine, the computer, the lift and so on are mundane features of organisational life that bring the body to particular points in space and organise them there, although their relation to social processes are routinely obscured. In this chapter, we have tried to develop an approach to organisational space that incorporates materiality and embodiment into understanding social processes and relations. In the following chapter, we explore the varieties of 'alternative organisations of space' that challenge the taken-for-granted approach to social space.

Note

[1] An earlier version of this chapter was published in *Organization*, 2005, 12, 5, 649–78.

7 alternative spaces: the radical organisation of space?

BUILDING ORGANISATION: SECURING AND OBSCURING POWER • BUILDING PEOPLE:
IDENTITIES AND SPACES • A POLITICAL ECONOMY OF ORGANISED SPACE • BOUNDARY
CROSSINGS: THE BRITISH COLONIAL WOMAN • BUILDING A SOCIAL MATERIALITY:
SPATIAL AND EMBODIED POLITICS IN ORGANISATION • ALTERNATIVE SPACES:
THE RADICAL ORGANISATION OF SPACE? • CONCLUSIONS: DISORGANISING SPACE

> To change life ... we must first change space.
>
> (Lefebvre 1991: 190)

Change is as much a part of the social arrangement of space as is fixed stability. Yet, the human capacity to appreciate 'change' in which 'we' have had no part is very limited indeed. At its most obvious, conceptions of geological time make a meaningful juxtaposition with the span of one human life hugely problematic. Movements in the landscape of millimetres per annum often escape human notice. Easier but by no means easy is our capacity to appreciate and understand the social transformation of space over recorded historical periods. But here, cultural relativism is often the lens through which the past use and abuse of space is viewed. Coming forward, whilst societal memory of the recent past is important the capacity to appreciate significant change is often delimited by the lifespan norm of three score years and ten. Given this set of methodological problems to perceiving change, our individual appreciation of the 'changing' landscape is often limited to contemporary appearance in which massive shifts pass unnoticed because of their 'slow' rate of change compared to a human generation. What passes for change in the built environment is often the removal of the tarnish accreted upon the old and a subsequent brush-up and polish. A change of livery or the application of a new coat of paint in the built environment can be conceptualised by the passer-by as significant improvement. 'Refurbishment' of existing spatial arrangements, often marking a change in ownership, has come to stand for significant change where the façade of buildings and the presentation of open spaces are altered in appearance. The refurbishment of social arrangements may also be undertaken at the same time, so that by putting a decorative gloss upon the prevalent socio-spatial organisation, it is made fit for purpose into the medium-term future.

Sometimes, of course, 'imaginary spaces' change space dramatically. Sometimes, the organising of space differently has profound social effects. Sometimes, new spaces are created when boundaries are transgressed. Sometimes, social relationships are secured by the changed use of space. But it is easy to underestimate the difficulties in changing socio-spatial arrangements and to mistake 'refurbishment' for these more fundamental changes. In this chapter, we seek to explore the 'radical' organisation of space. How far this might be differentiated from 'refurbishment' and how far the radicalisation of space is possible in the modern world are questions which we will address.

As we have shown in previous chapters, space is often portrayed as knowable, measurable and capable of exploitation and occupation. Key here is Von Humboldt, who, having travelled widely in South America carrying with him huge amounts of calibration devices, developed a method of drawing iso-lines by which points of equal measurement on the Earth's surface could be connected. This visualisation technology opened up a universalising 'grid of intelligibility' for all who used it. Points on the Earth's surface once separated by distance, difference and destiny became part of a unifying map of sameness. Difference, indeed uniqueness, became submerged in a current of connectivity and uniformity. Useful knowledge was transmitted back to Europe through a grid of iso-lines.

The Himalayas, for example, were mapped in the 1870s using Humboldtian methods but these surveys were undertaken not in the search for intrinsic knowledge. Knowledge in the form of these particular maps was exclusively for military use by the British state in 'protecting' India, a link to the pervasive organisation of warfare we noted in Chapter 4. The British wished to know possible invasion routes into India from Russia (Stewart 2006). Discourses of space in the Western capitalist world often involve a similar language of ownership and of exclusive possession but this closing protectionism is too obvious to accept as unproblematic. Discourses of this kind also involve a language of future possession and the opening-up of space. Mountain passes can be traversed both ways. Political maps typically express possession in terms of 'colour' differentiation and appear to respectfully close down boundaries. But of course they also open up new opportunities for capture and expansion. They show the next target for infiltration and annexation. Interestingly, in this context it is said that more professional geographers work for the CIA than for any other employer in the USA. All maps, furthermore, are essentially political. As forms of representation of space, they incorporate inclusions and exclusions, assumptions and interests in the way that they portray and construct spaces. Maps are valuable possessions therefore, and the possession of them creates social power and social conflict. For example, in fiction, the battles over the ownership of the map held by Jim Hawkins in *Treasure Island* can be thought to concretise this materiality of a map beautifully. A recent BBC series entitled *Map Man* (2004–2005) illustrates this through a number of examples. In the County of Northumberland, a map of the seventeenth century hides all the centuries of conflict over ownership in the Border Wars and in the subsequent period of the Reiver disputes. The map smoothes over this history and by asserting that all is settled, seeks to make it so. Maps of the Scottish Highlands were undertaken by cartographers with a view to being useful to the King in subduing rebels. Cycling maps of the Lake District were created to fill the gap in the market created by the new tourists using a new technology. These maps had a huge market and sold thousands more than the standard Ordinance Survey coverage of the area. They were presented as so good as to be predictive of the real experience that the cyclist would confront.

However, there are many alternatives to the ways in which space is customarily conceptualised, used and abused. Some lie deep in the historical record, some within living memory and some merely on the surface of the contemporary. Some offer radical hope for the future transformation of the social world. Others less so. To help us in our exposition in this chapter we have adopted a crude conceptualisation of 'alternative' spaces. This conceptualisation moves in large measure from the contemporary/empirical towards the historical/theoretical. Our conceptualisation also notes the importance to these spaces of very different forms of organisation. Alternative spaces imply alternative organisation – new modes of organising – just as to organise in an alternative way implies that alternative spaces are constructed.

First, then, we identify 'margin spaces' that exist at the ends of the envelope in which humans might live. One way from a 'margin space' leads back to the conventions of the built environment but the other way from it is a material *cul-de-sac* beyond which humans might not go without breaking some laws of nature and/or placing themselves in extreme danger. Roofs and cellars in the vertical plane are examples of this. Humans in margin spaces tend to meet the birds and the worms. Their organisational form reflects this marginality in space and their embracing of risk.

Second, we point to 'liminal spaces' which exist at the margins of the orthodox but abut to other conventional spaces. Liminal spaces are where different human worlds meet and to a greater or lesser extent overlap; and in this meeting they create new opportunities for difference. Border areas in the horizontal plane are clear examples of this. Humans in liminal spaces tend to meet other humans whose culture they do not fully share. Organisationally, the fluidity of boundaries is notable.

Third, there are 'alternating spaces' where the same space is used differently at different points within a 'short' cycle. 'Short' in this sense stands to relationship to the human generation as the relevant finite measure. Spaces such as these then operate in the temporal plane and the clearest example of this is the diurnal rhythm in the use of space in city centres. For example, Chicago used to be known as 'white by day, black by night'. Other instances exist, such as the Ise Shrine in Japan, originally built around 690, which is ceremonially rebuilt every 20 years on an adjacent site. The social organisation of such space is fraught. Human beings in alternating spaces must be careful, Cinderella-like, about 'the chimes of midnight' because being caught in the shift can be difficult or dangerous. It is often disconcerting for dwellers of the one temporal realm to see their parallel halves. There are some powerful photographs from the late 1960s of fruit and vegetable traders at London's Covent Garden Market (now a site of boutique consumption) looking with some hostility upon tuxedoed revellers on their way home through the Market.

Fourth, there are 'alternative spaces' within mainstream uses of space where an area is cordoned off in some way or another and non-standard uses are put to that enclosure. The organisation of the enclosure may be decidedly different from the organisation of the open 'plain'. Attempts at building self-sustaining communities or the establishment of clubs of a private and secure nature are examples of the former organisational configuration. There is an attempt to live within palisades in order to keep in 'the best' and keep out 'the beast'. These alternative spaces may not be 'radical' in any sense but this is always a matter for debate.

Fifth, there is 'opening space' where previously closed sites are rendered open to the populace whose movement through them is encouraged. The Situationists' opening-up of the urban scene through crime and sabotage lies within this approach, whilst the British Ramblers Association's attempts to bring down enclosures and fencing is another example of this at the practical level. At the theoretical level, so too is the concept of 'nomadism' derived from the work of Deleuze and Guattari.

Sixth, and finally, there is the possibility of an 'alternative space' in which the radical re-conceptualisation of space might be possible where possession and ownership disappear as defining concepts. This would require a de-totalisation of the current social formation. 'Property is theft' declared Proudhon who advocated the overthrow of property rights as the starting point for radical change. The emphasis adopted in this section is upon property and ownership that 'are institutional facts which are inextricably bound up with materiality' (Renfrew 2004: 28).

Margin spaces

One margin space of note is the rooftop. Members of the 'general public' rarely see the roofs of any building in any detail since in most streets the pressures on one's senses, simply to manoeuvre in horizontal space, force the eyes to focus on or about ground level. To climb onto one's own roof often requires scaffolding. Only from within tall buildings can one look down comfortably upon the roofs of others. Movies make much of this type of margin space. The strangeness of the view of roofs via vertigo-inducing helicopter shots of skyscrapers, taken from above, are often to be found in adventure or action films. From Mary Poppins and her adventures with chimney sweeps, the balletic avoidance of bullets in *The Matrix* on urban rooftops, and Robert de Niro's stalking of his unsympathetic victim from the New York roofs in *Godfather II*, roofs make for good dramatic scenes in which to showcase the unusual, the unknown and the downright bizarre. They are margin spaces. There has been much interest in roof runners recently. These are the fit, young and agile climbers who choose to see the space upon roofs within the city as offering them ways of exploring a new urban world. A BBC 'ident' (corporate advertising logo) in the early 2000s caused much interest when it showed perhaps the most famous of these roof runners about his trade. It has been suggested that it was dropped from schedules after adverse comment about its encouragement of trespass. This athletic endeavour is indeed an alternative approach to space, finding challenges to the body amongst the rooftops. It is largely illegal, given owners of property see their roofs as part of the building and primarily as the ingress for burglars. Yet its portrayal as a space at the margin – of danger as well as legality – makes it attractive. It is conceptualised as an extreme sport that happens to challenge property rights.

Similarly, graffiti artists too, appear to favour dangerous spaces at the edge of the spatial envelope. The margins of the railway, or the central reservation of the motorway or underground tracks are a favourite of theirs so that there is a thrill in getting into the space in the first place and avoiding fast-moving pieces of metal hurtling past them. These places are close to 'normality' in physical space but very far away in social space. Whilst it might seem obvious that graffiti would be put in its extraordinary place whilst no trains were in operation (i.e. in the early hours of the morning) it appears that that is seen as far too easy. That does not involve enough risk. The organisational form adopted in the pursuit of the art is often gang based, but within this is highly individualised, with the name of the artist given prominence within the art form so that his or her heroic status might be established and remembered.

Moving downwards from the rooftops via the electrified rail line to the surface of the earth we first meet those that live in hovels. The word 'hovel' refers to a home that has been dug out below ground level and then built into the earth itself so that scarce and expensive building material might be used only on the upper sections and roof. Dwellers of hovels thus live half in the earth and half in 'houses'. It is an unusual form of semi-detachment. Hovels put their inhabitants so well into the earth that they live out the consequences in how they are viewed as 'soiled' and at the 'margin'. Beyond the exclusion of poverty lies exclusion based on criminality. As well as the medieval threat of the dungeon, we confront the obvious notion of the 'underworld'; the place in which criminals live beneath the veneer of bourgeois society. There is a clear and unremitting linkage across human time between, for example, 'autochthons', Dickensian rookeries, Hell's Kitchen, 'troglodytes', 'cave men', Neanderthals, H.G. Wells' Morlocks (fierce eaters of the sweet Eloi in *The Time Machine*), denizens of the sewers and the creatures of Hell. It is a linkage based on the subterranean similarity in their dwelling places. Under the ground is the place and space of all of society's and of Heaven's marginals. Organisation in these realms is meant to be violently different. Down at the roots of the mountain, Tolkien tells us that

> even in the tunnels and caves the goblins have made for themselves there are other things living unbeknown to them that have sneaked in from outside to lie up in the dark. Some of these caves, too, go back in their beginnings to ages before the goblins, who only widened them and joined them up with passages, and the original owners are still there in odd corners slinking and nosing about. (1975: 69)

In similar vein, Milton (*Paradise Lost*, Book 1: lines 60–6) describes Satan's bottomless perdition thus,

> The dismal Situation waste and wild;
> A Dungeon horrible, on all sides round
> As one great furnace flam'd, yet from those flames
> No light, but rather darkness visible
> Serv'd onely to discover sights of woe,
> Regions of sorrow, doleful shades, where peace
> And rest can never dwell, hope never comes.

Sometimes, however, the underground dweller is afforded hope and prestige as well as opprobrium. Sometimes both at the same time. In 1944, as the Red Army pushed the Nazi divisions westwards, there was an encouragement from Moscow for the Polish resistance to show itself and disrupt the retreat. This led to the carnage of the Warsaw Uprising where the Polish resistance took to the cellars and sewers of the Polish capital and sought to offer resistance from beneath the pavements. They faced asphyxiation from noxious, if natural, fumes, cave-ins from knocking through between areas, German listening devices and canisters of poisonous gas.

This resistance was not a success given that no assistance from outside was forthcoming, despite the apparent offer of support from advancing Russian forces. Nevertheless the 'margin space' proffered by the underground world did allow some sort of alternative organising for a while which Norman Davies (2004), in *Rising, '44* details as a social structure of resistance. Thirty years later in Saigon, the Viet Cong had built a whole series of tunnels beneath the city from which to launch attacks upon the South Vietnamese Army and the American forces. Whilst the US Army were aware of their existence and used sniffer dogs to identify entry points, by the simple use of American soap by the Vietnamese underground dwellers, the dogs were rendered unable to detect these points. The network was vast, covering many acres and in general the surface forces were totally unaware of their extent. There was much publicity about this underground world in the late 1970s when its role in Vietnamese military victory became clear.

It should be recognised, however, that spaces such as we have discussed in this section are almost always in the form of resistance. They rarely allow permanent control of the space occupied and except in rare conditions do not offer much influence, if any, on what is going on at surface level. The Vietnamese organisation of margin space became successful once the tanks rolled in across conventional space; the other, in Warsaw's margin space, was a failure because Stalin discouraged his tanks from moving in across the surface till the resistance had ended. Life that is lived within margin space is life on the dangerous spatial edge and alongside the heroic, often takes a guerrilla form of organisation.

Liminal spaces

The sort of space to which reference is made in this section is space on the border, space at the boundary of two dominant spaces, which is not fully part of either. This is not the same as the first 'margin space' category, although there are some similarities. Border zones are not 'the edge' between inhabitable space and unliveable space where the margin exists. For us, the border zones are the boundaries between different types of habitable space. Much has been written about border regions across the world and far from being rigid demarcations they may well be areas of intense collaborative activity. Yet they do not share the identity of the twin areas which create them. Two very British examples may suffice. First, let us consider Kirk Yetholm, which lies two miles inside Scotland at the Northern end of the Pennine Way. For centuries its location made it ideal for the Gypsy Kings and Queens to live there in their 'palace'. It is a liminal space offering escape into England on one hand or retreat further into Scotland on the other, should trouble be brewing – which it regularly did. Its special characteristics including being almost surrounded by a river, allowed it a protection from the outside world but it was a place of choice for those who wished to live in a border zone owing allegiance to both and neither of the neighbouring state powers. Its economic life was also enriched by liminarity. Trading took place in rare goods and taxable items of state interest. Its custom was to avoid customs. Similarly, High Bentham in North Yorkshire is another such place. It lies two miles inside Yorkshire across the Lancashire border but is about 80 miles by very slow roads from its county town and High Sheriff. The village has an 'alternative' flavour, boasting for years a number of communes and a large gypsy community associated with a regular 'horse fair'. It exists in space at the limits of two municipal entities and owes allegiance to both and neither.

Such places are reflective to a greater or lesser extent of places such as Tijuana, Chaman and Portbou and a thousand other border towns around the world. These places, and the seaports which fulfil the same function, are often de-sanitised spaces where state rules of moral propriety have been backgrounded. It is not necessarily that they are at the 'end' of the reach of the central state apparatus because such sites are often heavily militarised. It is more that they are the shadow areas of the state where edginess is encouraged to exist. De-sanitisation is allowed at the fringes because what is sanitary is not always in the best interests of some economic, political, military and personal positions.

No Man's Heath is a settlement on the point where three English counties meet: Leicestershire, Derbyshire and Warwickshire. It is called No Man's Heath because its liminal position meant that no one could easily call it their own. More importantly, the police of these three counties could not expect their jurisdiction to hold in the area because it is possible at this point in space to step a few paces in one direction and move counties. A few more paces would take the fugitive from the police of two counties into a third county and away from the forces of law and order. It was a priceless spot upon which to carry out the illegal sport of bare-knuckle fighting. There were interests well served then, by the existence of a place such as this where violence could flourish. No Man's Heath was a place of intense de-sanitisation away from the grasp of the 'civilising process'. So too are the gory video games involving mass murder which are widely available for a variety of expensive electronic equipment. In letting loose the dogs of war, the next generation of these games takes you possibly (but not us), into virtual space.

Why, the reader might ask, do we see virtual space as liminal and not as an alternative form of space? For 'VR is a computer generated visual, audible and tactile multi-media experience...(that) aims to surround the human body with its artificial sensorium of light, sound and touch' so that 'a total sensory immersion in the artificial environment' is possible (Featherstone and Burrows 1995: 3–6). There are those converted zealots who see virtual reality as offering a different model of spatial arrangements, in the sense that humans can now escape to some extent the bounds of the body and its place in space. It cannot be missed that there is a developing argument that virtual reality technologies produce disruption, or even transcendence of somatic knowledge of place and space. The body can be thought to be 'present' in more than one place at a time. Rather than location in a specific point on the planet's surface objectively placed within a grid of intelligibility such as GPS, the focus is on the lived experience of being-in-the-world.

Many Hollywood blockbusters have embraced this notion of virtual reality as a powerful attraction to cinema audiences. *Total Recall*, for example, envisages a world where holidays are possible from everyday reality by entering a private organisation's facility which offers a virtual holiday and all its safe joys. The paying tourists simply attach themselves to a VR machine and enjoy a holiday of a lifetime. On the USS Enterprise the 'holodeck' offers exactly the same sort of relief from everyday reality where 'eyephones', 'datasuits' and 'data gloves' give extra-ship experiences for the bored Star Treker. In *Disclosure* the possibility of a virtual reality machine which would allow the user to enter a different space and a different material existence is mooted. Whilst such machines are not yet developed, the computer-generated graphics in movies dealing with spaces of the imagination such as Narnia and Middle Earth do conjure a world that is liminal. Like the south island of New Zealand where they are filmed, it exists at the boundaries of our experience. New somatic worlds of experience do appear to be in the process of manufacture in Hollywood and elsewhere.

However, the availability of such technologies is not widespread. Moreover, these Hollywood movies are often very long and the ache in one's bottom reminds one that whatever the eye thinks of the presentation, the cinema seat is all too materially present. When VR suits are taken off, re-immersion into the embodied world means that many users report nausea and disorientation (Heim 1995). Coming out of these suits too reminds the user that their bodies, unlike the one they have just so recently left, are prone to all the pain that flesh is heir to. The disembodied nature of electronic communications allows people to masquerade behind their avatar, allowing gender, age, appearance and location to be faked. Much has been made of the possibilities here for identity work. At first, when call centre work was exported from the UK to Asia, attempts were made to hide location from needy phone callers who liked to think that help was local. When one speaks to a graduate in Bangalore or Hyderabad today who knows something about one's ailing computer, the conversation now begins with enquiries about the differing weathers in both parts of the world. No attempt is made to convince the inquirer that both persons are in close proximity. Distance is celebrated and discussed openly so that there is no longer much pretence of inhabiting the same virtual space.

Virtual reality then 'skirt[s] the borderland between psychic and social space' (Grosz on the backcover of Pile 1994) and is thus a liminal space inhabiting a place between real spaces in which it seeks to make a living. For us, it is not an alternative space in which people could spend their lives, for liminal space is typically organised around brief encounters of apparent psychic and corporeal exchange at the borders.

Alternating spaces

Liminal spaces exist between major organised spaces. Alternating spaces are those places where space is regularly and differentially organised according to the passage of time. This differential split in time for the use of the same space can sometimes be seen as 'resistance through accommodation'. For example, students and local residents often use city centres at different times, occupying the same streets but one in daylight, the other in the hours of darkness. In the City of Durham, we have been told, locals from the surrounding villages use the city centre on Fridays and Saturdays, whilst students at Durham University go to the same pubs and clubs in the town centre on weekdays. This is a *modus vivendi* typical of the diurnal and nocturnal rhythms in nature where feeding and sleeping take place, non-competitively, in shifts. It allows one species to accommodate to the demands on another, yet co-exist. In social space, similar processes of accommodation might be recognised. The spaces within the London Underground, the majority of office buildings, stations and airports all tend to change, depending upon the hour. Safety work, the movement of cargo and bulk goods rather than people, cleaning and maintenance and a variety of other tasks all go on when darkness descends. So there are alternative uses of space going on all around us but at different points in the daily cycle. Skate boarding by pre-university students takes place on the steps of the University of Leicester in the evening and at the weekends. Parks are very different by night than they are by day. Despite the efforts of Haussman and other Parisian officials to utilise 'hard-headed managerialism and scientific socialism' (Harvey 2003: 3) in order to light up the boulevards and open spaces of Paris and protect its citizens from crime, no amount of gas lighting could prevent the alternating use of space. Back in the Vietnam War, the US forces concluded that since they controlled the countryside of the Mekong delta by day but the VietCong controlled it by night, the obvious thing to do was to create day from night. Attempts were made to develop a military satellite that would reflect the sun's rays from space onto South Vietnam each night to create perpetual day across the countryside. This was a high technology solution to the perceived problem of alternating spaces. But it was never delivered.

Of course, as we have already indicated, some alternating spaces are tied not to daylight but to other rhythms. Along the edge of oceans, the tide claims and secedes territory which create different uses of space at different temporal points. On the self-same spot in the midst of

Morecambe Bay in North West England, one might find, all at different points in the turn of the tide, first cockle pickers working *in* the sands, then Bay walkers crossing *over* the sands for pleasure in escorted groups, and later as the tide comes in fully, fishermen in boats *above* the sands. Alternating spaces here are productive of fishing and leisure, but also point to the dangers of drowning. The latter creates pressures for local authorities to come up with high technology solutions for the protection of life and property, such as flood defences and barriers, which in their own way create alternating spaces. Within tidal ranges elsewhere, if the surf is up, other claims are made on the sea by the complex organisation of watersports compared to when the sea is flat calm. Also, alternating spaces are to be found on land far from the seas and oceans, yet affected by other rhythms driven by the calendar. Human activity revolves around weekly, monthly and annual events so that in the metropolitan capitals of the globe, shrines, memorials, churches, parade grounds, royal residences, sports stadia and leisure sites, one can witness cycles in the use of space. All of these spaces alternate between relative busyness on particular days, and more typically long periods of inactive emptiness. Alternating spaces usually enter our consciousness only when busy and the lights are switched on. The movement of the Queen's Royal Court in its progress from place to place briefly highlights the one 'activated' palace but backgrounds the now inactive one she has just left. Organisational principles, to be operant in these sorts of places, have to be regularly temporary, but highly regulated. The change in requirement and on/off status for an alternating space can require very rapid responses indeed and the 'switching social technology' to achieve this bi-polar state is often slick and highly managed.

Alternative spaces

What we mean here are spaces for 'difference' that exist within dominant societal and spatial forms. Building upon what we raised earlier, it is relatively easy to see some spaces as the attempt to sanitise space by raising barriers to the ingress of 'deviance'. We look particularly at the attempts to establish 'model communities'. These we deal with first in this section. We then turn to attempts to raise barriers to the ingress of 'the normalising urge' and to therefore de-sanitise space on behalf of the people enclosed. Smokers' rooms within office buildings would be but one example of this sort of space.

Spatial constructions of community

Hayden's major work on utopia, *Seven American Utopias: The Architecture of Communitarian Socialism 1790–1975*, examines how several utopian communities turned their beliefs into built forms: the Shakers, Mormons, Fourierists, Perfectionists, Inspirationists, Union Colonists and Llano Colonists. Hayden explains her work as being about 'the relationship between the members of these experimental communities, their forms of social organisation, and the complex, collective environments they created' (1976: 3). She contrasts the creative practice of designing and building these communities with the 'dreary extravagance of much utopian writing' (p. 3). Central to the physical creation of community, she argues, 'every group must achieve a balance between authority and participation, community and privacy, uniqueness and replicability' (p. 5). The following sections explore some of these issues, but in so short a space cannot convey the rich detail of Hayden's analysis.

Just as the utopian communities diverged from one another in ideals, so they developed different built forms for the expression of these beliefs. For example, the Shakers developed a series of differentiated spaces, 'envelopes of space and imaginary barriers' (1976: 69), to separate off the sexes, along with graduated levels of participation in the community. Different activities were spatially separated, often through conventional gendered division of labour, and thus contact between members of different groups was limited. Yet, within the religious meetings, these spatial constraints were largely removed, creating different experiences of 'earthly' and 'heavenly' spaces. In these ways, the Shakers constructed their community as a 'living building'. In contrast, the Fourierist community of New York State, established in 1843, was designed to bring community members together in varied social interactions and activities. The members had to fight off authoritarian designs for monumental buildings intended to give a grandiose exterior expression of Fourierism. These plans were promulgated by influential supporters of Fourier's ideals, yet who were not part of the community. The members themselves believed in participation in the design process, allowing buildings to be developed gradually as an expression of their community, and carrying out the building themselves rather than using external labour. They constructed their own, locally inspired, versions of the 'Galleries of Association', with diverse communal spaces balanced with individual rooms and provision for families to build private cottages.

Utopian communities also learnt spatial principles from each other. Hayden's comment on the multiple spaces of the Oneida Community of Perfectionists is that they had borrowed socio-petal designs from the Shakers and socio-fugal ones from the Fourierists (1976: 197). Although a religious community based on principles of 'Bible Communism', the Oneida Community was thoroughly radical in regard to personal and sexual relations. Its system of 'complex marriage' sought to prevent the exclusivity of long-term pairings, and this was institutionalised through various forms of spatial control. For example, they developed a pattern of 'mixed use' spaces, where communal areas such as sitting and dining rooms were interspersed with bedrooms. This increased sociability and prevented loneliness, but also acted as a form of surveillance to maintain complex marriage. Bedroom doors were visible from sitting rooms, discouraging exclusive relationships, and the bedrooms themselves were designed so they could not facilitate the splitting off of small groups as an alternative to the deliberately designed communal spaces (p. 212).

In contrast to this form of peer surveillance practised at Oneida, Hayden analyses the way the Shaker community embodied and enacted the discipline of the community, whilst simultaneously negotiating the importance of the individual. 'Spatial discipline was enforced less by surveillance or admonitions than by Shaker design and crafts' (1976: 69). Not only clothes but also furniture was made to measure for the individual, using the skills within the community. A strong emphasis was made on the design and innovation of tools and materials to fit the exact purposes of the community. Thus 'members were physically surrounded by the handiwork of other believers' (p. 71): they lived out the community in every detail.

The problem with utopian communities, of course, is that what may be experienced as a liberating alternative space for one person may be felt as an imprisoning organised hell to another. Lefebvre remained resolutely opposed to any sort of traditional utopianism in relation to thinking about innovative spatial forms, precisely because of their tendency towards 'closed authoritarianism' (Harvey 2000: 182). Before him, of course, Marx had argued against the French utopian group the Icarians, who were to go to America to set up their new life, specifically because (as with Coleridge's abortive 'pantisocracy' scheme) they were fleeing the European cities in order to set up a closed sectarian society in the wilderness. Such utopianism ends up, Marx argued, by being politically neutralised because it is isolated and walled off. But the Icarians and the phalanxes of Fourierians went off to their phalansteries in the North American wilderness nevertheless. The urge to sanitise their lives and close themselves off from the shocks and horrors of the world around them in Europe was a great spur to go west and avoid political and religious persecution in the new promised lands.

Pleasure domes

The second set of alternative spaces we come to might be presented as 'pleasure domes'. Put crudely, pleasure domes may be indeed about the sanitisation of the protected enclave from the outside world as in Disney and the like. Or on the other hand, the 'pleasure dome' may be about something very different. It may be concerned with the de-sanitisation of the world and the temporary suspense of dominant values as in 'the carnival'. Both are still driven by the notion of closed and controlled spaces that allow organisational behaviour to be influenced. Both are still places for processing people – but their relationship to the perceived legitimacy of the behaviour *vis-à-vis* contemporary norms differs. The de-sanitised space is hypo-normalised; the sanitised space is hyper-normalised.

Let us begin with hyper-normalised space in which pleasure comes from emphasising 'the best' and consider iconic Disney. The creation of fantasy worlds out of swamp land and orange groves is achieved by placing 'impossible' combinations of fauna and flora together in what J. M. Findlay (1992) calls 'magic lands'. Findlay reports that, within the Disney empire, plants are changed with some frequency to falsely suggest the movement of seasons in the parks. This also strongly hints, of course, at a very controlling approach to nature and the environment. Walt

Disney is reported to have said, 'I don't want the public to see the world they live in while they're in the park' (quoted in Bryman 1995: 113) which, as Bryman points out, implies both the elimination of negative aspects of city life and the physical inability to see the outside world because of screening devices and, we might add, the use of *trompes l'oeil* (Burrell and Dale 2004). Utilities are placed underground, staff-changing areas and storage facilities are all masked and so on. But in Disneyland the corporation could not afford to buy enough real estate to prevent the explosion of use in surrounding land, creating the new, somewhat tawdry city around it. In Disneyworld, huge acreage was taken up from the swampland thereby preventing the encroachment of the city into the park in too obvious a way. But as Bryman (1995: 114) reminds us, controlling the immediate environs of the park also allows control over hotel accommodation on a massive scale and represents another business opportunity associated with the city not the countryside. The facilitator of this city-garden-countryside amalgam was to be the relatively unknown 'Reedy Creek Improvement District' which has huge control over what happens in and around Disney sites with regards to land drainage, pest control, road maintenance, public transport, police, as well as land use and planning. The parks are private cities located originally in the countryside. Experimental Prototype Community of Tomorrow (EPCOT) had a very strong utopian orientation in its early planning. Disney said, *inter alia*, 'there will be no slum areas because we won't let them develop' (cited in Mosley 1986: 275). It was to be a planned, controlled community, and a showcase for American industry. Disney's EPCOT, however, as has been pointed out many times, is a Panglossian celebration of what is, not what could be (Bryman 1995: 144–5) and centres around diversified consumption.

The utopianism of theme parks then, revolves around the superficial presentation to the 'guest' of what we later describe as the subordinate pleasures of the carnivalesque and the tradition of Cockaygne, where a peasant life of permanent excitation of the senses through drink and sex predominated. But this sensual excess is highly constrained and sanitised within Disney's urban-like walled and controlled cities. They reflect ideas that arose from within the rational tradition of Arcadia rather than Cockaygne (see Parker *et al.* 2007). Theme parks represent sites where people-processing has reached new heights of sophistication and the thrills are carefully manufactured and controlled.

A half a century later and it appears, as Disney foresaw, that Florida is where utopian plans for the new cities, like Celebration, are being concretised (Hollis 1998: 216–19). 'Seaside', conceived by Robert Davis, is a resort stretching for miles along the beach at Boca Raton and which is controlled by a private company which offers utopian lifestyles based on 'neo-traditional plans' of a central village green, few commercial buildings ringed around it and limited car access. The spirit of Ebenezer Howard, designer of the 'garden city' concept, lives on. The 'utopian' community has also been permanently taken to sea in the world's most luxurious cruise liner – the 'World' – with apartments for sale starting at $2 million. Whilst based in Florida, built by Norwegians and 'flagged' in the Bahamas, this enormous ship began in January 2002 to roam the world's warmer seas seeking major cultural events and, most importantly for its wealthy residents, to be free of crime. And in order to do so it boasts a ratio of 1 security person per 12 passengers.

Much has been written about the sanitised Arcadian enclosure as a pleasure dome. This focus has been taken to an interesting level in *The Truman Show*, which was largely filmed in Disney's gated community, Celebration. This movie extends the portrayal of forces at work in such communities to a highly poignant form where they exist to control one single human being's entire life. It features much of what Disney has to offer but subverts it. For these planned and controlled places tend to be self-policing and self-selecting on class and ethnic grounds. *The Truman Show* looks and feels like a 'festival' for the eye devoted to fooling only Truman Burbank – and the millions in the audience targeted for all the 'placed' products. But as Truman begins to suspect his fate he behaves differently and offers dangerous resistance. As Tony Bennett (1995: 50–1) tells us, by the mid-Victorian period, the organisation of pleasure was changing and 'the festival form could only be realised by the rigorous exclusion of all those elements of misrule, riotous assembly and carnivalesque inversion associated with traditional popular festivals'. It is to this repertoire of resistance that Jim Carey resorts, as Arcadia shows its authoritarian nature. The twenty-first century town Celebration, from this portrayal at least, is definitely low on the carnivalseque and high on sanitisation.

Prior to our current time of attempted sanitisation, pleasure domes in the form of eighteenth-century gardens such as the Tivoli gardens in Copenhagen and Vauxhall in London were inverting, phallocentric places of gentlemanly pleasure which had a strong de-sanitised edge to them. They were hypo-normalised. Misrule and riotous assembly were by no means unknown. The 'masked' nature of much of the mingling allowed anonymity and some freedom from consequences. Gardens have often guaranteed privacy of a less contemplative kind for 'mazes were bewildering outdoor theatres of choice and chance where tall hedges shielded lovers from view as they indulged in amorous pursuit' (van Zuylen 1995: 54). The existence of such a space and those of a kindred nature were alternatives to the more controlled areas north of the River Thames. Theatres and places of entertainment since Elizabethan times had been kept outside the city walls of London, because of the fire hazard and moral hazard they offered to the city authorities. They were kept at a 'respectable' distance.

Recent research on Pompeii has also revealed the way in which spaces for activities of a sexual and sensual kind have been organised for millennia. Ray Laurence in *Roman Pompeii: Space and Society* (1994) devotes several chapters to the layout and placement of public houses, baths and brothels in pre-volcanic Pompeii. In a chapter entitled 'Deviant Behaviour' Laurence looks at prostitution, excessive drinking of alcohol and gambling. Elites, it appears, attempted in Pompeii to distance themselves from the rest of the population, yet lived in close proximity. Their families were to be protected from exposure to seeing such activities through complex arrangements of doors and streets and districts. Strangers and families would tend to stay on the main thoroughfares, whereas 'deviant' behaviours took place 'off the beaten track' and away from the main thoroughfares. The places of sensual pleasure were not physically far away from the 'respectable' places, but they remained obscured through this elaborate arrangement of spatial coding. In contrast, the baths occupied spaces of high interaction and appear to be have been planned as a whole block on the basis of the daily routine of the elite. Just as the Vasari Corridor was to provide an elite route in sixteenth-century Florence, the bathhouses of Pompeii were central places within the city because they 'centred' the power of the elite. Lawrence explains this further:

> " The activities of the elite structured city space, Their pattern of movement established a routine. In the morning, they received their clients at their house; from there they went to the forum accompanied by their clients, from the forum they went to the baths, and finally they returned home. The temporal aspect of this routine articulates city space.... Given the emphasis on display, it would seem likely that the elite need not have bathed locally near their homes, but would enjoy the display of walking to baths further away.... This regular pattern means that the elite were seen at a certain time and place each day. The elite were mobile and visible outside their localities. (1994: 129)

Foucault has shown how particular hierarchialised, differentiated spaces are constructed, through which societies make certain things visible. Bathhouses can be used by the elite for parading their identity to the wider world as in Pompeii. But in other societies, at other points in time, bathhouses might have had a very different reception. The function undertaken by a building can be architecturally assessed to see how that function might be received within a dominant value system. Laurence looks at the number and positioning of doors to attempt to assess how visible the function of buildings would be within the community which was Pompeii. He concludes from this sort of analysis that if you lived in Pompeii, baths were in your face. Public houses, gaming dens and brothels were not. As 'matter out of place' they were swept under the metropolitan carpet.

Thus, spatiality is sometimes also about concealment and evasion, as will be seen from our discussion of the San Franciscan bathhouses some 1900 years later.

Folds in space

Michel Foucault was interested in pleasure, particularly of a sexual kind, and sought to develop the study of this phemonenon(a) which he terms 'hedonics'. In Foucault's later work we are told that 'the subject is no longer sex *per se*, but modes of practice, developed and shared in communities and grounded in mutuality, whose goal is the pursuit of the good life' (Starkey and McKinley 1998: 233). Foucault (1986: 10–11) defines technologies of the self as 'those intentional and voluntary actions by which men not only set themselves rules of conduct, but also seek to transform themselves, to change themselves in their singular being, and to make their life an *ouevre* that carries certain aesthetic values and meets certain stylistic criteria'. Individuals become self-referencing subjects, not objects, who can 'transform themselves in order to attain a certain state of happiness, purity, wisdom, perfection or immortality' (Foucault 1988: 18). 'Techniques of the Self' are practices of freedom identified with a particular ethic – an ethic of care for the self. Foucault acknowledges that this particular ethic was one of personal choice for a very small elite. It was based upon a desire to live a beautiful life. Foucault then says 'I don't think we can say that this kind of ethics was an attempt to normalize the population' (Foucault 1987b: 341). It is precisely this kind of elite, with the time and resources to frequent the bathhouses of New York and San Francisco, that formed a Leisure Class, reminiscent of the patricians of Pompeii and the Victorian Aesthetes. And it was one of those Aesthetes, Oscar Wilde, who said that 'It's an odd thing but anyone who disappears is said to be seen in San Francisco'.

In his obituary of Foucault, Edward Said claimed, 'It was noticeable that he was more committed to exploring, if not indulging his appetite for travel, for different kinds of pleasure (symbolised by his frequent sojourns in California), for less and less frequent political positions' (quoted in Macey 1994: 475). The point to make here perhaps is to suggest that this assessment totally ignores the possibility that the personal was very much the political and that the different kinds of pleasure sought out by Foucault were as much political as any of his more obvious activities in Paris. Moreover, we might argue Foucault saw the bathhouses of San Francisco, in particular, as sites of alternative modes of organising. He reportedly gave talks in 1979 within several bathhouses, which he saw as having political importance because they were representative of Other forms of human expression. We shall call his analysis here, an organisational form of 'alternative space', and the bathhouses of San Francisco in 1973–1983 shall be our model.

Gilles Deleuze (1993) has spoken at length about the importance of the Baroque concept of 'layering' to the contemporary world by drawing upon

Leibnitz and his notion of 'the fold'. This is a provocative and evocative notion from the Baroque period. The term 'baroque' is Portuguese for a misshapen pearl which, although layered by the efforts of the oyster, is folded out of the order expected from a perfect example and we have already explored the fold of Baroque spatial practices in Chapter 2. Deleuze sees this folding notion as a way out of the constraints imposed by striated, gridded space which results from all those 'royal' successes in opening up space for 'imperial' exploitation and analysis. Rather than accept spaces of 'royal' control he prefers the 'fold' and space turned in upon itself. Whilst Harrison (2000: 219–20) finds Deleuze's analysis of the Baroque less than persuasive and historically inaccurate, a more sympathetic reading of 'enfolding' is possible.

Herein, the enfolding of shapes in upon each other is reminiscent of the rooms of the bathhouse within the Castro district of San Francisco in the 1970s and 1980s and its inner directedness as a city area. The 'outside' is held in suspicion by the 'insiders', and the reverse is also true. The San Franciscan bathhouses represented in the period 1973–1983 an alternative mode of organisation to that with which we are familiar. First of all, as no less an analyst than Manuel Castells has shown in *The City and the Grassroots*, many gay bars and bathhouses were located in the Castro area in which gays had established political power throughout the late 1960s. Voting had been organised and Harvey Milk's election as Mayor was but a representation of this organisation of protected space. The Castro would emerge as a gay 'city within a city' in the last quarter of the twentieth century. Yet in the face of the discourses concerning 'the development of public hygiene, medical doctrines of psychopathology, class- and race-based biologism' (Wright in Higgs, 1999: 167) and plain old police brutality, there were attempts at remaining closeted even within this protected city space. So, more protected still, were the bathhouses for they offered 'a safer and more private alternative to public venues' where gays were exposed to 'arrest, blackmail, beatings, robbery and murder' (1999: 170). The first two explicitly gay male bathhouses were Jack's Turkish Baths and Third Street Baths, and both opened in the 1930s. These offered more protection as enclosures for gay lifestyles, for included within them was the development of specific forms of argot representing a gay dialect. This form of discourse – a 'parlari' – kept out the uninitiated and avoided the censorship of the straight world. 'Are you a friend of Dorothy's?' became a universally recognised code within the Anglophone world and beyond.

Beyond this, the 'closet economy' developed in which the protection of gays by gays was enhanced by businesses forming alliances to provide services and mutual protection. Bars, baths, adult bookstores and mail order services formed the core of this closet economy which began to adopt a sense of being a (albeit all white) minority. All this led to the feeling of San Francisco being 'a refugee camp for homosexuals' where, according to McCaffrey (quoted in Wright 1999: 179) 'we have formed a ghetto, out of self protection. It is a ghetto rather than free territory, because it is still theirs. Straight cops patrol us, straight legislators make our laws, straight employers keep us in line, straight money exploits us'. Privacy was and is precious to San Franciscans we are told by Wright (1999: 182–3). Castro residents never divulge their address. They move often and have unlisted phone numbers. Within this ghetto there was even more to be 'hidden' from the straight police. For here we have to recognise that sadomascochism (S/M) is seen as more secret and perverse than the fashion statements of those who are into the leather scene (Guertsen in Whittle 1994: 144–5).

In summary then, we can see that the bathhouse in the Castro district is presentable as 'a fold' in the fabric of space, representing a layer within a layer within a layer as the district attempted self-policing and succeeded in developing organisational forms of control and self-management constructed around political, economic, discursive and spatial enclosures. It is the opposite of prison in obvious ways, yet shares with the penitentiary the same reliance upon walls. In the Castro area, the walls kept out the barbarians. In the mainstream, the walls keep the barbarians incarcerated. But two organisational forms, one dominant, one subordinate, face each other across a binary divide which takes the form of an enfolding wall.

Because of this enclosed nature of the bathhouses and the social fabric which surrounds them – the fact that this place is a fold in space – the precise characteristics of these organisations within the Castro are difficult to acquire. A website entitled 'The Bathhouse Diaries' (/entry 20020901) contains the following.

> " I started writing these stories because I noticed that no one had ever talked about what goes on in a bathhouse. You can find many erotic stories written about encounters at the baths. But there are hardly any books written about the politics and the whole culture that takes place behind the doors at a bathhouse. Believe me, it is a whole other world.

What is then described is the following: anonymous membership, an avoidance of eye contact, the fact that there was a 'business of pleasure', the high status of beauty, an emphasis on mutual choice, a reliance on performance enhancing drugs, architectural reflections of particular pleasures so that the client could tell from the outside what was to be expected inside, the purchase of private space when required and overall, a devotion to hedonics.

The first point worth making is that such characteristics are to be found in other forms of voluntary organisations today. And second, the bathhouse also shares in common certain features of other pleasure domes that have come into being. Whilst there is not space here to develop the argument in any careful way, bathhouses appear to have grasped the Baroque as a style or period which they, and other institutions formed around hedonism, might draw upon. If one looks at the list of features identified above, it is possible to make out certain elements of the Baroque, such as masked balls, with an emphasis on anonymity and the freedom from consequences thereby produced. The mask served to hide the wearer from direct eye contact and the gaze. The pleasure gardens of the Baroque palaces hid labyrinths in which Kings and Courtiers could engage in sexual liaisons. Beauty in the form of the voluptuousness of decoration and gown and body was central to the Baroque period. The importance of the tactile was quite clear so that touch was greatly valued as a sensory locus. Grottoes too are key architectural additions of the Baroque. Today, the rise of lead-lined secure rooms, such as that possessed until recently by the firm Arthur Andersen, which seek to evade eavesdropping surveillance, are quite noticeable as being in this tradition. So too is the contemporary emphasis on crypts/ labyrinths and maize mazes. This fits in with the argument of Buci-Glucksmann (1994) who uses the notion of the Baroque to understand the last years of the twentieth century in France. She suggests the ruin, the labyrinth and the library are the key institutional forms of the Baroque. In the early 1980s in San Francisco we might argue that the most obvious Baroque feature were the bathhouses.

However, given the widespread hostility to the bathhouses in the early 1980s, we might well expect that a different and opposed account of these Baroque organisational structures would be associated with an alternative and competing organisational logic. This counter move was forthcoming from a long tradition of 'organisational classicism' and was quickly provided from within the 'straight' dominant, bureaucratic organisational form. What is meant by 'classicism' is that style that is derived from those Greco-Roman-inspired encouragements of ratio-nalism found in the Enlightenment's Neo-Classical period. With its straight lines, a sense of proportion and a belief in observer rationality rather than 'participant emotion', classicism produces transparency and openness of form (cf. Lefebvre on abstract space). 'Classically' inspired analyses detest the twisted 'shambles' from whence revolt might come at any moment, and found the Baroque bathhouses extremely difficult to cope with. Put simply, the image of the grotto in a fold is by no means to everyone's taste. Randy Shilts, in particular, when discussing the rise of AIDS, takes the side of the institutions of public health and disease control, whose style of organisation, it should be noted, sought not to be 'enfolded' and hidden but to be revelatory, linear and mathematical in its transparent precision. Shilts (1987), thoughout, sees the organisation and politics of San Franciscan gay life as getting in the way of good public health. Its constant enfolding to protect its membership makes control and disease prevention very difficult indeed, he argues. In 1983, as Shilts describes, the suggested closure of the bathhouses created a deep division within the gay community of San Francisco. Faced by huge efforts on behalf of the city to shut them down, by the late 1980s the bathhouses had more or less closed for lack of business. But by the early 1990s, they were in business again as a circumvention of the ban on bathhouses had been achieved by a new system of 'private sex clubs'. Wright says that 'membership fees were nominal, the practice of phoning in reservations was adumbrated with lists of paid club members at the door or the mere formality of collecting a (forged) signature and entry fee, much as the old bath houses had done in the time before AIDS' (Wright in Higgs 1999: 187–8).

Some readers at this point may then say – but does this process not merely represent 'hyper-commodification' of gay life-styles within consumer capitalism? Does it not point to the fact that the bathhouses were commercial organisations serving a client need and had no real alternative organisational spatial form which represented a serious challenge to the orthodoxy? Does their closure not show that they were by no means a radical alternative to all the disciplinary technologies concentrated in the Castro of the AIDS 'epidemic'?

It is at this point that one reaches for the book by Foucault that has affected understanding in social science approaches to management more than any other. That book is *Discipline and Punish* and it provides us with the clearest expression of Foucault's thinking on organisational forms. True, he had discussed the concept of '*l'organisation*' in *The Archaeology of Knowledge* but it is in *Discipline and Punish* that he focuses upon the resemblance between organisational forms in offering ways of disciplining and punishing their membership. Of course, it also provides a very skewed understanding of what Foucault might have wished to say about organising in its totality but nevertheless one might begin with such a stance. What would the bathhouses of the late 1970s look like in terms of the concepts utilised by Foucault in that very same period?

Foucault's experiences in the San Franciscan bathhouses perhaps revealed to him forms of organisation dedicated to the hedonics of desire. The presence of the disciplinary technologies of dressage, the judges of normality, the confession, the gaze and the panopticon are remarkably absent (in the crucial sense of juridicial presence) within the bathhouses of San Francisco at the time of Foucault's Californian visits. In some sense, the dressage of the body which is sought by the management of large organisations, including the state, is missing therein. The picture that Foucault chooses to represent the concept of dressage in *Discipline and Punish* is of the tree being bent back into straightness by the restraints of strong bonds. The English play here on 'bent' and 'straight' will not be lost on the reader. In the bathhouses, the body of the individual male could be used in whatever way they thought fit. The confession, it appears, was not seen as completely desirable within the bathhouse, for it was a place of action rather than contemplation, a locale of pleasure not of introverted introspection. Whilst, of course, one might imagine that phantasy and sex talk would play some role, it appears that 'performativity' drove forward the calculation of conquests rather than conversation. Hedonism and the confession do not sit well with each other in the same physical space. Third, the conventional judges of normality were absent from the bathhouses – at least in their professional capacity. Public health inspections of the premises were fought off and resisted as best they could. What were regarded as normal straight sexual practices were deliberately subverted within the bathhouses and normality took on a different hue (Maupin 1978: 97). As Foucault himself said, 'I am no doubt not the only one who writes in order to have no face. Do not ask who I am and do not ask me to remain the same: leave it to our bureaucrats and our police to see that our papers are in order. At least spare us their morality when we write' (1972: 17). The gaze and the panopticon were also missing from the bathhouses in a very deliberate sense. These buildings were designed to provide this sort of privacy in a knowing way.

In summary, then, the Foucault of *Discipline and Punish* had lived in the realm of the Californian bathhouses. They were organisations that were as close to being 'beyond' discipline as one might wish to imagine and they were organisations of and for consumption. Moreover, for the Foucault of *The Use of Pleasure* they were sites of activity that reflected technologies of the self where small elite groups had banded together to create their own modes of understanding and behaviour within their own communities.

Opening spaces

This section seeks to consider that practice and theory of restructuring space centred on the pulling down of barriers and opening up that which has previously been hidden or barred to entry in some other way, being perhaps the opposite of the bathhouses. The focus, therefore, will be on the demolition or breaching of walls, the cutting of barbed wire, and the construction of new routes to and through spaces. We begin with so-called democratic architecture.

Democratic architecture

In recent years, there have been significant attempts to create a consciously open and transparent architecture for explicitly democratic buildings. Examples include the buildings of the European Union in Brussels, the Australian government building in Canberra (see Dovey 1999 for a full discussion), the Reichstag in Berlin and the Welsh Assembly Building in Cardiff. Politicians within the Berlin Reichstag are now overseen by the public who can take the spiralling walkway to the top of the building and look down, literally and metaphorically, upon their 'leaders'. The same principles are being applied to the Welsh Assembly in Cardiff where, once they have negotiated the scanners at the entrance, the public are allowed to look down on their ministers sitting at their PCs (Figure 7). Seats are available so that viewing could take the whole day, but thick 'safety' glass prevents the observer (or anything they care to throw) from falling into the auditorium below.

Figure 7 *The Welsh Assembly Building, Cardiff. This is an espoused example of democratic architecture where transparency is the emblematic theme of Norman Foster's design. The use of glass is central to such architecture, suggesting an openness and accessibility whilst in effect creating a physical barrier to participation. Foster uses a similar theme in the Reichstag in Berlin.*

Aldersey-Williams (1999) claims that 'Glass is now the material of choice for democrats in Strasbourg, in Berlin, in Edinburgh'. The Reichstag with its glass cupola gives the impression that no boundaries exist between the people and the elites who are supposed to represent them. The architecture gives the impression of bringing down spatial barriers, whilst hiding the real barriers that obviously do exist to the attainment of full democracy. The visitors' entrance, for example, is carefully screened from the politicians. We might argue, with Lefebvre and Orwell, that 'democratic architecture' renders institutions more non-democratic because it represents closure as openness and occlusion as transparency. Thus, 'glass appears revolutionary while achieving conservative ends' (1999). Glass opens up yet closes down. A glass wall is a sensory contradiction (1999). It is an inherent part of the property of the crystal panel to stand as a source of transparency but also of occlusion. Every piece of glass, thus conceived, is a source of distortion.

Of course, spaces have been made open and transparent without the presence of glass. The agora of Athens (Sennett 1994: 55–61) was an area of unpaved open ground of about ten acres into which all citizens, whether rich or poor, could come and meet and participate in Athenian democracy. Of course, 130,000 others with the status of slaves were excluded by dint of not being citizens, deemed not fit to speak or vote. But the point here is that this architectural expression of democracy was conceived of as open and flat ground. Much utopian imagery thereafter, revolves around city life made more open and rendered egalitarian. The utopia described by Harvey in *Spaces of Hope* (2000: 263–79) would be one such attempt. In his provocative appendix called 'Edilia', 'the insurgent architect' describes the organisational details of this new Eden. The basic units of habitation are the 'hearth' made up of 25 or so adults and children, whilst the largest social unit is the 'regiona' of 3 million people, which is an independent self-supporting bio-region. This manner of organisation is symbolised by the physical layout of the units. Whole city blocks have been knocked through to create communal living spaces, yet still respecting the privacy of the individual. Cultivation occurs within the city. Whilst there are arbours and closed gardens for recreation, there is intense horticulture. Probably based on contemporary Baltimore,

Harvey's highly organised and static structure takes the nature of the city for granted and says little about the dynamic processes of human interaction. His 'insurgent architect' is more a builder of static social mores than of the lived-in environment. But almost everywhere, utopianism has chosen to focus upon static mores – including the 'original' *Utopia* dreamt up by Thomas More. And the reader does not need to be reminded that one person's space of freedom is another's space of constraint.

Pulling down the palisades

Some of the most radical social transformations have been brought about by the opening-up of space through mobile groups of humans entering spaces hitherto unknown to them, or hitherto blocked to their advance by static defences. Migrations and invasions perhaps are the clearest examples and have the most transformative social impact, although they may be politically conservative or progressive. Virilio (1994) has written about the architecture of the Atlantic Wall which was a defensive line from Bergen to Biarritz, adopted by the Nazis to prevent any D-Day landings. It was developed, perhaps paradoxically, by an army that had prospered on 'lightning' mobility and the *blitzkreig*. It was perhaps the concrete 'pause' to movement that architecture often does represent, as most explicitly in Gehry's Guggenheim Museum at Bilbao. The Hitlerian spatial notion of *lebensraum* is itself based precisely on the opening-up of space previously controlled and fixed by those Others who used notions of the sanctity of national frontiers and accompanying static defence lines. Imperial armies that cross frontiers with scant disregard to the peoples they are about to affect, often end up building walls to protect their own frontiers from just such incursions. Hadrian's Wall is a point at which the Roman Empire stopped and where the palisades were built of turf and stone to keep out the *Britunculi*, the 'wretched Britons'. The Berlin Wall represented such a palisade in more recent times, its destruction a highly charged emotional and symbolic act. But even if we try and think about such processes and palisades within specific national contexts, as opposed to imperial or international arenas, the issue of power remains.

As we have described in previous chapters, the effect of enclosure of the common land had a profound effect upon the British countryside and was in many places resisted. The Anti-Enclosure movements were not well developed but they did exist and had some effect in mobilising further action against the populace. In the twentieth century, the Ramblers developed peaceful techniques to force landowners to open up access to some moorland areas in the North of England. The leaders of this voluntary organisation were frequently jailed and constantly reviled for their attitude to aristocratic property rights but (in what might be seen as the revenge of the *Britunculi*) the national parks of Britain in part owe their existence to the right-to-ramble activists.

The 'garden' concept throws the issue of mobility and opening space into stark relief. It has been shown in many places, including Euripides's description of how the Bacchae treated those of an Apollonian bent (Euripides 1973: 215–18) and The Old Testament's narrative in Genesis of the events leading up to the Expulsion, that the garden is a place of mystery, power and pain, as well as harmonious enlightenment, equality and pleasure. In the first, the garden is opened up to highly sexualised marauders who plunder all before them. Here the horrors of the world enter the garden. In the second source, the expulsion from the palisades opens up the horrors of the world to those thrown out. The opening of space can be pleasurable or painful.

What does become apparent is that gardens, as with other social spaces, are places of multiple interpretations. There are two strong medieval garden traditions of note here. Both of these are on offer as spaces of the past, present and future. These are the *hortus conclusus*, the enclosed private space for contemplation which included hints of the wilderness but all under very firm control, or the more public and corporeal spaces of the *hortus deliciarum*, the garden of delights or the pleasure dome, as in for example the 'Valley of the Ladies' in Boccaccio's *Decameron* (van Zuylen 1995: 43). Thus, on the one side, we have the securing of the garden against nature, the wilderness, the beastly, perhaps particularly through the control of female sexuality as mythically symbolic of these forces. On the other, we have the close association of the garden with the wild – fertility, phallocentric sexuality and Dionysian abandonment.

Both views are about the relative openness of space. Foucault (1970) recognises this when he says, 'Utopias afford consolation: although they have no real locality, there are nevertheless a fantastic untroubled region in which they are able to unfold: they open cities with vast avenues, superbly planted gardens, countries where life is easy, even though the road to them is chimerical' (quoted in Harvey 2000: 183).

The destruction of the palisades can open up conceptual and material space. But the nature of the space revealed and the uses to which it will be put offer no guarantees that there will have been a radicalisation of the space. Opened up space, such as required by the World Bank and the IMF for country-specific loans may merely force entry of that nation state into a global system of capitalism. Refusal to open up national space for particular forms of trade is sometimes followed by status as a 'failed state'. Enclosure then is not a uniformly conservative force.

Anarchism and the opening-up of space

In the 1960s, particularly in the USA, an attempt was made to articulate 'alternative architecture' which, as a portmanteau concept, had a variety of interrelated compartments to it. First, there was valorisation of the indigenous styles of architecture which, for example, in the case of adobe settlements were seen to come from a 'golden past' in which the untutored vernacular style had much to offer (Rudofsky 1964). Second, there was an encouragement of building 'earth shelters' that offered cheap, well-insulated structures by being constructed largely underground and covered by turf. Third, self-build architecture took the form of structures based on passages within linguistic structuralism concerned with *bricolage*. Here the rejection of rationalistic design and planning led to the celebration of ad hoc constructions using recycled materials which happened to come to hand. This use of tree trunks, corrugated iron, plastic and plywood tapped into a deep-rooted notion in US culture of an historically based rural self-reliance and an accompanying distrust of architects and planners. This romanticism within 'alternative architecture', of course, was reflective of very ancient standpoints that, in searching for the future, looked backwards to a rural idyll.

The 'Land of Cockaygne' is found in a medieval English ballad and describes an escape for the lower classes, particularly rural peasantry, from labour and serfdom. It stems from the conceptualisation of an ideal world with a 'happy confluence of man and nature in an earthly paradise with abundant resources and aesthetically pleasing surroundings' (Hollis 1998: 41). But it is centrally associated with an excess of food, drink and sex. It is a utopia therefore, focused on the physical pleasures, in a land of plenty. The picture created is one of idle but healthy peasants in a classless and 'lawless' society where private property rights do not govern. Later, the tradition became associated with medieval festivals and carnivals where the turning upside-down of the everyday world was attempted. Hierarchy had been questioned throughout the feudal period in various Peasants' Revolts that had occurred in Europe. In the English Civil War the Levellers asked the anarchist question, 'When Adam delved and Eve span, who was then the Gentleman?' The resort to the Bible, particularly the New Testament and its encouragement of the questioning of hierarchy through the story of Christ's birth in a stable and his washing of the disciples' feet, was quite common in this search for an inversion of the aristocratic principle from within the scriptures.

But anarchism is much more than pro-democratic anti-hierarchicalism. If one dares risk talking of 'it' as a singular impulse for a brief moment, it may be noted that it stands for a questioning of the state and its role in social life. It stands for small-scale, human-centred forms of organising, technologies and productive activity (Thompson 1968: chapter 14). It rests upon distributed decision making by the whole community who perhaps share common value systems resting upon rejection of a single leader, a centralised state apparatus and the Kafkaesque bureaucracy that serves it. The anarchists of the Kronstadt Revolt in St Petersburg, in the early days of the Soviet Union, wholeheartedly rejected the Bolshevik system of 'bureaucracy plus the firing squad'. What they sought was an opening-up of space, the availability of land for all, to allow the blossoming of decentralised localism wherever it could flourish.

Given this, it might be argued that anarchism (meaning without central rule) cannot be relevant to a globalising world economy in the twenty-first century. With its emphasis on small-scale, anti-state, pro-local democracy, anti-leadership, ultra-leftist views, what could be the possible use of such a stance to the contemporary world? Anarchism, however, is alive and functioning in the anti-globalisation movement (Bircham and Charlton 2001: 321–28). Anti-capitalist demonstrators in a variety of recent economic summit meetings have organised themselves and their supporters using quite explicit forms of anarchist organisation and rhetoric. Exploiting modern forms of communication but within a cell-like structure that emphasises the benefits of small-scale activism and acephalism, anarchists have discovered ways, again, of circumventing opponents committed to large-scale bureaucracies. Commentators such as Manuel Castells (1989, 2003) has shown the relevance of anarchism to Mexican Zapatistas and it is clear that more widely in Latin America, it is a widely accepted organisational principle.

However, anarchism's view of space is widely misunderstood. Key here is the conceptual rival to anarchism's notion of Cockayne – the Arcadian utopia which we have already met. This image is one in which 'the desire for satisfaction is tempered through moderation' (Hollis 1998: 14). Interestingly, the Arcadia of Virgil is a reinvention of that by the Greek lyric poet Theocritus in the third century BC of an earlier Arcadia, actually a part of Greece, which was presented as a wilderness (Schama 1996: 528). The original area of Arcadia in Greece was a pre-selenic wilderness, marked by beastliness and bestiality, inhabited by 'autochthons', original mankind sprung from the earth itself, whose divinity was Pan, half goat by form and animal-like in his nature. From the second, recreated Arcadia, 'this perfect pastoral state, all savage things have been banished' transformed by 'a sense of order which is the social invention of humanity rather than the pure work of nature' (1996: 528). In Virgil's reworking, then, the forests become fields, the cultivated replaces the wild, animals now conduct themselves like citizens and are grown full and fat on the land. Civilisation is in its full refinement and it is man [sic] who lords it over the beastly. It is in the countryside that leisure might be taken in a tamed, controlled environment of security. This, need it be said, is quite a contrast to that of Cockaygne. Arcadia, in the manner of Virgil, was re-popularised by Renaissance humanists who saw its images as an antidote to the greed of the rich, powerful upper classes. However, the rural utopia captured in the remodelling of the English countryside in the eighteenth century gave no ground to either the dreams of corporeal sensuality of the lower classes, nor those of social justice held by the humanists.

Anarchism, it might be argued, is the democratic impulse in its rawest, most intense form. It is the organising principle from the past (and the future?) which has questioned the state most actively and clung on to notions of small-scale decision making by involved members of a collective. Although there are multiple versions of anarchism, in which the mechanisms by which decisions are made differ, and the level of analysis from which the state is opposed are also open to debate, what we are concerned with here is the possibility for different, more democratic, conceptualisations of space to be developed and built in a deliberate fashion (Parker *et al.* 2007).

Situationism

Situationism grew up as a radical French philosophical school around the likes of Guy Debord and a journal that published just 12 issues, *Internationale Situationniste*. They exhibited enthusiasm and exuberance which they liked taking to the city streets in the steps of their surrealist and Dadaist forebears. They demanded a 'revolution in everyday life', not least of which would involve transformation of the urban environment. They were responsible for some of the most memorable graffiti which appeared on Parisian walls in May 1968 and were not sympathetic with usual left-wing ideology. Having said that, they began from an analysis of alienation which they saw not only as rooted in private property and wage labour but as disseminated throughout all aspects of society as offering a fallacious paradise. They called for refusals to work, criminality such as shoplifting, mindless violence and graffiti, a festival of plagiarism and a new Luddism. These actions were designed to 'spit in the face' of those temples for frenetic consumption such as shopping malls, package holidays, theme parks, reconstructed villages and the heritage industry.

They analysed the Watts Riots in Los Angeles with the slogan 'To each, according to his false needs'. In the face of the all-encompassing 'society of the spectacle', the Situationists stressed fun, energy and the right to enjoy life.

Today such perspectives continue to attract. For example, the Centri Sociali (social centres) have spread across Italy in the 1990s but refer back in part to the Situationist ideals of the 1960s. The 'membership' involves themselves in, for example, squatting in abandoned buildings thus threatening property rights, the 'expropriation' of food from supermarkets, the 'self reduction' of bus fares and cinema tickets and a focus on the 'Disobbedienti'. They seek to provide a self-managed space, autonomous from the Italian state.

Another strand of Situationism led to a focus on urban change in the work of Constant, who between 1956 and 1973 spoke of a New Babylon. This was to be a community of movement in which people would shift and change their positions and locations on a very regular yet unpredictable way. It was to be 'the antithesis of the society of lies' (Heynen 2001: 157–72). Inhabitants were freed from all ties, norms and conventions in what was designed to be a dynamic labyrinth. All forms of permanence were to be rejected and people encouraged to live a nomadic existence. They were to achieve this permanent revolution through an anaesthetising 'derangement of the senses' and the cultivation of fun and enjoyment through the development of the game-playing 'homo ludens'. New Babylon will consist, Constant argued, of 80 per cent public space so that private space will be reduced to a minimum. Although Constant broke with the Situationists and saw his plans as future-oriented, the Provos in Amsterdam declared that city as the first site of New Babylon in the late 1960s. Meanwhile, in Copenhagen's Christiania district, Situationism was also having a spatial effect. Here, a mass squat in 1971 had established a self-governing part of the Christanhavn district on the site of an old military barracks. Christiania is governed by a series of meetings which all residents on the 85-acre site may attend and it has its own currency. Access to residence on the site is governed by an 'area' interview and 'public acceptance' at that meeting. The inhabitants of Christiania have faced numerous threats to close the area down but have responded with large

Situationist protests that have so far allowed a continuity of existence for the freetown within the Danish state. Yet Christiania's existence, New Babylon, and Situationism in general were all products of the 1960s. And like so much of that period, perhaps they did not outlast the 1980s in any form that has escaped commodification and life as tourist attractions.

Nomadology

Gilles Deleuze and Felix Guattari are inheritors of some of the Situationist positions, and the intention here is to focus on the opening-up of space they call 'nomadology'. In the view of Deleuze and Guattari (1988: 268), Goethe and Hegel, their key intellectual enemies, uphold the importance of the plan(e) of organisation. The plan(e) of organisation covers the area that Deleuze and Guattari call stratification. It stands for hierarchy. It is part of the state apparatus. It is unpleasant. Nietzsche and Kleist, on the other hand, they argue, are concerned with the true soul of movement. This is to be found in the (decidedly unplanned) plane of consistency. At this most basic level, new planes of consistency can be constructed through more movement and nomadism by human beings.

Note then, that in their collective works, (an approach sometimes called 'DeleuzeGuattarian') they can be seen to stand against deep-seated organisation and in favour of a traversing consistency. It is easy to see then why one of Deleuze and Guattari's overarching theoretical endeavours is nomadism. Wandering is the key activity in which they seek to engage. There is no ultimate aim or direction. What is sought is a headlong flight from the centres of power. As Steffy (1997: 449) has noted, much of contemporary social theory has the feel of a geography in which a map of a two-dimensional space is laid out for us as a representation of 'reality'. It is certainly presented in cartographic terms by Deleuze and Guattari as a picture of the terrain where humans can de-territorialise and act in a nomadic way. 'We think too much in terms of history, whether personal or universal', said Deleuze, 'Becomings belong to geography...' (Deleuze and Parnet 1987: 2). Nevertheless, at the slightest opportunity Deleuze and Guattari move beyond the geographical metaphor to one which is much more geological. Indeed on the very first page of *A Thousand Plateaus* (Deleuze and Guattari 1988: 3) they explicitly privilege geology.

They like geological analogies and speak of ontological 'folds'. As we have already seen, their metaphor of choice from this discipline refers to the folding of matter whence we see geological processes of stratification. Just as a lump of dough is folded over and over by a baker, rendering the outlines of the original piece of material more and more difficult to discern, so too is the social and material world. This world of substance always forms the basis of their theorising. Not for them the idealist's notion of the importance of consciousness. Mutual enfoldment of one and the other, where there is an exchange of each other's mode of existence, creates a real socio-historical field from a pre-existing order. What existed separately before the fold, now finds itself virtually indistinguishable from its new partner, wrapped as they are, tightly together in a process of becoming. Deleuze and Guattari are unhappy with the notion, typically derived from a deep structuralism, that all is given and pre-ordained. Their orientation stands against the unchallengeable and the unquestioned. Fluidity is all. Determinism is out. No plans. No organisation.

Nomadology, merely one plateau within *A Thousand Plateaus*, had such an impact that it was produced and published separately in 1986. Here, Deleuze and Guattari offer notions, concepts and provocations which have a clear relevance for organisation theory's approach to space. The state has always attempted, they argue, to control nomad (or minor) science and subordinate it to 'royal' science. The *compagnonnages*, or association of journeymen which we would call guilds in English, were roving groups of skilled labour. The state sought to sedentarise them and thus submit them to regularisation and to governance. Indeed, the state seeks to capture all space and all movements within it, a theme we have explored in relation to the UK in Chapter 4. The space inhabited by the nomad, however, is a smooth space over which he [*sic*] slides and distributes himself. The nomadic thinker seeks to travel in an homogenous space outside the imperial boundaries. In a strange paradoxical way, the citizen of the city which is a highly striated space moves all the time across and between boundaries whilst the nomad 'does not move' (Deleuze and Guattari 1988: 51). He does not move because deterritorialisation converts the earth for him into one homogenous place – the steppes, the desert, the ice fields. For 'nomads have no history; they only have a geography' (p. 73). This passage below contains, in essence, much of their thinking on what it would be like to be a nomad:

> On the side of the nomadic assemblages and war machines, it is a kind of rhizome, with its gaps, detours, subterranean passages, stems, openings, traits, holes etc. On the other side, the sedentary assemblages and State apparatuses effect a capture of the phylum, put the traits of expression into a form or a code, make the holes resonate together, plug up the lines of flight, subordinate the technological operation to the work model, impose upon the connections a whole regime of arborescent conjunctions. (Deleuze and Guattari 1988: 109)

Space then in the DeleuzeGuattarian world is a kind of rhizome, with its gaps, detours, subterranean passages, stems, openings, traits, holes but it is also a place for the nomad. Much, though not all, of this chapter has focused upon just such features of opening up our conceptualisations of space. How, then, to proceed to use these forms of alternative space to create alternative forms of organising?

Alternative space: an end to private property?

The relationship between space and property is perhaps central to finding alternatives to current forms of organising space. Why should it be assumed that what is on the land, what is in the land and what is above the land should 'belong' to those who live there? Why should it be assumed that rights of access of this kind should be extended to those who do not live there but who nevertheless 'own' the land? Property rights are a difficult but crucial issue in finding alternative spaces. Giddens (1971: 40), following Marx, argues that private property first emerges in the ancient world but only in limited areas. In the Middle Ages, several new stages of the development of property are evident, beginning with feudal landed property, corporative moveable property, and then capital invested in manufactories in the towns. In all of these, property is bound to the community, and politics is a local matter. Gorringe (2002: 70) points to the different perspective on property which was embedded in feudal land relations. The only absolute property holder was the king, otherwise all property was held in ownership of the local lord in their relationship to the monarch. There was a reciprocal if unequal relationship between owners and tenants, which involved an exchange of use and services. Modern capitalism, however, rarely has any communal or local embeddedness. As power moved from the King to Parliament, so a different approach to property developed. This enshrined in law an absolute and permanent right to property, and the assumption that ownership allows (almost) total control over that property. As the community dissipates and private property advances, the law becomes central to its furtherance and protection. Scott (1979: 30) has shown how the fiendish complexity of 'ownership' and 'property' and the 'law' is central to preventing a way through to the development of a 'sociology of property'. He claims that by the late 1970s sociologists by and large had neglected 'property'. A quarter of a century later little has changed.

We started to look at this issue in Chapter 4, where we concentrated on the construction of a 'political economy of space' around private property and power. This was related to the changing relationship to land and locality through the forced enclosure of common land, and the changing nature of social relations through 'the market' and contracts. In this section, we take this discussion further by considering how a changing perspective on property could link to the creation of an alternative space.

The 'political economy of space' in the UK was shaped by those seeking positions of power and those already holding power. Thompson argues that it 'was a plain enough case of class robbery, played according to the fair rules of property and law laid down by a parliament of property owners and lawyers' (Thompson 1968: 237–8). The structure of property ownership in the UK is little changed today. Gorringe comments that

> Everywhere inequality is inscribed in space, though perhaps rarely as dramatically as in England and Scotland, a situation which can still be traced largely to the impact of the Norman invasion of 1066! Half of Scotland's 19 million acres is owned

> by 608 land owners, and 10 per cent by 18. In England the top
> 1 per cent of the population own nearly two thirds of the land.
> Details of ownership are shrouded in secrecy. (2002: 50–1)

His source for England is the Royal Commission on the Distribution of Income and Wealth of 1979, which was to be abolished three months into the first Conservative Government under Margaret Thatcher.

Given this wholesale inequality, it is not surprising that the question of property ownership has been central to attempts to re-conceptualise and reshape social space. In 1840, Proudhon wrote *What is Property?* which contains the phrase, known to many, that 'property is theft'. Proudhon was a worker himself, and sought to write in their interests. His book challenged the tenets of what was then called political economy and made him the most influential socialist in Paris. Marx liked the book, but became critical of Proudhon's position when Proudhon refused to act as the French correspondent for a Committee set up by Marx.

Marx also locates property ownership as a centrally important focus for political change. However, he turns from the property relations of the agrarian revolution to industrialisation. Marx saw not the agricultural labourer as the major historical actor but the factory worker. Crucial at this point in the discussion of the nineteenth-century approach to private property and its abolition is the notion of alienation. Marx saw that private property and alienated labour were different expressions of the same relationship. The emancipation of the workers could only come from the ending of private property, for private property mediates between civil society and the state. It is the essence of capitalism and the 'alienated man' is the key figure of that system. *Alienation* in English has two meanings but one word. In German, alienation is expressed through two words that have different meanings which are lost in the single English term. These are *Entfremdung*, which means estrangement from one's fellows, and *Entausserung*, which means dispossession from what is rightly one's own. This double meaning clearly links the existential sense of being human in a community with the possession of settled property. In *The Communist Manifesto* it is claimed that 90 per cent of the population no longer have any property and its non-existence for them allows the remainder to have capitalist property. It is asserted that of the ten points connected with revolutionising the means of production, the first in importance is the abolition of property in land and the distribution of the rents to public purposes. The seventh point is the extension of factories and the bringing of the wastelands into cultivation. Communism overall is meant to allow for the positive transcendence of private property and thus the consummated oneness of humanity with nature. Its removal has the effect of emancipating the senses. It is this strand of 'reclaiming the commons' that has had an impact on the 'anti-capitalist movement' in very recent times. The 'commons' once seen as the land freed from private ownership has now come in the twenty-first century to include bio-diversity, access to water, the maintenance of traditional knowledges, and openness of information.

Weber, too, saw that the most important cleavage in a market-based society was the ownership of property. The *Besitzklassen* are the owners of property who receive rents through their possession of land, mines, and natural resources. They command privileged access to education. They often form a status group which enjoys high prestige from others. With this amount of power and political sway, property owners may well be able to influence societal means and ends. Arguing as they usually do in terms of antinomies, Deleuze and Guattari (1988: 443–4) suggest that land, work and money represent an 'apparatus of capture' and come to sedentarise the world, whilst it is the opposites of territory, activity and exchange that truly represent an alternative. In their view there is no simple economic evolution or 'lineage' through the forms of 'gatherers – hunters – animal breeders – farmers – industrialists', nor through the sequence 'the nomads – semi-nomads – sedentaries', nor through 'dispersed autarky of local groups – villages and small towns – cities – states' (p. 430). Thus, as they are not natural and inevitable, the links between land and power can be broken.

Two questions occur here. The first concerns 'the repository' of the alternative ideas to spatial organisation. What, if any, spaces have not been captured by capitalism? What spaces have avoided 'the spatial fix' spoken of by David Harvey (1989, 2000)? The second question concerns the nature of change, whether of a revolutionary form or from some seeds of the future which may be already present in our social spaces.

Williams (2005) argues that many spaces have not yet been opened up to the commodity form of exploitation and there are economic forms of collaboration not yet fully controlled by capitalism and the market mechanism. These include local economic exchanges within the community where land, work and money have not yet fully replaced territory, activity and exchange. In local areas, bartering, exchange of expertise, and non-monetised exchange of all kinds goes on. Williams (2005: 275) claims that his book uncovers 'the view of a hegemonic, all-encompassing, totalising and victorious capitalism' as an illusion. There is an encouragement to think less of a dual society between the commodifed and the non-commodified and more of a pluralist set of economic arrangements. In our terms, Williams is suggesting the housing estates and voluntary associations are the place where alternative forms of economic life might exist. But do these represent places and spaces where property is re-conceptualised? Williams does not discuss property at all but focuses on the issue of commodification which is a related but by no means identical issue. Whilst 'property' places land in the legal realm, 'commodification' places objects in an economic relation one to another. For example, the legal basis of marriage and the commodification of husband and wife in the eyes of the other are not the same thing and have differing trajectories – but they are interrelated. Nevertheless, the idea that alternatives to some elements of capitalism exist within contemporary Britain and elsewhere may offer us hope. There are Anglophone repositories of such ideas, says Williams, in Australia, New Zealand, the USA, Canada and the UK. He is optimistic and favourably quotes Byrne *et al.*

> Understanding the household as a site of economic activity, one in which people negotiate and change their relations of exploitation and distribution in response to a wide variety of influences, may help to free us from the gloom that descends when a vision of socialist innovation is consigned to the wholesale transformation of the 'capitalist totality'. (1998: 16)

Here the 'local' is seen as a site of positive and radical potential.

Yet, having looked at the 'political economy of space' as one which enrols social and material relations across spatial scales and spheres, it is difficult to see one scale or sphere as being able to transform space autonomously. Byrne *et al.* admit the household is too privatised and individualised from community, and yet too caught up in the intertwined relations of reproduction, production and consumption to provide a genuinely alternative space in itself: 'We can view the household as hopelessly local, atomised, a set of disarticulated and isolated units, entwined and ensnared in capitalism's global order, incapable of serving as a site of class politics and radical social transformation' (Byrne *et al.* 1998: 16).

However, there have been some transformative developments in Scotland in recent years. Whereas the English Labour Party has long shied away from the socialist principle of nationalisation of the land, there have been moves to restore land to the community in Scotland, which has already taken place on the Isle of Eigg (Gorringe 2002: 68). There have also been calls to introduce a land tax which would bring down capital values and generate revenue that could be used to further return the land to the community (2002: 68). The collective memory of the 'clearances' carried out by landowners in Scotland against the local communities is still very much more live than awareness of the enclosure movements is in England.

We turn, then, to consider whether there are repositories in existence where 'private property' embedded in a capitalist set of relationships can be shown to no longer exist *de facto* or *de jure*, or can be demonstrated to have never existed? Clearly the nomadic peoples of the large Continental areas of central Asia, North Africa, North America and Central Australia would be good places to begin an analysis. But their ways of life, their languages, their understandings of what it is to be living in the land of which they are a symbiotic part in a relationship of trust for their grandchildren are all heavily threatened. Technology, imperial icons, some forms of education, religious conversion, alcohol, gambling and so on are all part of the apparatus of capture. So too are the 'reservations'. The use of these parcels of land to allow 'primitive' life to continue assume that it is any piece of land which will do, an assumption based upon capitalist 'abstract space'. Using the surveyors' notion of square area and acreage, the idea developed that a swap from ancestral homelands to the Badlands would be perfectly adequate because the amount of land 'owned' is equivalent. It fails to see any relevance in ancestry, closeness to the land or knowingness. And of course, native possession of the Badlands will last only so long as there are no mineral deposits there worth exploiting.

The Savage in *Brave New World* was a part too of an abstract space and an homogenising grid formed around the New Mexican reservation near Santa Fe. It was one of four reservations within 560,000 square kilometres of land set aside, each of which was surrounded by 5000 km of electrified wire at 60,000 volts. So there was 'no escape' (Huxley 1994: 89–146) for any of the 60,000 Indians and no communication with the outside world except for the occasional visit from an inspector. Apart from the wire, the natives were controlled by gas bombs and encouraged to drink mescal. And within the reservation all was dirt, flies and goitres. In fact, Huxley had visited this part of the USA in the 1920s and returned in the early 1940s to the Mojave Desert in California as his place to live out the Second World War.

The historical reality of this area's land was no less frightening than Huxley's description of the world to come. Santa Fe was founded in 1609 after Coronado's incursions into North America from the south. What was found were sedentary ways of life associated with the Hokokam people who grew maize using irrigation systems and who built pueblos of stone or adobe. Their leaders were replaced by the Spanish, who installed Christianity instead of the Indian religions. The Spanish also brought with them notions of private property for agricultural and mineral exploitation. Mexico subsequently emerged independent from Spain after bloody race wars led by Creoles in the 1820s, but by 1823, the Santa Fe trail had been opened up so that New Mexico came under US economic and political influence rather than Mexican. It was this state of New Mexico, which became an integral state of the USA in 1912, that Huxley was to visit merely a decade later and remember thereafter as his 'imaginary' Savage Reservation. The concept of 'reservation' wherein the old might be preserved and reserved for the future, therefore, does not stand up to scrutiny as a defensible area with some non-propertied, yet territorial entitlements. They are tolerated by the state and capitalist organisations, only so long as they do not threaten present and future economic interests. And at some point or other they nearly always do.

Under Socialism, it will not have escaped the reader, the state was supposed to take all private property into its possession. Following Marx, the acceptance that property was a key cause of alienation and exploitation led to wholesale changes in ownership patterns in the Russian and Chinese Revolutions of the twentieth century. But this was decidedly not a simple reversion of all property to the state. Property was redistributed in both post-revolutionary eras and thus the spread of the notion of private property was intensified rather than rolled back. At this macrolevel then, whilst significant changes were made property continued to be privately owned in many agricultural spheres. Ownership of the industrial means of production by the state was the focus of attention. What we now know of course is that the alleged failure of these excursions into socialism means that the reassertion of private property within them in virtually all spheres is well accepted as the way forward into the twenty-first century for both states.

It is difficult then to see any serious ideas emanating from either domestic households in the west or 'reservations' in the Continental spaces or ideologically left wing state action from which private property might be attacked and replaced. We have attempted to show that spaces and spheres tend to be mixed, and are not separate. So creating alternative spaces from one sphere alone is not at all easy. Additionally, these radical sites are often repositories of 'old' ideas of the meaning of space and are tolerated therefore only for so long as they do not threaten internationally grounded and 'modern' property rights. They are 'folds' for a good reason. They belong to a hidden but permitted world within the dominant social fabric.

But if property is so crucial, so grounded, so embedded in what passes for normality, how might one go about changing the relationship between property and space? Is it at the individual level, the local level, the civic level or the state level at which the concept and reality of private property is attacked? If it is not from within the old order and its organisational principles that property rights change, how might such de-totalisation come about?

Let us first deal with catastrophism and the posited rapid and significant decline in the human population. What would this do for property rights? Hay (1966: 34) notes that in '1470 the number of households was halved in most European villages compared with the start of the fourteenth century; the reconquest by forest and waste of the arable is "an episode equal in importance to the drama of the earlier clearances". Of course, he is talking largely of the impact of the Black Death where between one third and one half of the human population perished. After it, good arable land was broken up into modest sized units and control given over to the share farmer. Serfdom was pushed to the margins of society. The price of land fell and some peasants refused to pay the tithe or any rent to the landowner. Significant changes to 'wages' and 'work' took place which came about because 'land' was re-conceptualised as no longer being scarce.

Various forms of catastrophism, which the television series *Horizon* has recently made its own, fall alongside post-nuclear war scenarios, biological warfare and asteroid impacts which see fundamental changing relationships between humans and the landscape. Other forms of total-ising change that can be foreseen might tend to be focus on possible but dramatic land scarcity. One scenario might be associated with rising sea levels whereby entitlements that have lasted for generations in land up to 150 feet above sea level, might 'suddenly' disappear under the melted water of the polar ice caps. Dealing with this enforced migration inland and upwards, particularly from the wealthy areas of South East of England or Manhattan may well change societal notions of land enti-tlement. It might well instil thoughts within the state of the benefits of land nationalisation. Scarcity of land of a profound dispossessing kind might well throw up revolts more reminiscent of earlier times. These forces towards immediate land release through human carnage or imme-diate land scarcity through natural cataclysm might take place anywhere on the globe, as they have through human history. It is in the nature of catastrophes that they are not common, but these narratives articu-late the widespread need for us to develop a different relationship with land and locality that no longer expresses an exploitative approach to its materiality.

What chances then are there for the radical (re)organisation of space? In this chapter, we have identified a number of spaces that might be worthy of consideration. There are margin spaces with their danger and edginess. Liminal spaces were identified where boundaries melt away to some extent. Alternating spaces also offer the possibility of some oscillation type change. Alternative spaces also exist in some numbers where the act of enclosure creates a separation of one place from the wider world. Opening space creates new forms of socio-spatial configuration where access into an area is widened. Finally, an attempt was made to discuss alternative space where a de-totalisation of the dominant forms of organisation comes about.

This chapter concludes that a built environment which offers us spaces and places for more democratic and egalitarian experiences of power, consumption, production and administration remain yet to be fully explored, to say nothing of their realisation. However, some elements of a different orientation to social space might be articulated. These include the need for a redistributive justice, which works for a greater egalitarianism of resources. In relation to a transformation of property it requires an attitude of 'stewardship' to the land. This does not see ownership as an absolute and permanent right of possession and control, but as a responsibility and trust for the community and for the future. In this it incorporates both a concern for satisfying the needs of all and for safeguarding the environment. Inherent in all of this is an emphasis on the lived social and material relations of community. This implies both the active participation of all, but also affirms a 'unity in diversity'. All of these are related to changing our approach to spatial relations, to a 'situatedness' (Gorringe 2002: 254–6) or 'dwelling' (Heidegger 1971). For as Lefebvre insisted, 'To change life...we must first change space' (1991: 190), and indeed this is a considerable challenge.

INTRODUCTION: THE SPACES OF ORGANISATION AND THE ORGANISATION OF SPACE

LDING ORGANISATION: SECURING AND OBSCURING POWER • BUILDING PEOPLE:
IDENTITIES AND SPACES • A POLITICAL ECONOMY OF ORGANISED SPACE • BOUNDARY
CROSSINGS: REPRODUCING ORGANISED SPACE • BUILDING A SOCIAL MATERIALITY:
SPATIAL AND EMBODIED POLITICS IN ORGANISATION • ALTERNATIVE SPACES:
THE RADICAL ORGANISATION OF SPACE? • CONCLUSIONS: DISORGANISING SPACE

8 conclusions: disorganising space

An attempt will be made in this final chapter to draw together some of the connections we have made through the book between space and organisation through looking at the spatial politics of the World Trade Center and its Manhattan site. The events of September 11, 2001, may at first sight appear to be a dramatic and exceptional example of the relationship between space and organisation, but there is also a significance to this moment of dissociation, the disorganisation of its social space, that allows us to glimpse many processes and interactions in the mutual enactment of the social and the material that are normally embedded in routes and routines and thus taken-for-granted.

The conventional approach to the analysis of the Manhattan skyline has its own appeal, of course. This wisdom is rooted in the notion of the iconic skyscraper which stands for power in the obvious phallic way, dominating the landscapes below. It is the combination of the material mass of the skyscraper alongside its symbolic valorisation which make the skyscrapers of Manhattan, for example, so potent. There are some connections here with Lefebvre's analysis of the 'abstract space' of capitalism, with its visual-geometric-phallic facets. However, the abstract space of the World Trade Center is not shown primarily in its symbolic architecture, or even in its destruction, but rather in its more hidden history of property ownership and land rents, and its place in the ongoing capitalist logic of accumulation and extraction of value. In September 2001, the spectacularised and mediatised violence of the terrorists met the underlying violence of capitalism. Its representation as an architectural icon of the New York skyline or as a space of human tragedy serve only to obscure those relations of domination under the guise of apparent transparency embedded in the language of 'freedom' and democracy', the market and the career. The World Trade Center is but one node in a 'political economy of space' that goes far beyond the building itself, however iconic.

Yet the attack on the World Trade Center in New York in 2001 appears to be the very negation of social and political space. The destruction of the Twin Towers, along with smaller buildings, is frequently described as an absence rather than a presence. 'Ground Zero' is the phrase used to capture this collapse. What towered high in the air is now in fragments on the ground. The functional spaces became a void in mere minutes. What is often forgotten is that (as we pointed out earlier) the term comes from the military. It is a euphemism, finding favour in the period of 'mutually assured destruction' (MAD), to describe the intended target for a nuclear bomb. It was first used to identify the centre of the destruction brought about by the dropping of the bomb on Hiroshima. It allows the calculation of blast damage from the point of origin. Thus it is the precise point on the surface of the earth at which or above which a nuclear detonation has been made. So Ground Zero is a place of explosive destruction, a target, a place that is no place. Yet the very materiality of this absence is captured by the photographs of Joel Meyerowitz, who describes the thousands of tons of steel and cable and concrete rubble in the aftermath of their collapse (Newsnight, BBC2, 11 September, 2006). The gaping hole quickly becomes full of social and ideological meanings. The debris becomes socially constructed so that cross-beams, melted in the heat, are rendered symbolic as a cross. The escape of some on the still-standing 'survivors' staircase' of the north tower is heralded as a miracle. The residual material of the collapse became a source of 'external symbolic storage' (Donald 1991) (Figure 8).

One set of debates in the aftermath has been about the materiality of the buildings themselves, asking why the Twin Towers collapsed so easily. As this question has been examined by various parties, the mutual enactment of social and material processes becomes apparent. The straightforward answer appears to have been that the explosion of the impacting aircraft blew the fire-protective coating off the main structural steel beams within the towers, exposing the steel to the full force of the subsequent heat. Structural engineers and architects had not calculated on an explosive impact of these proportions[1]. Ties which kept the plate of each floor rigid against the metal framework of the buildings melted in

Figure 8 Ground Zero, New York, December 2001. The 'ruin' awaits the work of all architects perhaps, but the ruination of the Twin Towers in one morning created bodily, political and symbolic turmoil across the globe. At the same time, it presented economic opportunities to real estate companies and other architectural practices.

the inferno and one by one the floors collapsed on top of the floor below, rendering it unstable, creating an accelerating effect which allowed the buildings to collapse. The central core and the method of attaching floors to it were not strong enough to support the buildings. The corners of the buildings contained the escape stairwells which were protected from the fire but not from the force of the collapsing floors. The stairwells in the two buildings have figured in many of the individual narratives. Lifts, which make living in skyscrapers routinely possible, were rendered inoperable on the outbreak of the fire, forcing thousands of people into the stairwells. These were the meeting places where friends and colleagues met and said goodbye as well as moving in concert. Many were talking on their cell phones, trying to speak to others in the building or those who might be worried. Safety officers tried to keep the calm and ensure the direction of movement was downwards. Firefighters moved upwards as office workers descended.

Lifts and stairs demonstrate an entwining of the social and the material that is taken for granted in everyday life. It may take an extreme displacement of everyday life and space such as 9/11 to alert us to their influence in social–spatial relations. Markus (1993: 280) puts this well: 'The traditional means for movement were cloisters, corridors and staircases – static spatial systems through which people and objects moved. Lifts and hoists reversed this; there was now a dynamic system where a piece of moving space contained static people or objects'. With the lifts in the Twin Towers being inoperable, this dynamic system was re-reversed. The corporeal effect was immense as now people had to move. The development of the high-speed lift by Elisha Graves Otis in the nineteenth century had made possible the economic occupation of skyscrapers. His 'safety elevator' was first exhibited in the New York Exposition in 1853. Giedion (1967: 209) describes it thus, 'In each demonstration Mr. Otis stepped on to the platform, which was then hoisted above the ground. As the hoisting rope was cut, the elevator came to a stop, whereupon Mr. Otis made the historical remark, "All safe, gentlemen!"'. By 1857 passenger lifts were becoming available for department stores and then hotels. The first office building with passenger lifts was the ten-storey Equitable Building in New York, completed in 1871. In the 1880s, Siemens demonstrated an electric lift to which the

Otis Elevator Company replied in 1903 with the traction elevator. In any event, the Eiffel Tower used lifts to great advantage and solved the problem of concentrated human traffic by a system of lifts where four double-decked elevators ran from ground level to the first platform, two ran from there to the second platform and the rest of the ascent was made in two stages using hydraulic elevators. The 1000 foot ascent in 1889 took seven minutes and could cope with 2350 passengers per hour (Giedion 1967: 211).

The safe elevation of such numbers to such heights concentrates the attention on the nature of the human body and its physical limitations. We all know that falling such distances means almost certain death but much of what we take for granted in the built environment relies upon the rendering of the body as apparently unproblematic. Thus the embodied nature of human beings is revealed by our susceptibility to gravity and the length of time it would take to physically climb to a height of a thousand feet or more. But it would be foolish to think that elevators remove physicality. Lifts are interesting liminal spaces, where people are brought together in a confined space often with strangers. Decisions have to be made about where to face, the level of eye contact and the possibility of conversation. The senses become heightened in lifts so that smells and the intimacies of touch become worries. Conversations if they take place at all are in whispers. Bodies are held rigidly in the grip of fierce self-control. The social fear of being trapped in a lift is quite common with its dangers and social embarrassments. Roald Dahl played with the constraints of the lift in making his great glass elevator move in all directions, eventually transcending the buildings entirely through the roof. Bruce Willis' character in *Die Hard* uses the elevator as a weapon. The CEO of the BATA Shoe Corporation placed his office in the lift so that he could have mobility between floors. Elevators are targets for vandals and graffiti artists. In the era of company mission statements, many organisations placed copies of these aims on lift walls. Various scientific and research institutes have sought to utilise this peripheral travelling space and time through locating blackboard and chalk in lifts so as to allow the continuation of everyday creative business. Alternatively, they may be used as a semi-private space within the organisation for snatched moments of private business or intimacy.

Lift engineers since Otis have concerned themselves with the speed, safety, reliability and cost of the elevator. It should be noted that the core and elevator system of the Twin Towers were unusual. 'Because it was feared the pressure created by the buildings' high speed elevators might cause conventional elevator shafts to buckle, engineers used a plaster board system fixed to a steel core to house the elevators. This made the shafts more flexible, though also more flammable' (Hawkins, 'Science in Engineering', Channel 4, December 2001). In the wake of 9/11, the buildings soon to be standing on the site of the World Trade Towers will reflect the latest thinking about 'core' protection. Opened in 2006, 7 World Trade Center, replacing the third smaller tower that collapsed in the attacks, is said to be one of the most terrorist-proof buildings in the world (Rose 2006: 21–2). Its lifts and stairwells are protected by two-feet thick walls of concrete and steel, wider exit stairs, better emergency systems and fireproofing. It is envisaged that the Freedom Tower will incorporate even more safety features and its lifts will have to carry five million people a year up to the observation deck.

As we have said, the lift was an essential development to allow the proliferation of the skyscraper. The USA has long been associated with the development of the tallest buildings, where they represent a particular fusion of corporate and commercial interests and values:

> In the twentieth century, [the skyscraper] was to become the paradigmatic statement, not only of American architecture and urbanism, but of the economic ideology, mode of production and ethos from which it was largely (if not entirely) produced: capitalist land values, speculative office development and big business materialism in the United States. (King 2004: 11)

Thus the World Trade Center was not only a material target, but very much a 'representational space', a space of the symbolic and imaginary (Jones 2006; Legge 2002).

As King says,

> American commitment to the 'symbolism of height' gauged in relation to a socially constructed and imagined universe, first produced by the world of commerce and fuelled by the competitive spirit of New York and Chicago, the two prime centers of American capitalism, was also shared (not surprisingly) by the world of politics. (2004: 9)

The tallest of the first cluster of skyscrapers, erected in the early 1870s, was the Tribune Building, the headquarters of the New York Tribune newspaper. Its predominance came out of conflict with corporate rivals (King 2004: 6). Within ten years, its supremacy was overtaken by the broader political symbol of the Washington Monument. Of course, the political and the economic spheres are inextricably bound together and the battle for spatial and symbolic dominance through the world's tallest buildings intended to convey the message of the supremacy of the nation and its commerce. This continues in the symbolism invested in the name of the proposed 'Freedom Tower' to replace the World Trade Center, in its height in feet at 1776 (the year of American Independence, and even taller than the WTC) and in Libeskind's original (now defunct) design, echoing the Statue of Liberty. This overt symbolism may appeal to a US wanting to reassert its superiority, but reconfirms its imperialist agenda (Jones 2006).

King describes this confluence of material and representational supremacy as 'cultural jingoism' (2004: 7), and sees its epitome in a collage created in 1889, which shows a composite drawing of the 'tallest buildings in the world' with the Washington Monument at the centre and apex of the picture. In its presentation of height as the defining feature of dominance and supremacy, it ignores all the other aspects of these multifarious buildings in their cultural, religious, historical significance and meaning. Such competitive representations are common today with, for example, SkyscraperPage.com, projecting 'a "local" discourse to a global world' (p. 7).

Buildings in Shanghai, Hong Kong, Kuala Lumpur, Taipei and Jakarta have overtaken the US in terms of height, but this does not necessarily mean that the cultural and economic dominance of the US is weakening. Many of these buildings have been designed and built by American architects and companies (Sklair 2005). However, it may be that the American form and symbol can be taken and subverted in more constructive ways than in 9/11. Some have seen the Petronas Tower of Kuala Lumpur as representing an Islamic architecture. King argues that 'meanings invested in the Petronas Building, designed by American architect Cesar Pelli, are apparently bound up with rivalries between the Chinese and non-Chinese business class, between Muslim and non-Muslim. Like other subjects, and objects, skyscrapers can have many identities' (2004: 19).

Skyscrapers have often become central to indicate dominance in areas where material supremacy required an outer expression, such as in financial services where products and services are intangible. Indeed, the majority of the organisations and institutions housed in the WTC were of this type. Franck and Schneekloth (1994) argue that social and economic functions are conceived through the lens of existing building types. Montgomery Schuyler in 1897 expressed this when he said that the skyline of Manhattan was 'not an architectural vision, but it does, most tremendously, look like business' (in van Leeuwen 1988: 84). The World Trade Center, however, was not just important in terms of symbolising capitalist power. In relation to Lefebvre's 'spatial practices', it was an important element in the routes and routines of finance capitalism, in its everyday practices and in the historical social relations embedded within it. Berman (2002: 7) writes that the real life of the World Trade Center 'belonged to the swampy history of Manhattan real estate deals'. Twenty years before the collapse of the World Trade Center, Zukin (1982) argued that in Lower Manhattan three processes 'manufactured' a particular social space by and for patrician real estate agents. First there was 'hi-tech', capital intensive, high-rise development in the form of the World Trade Center in 1972. Second, alternative spaces outside the Central Business District (CBD) which complemented rather than rivalled patrician plans were developed and third, these real estate elites used strategic low-cost arts patronage to prevent obstacles to redevelopment from low-rent housing. Fainstein (1994) maintains that, from the mid-1970s, local government in New York became increasingly entrepreneurial in stimulating private investment. Much of this was achieved through the organisation of Urban Development Corporations (UDCs). These hybrid forms retained many government powers but did not have to conform to the more transparent and representational aspects of the public sector such as holding public meetings, providing detailed reports and facilitating community participation. Although responsible to elected representatives, they operated like private firms, prioritising strictly commercial values such as profit taking and hence the interests of real estate holders over the community. Thus, New York City government actively brought down the occupancy costs of companies such as Chase Manhattan and Morgan Stanley whilst ignoring the needs of local drama groups, artists' workshops, galleries, coffee houses and book stores (Fainstein 1994: 138).

It is in this context of financial capital, land values, global capitalism and cultural imperialism that the World Trade Center stood as a major confluence of representations of space. Its collapse then is profoundly iconoclastic.

Harvey (2002: 57) argues that the BBC and many websites treated the attack on the Twin Towers as an attack upon the symbol of US global financial and military power. At the same time, the US media tended to see the attack as a local horror, and then as an attack upon 'freedom', 'American values' and the 'American way of life'. For Harvey (2002: 58), the Twin Towers 'marked in towering glass and steel the moment of transition from Fordism to flexible accumulation led by financialization of everything. They symbolized the new found dominance of finance capital over nation state policies and politics'. In this financialisation of everything, it is important to note the role played by organisations. Zukin, in the same collection as that of Harvey, opines that 'The towers belonged, first, to a global circuit of capital flows, where money – or its abstract symbols – passed through national stock exchanges, multinational banks, and global trading firms just as their local employees passed through the turnstiles at Cortlandt Street' (2002: 15). The Twin Towers' collapse, of course, can be conceptualised at the individual level or at the level of the 'humiliated' nation state in which they are located. The individualisation of the tragedy of 9/11 and the development of the place as iconic image of eventual triumph, hampers analysis of it as having much more to do with the particular construction of social-space and as being profoundly 'organisational' in nature.

Harvey (2002: 59) reminds us with regard to the process of individualisation that

> the brilliant short obituaries in the New York Times, coming day after day for weeks after the event, celebrated the towers and special qualities of those that died, making it impossible to raise a critical voice as to what role bond traders and others might have had in the creation and perpetuation of social inequality either locally or worldwide.

In fact about 300 companies occupied the Twin Towers, many of them servicing the needs of the occupants in the form of travel services, or the bond traders in the form of debt collection agencies, or television companies looking for high status (and just high) addresses.

In contrast to the individual obituaries in the newspapers, the following account was written in Manhattan on 24, September 2001 from the perspective of real estate concerns:

> Although the entire World Trade Center complex, 13.4 million square feet, was destroyed in the horrific terrorist attack on September 11, 2001, those buildings constitute less than four percent of Manhattan's entire office inventory of approximately 353.7 million square feet, according to a report by Insignia/ESG, New York City's largest commercial real estate brokerage concern. Seventy percent of the Downtown market survived intact, as some 28.7 million sq. ft of Downtown office space was affected by the incident – either destroyed or damaged. (www.buildings.com/Articles/detail.asp?ArticleID=341)

The report noted which buildings had suffered structural damage, and which could be repaired and returned to the use of the 'displaced tenants' within only a few months:

> Although none of us will ever forget the horrific human toll at the World Trade Center, we firmly believe that the recovery of Downtown will move forward with dispatch, said John F. Powers, vice chairman of Insignia/ESG. By no later than January 1, 2002, we believe that the majority of dispossessed tenants will have returned to the buildings that sustained window and facade damage, and much progress will have been made in repairing the three most structurally damaged properties. Downtown Manhattan will continue to be one of the largest and most attractive office districts in the nation. (www.buildings.com/Articles/detail.asp?ArticleID=341)

We feel that the language in this website document for property managers in Manhattan, written under two weeks after the attack on the Twin Towers, has an immediately shocking effect. Even though there is talk of the 'horrific' consequences, these are overshadowed by the emphasis on the opportunities and needs of 'business as usual'.

> " The vast majority of displaced tenants to date have been able to find space in Manhattan, which had 25.8 million square feet of available space at the time of the incident, according to Insignia/ESG. Relatively little of that available space was already built-out and much of the space was not scheduled to be available for occupancy until later in the year. Despite this, only a handful of displaced tenants have relocated outside Manhattan. The Hoboken/Jersey City waterfront – an extension of the Downtown Manhattan market-has garnered the most interest outside Manhattan.
>
> As of September 21st, only ten days after the terrorist disaster, ten deals have been confirmed for tenants with requirements of at least 79,000 sq. ft. Insignia/ESG sources indicate another 3.5 million sq. ft. of leases are pending...
>
> 'Although there was a marked slowdown in leasing velocity in Manhattan this year, Manhattan's overall availability rate stood at just above seven percent,' said Powers. 'Ironically, largely due to the high volume of sublease space thrown onto the market following the demise of the dot-coms, the market is better poised to accommodate displaced WTC center tenants now than it would have been nine months ago'.
>
> *Source*: Insignia/ESG in Buildings.com, an Internet magazine for 'facilities decision makers' (www.buildings.com/Articles/detail.asp?ArticleID=341)

At a time when the attention of the world is on the horrific fate of those who died or the traumatic experiences of the survivors, the focus here is on the organisations who are 'displaced tenants'. During the short time since 9/11, it is clear that property managers have been taken up with finding alternative premises for callous capitalism to continue its inexorable logic. This piece exposes the ongoing processes of global capitalism with its economic and commercial requirements at a time where the individual tragedy and national emergency is one of total disrupture and a feeling that life would never be the same again. However, in this very dismissal of individual experience we can also discern some of the ways in which the abstract spaces of capitalism shape the identities and 'choices' of those who are bound up within them. It is at the level of the organisation, however, where the processes of normalisation are most evident in this piece. Individual tragedy is dispensed with quickly and the text moves on to talk of solutions to corporate problems. This is what drives the system 'forward'. The organisation of space that governed

Lower Manhattan, and the World Trade Center is one of the maximum extraction of value from land and the perpetuation of a system of global capitalism. These were not destroyed, barely disrupted, by 9/11. It is this obscured space of capital power relations that we will first consider.

Putting quite a different perspective on the claims of the property managers of Manhattan, Zukin notes that although 25 million square feet of office space were wiped out in the attacks of September 2001, the context was that there were already high vacancy rates and a movement outwards from premium-cost Manhattan, especially into New Jersey. The changing forms and fortunes of finance capitalism may not in the event have much to do with terrorist attacks and everything to do with managing the periodic crises and contradictions within capitalism itself. Cantor Fitzgerald, the stock and bond traders who suffered the greatest loss of lives in 9/11 declared a fourth quarter profit in 2001. This reflected an ongoing strategy by the company to replace human traders with an electronic system, run through the trading firm eSpeed (2002: 17–19). The resonances between lives destroyed in the terrorist attacks and those destroyed in the (more routine and regular) processes of corporate 'downsizing' are revealing.

The terrorists had succeeded in killing nearly 3000 people, but in attacking a symbol of Western culture and capitalism they did nothing to change the basis of this system. As usual, capitalism made money from the destruction. A meeting had been scheduled for September 13, 2001, in which David Childs, a corporate architect, was to talk to Larry Silverstein, the new owner, about the World Trade Towers. Childs is the senior Partner in SOM, whose New York offices are on Wall Street. The agenda was to have been refurbishment of the 78th floor where a lift interchange was located. Instead of minor refurbishment, Childs now has the opportunity to be the principal architect of the Freedom Tower, one of the highest profile architectural commissions in the world.

Childs, for SOM, and Daniel Libeskind (a more radical architect, his Jewish Museum in Berlin having been discussed in Chapter 2) had been involved in a battle of the architects for control of Ground Zero (Jones 2006). Libeskind won the competition but was not first choice with powerful corporate business. The compromise that was reached of dual involvement came about because the developer Silverstein pointed to the clause which stated that he could appoint any architect he chose and he chose Childs. However, the Freedom Tower, that was the compromise building between the radical architect with populist leanings and the representative of corporate architecture, will not be built because New York police called for a radical rethink of the skyscraper's base to prevent truck bombs having a chance of being successful. The inter-organisational network formed around Ground Zero, which is based upon co-operating and competing architectural practices, clients and tenants, agencies of the city and the State of New York, was also entered by the New York Police Department (NYPD). The management of such networks is notoriously difficult so Libeskind gave up on the whole project leaving the corporate favourite, Childs, in charge. Already 7 World Trade Center, also designed and built by SOM, has been completed. It is one of the most terrorist-proof buildings in the world but it looks like any other corporate building on the outside. Liebskind's image of exciting architecture has been ditched in favour of two-feet thick steels to protect lifts and stairwells. The Freedom Tower, designed to be completed in 2011, will be 102 storeys high, will be surrounded by bollards at the insistence of the NYPD and will look highly conventional. Steve Rose (2006) opines that the new tower will be braced for disaster and infused with paranoia.

Andrew Benjamin (2000: 149) argues that all architecture is marked by melancholy, for each building is what it is, but simultaneously is 'that which it is not'. The latter absence creates a feeling in all those at the site of 'a loss', a negation of what might have been. He argues therefore that (p. 152) a building 'is always ruined in advance. Here melancholia works with the ruin of completed form'. Brand new buildings therefore bring about a melancholia – a sadness, dejection and depression – for 'that which they might have been' and come quickly to represent for those at the site, a ruin in completed form. Architecture, then, embodies within itself its own destruction.

The metaphor of death and the attempt to transcend it haunts architecture. Giedion (1967: 709) maintained that 'it is important to note that solutions which came out of the universal vision of the eighteenth century still remain valid long after the death of the society for which they were formulated'. In similar vein, Mumford (1961: 446) argues that between 1820 and 1900, 'the destruction and disorder within great cities is like that of a battlefield', but out of that battlefield came 'the main elements of the new urban complex (that) were the factory, the railroad and the slum'.

And this is a difficulty. De-materialisation in itself may just be part of a circuit of rebuilding and renovation that continually organises and re-organises the dominant political economy of space, but without actually challenging it.

The collapse of the World Trade Center in 2001 created, for a momentary and monetary pause, a de-materialised non-architecture at ground zero and way beyond. Thirty years earlier, the controlled collapse of the Pruitt-Igoe public housing Estate in St Louis was seen to represent the end of the modernist effort to engineer social arrangements through public housing. It too produced a de-materialised non-architecture – a pile of rubble. That is what deliberate or accidental demolition produces. Gossel and Leuthauser put it this way:

> 15th July 1972 saw the memorable dynamiting of the Pruitt-Igoe Estate in St Louis, Missouri. Its monotonous, eleven storey slab skyscrapers, built 20 years earlier by Minorou Yamasaki, had been an award-winning model settlement by all the standards then held progressive. It represented the successful creation of inexpensive housing for many, surrounded by public parks and in disciplined rows of housing units. But in the long corridors between its anonymous apartment doors, chaos reigned. Vandalism and crime could no longer be controlled. (2001: 293)

Curtis (1996: 449) maintains that the officials in St Louis ordered the demolition of the Estate after an arson attack by the populace taking revenge against the professional planning trick foisted upon them. Indeed there had been arson attacks on a regular basis. The symbolism of this was taken up by Charles Jencks (1977: 9) in order to argue that modernism had died that day. From a different perspective, Hayden (2002: 168) says that 'Pruitt-Igoe came to stand for the confrontation between the public housing bureaucracies and the ghetto residents who objected to the building program as much as to the aesthetic'. The architect was widely seen then as having produced a deeply flawed design.

It was this same Minorou Yamasaki whose winning design of 1969 produced the Twin Towers of the World Trade Center. Yamasaki (1912–1986) was an American architect of Japanese descent whose later work focused on screen-like properties where façades covered and hid the structural properties beneath. His façades took on a symbolic nature. Profiled concrete blocks were used as the façade of the American Concrete Institute in Detroit, metal grilles for the Reynolds Metals sales office in Michigan and pipe like qualities for the Michigan Consolidated Gas Company office building, again in Detroit. Architecture was becoming a stark aerial marketing device for the client. Architecturally, says Curtis (1996: 597), the Twin Towers were the end of the line for a minimalist notion of a free-standing object standing in a plaza using the curtain wall/box formula. But Curtis was not to know just how much the Twin Towers were to represent, for some, an eschatocol, the conclusion of the chapter of decorated marketing diagrams, in a burning pyre.

Arson comes to all architects who wait. Frank Lloyd Wright's home in Taliesin, Wisconsin was burnt down three times (Handlin 1985: 152), and on each occasion rebuilt. The burning of Watts, in Los Angeles, St Pauls in Bristol, Toxteth in Liverpool and the firebombing of US banks in 1911 all point to the role of arson in socio-architectural revolt. The imperialist form of arson is also crucial. The burning of the Chinese Emperor's Summer Palace by British troops during the Opium Wars exemplifies the use of arson on important buildings to punish the leadership of a society. Calculating that the Chinese nobility would be impressed but not directly harmed by the attack upon the hundreds of buildings within the Summer Palace, British officers took the gamble to incinerate the Emperor's property. The earlier burning of the 'original' White House in Washington by British troops shows a consistency of imperial style.

Remarkably, Markus (1993: 275–6) skirts over this connection between social relationships and arson in buildings. So much so that he speaks of 'new relations' (p. 275) in work around control, surveillance, discipline and worker solidarity, and as the reader turns the page we confront, without any explanation, the need to 'fireproof the machine'. We are told, presciently as it happens, that in the nineteenth century,

> fires become more disastrous when there is a collapse; the weight of the new structures, once a fire started in an upper floor, virtually knocked a hole through the mill. Moreover, the cast iron, unlike heavy timber members, when suddenly cooled by water, cracked and failed abruptly... so that there was progressive collapse of the entire precarious structure. (1993: 275–6)

But in the lacuna of Markus' work, what we can read is the impetus to rebuild, to reconstitute the spaces of destruction and de-materialisation into ever-changing versions of the 'spatial fix' of capitalism.

One might identify at this point at least two other forms of 'spatial fix' open to capitalism. The first oversees a process whereby the industrial buildings of the past become fitted for the consumer capitalism of the present: the Musee d'Orsay, the Reichstag and the Tate Modern all inhabit buildings whose entanglement with the past was huge. A railway station becomes a museum, government offices become modified versions of their original purpose and an electricity generating turbine hall becomes an exhibition centre. Conservation of form ensues but at the expense of function. New functions are found and seized upon in order to maintain the structure and enhance its cultural capital. After Pruitt Igoe, Nuttgens (1988: 172) claims that 'in continental countries and the United States, rebuilding and restoration became more popular'. However, conservation can be very conservative.

A second spatial fix for capitalism is appearing in the People's Republic of China. Here, today,

> Young Chinese architects, straight from college, could be found sitting in cramped kitchens in Shenzen and Guangzhou designing the facades of instant build office towers on laptops. They would cull images of office towers from around the world seen in glossy magazines, scan them into their computers and stretch the images vertically or horizontally to fit the concrete frame of the latest Chinese office block. The results were built soon afterwards. (Glancey 2003: 177)

So China may be the (new) place of cheap concrete buildings built on mass production lines by architects who are productive of abstract space in the service of the state. Yet, these buildings, too, will contain their own ruin. Standing upon ruined villages, new dams and towns and cities take shape. But the built environment cannot be de-materialised, for the rubble itself is heavily influential in what is to follow. The built environment cannot be disentangled from the everyday movements of people fulfilling the mundane necessities of life, for shelter is one of the basic human needs. Nor can 'important' buildings be disentangled from the symbolic role they are presumed to play. For, buildings represent the expression of order in a world prone to entropy and the destruction of buildings, oft times associated with war, is a disordering that does not often last long. However, whilst buildings might stand for this creative achievement, they also reflect back to *homo faber* a long-standing melancholic ruination.

In conclusion, we would like to point to the relationship between the organisation and the disorganisation of space, where some of the possibilities for disrupting the dominant relations of power and identity construction that have been analysed throughout the book might lie. If our capacity to think differently, to live differently and to hope differently are stifled through the production of the spaces within which we live both socially and materially, then perhaps we need to look for the chance of a 'pause' where disorganisation dwells and where the inherent organising processes are revealed as completed ruins and may be subverted. And in that pause a distinction between destruction and disorganisation might also be made. What we have seen above is that destruction is always already a part of built space, but that it need not imply any change in the relations of power and identity that are embedded in that materiality. Whilst destruction is a creative part of capitalism's 'spatial fix', 'disorganisation' is perceived meanwhile to be abhorrent and offering up far less opportunity for profit. But in our view disorganisation offers a pause in which the world could draw a deep breath and might, just might, restructure its thinking about how space should be organised, differently and better.

We have analysed in this book the spaces of organisation and the organisation of space in the hope that by so doing we have constructed a place that can be creatively *disorganised* by enthusiasts who have the energy for the task ahead.

Note

[1] Similar debates about the degree to which designs should incorporate these scenarios were had after a gas explosion in one flat led to the partial collapse of the 22-storey Ronan Point tower in London in 1968.

bibliography

Abbott, E. 2006. *Flatland*. London: Dodo.

Ackermann, K. (ed.) 1991. *Building for Industry*. United Kingdom: Watermark.

Ackroyd, S. and Crowdy, P. 1990. 'Can Culture Be Managed?' *Personnel Review* 19 (5): 3–13.

Adam, B. 2003. 'Reflexive Modernization Temporalised', *Theory, Culture and Society* 20: 59–78.

Adorno, T. 2001. *The Culture Industry*. London: Routledge.

Ainley, R. (ed.) 1998. *New Frontiers of Space, Bodies and Gender*. London: Routledge.

Aldersey-Williams, H. 1999. 'Cracking Form: Glass Architecture', *New Statesman*, 17 February.

Aldridge, A. 2003. *Consumption*. Cambridge: Polity.

Alferoff, C. and Knights, D. 2003. 'We're all Partying here: Target and Games, or Targets as Games in Call Centre Management' in Carr, A. and Hancock, P. (eds) *Art and Aesthetics at Work*. Basingstoke: Palgrave, pp. 70–92.

Allen, T., Bell, A., Graham, R., Hardy, B. and Swaffer, F. 2004. *Working without Walls: An Insight into the Transforming Government Workplace*. Norwich: HMSO.

Alvesson, M. and Willmott, H. (eds) 1992. *Critical Management Studies*. London: Sage.

Alvesson, M. and Willmott, H. (eds) 2003. *Studying Management Critically*. London: Sage.

Anderson, B. 1983. *Imagined Communities*. London: Verso.

Anderson, L. n.d. 'Architecture' can be accessed at http://www.webtribe.net/~franktalk/truth/architecture.html.

Anthony, P. 1977. *The Ideology of Work*. London: Tavistock.

Appadurai, A. (ed.) 1986. 'Introduction: Commodities and the Politics of Value' in *The Social Life of Things*. Cambridge: Cambridge University Press.

Armstrong, P. 1991. 'The Influence of Michel Foucault on Historical Research in Accounting' paper presented to Academy of Accounting Historians Research Methodology Conference, Mississippi.

Armstrong, P. 2004. 'Interior Design as a Disabling Profession', paper presented to European Academy of Management Conference, St Andrew's, Scotland, May.

Attfield, J. and Kirkham, P. (eds) 1995. *A View from the Interior: Women and Design*. London: The Women's Press.

Austen, J. 1983. *Mansfield Park*. Glasgow: FontanaCollins.

Bachelard, G. 1994. (French original 1958) *The Poetics of Space*. Boston: Beacon Press.

Baldry, C., Bain, P. and Taylor, P. 1998. 'Bright Satanic Offices' in Warhurst, C. and Thompson, P. (eds) *Workplaces of the Future*. Basingstoke: Macmillan, pp. 163–83.

Banham, R. 1986. *A Concrete Atlantis*. Cambridge, MA: MIT Press.

Barbrook, R. and Cameron, A. 2001. 'Californian Ideology' in Ludlow, P. (ed.) *Crypto-Anarchy, Cyberstates, and Pirate Utopias*. Cambridge, MA: MIT Press.

Baudrillard, J. 1998. *The Consumer Society: Myths and Structures*. London: Sage.

Bauman, Z. 1991. *Modernity and Ambivalence*. Cambridge: Polity.

Bauman, Z. 1998. *Work, Consumerism and the New Poor*. Buckingham: Open University Press.

Bauman, Z. 2000. *Liquid Modernity*. Cambridge: Polity.

Bauman, Z. 2001. *Liquid Love*. Cambridge: Polity.

Bell, E. and Taylor, S. 2003. 'The Elevation of Work', *Organisation* 10 (2): 329–49.

Bell, E. and Taylor, S. 2004. 'From Outward Bound to Inward Bound: The Prophetic Voices and Discursive Practices of Spiritual Management Development', *Human Relations* 57 (4): 439–66.

Benjamin, W. 1999. *The Arcades Project*. Cambridge, MA: Harvard University Press.

Benjamin, A. 2000. *Architectural Philosophy*. London: Athlone.

Benko, G. and Strohmeyer, U. (eds) 1997. *Space and Social Theory*. Oxford: Blackwell.

Bennett, T. 1995. *The Birth of the Museum*. London: Routledge.

Benson, S. 1979. 'The Palace of Consumption and Machine for Selling; the American Department Store 1880–1940', *Radical History Review* (21): 199–221.

Berg, M. 1985. *The Age of Manufactures: 1700–1820*. London: Routledge.

Berg, P. and Kreiner, K. 1990. 'The Corporate Architecture' in Gagliardi, P. (ed.) *Symbols and Artifacts*. Berlin: de Gruyter.

Bergdoll, B. 2002. *European Architecture 1750–1890*. Oxford: Oxford University Press.

Bergoneron, L. and Maiullari-Pontois, M. T. 2000. 'The Factory Architecture of Albert Kahn', Architecture Week, 1 November, http://www.architectureweek.com/2000/1101/culture_1.1.html.

Berman, M. 2002. 'When Bad Buildings Happen to Good People' in Sorkin, M. and Zukin, S. (eds) *After the World Trade Center: Rethinking New York City*. New York: Routledge.

Beynon, H. 1973. *Working For Ford*. Harmondsworth: Penguin.

Bircham, E. and Charlton, J. 2001. *Anticapitalism: A Guide to the Movement*. London: Bookmarks.

Birke, L. 1999. *Feminism and the Biological Body*. Edinburgh: Edinburgh University Press.

Blau, J. 1984. *Architects and Firms: A Sociological Perspective on Architectural Practice*. Harvard: MIT Press.

Bohm, S. 2006. *Repositioning Organization Theory*. Basingstoke: Palgrave Macmillan.

Boland, R. 2001. 'The Tyranny of Space in Organisational Analysis', *Information and Organisation* 11: 3–23.

Bolton, S. 2005. *Emotion Management in the Workplace*. Basingstoke: Palgrave Macmillan.

Booth, C., Darke, J. and Yeandle, S. (eds) 1996. *Changing Places: Women's Lives in the City*. London: Paul Chapman.

Bourdieu, P. 1984. *Distinction*. London: Routledge.

Boyle, M.-E. 2003. 'Reconciling Aesthetics and Justice In Organization Studies' in Carr, A. and Hancock, P. (eds) *Art and Aesthetics at Work*. Basingstoke: Palgrave Macmillan, pp. 51–66.

Bradley, H. 1999. *Gender and Power in the Workplace*. Basingstoke: Macmillan.

Braidotti, R. 1994. *Nomadic Subjects*. New York: Columbia University Press.

Brand, S. 1994. *How Buildings Learn*. London: Phoenix.

Bruce, S. 2000. *Uttering No Human Sound: Silence and Sign Language in Western Medieval Monasticism*. Ann Arbor, MI: University Microfilms International.

Brueggemann, W. 1999. *The Covenanted Self*. Minneapolis, MN: Augsberg Fortress.

Bryman, A. 1995. *Disney and His Worlds*. London: Routldege.

Bryman, A. 2004. *Disneyization*. London: Sage.

Buchanan, I. 2005. 'Space in the Age of Non-Place' in Buchanan, I. and Lambert, G. (eds) *Deleuze and Space*. Edinburgh: Edinburgh University Press.

Buci-Glucksmann, C. 1994. *Baroque Reason: The Aesthetics of Modernity*. London: Sage.

Burawoy, M. 1979. *Manufacturing Consent*. Chicago: University of Chicago Press.

Burawoy, M. 1985. *The Politics of Production*. Chicago: University of Chicago Press.

Burke, B. 1986. *The Italian Renaissance*. Cambridge: Polity.

Burrell, G. 1980. 'The Propensity to Strike in Relation to Social Power', unpublished PhD thesis, University of Manchester.

Burrell, G. 1984. 'Sex and Organisational Analysis', *Organisation Studies* 5 (2): 97–118.

Burrell, G. 1992a. 'The Organization of Pleasure' in Alvesson, M. and Willmott, H. (eds) *Critical Management Studies*. London: Sage, pp. 65–89.

Burrell, G. 1992b. 'Back to the Future' in Redd, M. and Hughes, M. (eds) *Rethinking Organization*. London: Sage, pp. 165–83.

Burrell, G. 1998. 'Linearity, Text and Death' in Grant, D., Keenoy, T. and Oswick, O. (eds) *Discourse and Organisation*. London: Sage, pp. 134–51.

Burrell, G. and Dale, K. 2003. 'Building Better Worlds? Architecture and Critical Management Studies' in Alvesson, M. and Wilmott, H. (eds) *Studying Management Critically*. London: Sage, pp. 177–96.

Burrell, G. and Dale, K. 2004. 'Utopiary' in Parker, M. (ed.) *Utopia and Organisation*. London: Sage, pp. 106–27.

Burton, J. 1994. *Monastic and Religious Order in Britain 1000–1300*. Cambridge: Cambridge University Press.

Butler, J. 1993. *Bodies that Matter*. London: Routledge.

Butler, J. 2004. *Undoing Gender*. New York: Routledge.

Byrne, K., Forest, R., Gibson-Graham, J. K., Healy, S. and Horvath, G. 1998. Imagining and Enacting Non-Capitalist Futures Rethinking Economy Project, Working Paper No. 1, http://www.arts.monash.edu.au/projects/cep/knowledges/byrne.html.

Caesar, J. 1984. *The Conquest of Gaul*. Harmondsworth: Penguin Classics.

Callon, M. 1991. 'Techno-economic Networks and Irreversibility' in Law, J. (ed.) *A Sociology of Monsters*. London: Routledge, pp. 132–64.

Campbell, C. 1983. 'Romanticism and the Consumer Ethic', *Sociological Analysis* 44 (4): 279–96.

Campbell, C. 1987. *The Romantic Ethic and the Spirit of Modern Consumerism*. Oxford: Macmillan.

Campbell Cole, B. and Elias Rogers, R. (eds) 1985. *Richard Rogers+Partners*, London: Architectural Monographs.

Carmona, S., Ezzamel, M. and Gutierrez, F. 1997. 'Control and Cost Accounting Practices in the Spanish Royal Tobacco Factory', *Accounting, Organisations and Society* 22 (5).

Carmona, S., Ezzamel, M. and Gutierrez, F. 1998. 'Towards an Institutional Analysis of Accounting Change in the Royal Tobacco Factory of Seville', *The Accounting Historians Journal* 25 (1).

Carmona, S., Ezzamel, M. and Gutierrez, F. 2002. 'The Relationship between Accounting and Spatial Practices in the Factory', *Accounting, Organisation and Society* 27: 239–74.

Casey, C. 1995. *Work, Self and Society*. London: Routledge.

Casey, C. 1996. 'Corporate Transformations', *Organization* 3 (3): 317–39.

Casey, E. 1998. *The Fate of Place*. Berkeley: University of California Press.

Castells, M. 1983. *The City and the Grassroots*. London: Edward Arnold.

Castells, M. 1989. *The Informational City*. Oxford: Blackwell.

Castells, M. 2003. *The Power of Identity*. Oxford: Blackwell.

Castree, N., Coe, N., Ward, K. and Samers, M. 2004. *Spaces of Work: Global Capitalism and Geographies of Labour*. London: Sage.

Certeau de, M. 1984. *The Practice of Everyday Life*. Berkeley, CA: University of California Press.

Chapman, T. and Hockey, J. 1999. *Ideal Homes?* London: Routledge.

Child, J. 1969. *British Management Thought*. London: Collier.

Ching, F. 1996. *Architecture: Form, Space and Order*. New York: Van Nostrand Rheinhold.

Clark, I. 1985. *The Spatial Organisation of Multinational Corporations*. London: Croom Helm.

Clark, P. 1990. 'Chronological Codes and Organisational Analysis' in Hassard, J. and Pym, D. (eds) *The Theory and Philosophy of Organizations*. London: Routledge.

Clarke, L. 1992. *Building Capitalism*. London: Routledge.

Clegg, S. 1975. *Power, Rule and Domination*. London: Routledge and Kegan Paul.

Clegg, S. 1979. *The Theory of Power and Organisation*. London: Routledge and Kegan Paul.

Clegg, S. 1989. *Frameworks of Power*. London: Sage.

Cockburn, C. 1983. *Brothers: Male Dominance and Technological Change*. London: Pluto.

Cohen, L., Wilkinson, A., Arnold, J. and Finn, R. 2005. 'Remember I'm the Bloody Architect', *Work, Employment and Society* 19 (4): 775–96.

Cohn, S. 1981. *Feminization of Clerical Labor in Great Britain: A Contrast of Two Large Clerical Employers 1857–1937*. Ann Arbor, MI: University Microfilms International.

Coleman, D., Danze, E. and Henderson, C. (eds) 1996. *Architecture and Feminism*. New York: Princeton Architectural Press.

Collinson, D. 1992. *Managing the Shopfloor*. Berlin: de Gruyter.

Collinson, D. 2003. 'Identities and Insecurities: Selves at Work', *Organization* 10 (3): 527–47.

Collinson, D., Knights, D. and Collinson, M., 1990. *Managing to Discriminate*. London: Routledge.

Cooper, R. 1990. 'Organisation/Disorganisation' in Hassard, J. and Pym, D. (eds) *The Theory and Philosophy of Organisations*. London: Routledge, pp. 167–97.

Cooper, R. 1993. 'Technologies of Representation' in Alionen, P. (ed.) *The Semiotic Boundaries of Politics*. Berlin: de Gruyter.

Corbett, J. M. 1994. *Critical Cases in Organisational Behaviour*. Basingstoke: Palgrave Macmillan.

Corbett, J. M. 2003. 'Sound Organisation: A Brief History of Psychosonic Management', *Ephemera* 3 (4): 265–76.

Corbett, J. M. 2006. 'Scents of Identity: Organisation Studies and the Conundrum of the Nose', *Culture and Organisation* 12 (3): 221–32.

Corbin, A. 1989. *The Foul and the Fragrant*. London: Picador.

Corrigan, P. 1997. *The Sociology of Consumption*. London: Sage.

Cowan, R. 1976. 'Two Washes in the Morning and a Bridge Party at Night: The American Housewife between the Wars', *Women's Studies* 3 (2): 141–71.

Cowan, R. 1979. 'From Virginia Dare to Virginia Slims: Women and Technology in American Life', *Technology and Culture* 20 (1): 51–63.

Cowan, R. 1983. *More Work for Mother?* New York: Basic Books.

Crang, M. and Thrift, N. 2000. *Thinking Space*. London: Routledge.

Crossley, N. 1996. 'Body-Subject/Body-Power: Agency, Inscription and Control in Foucault and Merleau-Ponty', *Body and Society* 2 (2): 99–116.

Cruickshank, D. 1992. 'Private Parts' in Rivers, T., Cruickshank, D., Darley, G. and Pawley, M. (eds) *The Name of the Room*. London: BBC Books.

Cruickshank, D. 2002. *Britain's Best Buildings*. London: BBC publications.

Curtis, W. 1996. *Modern Architecture Since 1900*. London: Phaidon.

Czarniawska, B. 2004. 'On Time, Space and Action Nets', *Organization* 11 (6): 777–95.

Dale, K. 1997. 'Identity in a Culture of Dissection: Body, Self and Knowledge' in Hetherington, K. and Munro, R. (eds) *Ideas of Difference*. Oxford: Blackwell, pp. 94–113.

Dale, K. 2001. *Anatomising Embodiment and Organisation Theory*. Basingstoke: Palgrave.

Dale, K. 2005. 'Building a Social Materiality', *Organization* 12 (5): 649–78.

Dale, K. and Burrell, G. 2003. 'Aesthetics and Anaesthetics' in Hancock, P. and Carr, A. (eds) *Art and Aesthetics at Work*. Basingstoke: Palgrave.

Dant, T. 1999. *Material Culture in the Social World*. Milton Keynes: Open University Press.

Dant, T. 2005. *Materiality and Society*. Milton Keynes: Open University Press.

Darley, G. 1992. 'The Power House' in Rivers, T., Cruickshank, D., Darley, G. and Pawley, M. (eds). *The Name of the Room*. London: BBC Books.

Darley, G. 2003. *Factory*. London: Reaktion.

Davies, C. and Rosser, J. 1986. *Processes of Discrimination: A Study of Women Working in the NHS*. London: Department of Health and Social Security.

Davies, N. 2004. *Rising '44: The Battle for Warsaur*. London: Pan.

Davis, M. 1995. 'Fortress Los Angeles: The Militarisation of Urban Space' in Kasinitz, P. (ed.) *Metropolis*. Basingstoke: Palgrave Macmillan.

Dear, M. 1997. 'Postmodern Bloodlines' in Benko, G. and Strohmayer, U. (eds) *Space and Social Theory*. Oxford: Blackwell.

Debord, G. 1967. (Eng. transl. 1977) *The Society of the Spectacle*. Detroit: Black and Red.

De Marrais, E., Gosden, C. and Renfrew, C. (eds) 2004. *Rethinking Materiality*. Cambridge: McDonald Institute for Archaelogical Research.

Deetz, S. 2003. 'Disciplinary Power, Conflict Suppression and Human Resources Management' in Alvesson, M. and Wilmott, H. (eds) *Studying Management Critically*. London: Sage, pp. 23–45.

Deleuze, G. 1993. *The Fold*. London: Athlone Press.

Deleuze, G. and Guattari, F. 1988. *A Thousand Plateaus*. London: Athlone Press.

Deleuze, G. and Parnet, C. 1987. *Dialogues*. London: Athlone Press.

Dicken, P., Peck, J. and Tickell, A. 1997. 'Unpacking the Global' in Lee, R. and Wills, K. (eds) *Geographies of Economies*. London: Arnold, pp. 158–66.

Dickinson, P. and Svenson, N. 2000. *Beautiful Corporations: Corporate Style in Action*. London: Prentice Hall.

Dicks, B. 2000. *Heritage Place and Community*. Cardiff: University of Wales Press.

Doel, M. 1999. *Poststructuralist Geographies*. Edinburgh: Edinburgh University Press.

Donald, M. 1991. *Origins of the Modern Mind*. Cambridge, MA: Harvard University Press.

Dostoyevsky, F. 1998. *Crime and Punishment*. Oxford: Oxford University Press.

Douglas, M. 1966. *Purity and Danger*. London: Routledge.

Dovey, K. 1999. *Framing Places: Mediating Power in Built Form*. London: Routledge.

du Gay, P. 1996. *Consumption and Identity at Work*. London: Sage.

du Gay, P., Hall, S., James, L., Mackay, H. and Negus, K. 1997. *Doing Cultural Studies*. Milton Keynes: Open University Press.

Duffy, F. 1980. 'Office Buildings and Organisational Change' in King, A. (ed.) *Buildings and Society*. London: RKP, pp. 255–82.

Duffy, F. 1982. 'Introduction' to Klein, J. *The Office Book*. London: Frederick Muller.

Duffy, F. 1992. *The Changing Workplace*. London: Phaidon.

Duffy, F. 1997. *The New Office*. London: Conran Octopus Ltd.

Durkheim, E. 1972. *The Division of Labour*. London: Routledge and Kegan Paul.

Easlea, B. 1983. *Fathering the Unthinkable*. London: Pluto Press.

Edwards, B. (ed.) 2001. 'Green Architecture', *Architectural Design* 71 (4) New York: Wiley.

Eichler, N. 1982. *The Merchant Builders*. Cambridge, MA: The MIT Press.

Elias, N. 1994. *The Civilising Process*. Oxford: Blackwell.

Eribon, D. 1991. *Michel Foucault*. Cambridge, MA: Harvard University Press.

Etzioni, A. 1964. *Modern Organizations*. New York: Prentice Hall.

Euripides, 1973. *The Bachae and Other Plays* ed. and trans. Vellacott, P. Harmondsworth: Penguin.

Ezzamel, M. 2004. 'Work Organisation in the Middle Kingdom, Ancient Egypt' *Organization* 11 (4): 497–537.

Ezzy, D. 1998. 'Theorizing Narrative Identity: Symbolic Interactionism and Hermeneutics', *Sociological Quarterly* 39 (2): 239–53.

Fainstein, S. 1994. *The City Builders: Property, Politics and Planning in London and New York*. Oxford: Blackwell.

Falk, P. and Campbell, C. (eds) 1997. *The Shopping Experience*. London: Sage.

Featherstone, M. 1991. *Consumer Culture and Postmodernism*. London: Sage.

Featherstone, M. and Burrows, R. 1995. 'Cultures Of Technological Embodiment: An Introduction' in Featherstone, M. and Burrows, R. (eds) *Cyberspace Cyberbodies Cyberpunk*. London: Sage, pp. 1–19.

Featherstone, M. and Lash, S. (eds) 1999. *Spaces of Culture*. London: Sage.

Felstead, A., Jewson, N. and Walters, S. 2005. *Changing Spaces of Work*. Basingstoke: Palgrave.

Findlay, J. 1992. *Magic Lands: Western Cityscapes and American Culture after 1940*. Berkeley, CA: University of California Press.

Findlay, L. 2005. *Building Change: Architecture, Politics and Cultural Agency*. London: Routledge.

Firestone, H. and Crowther, S. 1926. *Men of Rubber: The Story of Business*. Garden City, NY: Doubleday, Page & Co.

Fiske, J. 1989. *Understanding Popular Culture*. London: Routledge.

Flecker, J. and Hofbauer, J. 1998. 'The New Model Worker' in Thompson, P. and Warhurst, C. (eds) *Workplaces of the Future*. Basingstoke: Palgrave, pp. 104–23.

Florida, R. 2002. *The Rise of the Creative Class*. New York: Basic Books.

Ford, H. 1926. *Today and Tomorrow*. London: William Heinemann Ltd.

Ford, H. 1931. *Moving Forward*. London: William Heinemann Ltd.

Forty, A. 1986. *Objects of Desire*. London: Thames and Hudson.

Fossi, G. 1999. Introduction to '*The Uffizi: The Official Guide*'. Florence: Giunti.

Foucault, M. 1970. *The Order of Things*. London: Tavistock.

Foucault, M. 1972. *The Archaeology of Knowledge*. London: Tavistock.

Foucault, M. 1977. *Discipline and Punish*. Harmondsworth: Penguin.

Foucault, M. 1980. *Power/Knowledge: Selected Interviews and Other Writings 1972–1977* ed. Gordon, C. Brighton: Harvester Press.

Foucault, M. 1981. *The History of Sexuality, volume 1*. Harmondsworth: Penguin.

Foucault, M. 1985. *The History of Sexuality, volume 2: The Uses of Pleasure*. Harmondsworth: Penguin.

Foucault, M. 1986. *The History of Sexuality volume 3: The Care of the Self*. Harmondsworth: Penguin.

Foucault, M. 1986. 'Of Other Spaces', *Diacritics* 16 (1): 22–37.

Foucault, M. 1987a. 'What Is Enlightenment?' in Rabinow, P. (ed.) *The Foucault Reader*. Harmondsworth: Penguin, pp. 32–50.

Foucault, M. 1987b. 'On the Genealogy of Ethics: An Overview of Work in Progress' in Rabinow, P. (ed.) *The Foucault Reader*. Harmondsworth: Penguin, pp. 340–72.

Foucault, M. 1988. 'Technologies of the Self' in Martin, L., Gutman, H. and Hutton, P. (eds) *Technologies of the Self*. London: Tavistock.

Fox, A. 1985. *History and Heritage*. London: Allen and Unwin.

Foxell, J. and Spafford, A. 1952. *Monarchs of All They Surveyed: The Story of the Post Office Surveyors*. London: HMSO.

Frampton, K. 1992. *Modern Architecture: A Critical History*. London: Thames and Hudson.

Franck, Karen A. and Lynda H. Schneekloth (eds) 1994. *Ordering Space Types in Architecture and Design*. New York: Van Nostrand Reinhold.

Franklin, Caryn. 2001. *Nice Work*. BBC2/Open University.

Frederick, C. 1912. 'The New Housekeeping', *Ladies Home Journal* 26.

Frederick, C. 1919. *Household Engineering: Scientific Management in the Home*. Chicago: American School of Home Economics.

Frederick, C. 1929. *Selling Mrs Consumer*. New York: Business Bourse.

Freeman, J. 2004. *The Making of the Modern Kitchen*. Oxford: Berg.

Friedan, B. 1963. *The Feminine Mystique*. New York: Dell Publishing Co.

Friedman, A. 1999. *Women and the Making of the Modern House*. New York: Harry Abrams.

Gabriel, Y. and Lang, T. 1995. *The Unmanageable Consumer*. London: Sage.

Gagliardi, P. (ed.) 1990. *Symbols and Artefacts*. New York: de Gruyter.

Gagliardi, P. 1996. 'Exploring the Aesthetic side of Organisational Life' in Clegg, S. and Hardy, C. (eds) *Studying Organisation*. London: Sage, pp. 311–26.

Gans, H. 1967. *The Levittowners*. New York: Vintage Books.

Garrett, L. 1994. *The Coming Plague*. Harmondsworth: Penguin.

Gatens, M. 1996. *Imaginary Bodies*. London: Routledge.

Gerulaitis, L. 1976. *Printing and Publishing in Fifteenth Century Venice*. Chicago: American Library Association.

Gerth, A. and Mills, C. (eds) 1968. *From Max Weber*. London: Routledge.

Ghirardo, D. 1996. *Architecture after Modernism*. London: Thames and Hudson.

Giddens, A. 1971. *Capitalism and Modern Social Theory*. Cambridge: Cambridge University Press.

Giddens, A. 1974. 'Elites in the British Class Structure', in Stanworth, P. and Giddens, A. (eds) *Elites and Power in British Society*. Cambridge: Cambridge University Press, pp. 1–22.

Giddens, A. 1990. *The Consequences of Modernity*. Cambridge: Polity.

Giddens, A. 1991. *Modernity and Self-Identity: Self and Society in the Late Modern Age*. Cambridge: Polity.

Giedion, S. 1967. *Space, Time and Architecture*. Cambridge, MA: Harvard University Press.

Gilbert, N. and Mulkay, M. 1984. *Opening Pandora's Box*. Cambridge: Cambridge University Press.

Gilbreth, L. 1927. *The Homemaker and Her Job*. New York: D. Appleton and Co.

Gilbreth, L. 1930. 'Efficiency Methods Applied to Kitchen Design', *Architectural Record*, March: 291–92.

Girouard, M. 1990. *The English Town*. New Haven: Yale University Press.

Glancey, J. 1998. *Twentieth Century Architecture*. London: Carlton.

Glancey, J. 2003. 'The Wonderful World of Disney', *Guardian*, 27 October.

Gloag, J. 1949. *The Englishman's Castle*. London: Eyre and Spottiswood.

Glucksmann, M. 1990. *Women Assemble*. London: Routledge.

Glucksmann, M. 2000. *Cottons and Casuals*. Durham: SociologyPress.

Godlewska, A. and Smith, N. (eds) 1994. *Geography and Empire*. Oxford: Blackwell.

Goffman, E. 1961. *Asylums*. New York: Anchor Books.

Goffman, E. 1969. *The Presentation of Self in Everyday Life*. Harmondsworth: Penguin.

Gorringe, T. 2002. *A Theology of the Built Environment*. Cambridge: Cambridge University Press.

Gossel, P. and Leuthauser, G. 1991. *Modern Architecture*. London: Phaidon.

Gossel, P. and Leuthauser, G. 2001. *Architecture in the Twentieth Century*. Cologne: Taschen.

Gottdiener, M. 1997. *The Theming of America*. Boulder, CO: Westview Press Incorporated.

Gouldner, A. 1969. 'The Unemployed Self' in Fraser, R. (ed.) *Work*, Vols I and II, Harmondsworth: Penguin.

Gouldner, A. 1970. *Wildcat Strike*. New York: Free Press.

Gowler, D. and Legge, K. 1983. 'The Meaning of Management and the Management of Meaning' in Earl, M. (ed.) *Perspectives on Management*. Oxford: Oxford University Press.

Graham, S. and Marvin, S. 1997. 'More than Ducts and Wires' in Healey, P., Cameron, S., Davoudi, S., Graham, S. and Madari-Pour, A. (eds) *Managing Cities*. London: Wiley.

Gregory, D. 1994. *Geographical Imaginations*. Oxford: Blackwell.

Grey, C. 1994. 'Career as a Project of the Self and Labour Process Discipline', *Sociology* 28 (2): 479–97.

Grey, C. 2001. 'Re-imagining Relevance', *British Journal of Management* 12, December (Special Issue): S27–S32.

Grosz, E. 1994. *Volatile Bodies*. Bloomington, IN: Indiana University Press.

Grosz, E. 1995. *Space Time and Perversion*. London: Routledge.

Grosz, E. 2001. *Architecture from the Outside*. Cambridge MA: MIT Press.

Guertsen, W. 1993. 'The Pleasure of Pain: Sado-masochism as leisure', in Brackenridge, C. (ed.) *Body Matters: Leisure Images and Lifestyles* (LSA Publication No. 47). Eastbourne: Leisure Studies Association, pp. 19–24.

Guillen, M. 1997. 'Scientific Management's Lost Aesthetic: Architecture, Organization and the Taylorised Beauty of the Mechanical', *Administrative Science Quarterly* 42: 682–715.

Halford, S. and Leonard, P. 2001. *Gender, Power and Organisations*. Basingstoke: Palgrave Macmillan.

Hambling, D. 2005. *Weapons Grade*. London: Constable.

Hamilton, G. 1995. *Cottage Gardens*. London: BBC Publications.

Hancock, P. and Tyler, M. 2000. 'The Look of Love' in Hassard, J., Holliday, R. and Willmott, H. (eds) *Body and Organisation*. London: Sage, pp. 108–29.

Handlin, D. 1985. *The American Home: Architecture and Society 1815–1915*. London: Thames and Hudson.

Handlin, D. 1997. *American Architecture*. London: Thames and Hudson.

Hardt, M. and Negri, A. 2001. *Empire*. Cambridge, MA: Harvard University Press.

Hardt, M. and Negri, A. 2005. *Multitude*. London: Hamish Hamilton Ltd.

Harbison, R. 2000. *Reflections on Baroque*. London: Reaktion Books.

Hargrove, E. and Conkin, P. 1983. *TVA: Fifty Years of Grass Roots Bureaucracy*. Urbana: University of Illinois.

Harrison, J. 1984. *The Common People*. Glasgow: Fontana.

Harvey, D. 1983. 'Class-monopoly Rent, Finance Capital and the Urban Revolution' in Pipkin, J., LaGory, M. and Blau, J. (eds) *Remaking the City*. Albany, NY: State University of New York Press, pp. 334–63 (first published in *Regional Studies*, 1974, 8: 239–55).

Harvey, D. 1985a. *The Urbanization of Capital*. Oxford: Basil Blackwell.

Harvey, D. 1985b. *Consciousness and the Urban Experience*. Oxford: Blackwell.

Harvey, D. 1989. *The Condition of Postmodernity*. Oxford: Basil Blackwell.

Harvey, D. 1996. *Justice, Nature and the Geography of Difference*. Oxford: Basil Blackwell.

Harvey, D. 2000. *Spaces of Hope*. Edinburgh: Edinburgh University Press.

Harvey, D. 2001. *Spaces of Capitalism*. Edinburgh: Edinburgh University Press.

Harvey, D. 2002. 'Cracks in the Edifice of the Empire State' in Sorkin, M. and Zukin, S. (eds) *After the World Trade Center: Rethinking New York City*. New York: Routledge.

Harvey, D. 2003. *Paris: Capital of Modernity*. London: Routledge.

Hatch, M.-J. 1990. 'The Symbolics of Office Design: An Empirical Exploration' in Gagliardi, P. (ed.) *Symbols and Artifacts: Views of the Corporate Landscape* Berlin: De Gruyter, 129–46.

Hatch, M.-J. 1998. *Organization Theory*. Oxford: Oxford University Press.

Hay, D. 1966. *Europe in the Fourteenth and Fifteenth Centuries*. London: Longman.

Hayden, D. 1976. *Seven American Utopias: The Architecture of Communitarian Socialism 1790–1975*. Cambridge, MA: MIT Press.

Hayden, D. 1981. *The Grand Domestic Revolution*. Cambridge, MA: MIT Press.

Hayden, D. 2002. *Redesigning the American Dream*. New York: W. W. Norton and Company.

Hayward Gallery. 1995. 'Art and Power: Images of the 1930s'. London.

Heaney, S. 1999. *Beowulf: A New Translation*. London: Faber and Faber.

Heidegger, M. 1971. 'Building, Dwelling, Thinking' in *Poetry, Language, Thought*, trans. Hofstadter, A. New York: Harper and Row.

Heilbron, J. 1985. *The Rise of Social Theory*. Cambridge: Polity.

Heim, M. 1995. 'The Design of Virtual Reality' in Featherstone, M. and Burrows, R. (eds) *Cyberspace Cyberbodies Cyberpunk*. London: Sage, pp. 65–77.

Held, D. 1980. *Introduction to Critical Theory*. Cambridge: Polity.

Henley, S. 2003. 'The Twenty First Century Model Prison', Proceedings, 4th International Space Syntax Symposium, London, http:// www.spacesyntax.co.uk.

Henriques, J., Hollway, W., Urwin, C., Venn, C. and Walkerdine, V. (eds) 1984. *Changing the Subject*. London: Methuen.

Hernes, T. 2004. *The Spatial Construction of Organization*. Amsterdam: John Benjamins.

Heynen, H. 2001. *Architecture and Modernity*. Cambridge, MA: MIT Press.

Higgs, D. (ed.) 1999. *Queer Sites: Gay Urban Histories since 1600*. London: Routledge.

Hildebrand, G. 1974. *Designing for Industry: The Architecture of Albert Kahn*. Cambridge, MA: MIT Press.

Hill, C. 1969. *Reformation to Industrial Revolution*. Harmondsworth: Penguin.

Hillier, B. 1997. *Space Is the Machine*. Cambridge: Cambridge University Press.

Hillier, B. and Hansen, J. 1984. *The Social Logic of Space*. Cambridge: Cambridge University Press.

Hillis, K. 1999. *Digital Sensations*. Minneapolis, MN: University of Minnesota Press.

Hiss, T. 1990. *The Experience of Place*. New York: Vintage.

Hochschild, A. 1983. *The Managed Heart*. London: University of California Press.

Hochschild, A. 1989. *The Second Shift*. New York: Avon Books.

Hodder, I. (ed.) 1998. *The Meanings of Things*. London: Harper Collins.

Hofbauer, J. 2000. 'Bodies in a Landscape' in Hassard, J., Holliday, R. and Willmott, H. (eds) *Body and Organisation*. London: Sage, pp. 166–91.

Holliday, R. and Hassard, J. (eds) 2001. *Contested Bodies*. London: Routledge.

Hollis III, T. 1998. *The ABC-Clio World History Companion To Utopian Movements*. Santa Barbara: ABC-Clio.

Hollway, W. 1991. *Work Psychology and Organisational Behaviour*. London: Routledge.

Horn, W. and Born, E. 1979. *Plan of St. Gall*. Berkeley: University of California Press.

Horsfield, M. 1997. *Biting the Dust*. London: Fourth Estate.

Hoskin, K. 1995. 'The Viewing Self and the World We View', *Organization* 2 (1): 141–62.

Hoskin, K. and Macve, R. 1986. 'Accounting and the Examination: A Genealogy of Disciplinary Power', *Accounting, Organisations and Society* 11 (2): 105–36.

Hoskin, K. and Macve, R. 1994. 'Reappraising the Genesis of Managerialism', *Accounting, Auditing and Accountability Journal*, 7 (2), 4–29.

Hughes, R. 1991. *The Shock of the New, 2nd ed.* London: Thames and Hudson.

Humphrey, C. and Vitebsky, P. 2003. *Sacred Architecture*. London: Duncan Baird Publishers.

Huws, U. 1984. *The New Homeworkers*. London: Low Pay Unit.

Huxley, A. 1994. [1931] *Brave New World*. London: Flamingo.

Huxley, J. 1943. *TVA: Adventure in Planning*. Cheam, Surrey: The Architectural Press.

Hyde Minor, V. 1999. *Baroque and Rococo*. London: Lawrence King Publishing.

Iannucci, A. 2005. In The Thick of It. BBC4.

Inge, J. 2003. *A Christian Theology of Place*. Aldershot: Ashgate.

Jacques, R. 1996. *Manufacturing the Employee*. Thousand Oaks, CA: Sage.

James, S. 1999. 'The Community of the Soldiers: A Major Identity and Centre of Power in the Roman Empire' in Forcey, C. and Witcher, R. (eds) *Proceedings of the Eighth Theoretical Roman Archaeology Conference*. Leicester, Oxford: Oxbow, pp. 14–25.

Jameson, F. 1991. *Postmodernism or the Cultural Logic of Late Capitalism*. London: Verso.

Jarvis, B. 1998. *Postmodern Cartographies*. London: Pluto.

Jencks, C. 1977. *The Language of Post-modern Architecture*. New York: Rizzoli.

Jencks, C. 1985. *Modern Movements in Architecture, 2nd ed.* Harmondsworth: Penguin.

Jermier, J., Knights, D. and Nord, W. (eds) 1994. *Resistance and Power in Organisations*. London: Routledge.

Jodidio, P. 2001. *New Forms: Architecture in the 1990s*. Cologne: Taschen.

Johnson, S. 1983. *Late Roman Fortifications*. London: Batsford.

Jones, E. 1985. *Industrial Architecture in Britain 1750–1939*. London: B. T. Batsford.

Jones, P. 2006. 'The Sociology of Architecture and the Politics of Building: The Discusive Construction of Ground Zero', *Sociology* 40 (3): 549–65.

Julier, G. 2000. *The Culture of Design*. London: Sage.

Kamata, K. 1974. *Automobile Factory Of Despair*, reprinted in 1983 as *Japan in the Passing Lane*. London: Unwin.

Kamleh-Chapman, Wisam. n.d. report submitted for MBA at Tanaka Business School, Imperial College, London.

Kane, P. 2004. *The Play Ethic*. Basingstoke: Macmillan.

Kanter, R. 1977. *Men and Women of the Corporation*. Cambridge MA: Harvard University Press.

Kaplan, R. and Kaplan, S. 1998. *With People in Mind: Design and Management of Everyday Nature*. Washington DC: Island Press.

Kavanaugh, D. and Araujo, L. 1995. 'Chronigami: Folding and Unfolding Time', *Accounting, Management and Information Technologies* 5 (2): 103–21.

Kermode, F. 1968. *Sense of an Ending*. Oxford: Oxford University Press.

King, A. (ed.) 1980. *Buildings and Society*. London: RKP.

King, A. 1990. 'Architecture, Capital and the Globalisation of Culture' in Featherstone, M. (ed.) *Global Culture: Nation, State, Modernity*. London: Sage.

King, A. 2004. *Spaces of Global Cultures*. London: Routledge.

Klein, J. 1982. *The Office Book*. London: Frederick Muller.

Klein, N. 2001. *No Logo*. London: Flamingo.

Knights, D. 1990. 'Subjectivity, Power and the Labour Process' in Knights, D. and Willmott, H. (eds) *Labour Process Theory*. London: Macmillan.

Knights, D. and Willmott, H. 1986. *Managing the Labour Process*. Aldershot: Gower.

Knights, D. and Willmott, H. 1989. 'Power and Subjectivity at Work', *Sociology* 23 (4): 535–58.

Korczynski, M. 2003. 'Communities of Coping: Collective Emotional Labour in Service Work', *Organization* 10 (1): 55–79.

Kornberger, M. and Clegg, S. 2003. 'The Architecture of Complexity', *Culture and Organisation* 9 (2) June: 75–91.

Lampugnani, V. M. 1988. *Encyclopaedia of 20th century Architecture*. London: Thames and Hudson.

Landes, D. 1969. *The Unbound Prometheus*. Cambridge: Cambridge University Press.

Landes, D. 1986. 'What Do Bosses Really Do?' *The Journal of Economic History* XLVI (3): 585–623.

Lash, S. and Urry, J. 1987. *The End of Organized Capitalism*. Cambridge: Polity.

Latour, B. 1992. 'Sociology of a Few Mundane Artifacts' in Bijker, W. and Law, J. (eds) *Shaping Technology, Building Society: Studies in Sociotechnical Change*. Cambridge, MA: MIT Press.

Latour, B. 1999. 'On recalling ANT' in Law, J. and Hassard, J. *Actor Network Theory and After*. Oxford: Blackwell.

Latour, B. and Woolgar, S. 1979. *Laboratory Life*. Beverly Hills, CA: Sage.

Laurence, R. 1994. *Roman Pompeii: Space and Society*. London: Routledge.

Law, J. 1994. *Organising Modernity*. Oxford: Blackwell.

Law, J. and Hassard, J. (eds) 1999. *Actor Network Theory and After*. Oxford: Blackwell.

Law, J. and Hetherington, K. 2000. 'Materialities, Spatialities, Globalities' in Bryson, J., Daniels, P., Henry, N. and Pollard, J. (eds) *Knowledge, Space, Economy*. London: Routledge.

Lawrence, C. 1989. *Medieval Monasticism*. Harlow: Longman.

Lazonick, W. 1978. 'The Subjection of Labour to Capital', *Review of Radical Political Economy* 8 (1): 1–31.

Lazonick, W. 1979. 'Industrial Relations and the Case of the Self-acting Mule', *Cambridge Journal of Economics* 3: 231–62.

Le Bohec, Y. 2000. *The Imperial Roman Army*. London: Routledge.

Leach, D. 1999. 'Introduction' in Leach, D. (ed.) *Architecture and Philosophy*. London: Routledge.

Leach, N. (ed.) 1997. *Rethinking Architecture*. London: Routledge.

Lefebvre, H. 1976. *The Survival of Capitalism*. London: Allison and Busby.

Lefebvre, H. 1991. *The Production of Space*. Oxford: Basil Blackwell.

Lefebvre, H. 2000. *Everyday Life in the Modern World*. London: The Athalone Press.

Legge, K. 1995. *Human Resource Management: Rhetorics and Realities*. Basingstoke: Macmillan.

Legge, K. 2000. 'The Ethical Context of HRM: The Ethical Organisation in the Boundaryless World' in Winstanley, D. and Woodall, J. (eds) *Ethical Issues in Contemporary Human Resource Management*. Macmillan Business.

Legge, K. 2002. 'The Making of an Icon: The Construction/Deconstruction of September 11th', unpublished paper presented at the 18th EGOS Colloquium, Barcelona, July.

Lehtonen, T.-K. and Maenpaa, P. 1997. 'Shopping in East Centre Mall' in Falk and Campbell (eds) *The Shopping Experience*. London: Sage.

Levin, D. (ed.) 1993. *Modernity and the Hegemony of Vision*. Berkeley: University of California Press.

Leyshon, A. Lee, R. and Williams, C. (eds) 2003. *Alternative Economic Spaces*. London: Sage.

Libeskind, D. 2004. *Breaking Ground*. London: John Murray Publishers.

Lilley, S. 1998. 'Regarding Screens for Surveillance of the System', *Accounting Management and Information Technologies* 8: 63–105.

Littler, C. 1982. *The Development of the Labour Process in Capitalist Societies*. London: Heinemann.

Loeffler, J. 1998. *The Architecture of Diplomacy: Building America's Embassies*. New York: Princeton Architectural Press.

Lubar, S. and Kingery, W. (eds) 1993. *History from Things*. Washington: Smithsonian Institution Press.

Luke, T. 1996. 'New World Order or Neo-World Orders: Power Politics and Ideology in the Informationalizing Glocalities' in Featherstone, M., Lash, S. and Robertson, R. (eds) *Global Modernities*. London: Sage.

Luke, T. 1999. 'Simulated Sovereignty, Telematic Territoriality' in Featherstone, M. and Lash, S. (eds) *Spaces of Cultures*. London: Sage.

Lukes, S. 1973. *Emile Durkheim*. Harmondsworth: Penguin.

McLuhan, M. 1962. *The Gutenberg Galaxy*. Toronto: University of Toronto Press.

McGrath, P. 2005. 'Thinking Differently about Knowledge-Intensive Firms: Insights from Early Medieval Irish Monasticism', *Organization* 12 (4): 549–66.

McNally, D. 1984. *Sacred Space: An Aesthetic for the Liturgical Environment*. Ann Arbor, MI: University Microfilms International.

Mackay, H. 1997. *Consumption and Everyday Life*. London: Sage.

Macey, D. 1994. *The Lives of Michel Foucault*. London: Vintage.

Maine, H. 1878. *Ancient Law*. London: George Routledge and Sons.

Mandel, E. 1990. 'Introduction' to Marx, K. 1990. (originally published in 1867) *Capital: Volume 1*, Harmondsworth: Penguin, pp. 11–86.

Marglin, S. 1974. 'What do the Bosses Do?', *Review of Radical Political Economics* 6 (2): 60–112.

Markus, T. 1989. 'Class and Classification in the Buildings of the late Scottish Enlightenment' in Devine, T. M. (ed.) *Improvement and Enlightenment*. Edinburgh: John Donald.

Markus, T. 1993. *Buildings and Power: Freedom and Control in the Origin of Modern Building Types*. London: Routledge.

Marsden, R. 1999. *The Nature of Capital: Marx after Foucault*. London: Routledge.

Marx, K. 1990. (originally published in 1867) *Capital: Volume 1*. Harmondsworth: Penguin.

Massey, D. 1995a. 'Places and their Pasts', *History Workshop* 39: 182–93.

Massey, D. 1995b. 'Masculinity, Dualisms and High Technology', *Transactions of the Institute of British Geographers* 20: 487–99.

Massey, D. 2005. *For Space*. London: Sage.

Mauss, M. 1973. [1935] 'Techniques of the Body', *Economy and Society* 2 (1): 70–88.

Maupin, A. 1978. *Tales of the City*. San Francisco: The Chronicle Publishing Co.

Mayo, E. 1949. *The Social Problems of an Industrial Civilisation*. London: Routledge and Kegan Paul.

McDowell, L. 1997. *Capital Culture*. Oxford: Blackwells.

Merleau-Ponty, M. 1962. *The Phenomenology of Perception*. London: Routledge.

Merleau-Ponty, M. 1973. *The Visible and the Invisible Evanston*. Illinois: Northwestern University Press.

Merleau-Ponty, M. 1989. *Phenomenology of Perception*. London: Routledge.

Miele, C. (ed.) 1996. *William Morris on Architecture*. Sheffield: Sheffield Academic Press.

Miles, S. and Miles, M. 2004. *Consuming Cities*. Basingstoke: Palgrave Macmillan.

Miller, D. 1987. *Material Culture and Mass Consumption*. Oxford: Blackwell.

Miller, J. 1993. *The Passion of Michel Foucault*. London: HarperCollins.

Miller, D. 1995. 'Consumption as the Vanguard of History' in Miller, D. (ed.) *Acknowledging Consumption*. London: Routledge.

Milton, J. 1980. *The Complete Poems*. London: JM Dent and Sons.

Minchinton, W. (ed.) 1972. *Wage Regulation in Pre-Industrial England*. Newton Abbot: David and Charles.

Mintzberg, H. 1983. *Power in and around Organisations*. Engelwood Cliffs, NJ: Prentice Hall.

Mitchell, T. 1988. *Colonising Egypt*. Cambridge: Cambridge University Press.

Monbiot, G. 2001. *The Captive State*. London: Pan.

Morgan, G. and Knights, D. 1991. Gendering Jobs: Corporate Strategy, Managerial Control and the Dynamics of Job Segregation', *Work, Employment and Society* 5 (2).

Mosley, L. 1986. *Disney's World*. Briarcliff Manor, NY: Stein and Day.

Morley, D. 2000. *Home Territories*. London: Routledge.

Morley, D. and Robins, K. 1995. *Spaces of Identity*. London: Routledge.

Morris, T. and Pinnington, A. 1998. 'Evaluating Strategic Fit in Professional Service Firms', *Human Resource Management Journal* 8 (4): 76–87.

Mulholland, K. 1998. 'Survivors' versus 'Movers and Shakers': The Reconstitution of Management and Careers in the Privatised Utilities' in Warhurst, C. and Thompson, P. (eds) *Workplaces of the Future*. Basingstoke: Palgrave Macmillan, pp. 184–203.

Mumford, L. 1961. *The City in History*. New York, Harcourt: Brace Jovanovich.

Munt, S. 2001. 'The Butch Body' in Holliday, R. and Hassard, J. (eds) *Contested Bodies*. London: Routledge, pp. 95–106.

Myerson, J. 1998. *Design for Change: The Architecture of DEGW*. Basel: Birkhauser.

Natter, W. and Jones III, J. P. 1997. 'Identity, Space, and Other Uncertainties' in Benko, G. and Strohmayer, U. (eds) *Space and Social Theory*. Oxford: Blackwell, pp. 141–61.

Neale, R. 1975. *Feudalism, Capitalism and Beyond*. London: Arnold.

Negri, A. 2005a. *Time for Revolution*. London: Continuum International Publishing Group.

Negri, A. 2005b. *The Politics of Subversion: A Manifesto for the 21st Century*. Cambridge: Polity.

Nesbitt, K. (ed.) 1996. *Theorizing a New Agenda for Architecture*. New York: Princeton University Press.

Ngo, D. and Shamir Zion, A. 2002. *Open House: Unbound Space and the Modern Dwelling*. London: Thames and Hudson.

Norberg-Schultz, C. 2000. *Principles of Modern Architecture*. London: Andreas Papadakis.

Nuttgens, P. 1988. *Understanding Modern Architecture*. London: Unwin Hyman.

O'Connell Davidson, J. 1993. *Privatisation and Employment Relations: The Case of the Water Industry*. London: Mansell.

O'Connell Davidson, J. 1994. 'Resistance in a Privatised Utility' in Jermier, J., Knights, D. and Nord, W. (eds) *Resistance And Control*. London: Routledge.

Olins, W. 1989. *Corporate Identity: Making Business Strategy Visible by Design*. Cambridge MA: Harvard University Press.

Orwell, G. 1948. *Nineteen Eight Four*. Harmonsworth: Penguin.

Owings, N. A. 1973. *The Spaces in Between: An Architect's Journey*. Boston: Houghton Mifflin.

Packard, V. 1957. *The Hidden Persuaders*. Harmonsworth: Penguin.

Parker, M. 2004. *Against Management*. Cambridge: Polity.

Parker, M., Fournier, V. and Reedy, P. 2007. *The Dictionary of Alternatives: Utopianism and Organization*. London: Zed Books.

Pawley, M. 1992. 'The Electronic Cottage' in Rivers, T., Cruickshank, D., Darley, G. and Pawley, M. (eds) *The Name of the Room*. London: BBC Books.

Pawson, J. 2003. *Monastery of Novy Dvur: House and Garden*, www.johnpawson.com/essays/monastery.

Peck, J. 1996. *Work Place*. New York: The Guildford Press.

Peddie, J. 1994. *The Roman War Machine*, Stroud: Alan Sutton Publishing Limited.

Peter, J. 2000. *An Oral History of Modern Architecture*. New York: H. N. Abrams.

Peters, T. 1990. 'Towards the Entrepreneurial and Empowering Organization' Presentation at The Royal Lancaster Hotel, London, 13 February.

Peters, T. and Waterman, R. 1982. *In Search of Excellence*. New York: Knopf.

Pevsner, N. 1943. *Outline of European Architecture*. Harmondsworth: Penguin.

Pevsner, N. 1975. *Pioneers of Modern Design*. Harmondsworth: Penguin.

Pevsner, N. 1976. *A History of Building Types*. London: Thomas and Hudson.

Pfeffer, J. 1981. *Power in Organisations*. Boston: Pitman.

Pfeffer, J. 1993. 'Barriers to the Advancement of Organisation Science', *Academy of Management Review* 18 (4): 599–620.

Phillips, A. and Taylor, E. 1980. 'Sex and Skill: Notes Towards a Feminist Economics', *Feminist Review* 6: 79–88.

Phizacklea, A. and Wolkowitz, C. 1995. *Homeworking Women*. London: Sage.

Pile, S. 1994. *The Body and the City*. London: Routledge.

Pile, S. and Thrift, N. 1995. *Mapping the Subject*. London: Routledge.

Pinnington, A. and Morris, T. 1996. 'Power and Control in Professional Partnerships', *Long Range Planning* 29 (6): 842–9.

Pinnington, A. and Morris, T. 2000. 'Transforming the Architect: Ownership Form and Archetype Change', Unpublished paper.

Pinnington, A. and Morris, T. 2002. 'Transforming the Architect', *Organization Studies* 23 (2): 189–210.

Pipkin, J., La Gory, M. and Blau, J. 1983. *Remaking the City*. Albany: SUNY Press.

Plant, S. 1992. *The Most Radical Gesture*. London: Routledge.

Platt, C. 1984. *The Abbeys and Priories of Medieval England*. London: Martin Secker and Warburg Ltd.

Platt, H. 1991. *The Electric City*. Chicago: University of Chicago Press.

Plumwood, V. 1993. *Feminism and the Mastery of Nature*. London: Routledge.

Rapp, R. 1976. *Industry and Economic Decline in Seventeenth Century Venice*. Cambridge, MA: Harvard University Press.

Renfrew, C. 2004. 'Towards a Theory of Material Engagement' in De Marrais, E., Gosden, C. and Renfrew, C. (eds) *Rethinking Materiality*. Cambridge: McDonald Institute for Archaelogical Research.

Ricoeur, P. 1984. *Time and Narrative*, vol. 1 trans. McLaughlin, K. and Pellauer, D. Chicago: University of Chicago Press.

Ricoeur, P. 1988. *Time and Narrative*, vol. 3 trans. Blamey, K. and Pellauer, D. Chicago: University of Chicago Press.

Rivers, T. 1992. 'Home Entertainment' in Rivers, T., Cruickshank, D., Darley, G. and Pawley, M. (eds) *The Name of the Room*. London: BBC Books.

Roethlisberger, F. and Dickson, W. 1939. *Management and the Worker*. Cambridge, MA: Harvard University Press.

Romanyshyn, R. 1989. *Technology as Symptom and Dream*. London: Routledge.

Rose, N. 1989. *Governing the Soul*. London: Free Association Books.

Rose, N. 1996. *Inventing Ourselves*. Cambridge: Cambridge University Press.

Rose, N. 1999. *Powers of Freedom*. Cambridge: Cambridge University Press.

Rose, S. 2006. *Guardian*, 11 September, p. 21.

Ross, K. 1988. *The Emergence of Social Space: Rimbaud and the Paris Commune*. Minneapolis: University of Minneapolis Press.

Ross, K. 1996. *Fast Cars, Clean Bodies: Decolonization and the Reordering of French Culture*. Cambridge, MA: MIT Press.

Rossiter, A. 1988. *From Private To Public: A Feminist Exploration Of Early Mothering*. Toronto: The Women's Press.

Roy, D. 1952. 'Quota Restrictions and Goldbricking in a Machine Shop', *American Journal of Sociology*, 57: 427–42.

Rudofsky, B. 1964. *Architecture Without Architects*. New York: MOMA.

Rutherford, J. 2000. 'A Foot in Each Sphere: Christine Frederick and early Twentieth Century Advertising', *The Historian*, 22 September.

Rykwert, J. 1988. *The Idea of a Town*. Cambridge, MA: MIT Press.

Saint, A. 1983. *Image of the Architect*. New Haven: Yale University Press.

Sánchez-Matamoros, J., Gutierrez Hidalgo, F., Espejo, C. and Fenech, F. 2005. 'Govern(mentality) and Accounting: The Influence of Different Enlightenment Discourses in Two Spanish Cases (1761–1777)', *Abacus* 41 (2): 181–210.

Sartre, J.-P. 1963. *Nausea*. Harmondsworth: Penguin.

Sassen, S. 2000. 'Excavating Power', *Theory, Culture and Society* 17: 163–70.

Scanlon, J. 1995. *Inarticulate Longings: The Ladies Home Journal, Gender and the Promises of Consumer Culture*. London: Routledge.

Schama, S. 1996. *Landscape and Memory*. London: Fontana.

Schama, S. 2001. *A History of Britain. Part 2*. BBC TV Programme, June.

Scarbrough, H. 1995. (ed.) *The Management of Expertise*. London: Macmillan.

Schmitt, B. H., Simonsen, A. and Marcus, J. 1995. 'Managing Corporate Image and Identity', *Long Range Planning* 28 (5): 82–92.

Scott, J. 1979. *Corporations, Classes and Capitalism*. London: Hutchinson.

Scully, V., Jr, 1994. *Modern Architecture: The Architecture of Democracy*. New York: Knopf.

Selznick, P. 1953. (originally published in 1949). *TVA and the Grass Roots*. Berkeley, CA: University of California Press.

Selznick, P. 1969. *Law, Society and Industrial Justice*. New York: Russell Sage Foundation.

Sennett, R. 1990. *The Conscience of the Eye: The Design and Social Life of Cities*. New York: Alfred A. Knopf.

Sennett, R. 1994. *Flesh and Stone*. London: Faber and Faber.

Sennett, R. 1997. 'Growth and Failure: The New Political Economy and its Culture' in Featherstone, M. and Lash, S. (eds) 1999. *Spaces of Culture*. London: Sage.

Sennett, R. 1998. *The Corrosion of Character*. New York: Norton.

Sewell, G. and Wilkinson, B. 1992. 'Someone to Watch Over Me', *Sociology* 26 (2): 271–89.

Shields, R. 1997. 'Spatial Stress and Resistance: Social Meanings of Spatialisation' in Benko, G. and Strohmayer, U. (eds) *Space and Social Theory*. Oxford: Blackwell.

Shields, R. 1999. *Lefebvre, Love and Struggle: Spatial Dialectics*. London: Routledge.

Shilling, C. 1993. *The Body and Social Theory*. London: Sage.

Shilts, R. 1987. *And the Band Played on*. New York: St Martins Press.

Shotter, J. and Gergen, J. (eds) 1989. *Texts of Identity*. London: Sage.

Sibley, D. *Geographies of Exclusion*. London: Routledge.

Sillitoe, A. 1960. *Saturday Night and Sunday Morning*, London: Pan.

Sklair, L. 2001. *The Transnational Capitalist Class*. Oxford: Blackwell.

Sklair, L. 2005. 'The Transnational Capitalist Class and Contemporary Architecture in Globalizing Cities', *International Journal of Urban and Regional Research* 29 (3): 485–500.

Slater, D. 1998. 'Public/Private' in Jenks, C. (ed.) *Core Sociological Dichotomies*. London: Sage.

Smith, J. 1987. 'Elton Mayo and the Hidden Hawthorne', *Work, Employment and Society* 1 (1).

Soja, E. 1980. 'The Socio-spatial Dialectic', *Annals of the Association of American Geographers* 70 (2): 207–25.

Soja, E. 1989. *Postmodern Geographies*. London: Haymarket.

Sorkin, M. and Zukin, S. (eds) 2002. *After the World Trade Center: Rethinking New York City*. New York: Routledge.

Spotts, F. 2002. *Hitler and The Power of Aesthetics*. London: Random House.

Stalley, R. 1999. *Early Medieval Architecture*. Oxford: Oxford University Press.

Stallybrass, P. and White, A. 1986. *The Politics and Poetics of Transgression*. London: Metheun.

Stanger, H. 2000. 'From Factory to Family: The Creation of Corporate Culture in the Larkin Company of Buffalo New York', *Business History Review* 74 (3): 407–34.

Stanilavsky quoted in Berg, P. and Kreiner, K. 1990. 'The Corporate Architecture' in Gagliardi, P. (ed.) *Symbols and Artifacts*. Berlin: de Gruyter.

Stanley, L. and Wise, S. 1993. *Breaking Out Again*. London: Routledge.

Starkey, K. and McKinley, A. (eds) 1998. *Foucault and Organisation Theory*. London: Sage.

Steele, F. 1973. *Physical Settings and Organisational Development*. Reading, MA: Addison-Wesley.

Steffy, B. 1997. 'Ontological Fallacies', *Organization* 4: 448–50.

Stewart, J. 2006. *Spying for the Raj*. London: Sutton.

Strati, A. 1999. *Organisation and Aesthetics*. London: Sage.

Sudjec, D. 2001. *Architecture and Democracy*. London: Lawrence King.

Sudjec, D. 2004. 'Novy Dvur and the Stylish Austerity of John Pawson', http://www. godspy.com/culture/Novy-Dvur-and-the-Stylish-Austerity-of-John-Pawson-by-Deyan-Sudjic.cfm, 13 October (accessed 26 April 2007).

Sudjec, D. 2005. *The Edifice Complex*. London: Allen Lane.

Sutcliffe, A. 1993. *Paris: An Architectural History*. New Haven: Yale University Press.

Sutton, I. 1999. *Western Architecture*. London: Thames and Hudson.

Swyngedouw, E. 1997. 'Neither Global nor Local: "Glocalization" and the Politics of Scale', in Cox, K. (ed.) *Spaces of Globalization: Reasserting the Power of the Local*. New York: Guilford Press, pp. 137–66.

Tajfel, H. 1982. 'Social Psychology of Intergroup Relations.' *Annual Review of Psychology* 33: 1–30.

Tarbell, I. 1913. 'The Cost of Living and Household Management', *Annals of the American Academy of Political and Social Sciences* 48, July: 127–30.

Taylor, F. W. 1911. *Principles of Scientific Management*. New York: Harper.

Thomas, K. 1971. *Religion and the Decline of Magic*. London: Weidenfeld and Nicholson.

Thompson E. P. 1967. 'Time, Work-discipline and Industrial Capitalism', *Past and Present* 38: 56–97.

Thompson E. P. 1968. *The Making of the English Working Class*. Harmondsworth: Penguin.

Thompson, P. 1986. *The Nature of Work*. Basingstoke: Palgrave Macmillan.

Thompson, P. and McHugh, D. 2002. *Work Organisations*, 3rd ed. Basingstoke: Palgrave Macmillan.

Thompson, P. and Warhurst, C. (eds) 1998. *Workplaces of the Future*. Basingstoke: Palgrave Macmillan.

Thrift, N. (ed.) 1996. 'A Phantom State? International Money, Electronic Networks and Global Cities'. *Spatial Formations*. London: Sage.

Thrift, N. 2005. *Knowing Capitalism*. London: Sage.

Tiedemann, R. 1999. *Editor's Introduction* in Benjamin, W. (ed.) *The Arcades Project*. Cambridge, MA: Harvard University Press.

Tolkien, J. R. R. 1975. *The Hobbit*. London: Unwin.

Tomlinson, A. (ed.) 1990. *Consumption, Identity and Style*. London: Comedia.

Tuan, Yi-Fu. 1977. *Space and Place*. Minneapolis: University of Minnesota Press.

Turner, B. 1990. (ed.) *Organisational Symbolism*. Berlin: de Gruyter.

Van Leeuwen, T. 1988. *The Skyward Trend of Thought*. Cambridge, MA: MIT Press.

Van Maanen, J. 1991. 'The Smile Factory' in Frost, P., Moore, L., Louis, M., Lundberg, C. and Martin, J. (eds) *Reframing Organisational Culture*. Newbury Park, CA: Sage.

Van Zuylen, G. 1995. *The Garden: Visions of Paradise*. London: Thames and Hudson.

Virilio, P. 1986. *Speed and Politics: An Essay on Dromodology*. New York: Semiotext(e).

Virilio, P. 1994. *Bunker Archeology*. New York: Princeton Architectural Press.

Virilio, P. 1997. *Open Sky*, trans. Rose, J. London: Verso.

Virilio, P. 2002. *Ground Zero*. London: Verso.

Von Simson, O. 1952. 'The Gothic Cathedral: Design and Meaning', *Journal of the Society of Architectural Historians* 11 (3): 6–16.

Wajcman, J. 1991. *Feminism Confronts Technology*. Cambridge: Polity.

Warhurst, C. and Thompson, P. (eds) 1998. *Workplaces of the Future*. London: Macmillan.

Warren, S. 2002. 'Creating Creativity: The Organisational Manipulation of Aesthetics in a Web Design Department', *The Pink Machine Papers*, 9 (2) Stockholm.

Warwick Organisation Behaviour Staff. *Organisational Studies: Critical Perspectives*. London: Routledge.

Watkin, D. 2001. *Morality and Architecture Revisited*. London: John Murray.

Watson, T. 1994. *In Search of Management*. London: Routledge.

Watson, T. 2001. *Organising and Managing Work*. London: Prentice Hall.

Webb, S. 2004. *Out of this World*. New York: Praxis Publishing.

Weber, M. 1930. *The Protestant Ethic and the Spirit of Capitalism*. London: Allen and Unwin.

Webster, G. 1998. *The Roman Imperial Army*, 3rd ed. Norman: University of Oklahoma Press.

Weinstein, M. 1972. 'Coercion, Space and the Modes of Human Domination' in Pennock, J. and Chapman, J. (eds) *Coercion*. New York: Aldine.

Weir, D. 1993. 'Not Doing the Business', *The Times Higher Education Supplement* 30, 22 April.

Wells, H. G. 1895 (1971). *The Time Machine*. Harmondsworth: Penguin.

Welsch, W. 1997. *Undoing Aesthetics*. London: Sage.

West Wing, 1999. Episode 3 'A Proportional Response', Series One, Warner Brothers.

Whiteley, N. 2002. *Reyner Banham: Historian of the Immediate Future*. Cambridge MA: MIT Press.

Whittle, S. 1994. *The Margins of the City*. Aldershot: Arena.

Wilkinson, P. 2000. *The Shock of the Old*. London: Macmillan.

Williams, C. 2005. *A Commodified World? Mapping the Limits of Capitalism*. New York: Zed Books.

Williams, R. 2000. *On Christian Theology*. Oxford: Blackwell Publishing.

Williams, S. and Bendelow, G. 1998. *The Lived Body*. London: Routledge.

Willis, P. 1977. *Learning to Labour*. London: Saxon House.

Winch, G. and Schneider. E. 1993. 'Managing the Knowledge-based Organisation', *Journal of Management Studies* 30 (6): 323–41.

Wolfe, T. 1988. *Bonfire of the Vanities*. London: Pan.

Wolff, J. 1981. *The Social Production of Art*. Basingstoke: Palgrave Macmillan.

Wolff, J. 1985. 'The Invisible *Flâneuse*: Women and the Literature of Modernity', *Theory, Culture & Society* 2 (3): 37–46.

Woolgar, S. 1991. 'Configuring the User' in Law, J. (ed.) *A Sociology of Monsters*. London: Routledge, pp. 57–102.

Woolgar, S. (ed.) 2002. *Virtual Society? Technology, Cyberbole, Reality*. Oxford: Oxford University Press.

Worthington, J. 1997. *Reinventing the Workplace*. London: Architectural Press.

Worthington, J. 2005. 'A Future for Architectural Education in Ireland', Discussion paper prepared for the Higher Education Authority (Ireland) and the Royal Institute of the Architects of Ireland, presented in Dublin 23 June, http://www.hea.ie/index.cfm/page/sub/id/1021.

Wright, L. 1999. 'San Francisco' in Higgs, D. (ed.) *Queer Sites*. London: Routledge.

Wrong, D. 1968. 'Some Problems in Defining Social Power', *American Journal of Sociology* 73: 673–81.

Yanow, D. 1993. 'Reading Policy Meanings in Organization-Scapes', *Journal of Architectural and Planning Research* 10: 308–27.

Yates, F. 1966. *The Art of Memory*. London: RKP.

Zuboff, S. 1988. *In the Age of the Smart Machine*. London: Heinemann.

Zukin, S. 1982. *Loft Living*. Baltimore, MA: Johns Hopkins University Press.

Zukin, S. 1988. 'The Postmodern Debate over Urban Form', *Theory, Culture and Society* 5 (2–3): 431–46.

Zukin, S. 1991. *Landscapes of Power*. Berkeley: University of California Press.

Zukin, S. 2002. 'Our World Trade Center' in Sorkin, M. and Zukin, S. (eds) *After the World Trade Center: Rethinking New York City*. New York: Routledge.

index

organisational practices   30, 39, 77, 78, 83, 87, 105, 131, 147, 166

organisational space   39, 45, 61, 77, 78, 82, 90, 100, 102, 113, 203, 213, 217, 222, 226, 229, 230

organisational symbolism   205, 208

'organised walking'   72

Otis Elevator Company   282–3, 284

Owings, N.   31, 95, 290, 312

ownership   26, 124, 125, 144–7, 151, 165, 166, 185, 199, 224, 231, 232, 233, 235, 270–2, 276, 278, 279

Packard Motor Co   92–3, 95

Panopticon   61, 67, 75, 90, 98, 206, 222, 256, 257

parade grounds   243

parcels of land   62, 63, 274

Paris   6, 27, 46, 49, 75, 98, 159, 242, 251, 271, 306, 315

Parker, M.   35, 40, 247, 265, 312

Pawley, M.   189, 312

Peddie, J.   82, 312

Pelli, C.   285

perceived space   8, 148, 183, 218

'performativity'   109, 110, 131, 211, 257

Peter, J.   27, 312

Petronas Tower, Kuala Lumpur   285

Pevsner, N.   24, 26, 92, 312

Pfeffer, J.   34, 43, 312

phallic format of abstract space   14–15, 158, 159, 161, 279

phantasmagoria   51–2, 74, 96, 97, 127, 131

phenomenological   8, 9, 44, 127, 206, 215

Philips, Bangalore, India   xi, 114–15

Pile, S.   241, 312

Pinnington, A. and Morris, T.   30, 310–1, 312

place-boundedness   2, 60, 100, 147–8, 151, 152, 203

place   5–6, 11, 18, 19, 44–5, 53, 54, 60, 97, 100, 147–53, 155, 171, 240, 241

'place-capturing'   57, 59

play   128–30, 227–8, 308

pleasure gardens and pleasure domes   246–50, 254, 261

pleasure   46, 73, 107–8, 115, 122, 126, 131, 172–3, 175, 246–50, 251, 254, 257, 261

police   15, 186, 239–40, 247, 252, 253, 257, 291

political economy of space   39, 133, 137–47, 158, 168, 270, 273, 280, 292

politics of the banal   6

politics of the elite   6

Pompeii   249–50, 251, 308

poorhouses   64

Post Office (UK)   55

power   xii, xiv, 6, 10, 11, 15, 16, 18, 26, 27, 36–7, 39, 43–98, 99, 103, 106, 107, 109, 110, 113, 118, 125, 127, 129, 132, 137, 138, 140, 142, 143, 153, 171, 174, 177, 200, 206, 207, 213, 217, 219, 224, 228, 233, 250, 260, 267, 270, 272, 279, 286, 287, 290, 295

power, labour   106, 123, 125, 139, 172

Price, C.   xiii

prisons   53, 89

private armies   164, 167

private property   150, 263, 265, 269–78

private space and privacy   39, 177, 185, 198, 213, 254, 261, 266, 283

privatisation (of society)   147, 187, 188, 191, 193, 197, 198, 200

privatisation (ownership of organisations)   167, 168, 218, 224, 229

'producing space'   7

professionalising the housewife   193, 196

property developers   27, 184

Proudhon, P.-J.   235, 271

'property'   10, 146, 147–53, 158, 167, 174, 235, 261, 263, 266, 269–78, 279, 288–90

Pruitt-Igoe public housing Estate, St Louis, USA   292, 294

public finance initiative (PFI)   45

public health   255, 257

public houses (pubs)   165, 249, 250

public transport   181, 184, 189, 247

Queen's Royal Court   243

queuing   44, 53, 229

(le) quotidien   6

real estate   101, 185, 247, 281, 286, 288

Redstone Arsenal, USA   166, 167

Rentokil   xi, xii

Reedy Creek Improvement District, Florida   247

Reich Chancellery, Berlin   48, 258–9, 294

rents   272, 279

representational space   8, 9, 11, 39, 97, 111, 143, 161, 220, 284

representations of space   8, 9, 11, 13, 39, 53, 78, 99, 219, 223, 287

Printed and bound by CPI Group (UK) Ltd, Croydon, CR0 4YY